Praise for
Sams Teach Yourself
Android™ Application Development
in 24 Hours, Third Edition

"True, Android has its own spin on the Java programming language, particularly if you come from a traditional mobile Java background. Don't be flummoxed! Use this book to quickly get over those initial hurdles so you can see Android's inner beauty. And Android is beautiful when presented in this effective and confidence-building format."

—**David Oliver**, President, Oliver+Coady, Inc.

"*Sams Teach Yourself Android Application Development in 24 Hours* begins in Hour 1 by providing a comprehensive overview of Android and the Eclipse development environment. In the subsequent hours, the authors provide in-depth coverage of a wide array of topics, from explanation of Android basics to advanced topics such as using the camera, location services, and connecting to the Flickr API. The concise explanations of Android concepts and focused project instruction make this book perfect for novice and intermediate Android developers."

—**Valerie Shipbaugh**, Assistant Professor, Stark State College

"Let Android Sherpas Carmen Delessio, Lauren Darcey, and Shane Conder be your guides. They will take you on an efficient journey through Android territory, whether you are just starting out or a pro looking for a second set of eyes. Just the right amount of time is spent on the important landmarks, without getting bogged down in the details only a local would need to know."

—**Jason Van Anden**, Developer of BubbleBeats and the I'm Getting Arrested Android apps

Carmen Delessio
Lauren Darcey
Shane Conder

Sams **Teach Yourself**

Android™
Application
Development

in **24**
Hours

Third Edition

 800 East 96th Street, Indianapolis, Indiana, 46240 USA

Sams Teach Yourself Android™ Application Development in 24 Hours, Third Edition

Library of Congress Control Number: 2013944817

Printed in the United States of America

First Printing October 2013

Trademarks

Warning and Disclaimer

Bulk Sales

Sams Publishing offers excellent discounts on this book when ordered in quantity for bulk purchases or special sales. For more information, please contact

U.S. Corporate and Government Sales
1-800-382-3419
corpsales@pearsontechgroup.com

For sales outside of the U.S., please contact

International Sales
international@pearsoned.com

Editor-in-Chief
Mark Taub

Executive Editor
Laura Lewin

Development Editor
Sheri Cain

Managing Editor
Kristy Hart

Project Editor
Andy Beaster

Copy Editor
Paula Lowell

Indexer
Tim Wright

Proofreader
Sarah Kearns

Technical Editors
Sebastian Delmont
Valerie Shipbaugh

Publishing Coordinator
Olivia Basegio

Interior Designer
Gary Adair

Cover Designer
Mark Shirar

Compositor
Gloria Schurick

Contents at a Glance

Table of Contents

Preface

What I wish I knew when I started Android development.

Android has become a leading platform for smartphones, tablets, and other devices. The size of the potential global audience for your apps is justification to learn Android. The goal of this book is to introduce the Android platform and empower you to create professional grade apps.

In 24 hours of focused material, you will learn the basics of Android development and move on to specific topics like working with data in the cloud, handling bitmaps and videos in an app, and using the Facebook Android SDK.

In the early days of Android, author Carmen Delessio worked on a major Android project for a large media company. The app launched and was a success. But, it really was not built in an Android way. Having built many Android apps since then, the material in this book is largely guided by the idea of including "What I wish I knew back then."

The material in this book covers common topics in professional Android development. The book is not intended to be an encyclopedia of all things Android. Plenty of Android resources are available and the documentation on the Android developer site has never been better. This book will start you on the path to developing professional Android apps and can be used as a guide to the additional material.

New in the Third Edition

There are three major changes from the second edition to the third edition of this book.

New features in Android are covered. The updates include significant coverage of fragments, the action bar, and the Android support package. This edition covers new open-source projects that help in Android development, differences in Android versions, and how to use the support package to develop for multiple versions of Android.

More topics are covered in the third edition. Topics that are covered in detail in this edition include using SQLite, creating content providers, and using the Facebook SDK.

The final change is structural. In the second edition of this book, a single app was developed and expanded on in each hour. As new features were added to the app, that feature was described in the book. This approach helped many Android developers get their start and was a way to build a real app along with the authors.

This third edition takes a topic-based approach. For each topic covered, an example project is developed. Some hours include multiple projects. The goal of these examples is to clearly illustrate the topic being covered, which might mean that the examples, particularly in the early hours, do not simulate real-world apps. In Hours 12–16, which cover cloud data and the Flickr API, the chapters are related to and build on each other. Hour 12 begins with retrieving Flickr data, and Hour 16 is a complete app that uses the Flickr data and displays images. The later hours in the book cover single topics such as using the camera or using the Facebook SDK. For each of those hours, an example project is developed.

Who This Book Is For

The examples in this book are created so that someone with programming knowledge can understand them, but Android apps are developed in Java. The book will be much more valuable and useful if you are familiar with Java.

If you are a Java programmer with an interest in Android development, this book will introduce you to Android and get you on track for professional Android development.

If you have started Android development, but have not proceeded past the basic examples, then this book is for you. It covers topics such as downloading data, using a database, and creating content providers. The book can take you from the basics to real development in a series of understandable steps.

How This Book Is Organized

Hours 1–4 are a hands-on "getting started" section for Android development. In these hours, you will set up your development environment, create and run an example app, and go over the details of how to set up and organize an Android project. Android resources are used to customize apps for different devices and languages and they are introduced in this section.

Hours 5–11 cover all aspects of developing user interfaces on Android, including layouts for basic controls as well as advanced controls such as ViewFlippers.

In Hours 12–16, you learn to develop an app using the Flickr API. The Flickr API includes an option to get recently uploaded photos. In Hour 12, the data for the API is received and parsed. Over several hours, you learn to develop an app that parses the Flickr data, stores it locally, and uses it to display the associated images.

Hours 17–22 cover specific topics: using contact and calendar data, location-based services, internationalization, working with cameras, using media, and developing a Facebook Android app.

Hour 23 includes tips and tricks for creating a responsive app and touches on Android topics that you might want to pursue further.

Hour 24 shows how to package and publish your app.

About the Authors

Carmen Delessio is an experienced application developer who has worked as a developer, technical architect, and CTO in large and small organizations.

Carmen developed the award-winning "BFF Photo" Android app, which won the Sprint App Challenge contest in the Social Networking category.

Carmen began his online development career at Prodigy, where he worked on early Internet applications, shopping apps, and fantasy baseball.

He has written for Mashable and AndroidGuys and is the author of *Sams Teach Yourself Google TV App Development in 24 Hours.*

He is a graduate of Manhattanville College and lives in Pound Ridge, New York, with his wife, Amy, and daughter, Natalie.

Lauren Darcey is a multi-published Android author with several Pearson books to her credit, along with earlier editions of this book. Lauren is technical leader of Mamlambo, Inc., a firm specializing in mobile development and consulting with Android, iOS, Blackberry, and other mobile platforms. She has more than two decades of software development experience under her belt and is a recognized authority in enterprise architecture and commercial-grade mobile development.

Shane Conder is also a multi-published Android author with several Pearson books to his credit, along with earlier editions of this book. Shane has extensive development experience and has focused his attention on mobile and embedded development for the past two decades. He has designed and developed many commercial apps for Android, iOS, BREW, Blackberry, J2ME, Palm, and Windows Mobile, some of which have been installed on millions of phones worldwide.

Dedication

For Amy and Natalie.

—Carmen Delessio

Acknowledgments

This book would not exist without the help and guidance of the team at Pearson (Sams Publishing). Thanks to Laura Lewin for constant encouragement and Olivia Basegio for her incredible work on the project.

Technical editors are an important part of every book. That is particularly true in this case. Sebastian Delmont is a Ruby on Rails expert who also happens to be an Android guru. Valerie Shipbaugh did her technical review by placing herself in the role of a reader who was new to Android. The feedback and guidance from Sebastian and Valerie make this a much better book.

We Want to Hear from You!

As the reader of this book, you are our most important critic and commentator. We value your opinion and want to know what we're doing right, what we could do better, what areas you'd like to see us publish in, and any other words of wisdom you're willing to pass our way.

We welcome your comments. You can email or write to let us know what you did or didn't like about this book—as well as what we can do to make our books better.

Please note that we cannot help you with technical problems related to the topic of this book.

When you write, please be sure to include this book's title and author as well as your name and email address. We will carefully review your comments and share them with the author and editors who worked on the book.

Email: consumer@samspublishing.com

Mail: Sams Publishing
         ATTN: Reader Feedback
         800 East 96th Street
         Indianapolis, IN 46240 USA

Reader Services

Visit our website and register this book at informit.com/register for convenient access to any updates, downloads, or errata that might be available for this book.

PART I

Getting Started

HOUR 1
Getting Started: Creating a Simple App

What You'll Learn in This Hour:

▶ Setting up your development environment

▶ Creating a simple app

▶ Personalizing your app

▶ Running your app on an emulator

The goal of this hour is to jump into Android development. To do this, you first need to set up a development environment. With the introduction of the Android Developer Tools (ADT) Bundle download, this process has become much easier for new Android developers. With the development environment in place, you will create a simple app and then modify it. This process will introduce you to the tools for creating user interfaces, running test apps, and debugging code.

Setting Up Your Development Environment

To jump into Android development, you have to first set up a working development environment. You do Android development in Java. Significant Android support is built into the Eclipse Integrated Development Environment (IDE). IntelliJ and Android Studio, which is built on IntelliJ, are other good choices. This book focuses on using Eclipse. To install Eclipse and the Eclipse plugin for Android (Android Developer tools), you download a single installation file called the ADT Bundle.

TIP

Attached Code

The source code examples in this book are available for download. You'll learn more about Eclipse projects in this hour. Generally, the code is included in one or more projects with names like Hour1App.

Installation Using the ADT Bundle

With the single download of the ADT Bundle, you receive all you need to begin Android development. The ADT Bundle includes the Eclipse IDE and all required tools to get started.

Download the ADT Bundle by following the download links provided on http://developer.android.com/sdk/index.html. Installation and environment setup instructions are available for both Windows and Macintosh machines.

The ADT Bundle is a zipped file. After you download and unzip it, you see the folder structure shown in Figure 1.1. Running the Eclipse application starts the development environment.

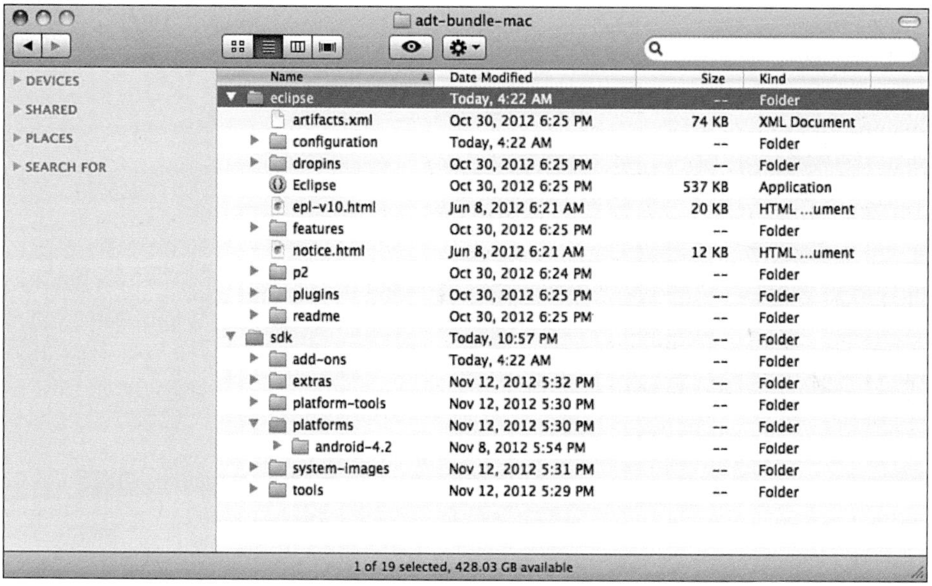
adt-bundle-mac
DEVICES
SHARED
PLACES
SEARCH FOR
Name
Date Modified
Size
Kind
eclipse Today, 4:22 AM -- Folder
artifacts.xml Oct 30, 2012 6:25 PM 74 KB XML Document
configuration Today, 4:22 AM -- Folder
dropins Oct 30, 2012 6:25 PM -- Folder
Eclipse Oct 30, 2012 6:25 PM 537 KB Application
epl-v10.html Jun 8, 2012 6:21 AM 20 KB HTML ...ument
features Oct 30, 2012 6:25 PM -- Folder
notice.html Jun 8, 2012 6:21 AM 12 KB HTML ...ument
p2 Oct 30, 2012 6:24 PM -- Folder
plugins Oct 30, 2012 6:25 PM -- Folder
readme Oct 30, 2012 6:25 PM -- Folder
sdk Today, 10:57 PM -- Folder
add-ons Today, 4:22 AM -- Folder
extras Nov 12, 2012 5:32 PM -- Folder
platform-tools Nov 12, 2012 5:30 PM -- Folder
platforms Nov 12, 2012 5:30 PM -- Folder
android-4.2 Nov 8, 2012 5:54 PM -- Folder
system-images Nov 12, 2012 5:31 PM -- Folder
tools Nov 12, 2012 5:29 PM -- Folder
1 of 19 selected, 428.03 GB available

FIGURE 1.1
Folder structure of ADT Bundle

Looking at Figure 1.1, you see that two main folders exist:

- Eclipse contains the Eclipse Integrated Development Environment and related tools.
- The sdk folder contains a number of subfolders, including tools, platforms, and platform tools.

Understanding What Has Been Installed

The Android environment distinguishes between Android SDK tools and platform tools. Tools are the core components of the Software Development Kit (SDK). They are used by all versions of Android. Platform tools are associated with a specific version of Android. In this example, the platform for version 4.2 of Android is installed. There are also folders called extras, add-ons, and system-images. When you use an emulator to test an Android app, you use a virtual device that is set up in the system-images folder. A virtual device or Android Virtual Device is referred to as an AVD. You can create an AVD by using a tool in Eclipse ADT called the Android Virtual Device Manager. You can access it from the Windows menu in Eclipse.

Figure 1.2 shows the app start-up screen for Android developer tools after you've installed the bundle. When you use the tools installed by the ADT Bundle, you are using Eclipse. (This book refers to the development environment as Eclipse.)

FIGURE 1.2
Selecting a workspace in Eclipse

Instantly Creating a Simple App

In this section, you create and run a simple app. Figure 1.2 shows that when you start Eclipse, you must set a workspace for development. Typically, the default is a good choice. The first time you use Eclipse, you see a welcome screen. After you close it, you see Eclipse, as shown in Figure 1.3.

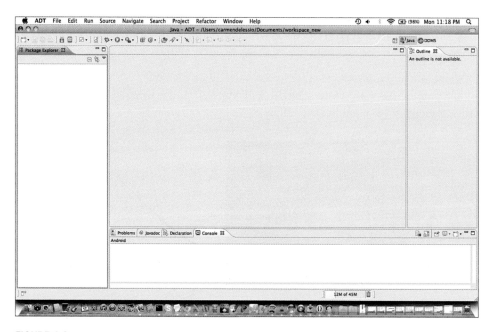

FIGURE 1.3
Starting Eclipse

Eclipse is a blank slate to start your app development efforts. You add projects for each app you want to create. The discussion starts with a simple app and looks closely at what can be automatically generated.

Creating a New Project

To create an app, the first step is to create a new project. To do this, follow these steps:

1. In Eclipse, choose File, New, and Android Application Project.

2. Fill in Hour1App for the Application Name. The Project Name and Package Name will be filled in automatically.

Your screen should look like what's shown in Figure 1.4.

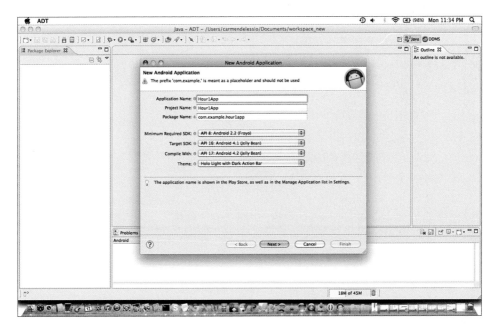

FIGURE 1.4
Naming your Android project

DID YOU KNOW?

Package Names

The package name in Figure 1.4 includes `com.example`, and a note tells you that you should change it. A Java package uniquely identifies an app. Typically, you use a reverse domain name structure. You can change the package name to anything you like. The apps in this book use `com.bffmedia` as the package name going forward.

3. Click Next. On the screen that appears, choose the checkbox to create a custom icon and create an activity. Your screen will look like Figure 1.5.

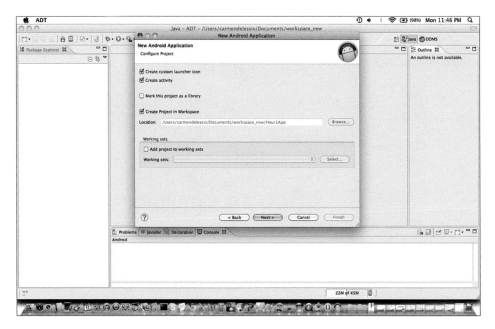

FIGURE 1.5
Configuring the project

4. Click Next. The icon screen appears. You can accept the default icon and choose an activity type for the app. Choose a Blank Activity and click Next. Your screen should look like Figure 1.6. Click Finish.

The project might take a minute or two to load, but your formally empty Eclipse ADT is starting to look full! Figure 1.7 shows the project in full. On the left, you see the Package Explorer for the Hour1App. Many folders have been created. The highlighted item is called activity_main.xml. The center of the screen shows a graphical representation of this XML file.

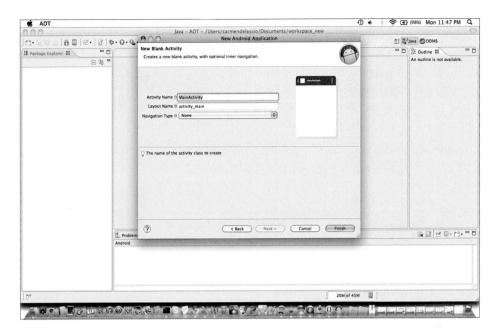

FIGURE 1.6
Creating a blank activity

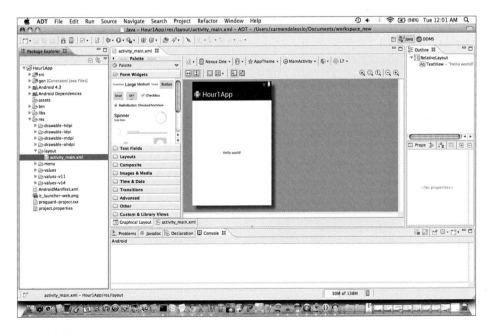

FIGURE 1.7
The newly created project

Understanding the Java Code and XML Layout

As mentioned, Figure 1.7 shows the graphical layout represented by the XML file activity_main. xml. In Android, this is a standard way to create the user interface. Creating or modifying a user interface on the fly is certainly possible, but for the most part, you will use XML files. You can modify these files through the graphical interface or by changing the XML directly. Both methods can be useful.

You just generated a simple app that shows the screen defined in the XML layout. There are methods in Java code to show that screen. To see the Java code, in the Package Explorer, expand the src folder and select the MainActivity.java file. Your screen should look like Figure 1.8.

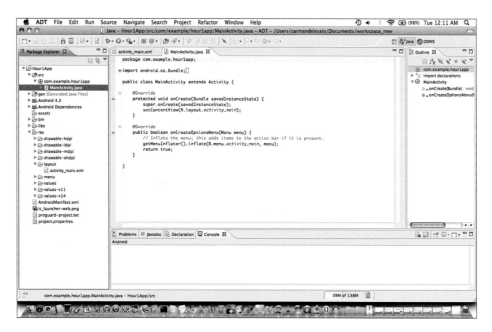

FIGURE 1.8
Source code for the app

In Figure 1.8, you can see that `MainActivity` extends a class called `Activity`. There are two methods: `onCreate` and `onCreateOptionsMenu()`. In the `onCreate()` method, you see the link between your source code and the XML layout file. A call is made to `setContentView()` with a reference to `R.layout.activity_main`. That is the XML file that you created.

You use the `onCreateOptionsMenu()` that is generated for handling menu items. Hour 7, "ActionBar and Menu Navigation," covers this in more detail.

Resource Files

Android converts files in the res folder to resources that are used within the app. The `activity_main.xml` file is in the folder res/layout/. When this is referred to as a resource within the app, it is `R.layout.activity_main`.

GO TO ▶ HOUR 3, "EXPLORING AN ANDROID PROJECT AND RESOURCES," to learn more about resources.

Running the App

To run the app, follow these steps:

1. Highlight Hour1App and right-click it with a mouse to show a list of options. You can also press the Control key and click a Mac. Choose Run As, and then Android Application (see Figure 1.9).

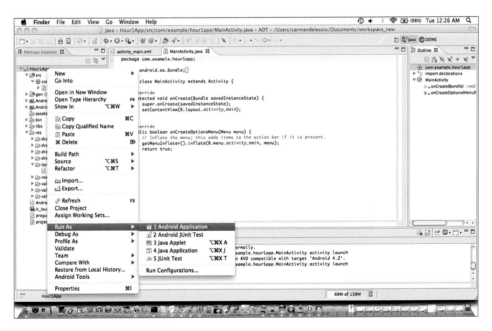

FIGURE 1.9
Running the app as an Android application

2. When you receive the error message "Android AVD Error," you can choose whether to create a new Android Virtual Device. Choose Yes.

An Android Virtual Device (AVD) is required to run the emulator. It defines the specifics of a device for testing in the emulator. Many different devices are available and you can create custom configurations. Creating a new AVD with the defaults provided is easy.

To do this, in the Android Virtual Device Manager screen:

1. Choose New to create a new AVD.

2. Select a device from the drop-down menu and give this AVD a name.

In Figure 1.10, the device selected is a Galaxy Nexus and the AVD Name is "GalaxyNexus."

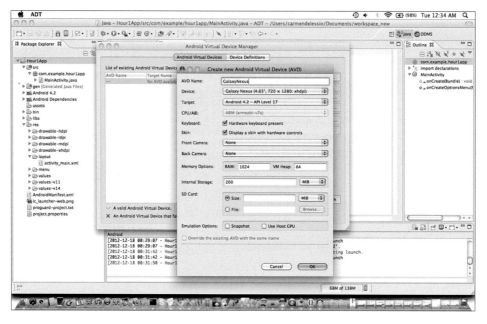

FIGURE 1.10
Android Virtual Device Manager

Now you can close the AVD Manager and run the app again. It should successfully run in the emulator using the Galaxy Nexus Android Virtual Device.

DID YOU KNOW?

Auto Monitor Logcat

When you run the app in the emulator, Eclipse asks whether you want to automatically monitor logcat. Logcat is an Android tool for showing the messages that are logged to the system. Logcat will be the first area you look when debugging, and you can add your own app messages. So, say "Yes" to monitoring logcat.

Personalizing the App

The instant app you created shows the words "Hello world!," as shown in Figure 1.11. You'll want to make this app your own by adding interactive features. To do this, you update the user interface by adding a field for entering data and a button. When the user clicks the button, the entered text appears in the center of the screen.

Updating the User Interface

The first step in making the app your own is to update the user interface.

TRY IT YOURSELF ▼

Updating the User Interface Using the Visual Editor

Using the visual editing tool that is built into the ADT, you can add a button and an `EditText` field. An `EditText` field is a text input field. To do so, follow these steps:

1. Find the activity_main.xml file in the res/layout folder. That is the file that was displayed when the app was created.

2. Choose a button from the Form Widgets section of the palette and drag it onto the app canvas. See Figure 1.11.

3. Select the Text Fields section of the palette. Choose the first type of `EditText` field and drag it onto the canvas. As you drag it, you see the words "Plain Text." Figure 1.12 shows your edits.

4. Save your changes.

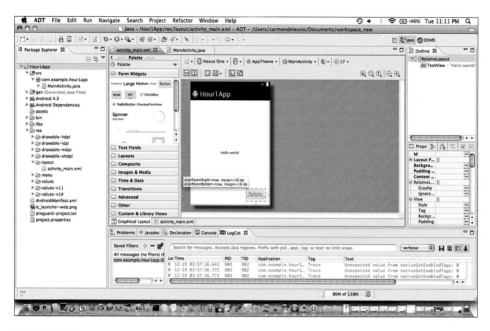

FIGURE 1.11
Adding a `Button`

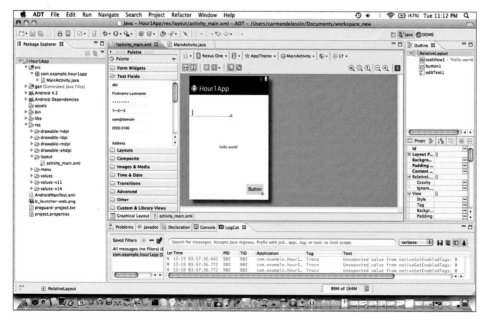

FIGURE 1.12
Adding an `EditText` field

Adding Action in Code

Now that you have the simple user interface for your app, add the code to refer to the Button and EditText. The next step is to update the TextView in the center of the screen. Listing 1.1 shows the XML code for Button that was created using the visual tool. The id for the Button is specified in line 2 as button1; the EditText is editText1; and the original TextView has the id textView1. These ids are important because they are used to refer to these user interface items in the code.

LISTING 1.1   Button Defined in XML Layout

```
1:  <Button
2:      android:id="@+id/button1"
3:      android:layout_width="wrap_content"
4:      android:layout_height="wrap_content"
5:      android:layout_alignParentBottom="true"
6:      android:layout_alignParentRight="true"
7:      android:layout_marginBottom="17dp"
8:      android:layout_marginRight="15dp"
9:      android:text="Button" />
```

The goal is to accept the information entered into the EditText and plop it into the TextView when the Button is clicked. The first step in doing that is making a connection between the user interface and the code. The second step is to add an action to the Button.

You need to modify the code that was generated. Select the MainActivity.java file in Eclipse. You modify the code in the onCreate() method, but first add the necessary imports for the user interface elements.

The new import statements are the following:

```
import android.widget.Button;
import android.widget.EditText;
import android.widget.TextView;
```

The complete list of imports is as follows:

```
import android.os.Bundle;
import android.app.Activity;
import android.view.Menu;
import android.view.View;
import android.view.View.OnClickListener;
import android.widget.Button;
import android.widget.EditText;
import android.widget.TextView;
```

These Java classes are included in Android in the widget package.

Add the code to the onCreate() method to associate the resources from the layout file with the code. Listing 1.2 shows the onCreate() method. Lines 5 through 9 define an EditText, TextView, and Button that you can now use in your code. The findViewById() method makes the association Line 4 tie this Activity to the XML layout file named activity_main. xml in the res/layout folder in your project. Lines 5–8 refer to the ids of each of the resources defined in that file.

LISTING 1.2   Referring to UI Widgets in Code

```
1:   @Override
2:     protected void onCreate(Bundle savedInstanceState) {
3:       super.onCreate(savedInstanceState);
4:       setContentView(R.layout.activity_main);
5:       EditText e =  (EditText)findViewById(R.id.editText1);
6:       TextView t =  (TextView)findViewById(R.id.textView1);
7:       Button b =  (Button)findViewById(R.id.button1);
8:   }
```

Listing 1.2 sets you up to read the data from the EditText field and populate the TextView when the Button is clicked. Listing 1.3 shows the code to do this.

LISTING 1.3   Responding to the Button Click

```
1:   @Override
2:     protected void onCreate(Bundle savedInstanceState) {
3:       super.onCreate(savedInstanceState);
4:       setContentView(R.layout.activity_main);
5:       final EditText e =  (EditText)findViewById(R.id.editText1);
6:       final TextView t =  (TextView)findViewById(R.id.textView1);
7:       Button b =  (Button)findViewById(R.id.button1);
8:       b.setOnClickListener(new OnClickListener() {
9:         public void onClick(View v) {
10:         t.setText(e.getText());
11:       }
12:     });
13: }
```

You add the *final* modifier to the declarations on lines 5 and 6. Final variables are not changed after they are assigned. That is true in this case, and it allows you to use these variables in the code for the Button. If the variable e is not declared final, you see this error in Eclipse:

```
Cannot refer to a non-final variable e inside an inner class defined in a different
method
```

This error occurs on line 10. In line 10, you use the variable e, but you are in an inner class. Line 8 declares a new instance of the class OnClickListener(). Using a variable that might change in a separate class like this is not allowed. By declaring e as a final variable, you can use it because you are assured it is not changing. You can also make the EditText a field in the class that would have global scope and be visible to all methods.

The code to update the TextView from the EditText field occurs on line 10. The text is read from variable e and set in variable t. Line 10 is in the onClick() method for Button b. Setting the onClickListener() in line 8 tells Button b to listen for clicks. When a click on the Button occurs, the onClick() method of the OnClickListener fires and the code runs to update the TextView.

Make these modifications, and run the app in the emulator to watch the interaction occur.

Summary

In this hour, the goal was to jump into Android development. The first step was to download and install a development environment for Android. Using that environment, you generated a simple application and then updated it. You learned that the user interface for an Android app can be created visually, and that it is actually an XML file. You saw how the Java code for Android development refers to resources in the XML layout. You added a simple action to the app by creating an onClickListener() method for a button.

Q&A

Q. Is it best to use the ADT Bundle to get started?

A. The ADT Bundle is the quickest and easiest way to start Android development, but if you have an existing Eclipse instance or are using an IDE other than Eclipse, you should be able to install the Android SDK, platform, and platform tools as separate pieces and continue to use the development environment that you are familiar with.

Q. Should I use the visual tool for creating user interfaces?

A. Generally, yes, but this chapter just introduces this tool. As you learn more about Android layouts, you might find yourself using both the tool and modifying XML directly.

Workshop

Quiz

1. In an activity, what method associates a resource for a `Button` to a variable of type `Button`?

2. How do you add a `Button` to the screen using the visual tool?

Answers

1. An activity includes a method called `findViewById()` that associates resources with variables in the code. Specifically, `findViewById()` is passed a resource id and returns the `Button` or other view associated with the resource. In this code, you must cast the view to the proper type.

2. Just drag and drop the `Button` from the palette to the app canvas.

Exercise

Use the visual editing tool to add additional items to the app. Those items should include a `CheckBox` and an `ImageView`, but this is a good opportunity to try many different user interface elements.

HOUR 2
Understanding an Android Activity

What You'll Learn in This Hour:

▶ Understanding an activity
▶ Starting an activity
▶ Passing information between activities
▶ Understanding intents
▶ Understanding the activity lifecycle

In Hour 1, you created an app that included an activity. In this hour, you consider activities in detail. Activities are a core component of Android. By examining activities, you can learn about both app development and how the Android system operates. This chapter covers how to launch activities and how to pass data between activities, as well as introduces Android intents by examining how they are used with activities.

Understanding an Activity

In Hour 1, "Getting Started: Creating a Simple App," you generated a simple app using Eclipse. The generation process created a class called MainActivity, which was an activity. You've used an activity already, and now in this chapter you examine activities more closely.

Activities have a well-defined lifecycle. An activity is created, started, resumed, paused, and destroyed. Those are some of the events in the lifecycle. For each event, you can override a callback method of the Activity class to do something when that event occurs. That is what you are doing when you override the onCreate() method. For example, in Hour 1, you modified the onCreate() method of MainActivity to create a Button and EditText field. This hour covers the activity lifecycle in detail.

Per the Android Developer documentation, "an activity is an application component that provides a screen with which users can interact in order to do something, such as dial the phone, take a photo, send an email, or view a map. Each activity is given a window in which to draw its user interface. The window typically fills the screen, but may be smaller than the screen and float on top of other windows."
(See http://developer.android.com/guide/components/activities.html.)

Starting an Activity

You can start activities in several ways. This section first covers starting one activity from another, and then examines how the initial activity in your app is launched.

Starting One Activity from Another

In Hour 1, you created a project called Hour1App and an activity called `MainActivity`. Follow the same process as "Creating a New Project" to create a project called Hour2App. When it's time to name the activity, call it ActivityA. In the example app, you'll start by having ActivityA start ActivityB.

▼ TRY IT YOURSELF

Create the Hour2App Project

Follow the same steps listed in Hour 1 to create a new project:

1. In Eclipse, choose File, New, and Android Application Project.

2. Name the project *Hour2App* and enter a Package Name.

3. Accept the default icon and choose to create a Blank Activity.

4. Use *ActivityA* for the Activity Name and *activity_layout* for the Layout Name.

5. Click Finish to create the project. See Figure 2.1.

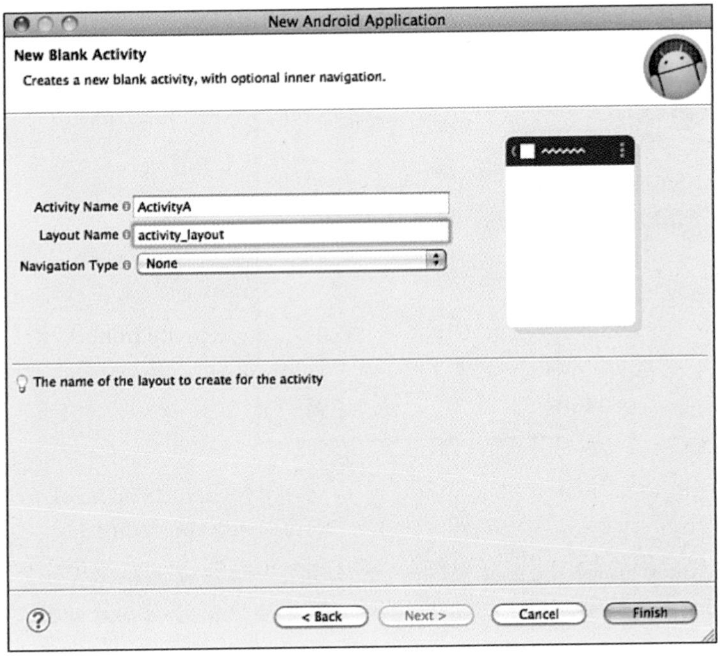

FIGURE 2.1
Final step to create Hour2App

The Hour2App now contains one activity and one layout. The layout is created for you and contains a `TextView` that displays "Hello world!." The goal is to create one activity that starts another. As such, you need two activities. For this demonstration app, you can use one layout for both activities.

The common layout is *activity_layout*. To create a second activity, you make a copy of *ActivityA*. In Eclipse, find ActivityA in the package you created in the /src folder. Right-click ActivityA and choose Copy. Highlight the package, right-click, and choose Paste. Eclipse provides a prompt for naming the second activity. Call the second activity *ActivityB*. Figure 2.2 shows a wireframe for the app you are creating. ActivityA will start ActivityB.

Figure 2.2 shows a button with the label Go in the activity. Create this button using the visual tools to drag as you did in Hour 1. You add the button to the *activity_layout* by dragging and dropping it from the palette to the layout canvas.

Now you want to change the properties for the button. After you add the button, you can use Eclipse to change the Text property of the button to contain the word *Go*. You might need to select the button to see the properties listed.

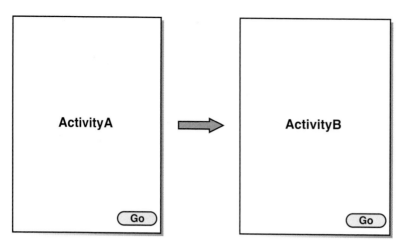

FIGURE 2.2
Wireframe for a two-activity app

With the layout in place, you can examine the code for launching ActivityB from ActivityA. Listing 2.1 shows that, as in Hour 1, you override the activity's onCreate() method and add code to handle the button click.

LISTING 2.1   Starting ActivityB from a Button Click (ActivityA.java)

```
1:   @Override
2:       protected void onCreate(Bundle savedInstanceState) {
3:       super.onCreate(savedInstanceState);
4:       setContentView(R.layout.activity_layout);
5:       Button b = (Button)findViewById(R.id.button1);
6:       b.setOnClickListener(new OnClickListener() {
7:        public void onClick(View v) {
8:       Intent intent = new Intent(ActivityA.this, ActivityB.class);
9:            startActivity(intent);
10:      }
11:   });
12: }
```

In line 8 of Listing 2.1, you create an Intent. The first parameter for the Intent is the current activity and the second parameter is the ActivityB class. In Android, Intents contain data about operations to be performed (covered in depth later this hour). For now, consider the Intent defined in line 8 as the mechanism to tie ActivityA to ActivityB. Line 9 starts the Intent. In Line 8, ActivityA.this is passed to refer to ActivityA because if you used the this keyword, you would be referring to the OnClickListener() class that was defined in line 6.

Of course, you can keep this simple and think of the `Intent` defined in line 8 as the setup for starting `ActivityB` in line 9.

To run the app, you must add `ActivityB` to the project's AndroidManifest.xml file. Every application must have an AndroidManifest.xml file. It presents essential information to the Android system about the application, including information about the available activities.

To add a reference to `ActivityB` to the AndroidManifest.xml file, find AndroidManifest. xml with the Hour2App project and select it. You edit the XML file directly by selecting the AndroidManifest.xml file tab, as shown in Figure 2.3.

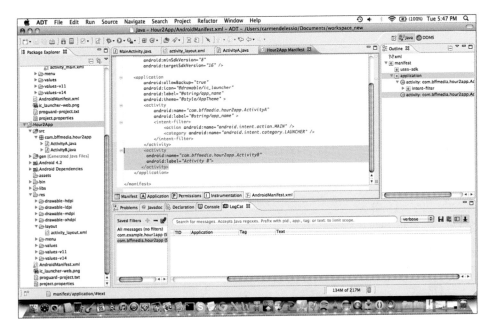

FIGURE 2.3
Editing the AndroidManifest.xml file

In the manifest file is an Application definition with `ActivityA` already defined. Add `ActivityB` within the Application section, as shown in Listing 2.2.

LISTING 2.2   Adding ActivityB to the Android Manifest

```
1:   <activity
2:   android:name="com.bffmedia.hour2app.ActivityB"
3:       android:label="Activity B">
4:   </activity>
```

Another way exists to add `ActivityB` using Eclipse. When editing the AndroidManifest.xml, choose the Application tab and then make updates in the Application Nodes section, as shown in Figure 2.4.

FIGURE 2.4
Modifying the AndroidManifest.xml file via Application nodes

With the definition of `ActivityB` in the AndroidManifest.xml file, you have a working project. The resulting app does very little, but it does define two activities and have one activity start another.

BY THE WAY

Don't Forget to Add the Activity to the AndroidManifest.xml File

If you do forget to add an activity, you get this fatal error:

```
Unable to find explicit activity class
{com.bffmedia.hour2app/com.bffmedia.hour2app.ActivityB}; have you declared this
activity in
your AndroidManifest.xml?
```

This helpful message tells you that class `com.bffmedia.hour2App.ActivityB` cannot be found. The hint is to check the AndroidManifest.xml file to see whether this activity has been declared.

Now it's time to expand on the code in ActivityB to have the `TextView` in each activity identify which activity is being displayed, and wire the `Button` in ActivityB to start ActivityA. Listing 2.3 shows the code for the `onCreate()` method of ActivityB.

LISTING 2.3   ActivityB Starting ActivityA (ActivityB.java)

```
1:   @Override
2:     protected void onCreate(Bundle savedInstanceState) {
3:       super.onCreate(savedInstanceState);
4:       setContentView(R.layout.activity_layout);
5:       TextView t =  (TextView)findViewById(R.id.textView1);
6:       t.setText("This is Activity B");
7:       Button b =  (Button)findViewById(R.id.button1);
```

```
8:     b.setOnClickListener(new OnClickListener() {
9:         public void onClick(View v) {
10:            Intent intent = new Intent(ActivityB.this, ActivityA.class);
11:            startActivity(intent);
12:    }
13:});
14: }
```

Lines 5 and 6 of Listing 2.3 define a TextView and set it to display "This is Activity B". Line 10 has ActivityB start ActivityA. The code for ActivityA is modified similarly to display "This is Activity A" in the TextView.

You can run this code in the emulator and easily switch between ActivityA and ActivityB by choosing the Go button in each activity. Figure 2.5 shows the app in the emulator.

After switching between ActivityA and ActivityB a number of times, if you use the Back button in the emulator, the app shows the activities in reverse order. That is, you will go back through each activity that you started. That might not be the behavior that you expected or wanted!

In Figure 2.5, the Back button is in the lower-left corner of the image.

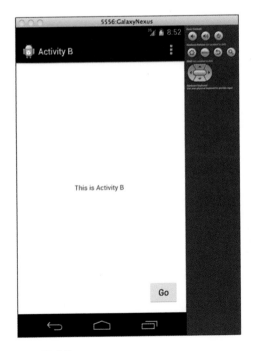

FIGURE 2.5
Hour2App running in the emulator

Back, Back, Back: Understanding the Back Stack

The behavior of the Back button for the Hour2App is the default behavior for Android apps. As an activity is started, it is added to the "back stack" for the application. The back stack is a stack of activities. The first activity is added to the stack and all subsequent activities are added to the stack when they start.

An activity may occur in the stack more than one time. In the Hour2App, ActivityA is added to the back stack when the app launches. Each time you click the Go button, you add either ActivityA or ActivityB to the stack. After clicking Go three times, the stack looks like ActivityB, ActivityA, ActivityB, ActivityA. The last ActivityA in this list was the activity started when the app launched.

Figure 2.6 shows the back stack. Thinking of each added activity as a card being added to a stack can be helpful.

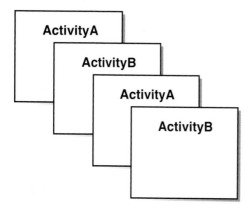

FIGURE 2.6
Visualizing the back stack

For most apps, the default behavior of the back stack gives the expected result. Options are available to change this behavior. One is to use intent flags to change the standard behavior. Listing 2.4 shows updated code to set two intent flags when you start each activity.

LISTING 2.4 Adding Intent Flags

```
1:  @Override
2:     protected void onCreate(Bundle savedInstanceState) {
3:     super.onCreate(savedInstanceState);
4:     setContentView(R.layout.activity_layout);
```

```
5:      TextView t = (TextView)findViewById(R.id.textView1);
6:      t.setText("This is Actvity B");
7:      Button b = (Button)findViewById(R.id.button1);
8:      b.setOnClickListener(new OnClickListener() {
9:          public void onClick(View v) {
10:             Intent intent = new Intent(ActivityB.this, ActivityA.class);
11:             intent.setFlags(Intent.FLAG_ACTIVITY_NEW_TASK|Intent.FLAG_ACTIVITY_
CLEAR_TOP);
12:             startActivity(intent);
13:         }
14:     });
15: }
```

Line 11 in Listing 2.4 sets the flags `Intent.FLAG_ACTIVITY_NEW_TASK` and `Intent.FLAG_ACTIVITY_CLEAR_TOP` for the intent created in line 10. Taken together these flags effectively keep one instance of each activity in the back stack. If you think of the stack as a set of cards, in this scenario, you have one card for ActivityA and one card for ActivityB. No matter how many times you navigate between the two activities, when you choose the Back button from ActivityB, you go to ActivityA, and when you choose the Back button from ActivityA, you exit the app.

In general, the best way to handle the back stack is to use the default model. As we introduce fragments and other navigational elements, like the ActionBar, we will revisit how the back stack is handled.

NOTE

What Is a Task in Android?

According to Android documentation, *"a task is a collection of activities that users interact with when performing a certain job."*

The activities are arranged in a stack based on the order in which they are opened. That is the back stack. Intent flags, such as `Intent.FLAG_ACTIVITY_NEW_TASK`, are based on this understanding of tasks. For additional information, see http://developer.android.com/guide/components/tasks-and-back-stack.html.

GO TO ▶ HOUR 7, "ACTIONBAR AND MENU NAVIGATION"

The Launch Activity

To start ActivityB from ActivityA, you created the ActivityB class and added it to the AndroidManifest.xml file. You then created an intent in ActivityA and started ActivityB.

That begs the question: How do you indicate that the app should start with ActivityA?

Remember that the basic code for ActivityA was generated for you. The AndroidManifest.xml file was also generated. The manifest file indicates the activity to launch when the app starts, as shown in Listing 2.5.

Lines 5 and 6 of Listing 2.5 define an action and category for ActivityA. By having the action set to MAIN and the category to LAUNCHER in the intent-filter, ActivityA is specified as the launch activity for this app. Think of the intent-filter as a set of rules that is checked when the Android system asks the question, "Is there an activity that can handle this?" In this case, the Android system is asking for a launch activity for this app. Lines 5 and 6 indicate that ActivityA can fulfill this request.

LISTING 2.5 **Android Manifest for the Launch Activity**

```
1:   <activity
2:       android:name="com.bffmedia.hour2app.ActivityA"
3:       android:label="Activity A" >
4:       <intent-filter>
5:         <action android:name="android.intent.action.MAIN" />
6:         <category android:name="android.intent.category.LAUNCHER" />
7:       </intent-filter>
8:   </activity>
```

Passing Information Between Activities

The app you have created does not do much, but the basics of starting one activity from another are in place. Apps get more interesting and useful when you pass data between activities. The two cases for passing data between apps are the following:

▶ Passing data from one activity to another; for example, ActivityA passes data to ActivityB.

▶ The first activity requests data from a second activity. So, ActivityA requests data from a new activity called ActivityC, and ActivityC returns data to ActivityA.

This section covers these two cases.

Using Extras and Bundles

To start an activity, you use an Intent (android.content.Intent). Data can be added to the intent that starts the activity. The intent and associated data is available when the new activity is started. Data is added to the intent as "extra" data. Data types such as strings, integers, and booleans can be passed as extras. A bundle of data and more complex data types can also be passed. Listing 2.6 shows ActivityA modified to add data to the intent that starts ActivityB.

Lines 6–11 in Listing 2.6 add data to the intent. In Line 6, a bundle is defined. A `Bundle(android.os.Bundle)` contains data defined by key-value pairs. On Line 7, the string "Hello" is added to the `Bundle` b and identified by the key `"greeting"`. Line 8 adds the bundle to the intent. Lines 9–11 put additional extra data into the intent.

LISTING 2.6   Adding Extra Data to an Intent

```
1:  Button b =  (Button)findViewById(R.id.button1);
2:  b.setOnClickListener(new OnClickListener() {
3:  public void onClick(View v) {
4:    Intent intent = new Intent(ActivityA.this, ActivityB.class);
5:    intent.setFlags(Intent.FLAG_ACTIVITY_NEW_TASK|Intent.FLAG_ACTIVITY_CLEAR_
TOP);
6:    Bundle b = new Bundle();
7:    b.putString("greeting", "Hello");
8:    intent.putExtra("greetingBundle", b);
9:    intent.putExtra("message", "World!");
10:   intent.putExtra("showAll", true);
11:   intent.putExtra("numItems", 5);
12:   startActivity(intent);
13: }
14: });
```

Listing 2.6 adds data to the intent that starts ActivityB. Listing 2.7 shows how that intent data is accessed and used. Line 5 of Listing 2.7 gets the intent that started ActivityB. With the intent, the bundle and other data defined in ActivityA can be accessed. Line 6 accesses the bundle, and line 7 retrieves the string from the bundle. Lines 8–10 retrieve the additional extra data from the intent. The data passed from ActivityA is displayed in ActivityB. Lines 12 and 13 display the passed data in the `TextView` in ActivityB (see Figure 2.7).

LISTING 2.7   Accessing Extra Data from an Intent

```
1:  @Override
2:  protected void onCreate(Bundle savedInstanceState) {
3:    super.onCreate(savedInstanceState);
4:    setContentView(R.layout.activity_layout);
5:    Intent intent = getIntent();
6:    Bundle bundle = intent.getBundleExtra("greetingBundle");
7:    String greeting = bundle.getString("greeting");
8:    String message = intent.getStringExtra("message");
9:    Boolean showAll = intent.getBooleanExtra("showAll", false);
10:   intnumItems = intent.getIntExtra("numItems",0);
11: TextView t =  (TextView)findViewById(R.id.textView1);
12:   t.setText("This is Activity B: "  + greeting + " "
13:             + message + " " + showAll + " " + numItems);
14: });
```

Naming Intent Extras

To illustrate how extras are used to pass data, Listings 2.6 and 2.7 use string literals such as a "greeting" for keys. One practice for naming extra keys is to start with the package name. So, you would use "`com.bffmedia.hour2app.greeting`" as the key. Defining a constant value for the key is a recommended practice, as follows:

```
private static final String GREETING= "com.bffmedia.hour2app.greeting";
```

Eclipse has a convenient technique for creating constants: Highlight the string literal and choose the menu options for Refactor, Extract Constant.

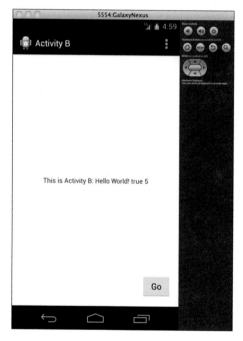

FIGURE 2.7
Displaying data from ActivityA in ActivityB

Returning a Result: Using StartActivityForResult

So far, you have created activities, started activities, and passed data from one activity to another using intents. Another way that activities interact is when one activity starts another with a request to return a result. ActivityA can start ActivityC and request a result from ActivityC. In that case, ActivityA uses `startActivityForResult()` and must handle the result and any data provided by ActivityC. ActivityC might or might not return data, but it will generally provide a result to ActivityA.

For example, in an app that uploads photos, your main activity might use `startActivity-ForResult()` to start an activity for selecting an image from the file system.

TRY IT YOURSELF ▼

Create ActivityC to Handle Data Requests

Let's create a simple app to demonstrate the use of `startActivityForResult()`.

1. Copy activity_layout.xml to a file called activity_c_layout.xml.

2. Modify the new layout file using the visual editor. There should be one `EditText` and two `Buttons`: one for Send Data and the other for Cancel.

3. Create an activity called ActivityC. (You can copy ActivityA to start.)

4. Update ActivityC to use the new layout in `setContentView`.

5. Refer to the buttons you created in the activity code.

6. Add ActivityC to the AndroidManifest.xml file.

7. See Listing 2.8 for the basic ActivityC code.

Listing 2.8 shows ActivityC with an `EditText` and two `Buttons`. The code sets up empty `onClickListener()` methods for each `Button`. The next step is to add code for each `Button`.

LISTING 2.8   Starting Code for ActivityC

```
1:  public class ActivityC extends Activity {
2:      @Override
3:      protected void onCreate(Bundle savedInstanceState) {
4:          super.onCreate(savedInstanceState);
5:          setContentView(R.layout.activity_c_layout);
6:          final EditText e = (EditText)findViewById(R.id.editText1);
7:          Button send =  (Button)findViewById(R.id.button1);
8:          send.setOnClickListener(new OnClickListener() {
9:              public void onClick(View v) {
10:                 // Add send button code here
11:             }
12:         });
13:         Button cancel =  (Button)findViewById(R.id.button2);
14:         cancel.setOnClickListener(new OnClickListener() {
15:             public void onClick(View v) {
16:     // Add cancel button code here
17:             }
18:         });
19:      }
20: }
```

In ActivityC, the Send Data button sends data back to the calling activity. The Cancel button ends the activity without sending data.

To send data back to the calling activity, you use an intent to pass the data. Listing 2.9 shows the code for the Send Data button. In line 3, a new intent called `result` is instantiated. In line 4, extra data is added to the intent. The data is the contents of the EditText. Line 5 uses the setResult() method. The first parameter is `Activity.RESULT_OK`, which indicates that the data has been set. The second parameter is the `Intent` that contains the data. Line 6 is a call to the finish method to end the activity.

So, clicking the Send Data button takes the data entered in the EditText view and returns it the calling activity as an extra within an intent.

LISTING 2.9   Returning a Result from an Activity

```
1:   send.setOnClickListener(new OnClickListener() {
2:     public void onClick(View v) {
3:       Intent result = new Intent();
4:       result.putExtra("Data", e.getText().toString());
5:       setResult (Activity.RESULT_OK, result);
6:       finish();
7:     }
8:   });
```

Listing 2.10 shows the code for the Cancel button. The setResult() method is used in line 3 with the single parameter `Activity.RESULT_CANCELLED`.

LISTING 2.10   Returning No Result from an Activity

```
1:   cancel.setOnClickListener(new OnClickListener() {
2:     public void onClick(View v) {
3:       setResult (Activity.RESULT_CANCELLED);
4:       finish();
5:     }
6:   });
```

You have created ActivityC with a way to handle passing data back to a calling activity. Now you need to actually call ActivityC from somewhere. To do that, add a Get Data button to ActivityA's layout. That button will start ActivityC. ActivityA will also need to handle the data returned from ActivityC.

Listing 2.11 shows the code for the Get Data2 button in ActivityA. Line 5 uses startActivity-ForResult to start ActivityC. The parameters are the intent and an integer to track the request.

LISTING 2.11   Using StartActivityForResult

```
1:   Button getData =   (Button)findViewById(R.id.button2);
2:   getData.setOnClickListener(new OnClickListener() {
3:   public void onClick(View v) {
4:     Intent intent = new Intent(ActivityA.this, ActivityC.class);
5:     startActivityForResult(intent, 0);
6:   }});
```

You must also modify ActivityA to handle the results from ActivityC, as shown in Listing 2.12. You must override the method onActivityResult() to handle the returned data. In line 2, you can see that the parameters to this method are requestCode, resultCode, and data. The requestCode is the value you passed when you called startActivityForResult(). In line 5 of Listing 2.11, you can see that zero was passed as the requestCode. The resultCode is the result set in ActivityC. It will either be Activity.RESULT_OK or Activity.RESULT_CANCELLED. If data is available, it will be passed in the intent parameter.

Line 3 of Listing 2.12 checks for a requestCode of zero and a resultCode of Activity. RESULT_OK. If this is the request you want and the result is OK, you get the data from the passed intent in line 4 and use that data in line 5 to populate the TextView in ActivityA. The result of Activity.RESULT_CANCELLED is ignored.

Figure 2.8 shows the relationship between ActivityA and ActivityC in the case of using startActivityForResult(). The Cancel button on ActivityC returns a result of Activity.RESULT_CANCELLED to ActivityA.

LISTING 2.12   Handling the Result

```
1:   @Override
2:     protected void onActivityResult(int requestCode, int resultCode, Intent data
) {
3:       if (requestCode == 0 && resultCode == Activity.RESULT_OK){
4:             String enteredData = data.getStringExtra("Data");
5:             t.setText(enteredData);
6:       }
7:       super.onActivityResult(requestCode, resultCode, data);
8:   }
```

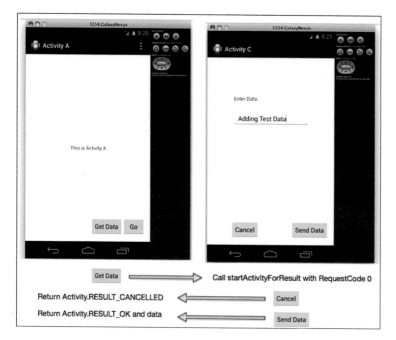

FIGURE 2.8
ActivityA requests information from ActivityC.

Understanding Intents

Intents have been used a number of times in this hour. They have been used to start an activity, pass data to an activity, and to request a result from an activity.

So far, you have used *explicit* intents, which means intents that refer explicitly by class name for the activity that you want to start. In the case of explicit intents, the action to perform is specified by the activity.

There are also *implicit* intents. Activities can start an implicit intent that does not specify a specific activity, but rather requests an action of some kind. For example, implicit intents can retrieve an image from the file system or take a picture with the camera. The request specifies the action to take, not the activity to run.

When a request for action is made using implicit intent, the Android platform determines which activity will handle the request or presents a list of available activities to the user to select. There might be many activities that can handle an implicit intent.

This section demonstrates the use of an implicit intent by showing you how to add the ability to handle `Intent.ACTION_SEND` for plain text to ActivityB. That means when any activity makes a request to handle `Intent.ACTION_SEND`, ActivityB will be one of the options. You will be adding this as a new capability for ActivityB.

You will modify ActivityB and change the AndroidManifest.xml file to indicate that ActivityB can handle this intent. You do this by adding an intent filter. Listing 2.13 shows the changes to the AndroidManifest.xml file for ActivityB. Line 5 in Listing 2.13 indicates that ActivityB will handle the `android.intent.action.SEND` action. This is one of many intent actions that are defined for Android. Line 7 indicates that ActivityB will handle plain text data. As you implement the changes to ActivityB to handle the intent, you can see how action and data are used.

LISTING 2.13   Changing IntentFilter in the Manifest File

```
1:    <activity
2:        android:name="com.bffmedia.hour2app.ActivityB"
3:        android:label="Activity B">
4:        <intent-filter>
5:          <action android:name="android.intent.action.SEND" />
6:          <category android:name="android.intent.category.DEFAULT" />
7:          <data android:mimeType="text/plain" />
8:        </intent-filter>
9:    </activity>
```

Recall that you added the ability for ActivityB to get data from ActivityA via an intent. Now you modify ActivityB to check the action associated with the intent. If the action equals `Intent.ACTION_SEND`, you'll handle the passed data. If it does not, assume the intent came from ActivityA.

Listing 2.14 shows the updates to ActivityB to handle the `ACTION_SEND` intent.

LISTING 2.14   Handling Intent.ACTION_SEND

```
1:    TextView t = (TextView)findViewById(R.id.textView1);
2:    Intent intent = getIntent();
3:    if (intent!=null){
4:        String action = intent.getAction();
5:        String type = intent.getType();
6:        if (Intent.ACTION_SEND.equals(action) && "text/plain".equals(type)) {
7:            t.setText(intent.getStringExtra(Intent.EXTRA_TEXT));
8:        }else{
9:            //handle intent data from ActivityA
```

Now ActivityB is ready to act on any intent for an activity that handles action `Intent.ACTION_SEND` with type "plain/text." You can see this work in a number of ways. Using the browser app, you can share a URL. Figure 2.9 shows the Share Page function in the browser. When you select that option, ActivityB appears as an option, as shown in Figure 2.10. The URL provided from the browser `ACTION_SEND` intent will be displayed in ActivityB as the passed data.

Each activity that can handle the `ACTION_SEND` intent is shown. Figure 2.10 shows that the available options are ActivityB and the Messaging app.

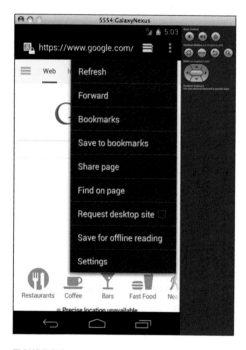

FIGURE 2.9
Sharing a page from the browser

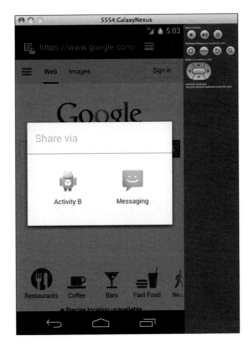

FIGURE 2.10
ActivityB displaying as an option to handle the browser `ACTION_SEND` intent

You have seen that when the `startActivity()` method is called with the intent parameter, the Android system matches the intent action with the appropriate activity on the Android system. The appropriate activity then launches. An intent object encapsulates a task request used by the Android operating system.

The Android system handles all intent resolution. An intent can be specific, such as a request for a specific activity to be launched, or somewhat vague, requesting that any activity matching certain criteria be launched. In this example, ActivityB launches directly from ActivityA. ActivityB also launches when it meets the criteria of handling the intent for `ACTION_SEND` for the specified mime type.

Passing Information with Intents

Intents can be used to pass data between activities. You use an intent in this way by including additional data, called *extras*, within the intent.

As you saw in Listing 2.6, to package extra pieces of data along with an intent, you use the `putExtra()` method with the appropriate type of object to include.

When you use the `startActivityForResult()` method, the result is passed in as a parameter to the `onActivityResult()` method with an intent parameter. The intent data can then be extracted and used by the parent activity.

Using Intents to Launch Other Applications

Apps may launch external activity classes in other applications.

There are well-defined intent actions for many common user tasks. For example, you can create intent actions to initiate applications such as the following:

▶ Launching the built-in web browser and supplying a URL address

▶ Launching the web browser and supplying a search string

▶ Launching the built-in Dialer application and supplying a phone number

▶ Launching the built-in Maps application and supplying a location

▶ Launching Google Street View and supplying a location

▶ Launching the built-in Camera application in still or video mode

▶ Launching a ringtone picker

▶ Recording a sound

Here is an example of how to create a simple intent with a predefined action (ACTION_VIEW) to launch the web browser with a specific URL:

```
Uri address = Uri.parse("http://developer.android.com/");
Intent androidDocs = new Intent(Intent.ACTION_VIEW, address);
startActivity(androidDocs);
```

This example shows an intent that has been created with an action and some data. The action, in this case, is to view something. The data is a uniform resource identifier (URI), which identifies the location of the resource to view.

For this example, the browser's activity then starts and comes into the foreground, causing the original calling activity to pause in the background. When the user finishes with the browser and clicks the Back button, the original activity resumes.

Applications may also create their own intent types and allow other applications to call them.

Understanding the Activity Lifecycle

In this hour, you learned how to start activities and how activities pass data and work with each other. An activity also has a number of internal states. Activities are created, started, paused, resumed, and destroyed. The states that an activity goes through are known as the activity lifecycle. The activity lifecycle includes creating, starting, pausing, resuming, and destroying activities.

The activity lifecycle is important because each point in the lifecycle provides an opportunity to take an action within the activity. There may be set-up work to do when an activity is started and clean-up work to do when an activity is paused.

So far, all the activities that you developed have used the onCreate() method to set up the user interface for the app. In onCreate(), you call setContentView() to tie the activity to the layout and define all the user interface elements such as EditText and Buttons.

When an activity is created, it is being set up. When it is started, the activity is visible to the user. A resumed activity is also visible to the user. A paused activity might be partially visible, for example, such as an activity seen behind a dialog window. A stopped activity is not visible to the user. Ultimately, an activity is destroyed

An activity that is visible to the user and that the user can interact with is considered to be in the foreground.

For each of these states, a callback method exists within the activity. Callback methods exist for onCreate(), onPause(), onResume(), onStop(), and onDestroy().

Figure 2.11 shows the important methods of the activity lifecycle. In Figure 2.11, onResume() is called both when the activity is first started and when it is resumed. It is called whenever the activity comes to the foreground. That makes it a good place to do things such as get intents and read extra data.

The onCreate() method is used to set up the user interface using setContentView() and to initialize any other static parts of the activity.

As shown in Figure 2.11, the onStart() method runs after an activity has been sent to the background. That makes the onStart() method a good spot to ensure that any required system resources are still available. For example, if your GPS is required, onStart() is a good place to ensure that GPS is available. The advantage of checking GPS in onStart() is that onStart() is called less frequently than onResume().

The onPause() method fires when the activity leaves the foreground. That might mean that a dialog window is showing and the activity will resume shortly, or it might mean it is the first step in the activity being stopped. This makes onPause() a good place to perform tasks such as stopping animations, saving uncommitted data, and releasing system resources. Anything released with the onPause() method should be reset in the onResume() method.

The onStop() method assures you that the activity is in the background. It is the place to release all resources that are not required for the user to interact with the activity. Killing threads in the onPause() or onStop() methods is best. Cleanup might occur in the onDestroy() method for any long-running processes that should continue after the activity is stopped.

You can match the methods for creating and cleaning up items. If something is created in onResume(), clean it up in onPause(). If something is allocated in onStart(), clean it up in onStop().

In practice, you might find yourself using onCreate(), onResume(), and onPause() for app initialization and cleanup.

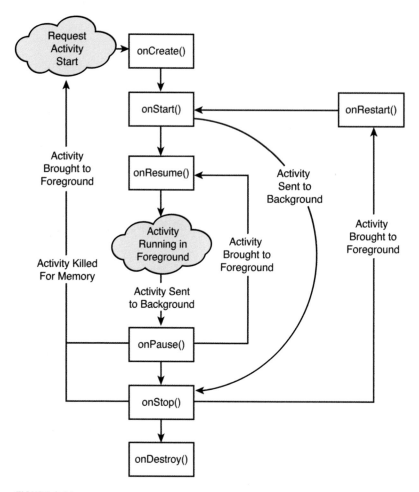

FIGURE 2.11
Important callback methods of the activity lifecycle

Table 2.1 shows the key callback methods for activities with recommendations on the functionality to handle in those methods.

TABLE 2.1   Key Callback Methods of Android Activities

Callback Method	Description	Recommendations
onCreate()	Called when an activity is created.	Initialize activity data. Set layout with setContentView() and set up user interface.
onStart()	Called when activity becomes visible.	Check to ensure that resources are enabled.
onResume()	Called when the activity is brought to the foreground, including when the activity is first created.	Acquire exclusive resources. Start audio/video. Get intents and extra data.
onPause()	Activity is not in the foreground. It might be partially visible, such as when it is covered by a dialog window.	Stop animations, save uncommitted data, release system resources.
onStop()	The activity is completely hidden and not visible to the user. The activity is in the background.	Release all resources not needed for the user to interact with the app. Clean up activity resources.
onDestroy()	Called when an application is shutting down.	Most cleanup should be done in onPause() and onStop(). Kill any long-running threads or processes here.

Summary

This hour covered activities from both an implementation and technical definition perspective. On the implementation side, you saw how to start one activity from another, how to pass data between activities, how one activity can request information from another, and how an activity can handle data shared from another application.

You also learned about the relationship between intents and activities, which provided the basis for understanding explicit intents and implicit intents. Explicit intents are direct calls to specific activities. Implicit intents are general calls to action in the system that are handled by any activity with matching criteria.

Q&A

Q. What is the relationship between activities and intents?

A. Intents contain a call to action and can carry additional data. The call to action in an intent usually results in an activity being started. The data provided in the intent is made available to the activity. When activities are started, they are passed intents.

Q. What is the importance of the activity lifecycle?

A. The activity lifecycle provides an opportunity to clean up an app as it is shutting down and to efficiently start and resume apps.

Workshop

Quiz

1. What two methods are used to start activities?

2. When an activity expects a result, what method must be implemented to handle the result?

3. What is the difference between a bundle and extra data?

Answers

1. The two methods are `startActivity` and `StartActivityForResult`. An intent is passed to both. `StartActivityForResult` also takes an integer value to track the request.

2. The method `onActivityResult` must be implemented. It will be passed a result code, a request code, and any data.

3. A bundle is a collection of data. An extra is used to add data to an intent. A bundle can be an extra. That is, a bundle can be defined, populated with data, and then added to an intent.

Exercises

1. Create an activity called `InputActivity`. It should have two `EditText` fields called `numEditText1` and `numEditText2` that accept numbers as input. Add a `Button` to the activity called "Add."

When the Add button is clicked, take the data entered in the two `EditText` fields and save the data in a bundle.

2. Create a second activity called `AddActivity` that adds two numbers passed in a bundle and displays the results in a `TextView`.

3. Pass the bundle from the `InputActivity` to the `AddActivity` and verify their results.

To convert the passed strings to numbers `(int)`, use the function `Integer.parseInt(string)`.

This is not a "real-world" example, but it shows the ability to create activities, design simple layouts, and pass data between activities in a meaningful way.

HOUR 3
Exploring an Android Project and Resources

What You'll Learn in This Hour:

▶ Exploring the Android project files

▶ Understanding common resources

▶ Using image resources

▶ Using styles

▶ Raw and asset folders

In both Hour 1, "Getting Started: Creating a Simple App," and Hour 2, "Understanding an Android Activity," you learned how to create Android projects and update specific project resources such as the layout files. This hour reviews the components of an Android project in detail and examines some of the types of resources that can be used in an Android project. The discussion begins with a review of the resources that are included on initial project creation followed by a closer look at some additional resources.

Exploring the Android Project Files

Android applications are made up of executable code (Java code, classes) and data (including resources such as graphics, strings, and so on). Most Android application resources are stored under the /res subdirectory of the project.

In Hours 1 and 2, you used Eclipse to create a new project. This hour examines precisely what is generated during that process.

Folders and Files at Project Creation

Create Hour3App using the same process you used in Hour 1 and Hour 2. That is, you create Hour3App as a new Android Application Project that includes a Blank Activity named MainActivity.java. Figure 3.1 shows the folder structure created by Eclipse for Hour3App.

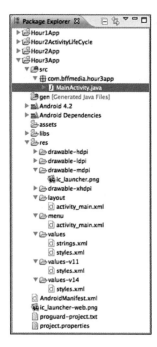

FIGURE 3.1
Folder structure for Hour3App

Let's take this from the top and review each folder. When you do this yourself, you should see the Hour3App Android project in the Eclipse File Explorer. The following files and directories have been created:

- ▶ **/src folder**—Required folder for all source code.

- ▶ **/src/com.bffmedia.hour3app/MainActivity.java**—The main entry point to this application, named MainActivity. This activity has been defined as the default launch activity in the Android manifest file.

- ▶ **/gen/ com.bffmedia.hour3app /R.java**—A generated resource management source file. Do not edit this file. This hour explains the role of R.java.

- ▶ **/Android 4.2 folder**—The Android platform.

- ▶ **/Android dependencies folder**—Includes the Android compatibility library.

- ▶ **/assets folder**—A required folder where uncompiled file resources can be included in the project.

- ▶ **/libs folder**—Contains any additional Java libraries that are added to the project.

▶ **/bin folder**—The output directory of the build. An Android app builds an APK file. That APK will be in the Bin file.

▶ **/res folder**—A required folder where all application resources are managed. Application resources include animations, drawable graphics, layout files, data-like strings and numbers, and raw files.

▶ **/res/drawable-***—Application icon graphic resources are included in several sizes for different device screen resolutions.

▶ **/res/layout/activity_main.xml**—Layout resource file used by Hour3App to organize controls on the main application screen.

▶ **/res/menu/activity_main.xml**—A menu for the activity can be defined here. This can be used as an action bar or menu and is covered in Hour 7, "ActionBar and Menu Navigation."

▶ **/res/values/strings.xml**—The resource file where string resources are defined.

▶ **/res/values/styles.xml**—The resource file where style resources are defined.

▶ **/res/values-11/styles.xml**—The resource file where style resources that are used in API version 11 are defined.

▶ **/res/values-14/styles.xml**—The resource file where style resources that are used in API version 14 are defined.

▶ **AndroidManifest.xml**—The central configuration file for the application.

▶ **Ic_launcher-web.png**—This is a 512x512 image. It is not used directly in the app, but will be used in the Google Play Store to promote the app. It was created when you set up the project using a custom icon.

▶ **Proguard-project.txt**—Proguard provides a mechanism to obfuscate Android binaries. ProGuard can be enabled by modifying the project.properties file. Additional options for ProGuard are added to the proguard.project.txt file.

▶ **project.properties**—Contains project specific info. In the initial build using Eclipse it indicates that the build is being done on Android version 17.

Understanding the R.java File

The R.java file must never be edited. It is a generated file. This section examines the contents of the R.java file because it is the link between the resource files and the Java source code.

When you create your project using Eclipse, an XML layout and source code for the activity is created. In the onCreate() method for the activity, the layout is associated with the code with a call to setContentView():

```
setContentView(R.layout.activity_main);
```

The method called setContentView() takes a resource id as a parameter. The resource ID is an integer. You can see an association between the name of the XML layout and the resource id in the code. The name of the layout file is activity_main.xml and the resource ID is R.layout. activity_main. The way that association occurs is in the R.java file. You'll see how.

When you build an Android project, an R.java file is generated that includes resource IDs based on the information in the /res/ folders. You are most familiar with /res/layout. The R.java file lives in the /gen/ folder.

The build process generates the R.java file based on the XML layout file and all the other resource files. The definitions for resource IDs for resources such as Buttons and TextViews are created the same way.

This snippet of the generated class R shows an inner class called layout that defines an int called activity_main. When you refer to R.layout.activity_main in the code, you are using the integer 0x7f030000:

```
public final class R {
  . . .
 public static final class layout {
        public static final int activity_main=0x7f030000;
    }
}
```

All the resources in the /res/ folders will be defined in the R.java file, which includes drawables and other resource types that covered in this hour.

Android Platform and Android Dependencies

Whenever you create an Android project, you must use an Android platform. The default project using the ADT sets the platform to Android 4.2. The content of the Android 4.2 folder is an Android.jar that was installed with the ADT Bundle download.

Android dependencies contain jar files that support Android. When Eclipse creates a project it includes the Android Compatibility Library.

If problems occur with Android dependencies, they can generally be fixed in Eclipse by choosing Android tools and then Fix Android properties for the project.

GO TO ▶ **HOUR 4, "NOT JUST SMARTPHONES: SUPPORTING TABLETS, TVS, AND MORE,"** for more information on the Android Compatibility Library.

Understanding Common Resources

Common resources for a project include layout files, image drawables, string definitions, and more.

The following sections consider resources in general and then a few common resource types more closely.

Using Resources

Grouping application resources together and compiling them into the application package has the following benefits:

- ▶ Code is cleaner and easier to read, leading to fewer bugs.

- ▶ Resources are organized by type.

- ▶ Resources help in dealing with the large variety of Android devices, often automatically.

- ▶ Localization and internationalization are straightforward.

- ▶ Raw files of all types can be accessed.

Resource files stored within /res subdirectories must abide by the following rules:

- ▶ Resource filenames must be lowercase.

- ▶ Resource filenames may contain letters, numbers, underscores, and periods only.

NOTE

Resources: How They Help in the Real World

One advantage of using resources is that the appearance of the entire app you are developing can be changed easily. For example, you might have defined a resource that specifies a blue gradient as a drawable image. Several places in your app might rely on that resource. If you have a last-minute request to change to from blue gradient to red, you should be able to just change it in the resource file.

Referencing Application Resources

All application resources are stored within the /res project directory structure and are compiled into the project at build time. Application resources can be used programmatically. They can also be referenced in other application resources.

Application resources are accessed programmatically using the generated class file called R.java. To reference a resource from within your Activity class, you must retrieve the application's

`Resources` object using the `getResources()` method and then make the appropriate method call, based on the type of resource you want to retrieve.

For example, to retrieve a string named `hello` defined in the `strings.xml` resource file, use the following method call:

```
String greeting = getResources().getString(R.string.hello);
```

To reference an application resource from another compiled resource, such as a layout file, use the following format:

```
@[resource type]/[resource name]
```

For example, the same string used earlier would be referenced as follows:

```
@string/hello
```

Working with System Resources

Applications can access the Android system resources in addition to private resources.

System resources are stored within the `android.R` package. Classes exist for each of the major resource types. For example, the `android.R.string` class contains the system string resources. To retrieve a system resource string called `ok` from within an `Activity` class, you first need to use the static method of the `Resources` class called `getSystem()` to retrieve the global system `Resource` object. You then call the `getString()` method with the appropriate string resource name, like this:

```
String confirm = Resources.getSystem().getString(android.R.string.ok);
```

To reference a system resource from another compiled resource, such as a layout resource file, use the following format:

```
@android:[resource type]/[resource name]
```

For example, you could use the system string for `ok` by setting the appropriate string attribute as follows:

```
@android:string/ok
```

Hour 11, "App Setting: Managing Preferences," demonstrates how to use `ListViews`. In a `ListView`, using a system resource to define the look of an item within the list is common. For example, `android.R.layout.simple_list_item_1` defines a layout that displays one line of text and is appropriate for showing an item in a list.

Working with Simple Resources

Simple resources such as string, color, and dimension values should be defined in XML files under the /res/values project directory in XML files. These resource files use XML tags that represent name-value pairs. You can manage string, color, and dimension resources by using the Eclipse resource editor by editing the XML resource files directly.

Working with Strings

You can use string resources anywhere your application needs to display text. You define string resources with the <string> tag, identify them with the name property, and store them in the resource file /res/values/strings.xml.

Here is an example of the string resource file that was created when you created the Hour3App using Eclipse:

```xml
<?xml version="1.0" encoding="utf-8"?>
<resources>
<string name="app_name">Hour3App</string>
<string name="hello_world">Hello world!</string>
<string name="menu_settings">Settings</string>
</resources>
```

String resources have a number of formatting options. Strings that contain apostrophes or single straight quotes must be escaped or wrapped within double straight quotes. Table 3.1 shows some simple examples of well-formatted string values.

TABLE 3.1   String Resource Formatting Examples

String Resource Value	Will Be Displayed As
Hello, World	Hello, World
"Hello, World"	Hello, World
Mother\ 's Maiden Name:	Mother's Maiden Name:
He said, \ "No.\ "	He said, "No."

You can access a string resource programmatically in several ways. The simplest way is to use the getString() method within your Activity class:

```
String greeting = getResources().getString(R.string.hello);
```

String resources should be used in layout files. When you are putting text on a button, the text should come from a string resource. The usage is as follows:

```
android:text="@string/hello_world"
```

Working with Colors

You can apply color resources to screen controls. You define color resources with the `<color>` tag, identify them with the `name` attribute, and store them in the file /res/values/colors.xml. This XML resource file is not created by default and must be created manually.

You can add a new XML file, such as this one, by choosing File, New, Android XML File and then filling out the resulting dialog with the type of file (such as values). This automatically sets the expected folder and type of file for the Android project.

Here is an example of a color resource file:

```
<?xml version="1.0" encoding="utf-8"?>
<resources>
<color name="background_color">#006400</color>
<color name="app_text_color">#FFE4C4</color>
</resources>
```

The Android system supports 12-bit and 24-bit colors in RGB format. Table 3.2 lists the color formats that the Android platform supports.

TABLE 3.2 Color Formats Supported in Android

Format	Description	Example
#RGB	12-bit color	#00F (blue)
#ARGB	12-bit color with alpha	#800F (blue, alpha 50%)
#RRGGBB	24-bit color	#FF00FF (magenta)
#AARRGGBB	24-bit color with alpha	#80FF00FF (magenta, alpha 50%)

The following `Activity` class code snippet retrieves a color resource named `app_text_color` using the `getColor()` method:

```
int textColor = getResources().getColor(R.color.app_text_color);
```

Working with Dimensions

To specify the size of a user interface control such as a `Button` or `TextView` control, you need to specify different kinds of dimensions. Dimension resources are helpful for font sizes, image sizes and other physical or pixel-relative measurements. You define dimension resources with the `<dimen>` tag, identify them with the name property, and store them in the resource file /res/values/dimens.xml. This XML resource file is not created by default and must be created manually.

Here is an example of a dimension resource file:

```xml
<?xml version="1.0" encoding="utf-8"?>
<resources>
<dimen name="thumbDim">100px</dimen>
</resources>
```

Each dimension resource value must end with a unit of measurement. Table 3.3 lists the dimension units that Android supports.

TABLE 3.3 Dimension Unit Measurements Supported in Android

Type of Measurement	Description	Unit String
Pixels	Actual screen pixels	px
Inches	Physical measurement	in
Millimeters	Physical measurement	mm
Points	Common font measurement	pt
Density-independent pixels	Logical Pixel	dp
Scale-independent pixels	Best for scalable font display	sp

The following `Activity` class code snippet retrieves a dimension resource called `thumbDim` using the `getDimension()` method:

```
float thumbnailDim = getResources().getDimension(R.dimen.thumbDim);
```

The use of device independent pixels and scale independent pixels is highly recommended. In Android, there are not fixed screen sizes, so using device independent values helps to assure your layout display well on different devices.

GO TO ▶ HOUR 5, "USING LAYOUTS," for additional information on designing a layout using device independent pixels.

Working with Drawable Resources

Drawable resources, such as image files, must be saved under the /res/drawable project directory hierarchy. Android devices have different sizes and different pixel density screens. Android provides a mechanism to show an appropriate image for each type of screen. When applications provide multiple versions of the same image for different pixel density screens, the appropriate image will be shown for the screen. That is, a high-density image will be shown on a high-density screen.

The Android project contains three drawable directories: drawable-ldpi (low density), drawable-mdpi (medium density), and drawable-hdpi (high density). The system picks the correct version of the resource based on the device the application is running on. All versions of a specific resource must have the same name in each of the drawable directories.

GO TO ▶ HOUR 4, "NOT JUST SMARTPHONES: SUPPORTING TABLETS, TVS, AND MORE," for additional information on designing a layout using device independent pixels.

You can drag and drop image files into the /res/drawable directory by using the Eclipse Project Explorer or use the import mechanism to specify one or more files to import.

Working with Images

The most common drawable resources used in applications are bitmap-style image files, such as PNG and JPG files. These files are often used as application icons and button graphics but may be used for a number of user interface components.

As shown in Table 3.4, Android supports many common image formats.

TABLE 3.4   Image Formats Supported in Android

Supported Image Format	Description	Required Extension
Portable Network Graphics	Preferred format (lossless)	.png (PNG)
Nine-Patch Stretchable	Preferred format (lossless)	.9.png (PNG) Images
Joint Photographic Experts	Acceptable format (lossy)	.jpg (JPEG/JPG) Group
Graphics Interchange	Discouraged but supported	.gif (GIF) Format (lossless)

NinePatch—What's That?

Android includes a drawable type known as a ninepatch. The class for a ninepatch is android.graphics.drawable.NinePatchDrawable. A ninepatch is designated with the extension .9.png. Android provides a tool called the Draw 9-patch tool for creating these images.

A ninepatch is a stretchable bitmap image that has some fixed elements. Parts of the nine-patch image stretch as the image grows and some parts are left unchanged. The use of a nine-patch is best shown by example. Standard Android buttons use a ninepatch image as a background. With a button, the center stretches, but the border of the button does not.

For more information on ninepatch, see http://developer.android.com/tools/help/draw9patch.html.

Using Image Resources Programmatically

Image resources are encapsulated in the class `BitmapDrawable`. To access a graphic resource file called /res/drawable/logo.png within an `Activity` class, use the `getDrawable()` method, as follows:

```
BitmapDrawable logoBitmap =
    (BitmapDrawable)getResources().getDrawable(R.drawable.logo);
```

You can use the resource identifier for an image directly within another control. An `ImageView` control displays an image. The image in an `ImageView` can be set by using a resource identifier for an image to the source attribute of the `ImageView`.

A condition in your app might cause you to change the image in an `ImageView`. The following `Activity` class code sets and loads the `logo.png` drawable resource into an `ImageView` control named `LogoImageView`, which must be defined in advance:

```
ImageView logoView = (ImageView)findViewById(R.id.LogoImageView);
logoView.setImageResource(R.drawable.logo);
```

Working with Other Types of Drawables

In addition to graphics files, you can also create specially formatted XML files to describe other drawable subclasses, such as `ShapeDrawable`. You can use the `ShapeDrawable` class to define different shapes, such as rectangles and ovals.

See additional documentation on drawables at http://developer.android.com/guide/topics/resources/drawable-resource.html.

You will define two simple shapes as drawable resources using XML. The goal is to create a gradient and to create shape that can be used as a background to frame an image. The gradient transitions from blue to black. The frame is a line that defines a rounded rectangle.

The gradient is a rectangle defined by the following XML. This is the content of the file gradient.xml, which is placed in a drawable folder:

```
<shape xmlns:android="http://schemas.android.com/apk/res/android"
android:shape="rectangle">
<gradient android:startColor="#0000ff" android:endColor="#000000"
    android:angle="270"/>
</shape>
```

The gradient has a start color (blue) and end color (black) and an angle of 270. The angle is the direction of the gradient. Zero is left to right and 90 is bottom to top. Use 270 to get blue to black and top to bottom.

Now, define shape that can act a border for images. The shape is a rectangle with rounded corners and padding. The shape is defined by the following XML. This is the contents of the file background.xml, which is placed in a drawable folder:

```
<shape xmlns:android="http://schemas.android.com/apk/res/android"
android:shape="rectangle">
<stroke android:width="2dp" android:color="#EEEEEE" />
<padding android:left="10dp" android:top="20dp"
         android:right="10dp" android:bottom="20dp" />
<corners android:bottomRightRadius="7dp"
         android:bottomLeftRadius="7dp"
         android:topLeftRadius="7dp"
         android:topRightRadius="7dp"/>
</shape>
```

This XML defines a rectangle shape. Stroke indicates the width of the line to draw (like the stroke of a pen). Padding pads the shape and the corners are defined with slight rounding.

To see the gradient and background in action, Hour3App uses the gradient drawable as the background for the RelativeLayout defined in activity_main.xml.

An `ImageView` is added to the project that uses the ic_launcher.png image as the source value. Use the background.xml as the background for the `ImageView`. The result is shown in Figure 3.2.

FIGURE 3.2
Using a gradient and shape drawable as a background

Adding Animations

Adding animation to an application can be a fun way to add style. Animations are appropriate if your app includes a splash screen and animations might fit well into certain aspects of your design. This section looks at a simple animation that uses an animation resource file. The goal is to make the image fade in when displayed.

Under the res/ folder, create a folder called anim to hold your animation files. You then create fadein.xml in that folder.

Fadein.xml specifies that the alpha value should move from 0.0 to 1.0 (invisible to fully visible) with a duration of 2000. That is, 2,000 milliseconds, so this means you are defining a fade-in animation that takes 2 seconds to go from invisible to visible, which is shown in Figure 3.3.

```
<?xml version="1.0" encoding="utf-8"?>
<alpha xmlns:android="http://schemas.android.com/apk/res/android"
android:interpolator="@android:anim/accelerate_interpolator"
android:fromAlpha="0.0" android:toAlpha="1.0" android:duration="2000" />
```

FIGURE 3.3
A fade-in animation

Using Styles in Views

Android styles can be used to set a multiple attributes for a view. For example, if you want to define a `TextView` to use a white text color, use italic, and use a font size of 20sp, you could define each of those individual values or define a style that uses all of those characteristics and assign that style to the `TextView`.

Let's look at two snippets of XML code that show the same result in regard to displaying a `TextView`. In the first snippet, the values are set directly in the `TextView` attributes:

```
android:text="TextView"
android:textColor="#ffffff"
android:textSize="20sp"
android:textStyle="italic"
```

The second case defines a style called `CustomText` in the styles.xml file in the res/values folder:

```
<style name="CustomTextStyle"   >
<item name="android:textColor">#ffffff</item>
```

```
<item name="android:textSize">20sp</item>
<item name="android:textStyle">italic</item>
</style>
```

Then, you can apply the style you defined to a `TextView` with the line:

```
style="@style/CustomTextStyle"
```

The result is that the `TextView` controls display in an identical manner.

By defining and using styles, you can give your app a distinct look and feel. Your results will be consistent and you can change the look of the app easily by changing the contents of the style files.

Using the Raw and Assets Folders

You add raw resource files to a project by including them in the raw/ resources project directory. You can do this by creating them as a new file, dragging them in from a file management tool, or any other way you're accustomed to adding files to Android projects in Eclipse.

Raw resources are files that are compiled into the project and accessible for your use. Because they are in the resource folder structure, they are provided with a resource id and are accessible using the R.raw. *resourcename* convention.

Assume that you have a raw resource file called instructions.txt. The goal is to read the file and display the contents.

To read the file, use the `openRawResource()` method to obtain an `inputStream`:

```
InputStream  instructions = getResources().openRawResource(R.raw.instructions);
```

Now the `inputStream` can be read to get the contents of the file as a `String`. A number of ways exist to do this in Java. This Java method reads an `InputStream` and returns a `String` with its contents:

```
public String inputStreamToString(InputStream is) throws IOException {
    StringBuffer sBuffer = new StringBuffer();
    DataInputStream dataIO = new DataInputStream(is);
    String strLine = null;
    while ((strLine = dataIO.readLine()) != null) {
        sBuffer.append(strLine + "\ n");
    }

    dataIO.close();
    is.close();

    return sBuffer.toString();
}
```

The assets/ folder can also be used to store files. The files are unchanged and no resource identifier is associated with them. The assets/ folder preserves the original filenames used. You use the class `AssetManager` (`android.content.res.AssetManager`) to access these files.

Summary

This hour examined the structure and contents of an Android project and took a closer look at how to create and use resources

Android applications can use many different types of resources, including application-specific resources and system-wide resources. Once defined, resources can be accessed programmatically as well as referenced, by name, by other resources. String, color, and dimension values are stored in specially formatted XML files, and graphic images are stored as individual files. Application user interfaces are defined using XML layout files. Raw files, which can include custom data formats, may also be included as resources for use by the application. Finally, applications may include numerous other types of resources as part of their packages.

Q&A

Q. **Must string, color, and dimension resources be stored in separate XML files?**

A. Technically, no. However, it is a good practice to follow. Keeping the resource types separate keeps them organized.

Q. **What are some of the technical and practical benefits of using resources?**

A. Using resources keeps your code cleaner and more readable. In practice, using resources and for colors, text, and styles allows you to consistently and quickly change the look and feel of your app just by changing the resource files.

Workshop

Quiz

1. What color formats are supported for color resources?

   A. 12-bit color
   B. 24-bit color
   C. 64-bit color

2. True or False: You can include files of any format as a resource.

   3. Which graphics formats are supported and encouraged on Android?

       A. Joint Photographic Experts Group (JPG)

       B. Portable Network Graphics (PNG)

       C. Graphics Interchange Format (GIF)

       D. Nine-Patch Stretchable Images (.9.PNG)

   4. True or False: Resource filenames can be uppercase.

Answers

   1. A and B. Both 12-bit and 24-bit color are supported.

   2. True. Any file can be added as a raw resource.

   3. B and D. Although all four formats are supported, they are not all encouraged. PNG graphics, including Nine-Patch Stretchable graphics, are highly encouraged for Android development because they are lossless and efficient. JPG files are acceptable but lossy, and GIF file use is outright discouraged.

   4. False. Resource filenames may contain letters, numbers, and underscores and must be lowercase.

Exercises

   1. Add a new color resource with a value of `#00ff00` to your Hour3App project. Within the activity_main.xml layout file, change the `textColor` attribute of the `TextView` control to the color resource you just created. View the layout in the Eclipse and then rerun the application and view the result on an emulator or device—in all three cases, you should see green text.

   2. Add a new dimension resource with a value of 22pt to your Hour3App project. Within the activity_main.xml layout file, set the `textSize` attribute of the `TextView` control to the dimension resource you just created. View the layout in the Eclipse Layout Resource Editor and then rerun the application and view the result on an emulator or device—in all three cases, you should see larger font text (22pt). What happens if you try it with different screen density settings in the emulator? What about the use of px, dp, or sp as the unit type?

   3. Add a new drawable graphics file resource to your Hour3App project (for example, a small PNG or JPG file). In Eclipse, add an ImageView control to the layout. Then set the ImageView control's src attribute to the drawable resource you just created. View the layout in the Eclipse layout resource editor and then rerun the application and view the result on an emulator or device—in all three cases, you should see an image below the text on the screen.

Not Just Smartphones: Supporting Tablets, TVs, and More

What You'll Learn in This Hour:

▶ A brief history of Android

▶ Handling device display and orientation

▶ Device features

▶ Platform versions and the compatibility package

▶ Launching apps on a device

Android was developed to run on different kinds of hardware and to support various screen sizes. For building a user interface for an Android app, support for multiple screen sizes and densities was included from the start. Density refers to the number of pixels in a physical area on the screen. With the capability to support multiple hardware devices and screen sizes, Android was eventually deployed on tablets and on Google TVs. This hour provides a brief history of Android, considers options for supporting multiple devices with different characteristics, reviews the SDKs that have been released, and introduces the Android Support Library. The Support Library brings some newer SDK features to older versions of Android.

A Brief History of Android

In October 2008, the HTC Dream (or G1) phone was released with the 1.0 version of the Android operating system. The phone was available to T-Mobile customers in the United States and via other providers in Europe.

At the time the G1 was released, the Android Software Development Kit (SDK) had been available to developers for a year, but few applications were available in the early days.

In March 2009, approximately 2,300 applications were in the Android market. By late 2011, the number of Android apps was more than 100,000, and by late 2012, more than 700,000 apps were available.

Android began as an independent company in 2003 and was purchased by Google in 2005. The Android operating system is based on Linux, and the development environment uses the Java language.

Android operating system releases are known by their dessert-based code names. Android 1.5, released on the G1 in 2009, was known as Cupcake. Donut, Eclair, Froyo, and Gingerbread followed Cupcake. Honeycomb was then released as a tablet-specific version of Android. Honeycomb was followed by Ice Cream Sandwich (ICS) and Jelly Bean.

In September 2011, Amazon released a seven-inch tablet known as the Kindle Fire. The first Kindle Fire ran a customized version of Gingerbread. The current generation Kindle Fire HD runs a custom version of Ice Cream Sandwich.

Google TV was originally released on the Eclair version of Android, but then received a major upgrade to Honeycomb.

That's a lot of devices, manufacturers, and OS versions. By understanding the options for working with different devices and features, simplifying the task of supporting a large number of devices and OS versions is possible.

Handling Device Display and Orientation

When you develop an Android app, the goal is to make sure that the app looks good wherever it runs. Android devices come with a variety of display settings, including different screen sizes, densities, aspect ratios, resolutions, and default orientations. You should consider these factors when designing the app.

To simplify working with different types of screen configurations, the Android system looks at two important characteristics: *screen density* and *screen size*.

Screen Density

Screen density is the physical density of the screen. It is the dots-per-inch (dpi) displayed.

Android defines four screen densities: *low density*, *medium density*, *high density*, and *extra high density*. These densities are not device specific; they allow similar devices to be placed in the same group.

You have already encountered one way that Android provides support for devices with different screen densities: In Hour 3, you examined the structure of an Android project and saw that multiple folders were provided for drawable resources. The folders correspond to the four defined screen densities. The screen density categories are used to group devices and are approximate values:

- ▶ **Low** (ldpi): 120dpi

- ▶ **Medium** (mdpi): 160dpi

- ▶ **High** (hdpi): 240dpi

- ▶ **Extra high** (xhdpi): 320dpi

Screen Size

Screen size is the actual physical size of the screen. Android characterizes screen size into four general sizes: *small*, *normal*, *large*, and *extra large*.

For each Android screen size, a range might exist of actual physical dimensions on the device. That is, two devices with *normal* screen size from the Android perspective might have screens with different physical dimensions. Android uses a generic screen size definition to simplify working with multiple sizes. There is a range for each size.

The minimum size of these generic screen sizes can also be considered in DIPs, or *density-independent pixels* (dip or dp). The screen sizes with their *approximate* size and minimum resolution in dips are as follows:

- ▶ **Small (2 inches)**: Minimum 426dp x 320dp

- ▶ **Normal (4 inches)**: Minimum 470dp x 320dp

- ▶ **Large (7 inches)**: Minimum 640dp x 480dp

- ▶ **Extra large (10 inches)**: Minimum 960dp x 720dp

As with densities, these screen sizes allow different devices to be considered together as part of the same group.

NOTE

Density-Independent Pixels (DIPs or DPs)

Screens have a density expressed in dots-per-inch (DPI). A density-independent pixel has the size of one physical pixel on a device with a 160dpi screen. So, a density-independent pixel is equivalent to one physical pixel on a medium device. For higher-density screens, the number of physical pixels increases with the DPI.

One device-independent pixel equals 1 physical pixel on a 160dpi screen.

One device-independent pixel equals 1.5 physical pixels on a 240dpi screen.

Physical pixels can be determined from the DPI as follows: $px = dp * (dpi / 160)$ where px is physical pixels, dp is the number of device-independent pixels, and dpi is the dpi of the device. Ten device-independent pixels are equivalent to 15 physical pixels on a 240dpi screen.

Handling Screen Size and Density

One option for handling devices with different screen sizes and densities is to do nothing. No, really! The Android system will adjust your user interface (UI) layouts and drawables to best match the device that the application is running on. Drawable images will be stretched based on device-independent pixels and Android will do the best it can with the layout.

Another way to look at "doing nothing" is that you are creating a device-independent UI that works well on all Android device screens.

An important caveat applies to the "doing nothing" method. You must use the layouts that support stretching and sizing. You must also specify the width and height of widgets using settings such as WRAP_CONTENT and MATCH_PARENT.

GO TO ▶ HOUR 5, "USING LAYOUTS," for more information on using layouts.

The key to a device-independent user interface is to use density-independent pixels in your layout! Android adjustments are based on using dp units.

Figure 4.1 shows the ic_launcher.png icons that are created by default for a project. The Android icon is shown from the extra-high density version to the low-density version. The medium-density version is 48 pixels wide and 48 pixels high (48 x 48). By understanding screen size and densities, you can figure out how to scale appropriately. A high-density screen is 240dpi and is 1.5 times denser than a medium-density screen. The high-density screen graphic is 72 pixels by 72 pixels, which is 1.5 times larger than the image for the medium screen. The other images are scaled similarly.

Keep in mind that the goal of having separate images like these is that the images will appear with the same proportions on devices of different densities. *All four images have the same dp size.* On the higher-density screens, the images will be shown more sharply.

FIGURE 4.1
Sizing graphics from extra-high density to low density

You can use two more techniques to handle different screen sizes. One is to create alternate resource folders, and the other is to use the <supports-screens> element in your manifest. You might choose to use these options to create a pixel-perfect experience, such as in certain types of games or other applications where the visual design is the dominant factor. Using the built-in flexibility of Android usually makes it unnecessary to create many alternate resource folders. Also consider which on-screen elements should grow to fill an area and which should be fixed in place. Using device-independent pixel sizes for elements, such as borders combined with layouts where other elements fill the parent or wrap content, can make a consistent design across devices.

Alternative Resources

Providing different versions of images in different resource folders applies the concept of using alternative resources. Having a drawable-mdpi folder specifies to the system where medium density images can be found. You can extend that concept to creating folders for different types of alternative resources.

In addition to the drawable density qualifiers such as `mdpi`, you can use size qualifiers of `small`, `normal`, `large`, and `xlarge`.

To create an alternate layout for an extra-large screen, you append `xlarge` to the layout folder:

```
/res/layout-xlarge/activity_main.xml
```

You can also address screen orientation by using alternative resources. The following section covers screen orientation in more detail. To support portrait and landscape orientation, the qualifiers `port` and `land` are available.

Table 4.1 shows a list of import resource directory qualifiers. Note that the Android SDK version can be directly targeted using resources.

You can combine resource qualifiers. The following is a valid resource directory for landscape orientation on an extra-large device:

```
res/layout-xlarge-land/my_layout.xml
```

TABLE 4.1   Important Resource Directory Qualifiers

Directory Qualifier Type	Values	Comments
Language	en, fr, es, zh, ja, ko, de, and so on	ISO 639-1 two-letter language codes
Region/locale	rUS, rGB, rFR, rJP, rDE, and so on	ISO 3166-1-alpha-2 region code in ALL UPPERCASE, preceded by a lowercase r
Screen dimensions	small, normal, large, xlarge	Screen size and density ratio
Screen aspect ratio	long, notlong	Screen aspect ratio to handle "wide screen" devices
Screen orientation	port, land	Portrait mode, landscape mode
Dock mode	car, desk	Device is in a specific dock state
Night mode	night, notnight	Device is in night or day mode
Screen pixel density	ldpi, mdpi, hdpi, xhdpi, nodpi	Screen density that the resource is for
Touch screen type	notouch, stylus, finger	No touch screen, Stylus-only, Finger touch screen

Directory Qualifier Type	Values	Comments
Is keyboard available	keysexposed, keyshidden, keyssoft	Keyboard available, keyboard not available to user, resources used only with software keyboard
Primary non-touch screen navigation method	nonav, dpad, trackball, wheel	Four-key directional pad, trackball, scroll wheel
SDK version	v1, v2, v3, v4, v5, v6, v7, v8, v9, v10, v11, v12, and so on	The SDK version's API level (for example, v4 is Android SDK 1.6, while v11 represents 3.0)

Adding <supports-screens>

You can add the `<supports-screens>` element to the AndroidManifest.xml file. The idea is to specify which screens your application supports. This limits the number of devices that can run your app, but provides for additional control over the user experience. If your app just does not work well on small screens, then using `<supports-screens>` to restrict access is a good option. Later, if you decide to add a small-screen version, you can remove this element.

Values are set to true or false for attributes based on screen size; for example, `android:smallScreens=false`.

BY THE WAY

More About <supports-screens>

For additional information on `<supports-screens>`, see the documentation on the AndroidManifest.xml file at http://developer.android.com/guide/topics/manifest/supports-screens-element.html.

Here are the techniques to support multiple screens:

▶ Use device-independent pixels in your layouts.

▶ Provide alternative graphics resources.

▶ Provide other alternative resources (this should only be needed in rare cases).

▶ Use the `<uses-screens>` element in the AndroidManifest.xml file.

Orientation

Android applications can run in landscape or portrait mode. For a phone or tablet, the orientation depends on how the user tilts the device screen. Google TVs are always in landscape mode. One approach to handling screen orientation is to design simple layouts that work in either portrait or landscape mode.

Another technique is to use alternative resources by specifying layout-land or layout-port resource directories.

To implement different screen orientations using alternative resources, do the following:

1. Create a new landscape-specific layout file to the /res/layout-land/ directory.

2. Make sure to include all the controls defined in default layout resources that are referenced in the Java code or other files.

3. Design a new version of the layout that meets your design expectation for landscape mode.

BY THE WAY

Toggling the Orientation of the Emulator

On Windows, you can toggle the orientation of the emulator by pressing Ctrl+F11 and Ctrl+F12. For Macintosh, use Ctrl+fn+F11.

Handling Orientation Changes Programmatically

An orientation change is considered to be a configuration change in Android. In each activity that you have created thus far, you have loaded a layout in the onCreate() method. An orientation change is an opportunity for a different layout to load. So, considering it a configuration change makes sense.

When a configuration change occurs, the current activity is restarted. The onDestroy() method of the activity is called followed by the onCreate() method. The application then reloads, taking the new configuration into account.

This gets complicated when the state of the activity has changed and should be retained after the configuration changes. To consider a simplified example, if you download an image and display it when you start your activity, if you do nothing, you will download the image a second time when the orientation changes.

Retaining Data Across Configuration Changes

One way to address retaining data across configuration changes is the use the `onSaveInstan-ceState()` method to save data about the application state. Considering the activity lifecycle, you would then restore the state during `onCreate()` or `onRestoreInstanceState()`. In the following example, the value 5 is stored with the key `"numAttempts"` during the `onSaveIn-stanceState()` method and restored during the `onCreate()` method:

```
protected void onSaveInstanceState(Bundle outState) {
super.onSaveInstanceState(outState);
outState("numAttempts", 5);
}
public void onCreate(Bundle savedInstanceState) {
if (savedInstanceState != null){
int numAttempts = savedInstanceState("numAttempts");
   }
}
```

TIP

Saving State

Often saving state in an activity might mean saving a limited number of items. For a complex form where the user has entered data in fields, losing that data on a configuration change will certainly be an unpleasant experience. So, save the state of your UI elements! That means checkboxes, text entries, or other selections.

Using android:configChanges

What if you don't need the activity to restart on an orientation change? If you are certain that you don't need to load resources on certain configuration changes, you can use the Android manifest to indicate that you will handle configuration changes yourself. When you do this, the activity is not shut down and restarted on a configuration change.

You can add code to the `onConfigurationChanged()` method and handle everything yourself.

And, in certain cases, you can indicate that you will handle configuration changes and *not* implement the `onConfigurationChanged()` method!

You can do that when no need exists to update the application based on a configuration change. In this case, you have all the resources you did before the configuration change and have avoided restarting the activity.

Adding the following to the AndroidManifest.xml file indicates that the `MyActivity` activity will handle configuration changes for `orientation` and `keyboardHidden`. The `keyboard-Hidden` attribute indicates that a slideout keyboard has been used:

```
<activity android:name=".MyActivity"
android:configChanges="orientation|keyboardHidden"
          android:label="@string/app_name">
```

Device Features

Different devices have different features. A particular phone or tablet might or might not have a camera. Some devices have two cameras. What about location-based services such as GPS? What about the availability of Near Field Communication (NFC) or Bluetooth? Any particular phone or device may or may not have these capabilities. Your app should check for these features before using them.

Android provides a way to specify whether a particular device feature is required or optional for your app. If a feature is optional, Android must provide a way to detect whether the feature is available.

The following sections consider the case of an app that optionally uses a camera. If a camera is available, the app would show additional options to the user.

The <uses-feature> Element in AndroidManifest.xml

The <uses-feature> element indicates that a specific device feature is used by the application. The Android system does not use this element directly, but services such as Google Play use it to determine how to interact with your app. Using the element is straightforward. You specify the feature and use an indicator for whether the feature is required. To indicate that a camera is used in the app but is not required, you would add the following:

```
<uses-feature android:name="android.hardware.camera" android:required="false"/>
```

Being accurate in the manifest is important. If the main purpose of your app is to log trip information, adding a photo using a camera would be a nice extra feature, but is not required. By indicating that the app uses the camera, but it is not required, enables users who do not have a camera on their device to use the app.

Detecting Feature Availability

If your app uses a camera, but the camera is not required, you need a way to check whether a camera is available. You do so with the android.content.pm.PackageManager class. The PackageManager class contains information about application packages that are installed on the device.

The getPackageManager() method is called from a context, so it can be called from within an activity. The following snippet instantiates a PackageManager and uses the hasSystemFeature() method to check whether a camera is available:

```
PackageManager pm = getPackageManager();
if (pm.hasSystemFeature(PackageManager.FEATURE_CAMERA)) {
  // add camera code here
}
```

This `PackageManager` code lists the features related to a camera. The full list of possible device features is available in the documentation for `PackageManager` at http://developer.android. com/reference/android/content/pm/PackageManager.html:

- ▶ FEATURE_CAMERA indicates the device has a camera facing away from the screen (not front-facing).

- ▶ FEATURE_CAMERA_ANY indicates the device has at least one camera pointing in some direction.

- ▶ FEATURE_CAMERA_AUTOFOCUS the device supports auto-focus.

- ▶ FEATURE_CAMERA_FLASH the device supports flash.

- ▶ FEATURE_CAMERA_FRONT indicates the device has a front-facing camera.

Platform Versions and the Compatibility Package

This hour began with a brief history of Android that mentioned the Android 1.5 release known as Cupcake. In fact, a name and *two numbers* are associated with each release of Android. One number is the version number, such as 1.5, and the other is API level. Table 4.2 shows the list, starting with Android 2.1.

TABLE 4.2   Android Versions and Android Levels

Version	Name	API Level
Android 2.1	Eclair	7
Android 2.2.x	Froyo	8
Android 2.3-2.3.2	Gingerbread	9
Android 2.3.3-2.3.7	Gingerbread	10
Android 3.0	Honeycomb	11
Android 3.1	Honeycomb	12
Android 3.2	Honeycomb	13
Android 4.0-4.0.2	Ice Cream Sandwich	14

Version	Name	API Level
Android 4.0.3-4.0.4	Ice Cream Sandwich	15
Android 4.1	Jelly Bean	16
Android 4.2	Jelly Bean	17
Android 4.3	Jelly Bean	18

Each new version of Android will have features for both users and developers. This hour covers some of these features at a high level. Though Table 4.2 shows multiple versions of Android, the effective list of versions is smaller. Some releases, such as 3.0, are quickly replaced by others and virtually no devices are running that particular version.

Honeycomb (3.0-3.2) was released as a tablet-only version. Most tablets received a fast update from 3.0 to 3.2 and have subsequently been upgraded to Ice Cream Sandwich or Jelly Bean.

At the time of this writing (June 2013), four main Android versions are in use: Froyo by 3% of users, Gingerbread by 36% of users, Ice Cream Sandwich by 25% of users, and Jelly Bean by 33% of users. This accounts for 97% of the devices in use.

The Android developer site includes information on the user and developer features that are available in each release: http://developer.android.com/about/versions/index.html.

In the AndroidManifest.xml file, you set a minimum SDK version and a target SDK version with the `<uses-sdk>` element. To support Ice Cream Sandwich and higher, you would set the minimum SDK versions to 14. Here's the format:

```
<uses-sdk android:minSdkVersion="integer"
          android:targetSdkVersion="integer"
android:maxSdkVersion="integer" />
```

What strategy should you use for setting SDK versions? The target SDK should be the highest version that you have tested on. The minimum API should be the lowest API level you need to run. If you use classes from API level 8, then set the `minSdkVersion` to 8. Setting `maxSdkVersion` is not typically necessary.

Introducing Fragments and the Action Bar

Honeycomb introduced fragments and the action bar to be used by developers and seen by users as an integral part of the user interface. You'll look at both of these features in detail in this book as you design more complex user interfaces.

A fragment represents a behavior or portion of the user interface within an activity. A fragment is sort of like a modular part of an activity that can be added or removed. It is something of a "subactivity."

One advantage of fragments is that they provide a mechanism for developing modular parts of a user interface that can be used in different ways on different devices. You can combine multiple fragments in either a tablet or phone user interface, but you can develop an app where multiple fragments are shown in the tablet design and only one in the phone design. You can use the same fragments in both devices.

The action bar is a persistent bar across the top of the screen in an app. It can provide navigation, status information, and contextual options.

Figure 4.2 shows the action bar for Gmail on a phone in landscape mode.

FIGURE 4.2
Gmail action bar

Fragments and the action bar are powerful features that are helpful to developers. The action bar is also highly visible to app users. Each version of Android offers other feature differences for developers, but these two are called out because fragments provide a way to create powerful user interfaces, and the action bar is central to app navigation.

Using the Support Library

The Android Compatibility package or support library provides a way to include new API features in older versions of Android. It is a library that you add to your project. The projects you have created so far using Eclipse all include the support library.

In any project, look in the Android-dependencies folder and you will see the filename android-support-v4.jar. That is the support library. Figure 4.3 shows that you can add the support library to a project by choosing Android Tools, Add Support Library.

The main advantage of the support library is that it implements a large subset of the fragments API.

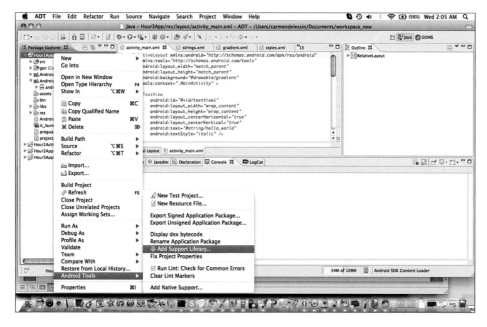

FIGURE 4.3
Adding the support library

The features supported by the library are listed at http://developer.android.com/tools/extras/support-library.html.

The support library does not provide an alternate action bar. For devices that do not support an action bar, the Android menu system can be used. A popular open source project called ActionBarSherlock also supports an action bar in older versions of Android.

GO TO ▶ HOUR 23, "PRO TIPS, FINISHING TOUCHES, AND NEXT STEPS," to learn more about ActionBarSherlock.

In addition to using the support library, targeting specific versions of Android is possible. To programmatically determine the version of Android, use the Build class (android.os.Build). Specifically, check the Build.VERSION class's SDK_INT value, as defined in android. os.Build.VERSION_CODES.

By determining specific Android versions and using the support library, using fragments for an app and including an action bar if it is supported and an alternate display if it is not is possible.

To call methods from the newer APIs and still support older versions, wrap the code in an if statement to check the version:

```
if (Build.VERSION.SDK_INT >= Build.VERSION_CODES. HONEYCOMB) {
 // do HONEYCOMB specific work
}
```

Strategy for Device Support

Though many versions of Android are running on different devices, coming up with a simple device strategy that fits your application is probably possible.

You can use the support library on versions of Android back to 1.6. It has new features including fragments. If you are creating a "normal" app, then using the support library is a good starting point. Using the support library with a separate implementation of the action bar for devices that support it is a good option.

GO TO ▶ HOUR 7, "ACTIONBAR AND MENU NAVIGATION," for more information on using the action bar.

If your app uses any Android version–specific features, then you need to use the appropriate version. Supporting only more recent versions of Android might be a good strategy for a cutting-edge app.

Beyond which versions to support, as a developer, you must decide whether you will have multiple versions of your app or one app that handles all devices. Google and the Android system have made a clear path to create one app that runs well on all devices.

Another strategy is to create a core library of common functions and create specific app versions if needed. Android provides you the ability to make any project a library project. Creating a specific version for tablets or for the Kindle Fire might be worthwhile for a particular app.

NOTE

Kindle Fire

The Kindle Fire is a popular Android device from Amazon. The original Kindle Fire runs Android version 2.3.3, and the newer Kindle Fires run Android 4.03. You can find additional information at https://developer.amazon.com/sdk/fire/specifications.html.

Launching Apps on a Device

This hour is about creating apps for different devices. The emulator is great for development, but if you are going to release apps onto Google Play or other markets, testing on one or more actual devices is best.

Setting Up Your Device

When configuring your device, you will make certain changes to the device settings and you need to make sure you can connect your device to a computer using a USB cable:

1. Go to the Settings application on your device and choose Developer Options.

2. Set USB debugging to `true` by checking that selection.

3. Go to the Security settings and set Unknown sources to `true`. This allows apps to be installed from places other than the Play Store.

4. Connect your device to your computer via a USB cable. If you are using a Windows machine you need to find and install the appropriate driver for your device.

Running from Eclipse

To run a specific project, select the project in Eclipse, right-click, and choose Run As Android Application. The Android Device chooser screen appears, as shown in Figure 4.4. You can choose to run on a device or an emulator.

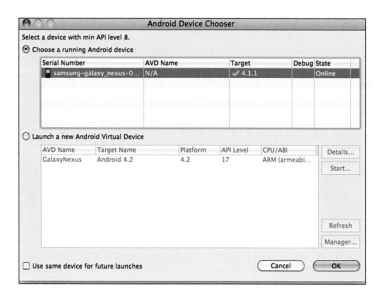

FIGURE 4.4
Android Device Chooser

Configuring how to run a specific project is easy. You can set the project to always ask which device to use. To do that, choose Run, Configurations in the Eclipse menu to access the Run Configurations screen shown in Figure 4.5.

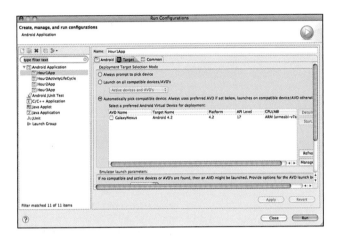

FIGURE 4.5
Run Configurations screen

Summary

In this hour, you learned about screen size and resolution and how to handle creating apps for devices with different screen characteristics, including how to load alternative resources. This hour also covered how to check for device features, such as whether a camera is available. You learned about the support library as well as how to handle different Android versions.

Q&A

Q. Is the variety of devices and OS versions what people mean by Android fragmentation?

A. To some extent, yes. The Android device market includes devices of different sizes, different features, and different Android versions. A manufacturer can also add software modifications. When people started to use the word *fragmentation* to talk about the large variation in Android devices, Apple had one version of the iPhone. For the iPhone, Apple controls the hardware and the software. That is different from Android where multiple hardware manufacturers and multiple versions of Android exist. That said, one significant consideration for designing and developing apps on Android was handling different screen sizes. With the introduction of the iPad and the iPad-mini, the work involved in supporting multiple screen sizes is affecting the Apple world as well. Android has had screen size support built in from the beginning, and Android's support package makes development easier across OS versions.

Workshop

Quiz

1. True or False: You can provide alternative resources for a specific version of the Android SDK, such as Honeycomb (Android 3.0).

2. Specify a resource directory for layouts that are in portrait mode and support a large screen.

3. What method can you use to preserve an object through an orientation change?

4. What is the purpose of the support library?

Answers

1. True. See Table 4.1 for the list of possible resource directory qualifiers.

2. The resource directory is res/layout-large-port/.

3. The method `onRetainNonConfigurationInstance()` preserves the object. To retrieve it, you use `getLastNonConfigurationInstance()`.

4. The support library brings newer Android features to older versions. You can add this library to your current project.

Exercises

1. Implement an orientation listener in one of your activity classes. You can use example code from an earlier hour in this book. Log an information message each time an orientation event occurs. You can do this using the `Log` class. Find out more at http://developer.android.com/reference/android/util/Log.html.

2. Create an activity that checks for the availability of a camera on a device. Display the camera information as part of the user interface. Run this on as many actual devices as possible. Try listing all camera features (front-facing, flash, and so on).

3. Provide a new landscape directory for the layout in Hour1App. You can copy the current layout directory by right-clicking and choosing Copy. Highlight the res directory and choose Paste. Give the new directory the name layout-land. Edit the activity_main.xml file to have an appropriate design for landscape mode (or just give it a blue background to make it different). Using an emulator or a device, run the app and change the orientation.

PART II

User Interface

HOUR 5
Using Layouts

What You'll Learn in This Hour:

▶ Getting started with layouts
▶ Using different types of layouts
▶ Tips for creating useful layouts

In the last hour, you learned that Android was developed to run on different hardware and to support various screen sizes. One way to support those different screen sizes was to introduce layouts for creating useful and flexible user interfaces. Layouts are usually created using XML files. The XML files are the templates for what the screen will look like. The Android system uses the layouts to properly display the user interface on different devices. This hour reviews the types of layouts and how to use them.

Getting Started with Layouts

Layout files are XML files that define what a screen—or portion of the screen—will look like in your Android apps. Layout files define the look of a user interface. The layout contains different types of view controls like EditTexts and Buttons. These view controls might reference other resources, such as strings, colors, dimensions, and drawables.

If you look at the Android documentation for a particular layout class such as LinearLayout, you can see that LinearLayout is an extension of a ViewGroup class. The ViewGroup class is defined as a view that can contain other views. A View in Android is the most basic component for building a user interface. Every Button, TextField, or Layout is a type of view. A ViewGroup is a container for other views referred to as child views. A LinearLayout is a specific type of ViewGroup that defines how each child view is drawn on the screen.

Having an idea of the class hierarchy of a layout is worthwhile. Thinking of a layout as a container for user interface elements that has specific rules applied when new elements are added is helpful. Different types of layouts use different rules for how to add child views.

Practically, you often use an XML layout file to define the views for the user interface, but you can also create any view programmatically. The layout is the container for other views whether they are defined in an XML file or created on the fly.

As you have seen, layout resource files are stored in the /res/layout directory hierarchy. You compile layout resources into your application as you would any other resources.

The included Hour5App project includes example layout files. These can be viewed as layouts in a visual editor and as XML files in a text editor. The files in the res/layout directory are activity_main.xml, padding_example.xml, weight_example.xml, and gridlayout_example.xml.

Designing Layouts Using the Layout Resource Editor

You can design and preview compiled layout resources in Eclipse by using the Layout Resource Editor (see Figure 5.1). Double-click the project file /res/layout/activity_main.xml from Hour1 within Eclipse to launch the Layout Resource Editor. It has two tabs: Graphical Layout and main.xml. The Graphical Layout tab provides drag-and-drop visual design and offers you the ability to preview the layout in various device configurations. The main.xml tab enables you to edit the layout XML directly.

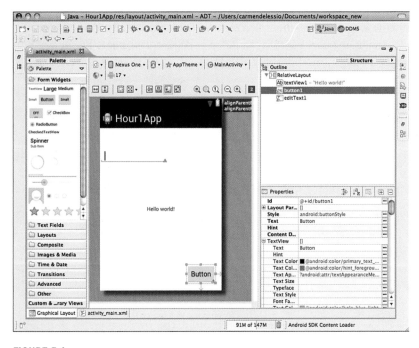

FIGURE 5.1
The Layout Resource Editor in Eclipse

Chances are, you'll switch back and forth between the graphical and XML modes frequently.

Editing Layouts Using XML

You can edit the raw XML of a layout file. As you create more apps, editing the XML layout file directly will become natural. By switching to the XML view frequently, you can gain an understanding of XML generated by each type of control. As you change properties using the visual editor, they are also changed in the XML. Over time, you might find yourself making some edits visually and others directly in the XML file.

Because you can edit the XML file as a text file, searching for certain terms or making other changes directly can be useful.

Using Layout Resources Programmatically

In Hour 1, you created a `Button` and an `EditText` control. Those view controls are defined in the activity_main.xml file in the/res/layout directory. They are defined in the XML within a `RelativeLayout` element.

When you used this layout in an activity, you called the method `setContentView()`. This line of code was included when the project was generated:

```
setContentView(R.layout.activity_main);
```

An activity has a `setContentView()` method to associate the activity with the view. When you want to access the controls defined within the layout, you use `findViewById()`. This line creates a new `Button` from a reference in the layout file and assigns it to the variable `myButton`:

```
Button myButton=   (Button)findViewById(R.id.button1);
```

The `findViewById()` method is available within an activity. It is also available from other views. When you use fragments or want to have a custom look in a `ListView` or `GridView`, you can create views on the fly from XML layouts. You *inflate* the layout file into a `View` object using the `LayoutInflater` class. You then use the new `View` to access controls such as `Buttons`. The following listing shows an example of creating a `LayoutInflater` and creating a `View`:

```
LayoutInflater inflater = LayoutInflater.from(context);
View exampleView = inflater.inflate(R.layout.example, container, false);
Button myExampleButton =   (Button)exampleView.findViewById(R.id.button1);
```

The details of how to use these parameters is covered when you use `LayoutInflaters` to create fragments later in this book.

GO TO ▶ HOUR 8, "ACTIVITIES AND FRAGMENTS," for more on using layouts in fragments.

Layout Types

Having a screen be encapsulated in one large parent layout is quite common. `RelativeLayout` and `LinearLayouts` are commonly used. Table 5.1 lists the most common Layout controls.

TABLE 5.1   Common Layout Controls

Layout Control Name	Description	Key Attributes/Elements
LinearLayout	Each child view is placed after the previous one, in a single row or column.	Orientation (vertical or horizontal).
RelativeLayout	Each child view is placed in relation to the other views in the layout, or relative to the edges of the parent layout.	Many alignment attributes to control where a child view is positioned relative to other child View controls.
FrameLayout	Each child view is stacked within the frame, relative to the top-left corner. View controls may overlap.	Alignment attributes for a child view may be set relative to the parent. The order of placement of child `View` controls is important, when used with appropriate gravity settings.
TableLayout	Each child view is a cell in a grid of rows and columns	Each row requires a `TableRow` element.

NOTE

Using an Include in a Layout XML File

The XML layout includes support for an `<include/>` element. To use this element, create a layout file to be embedded in other layouts and then reference it as a resource. You can reference the layout named basicHeader.xml in other layout files by using `<include layout="@layout/ basicHeader "/>` device.

Figure 5.2 shows the design of a user interface that uses `LinearLayout` and `TableLayout`. Doing this upfront work to plan out your design can make the implementation much easier.

In the splash screen design in Figure 5.2, a vertical `LinearLayout` control is used to organize the screen elements, which are, in order, a `TextView` control, a `TableLayout` control with some `TableRow` control elements of `ImageView` controls, and then two more `TextView` controls.

Figure 5.3 shows how this screen looks in a complete app.

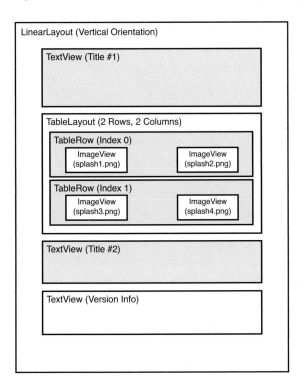

FIGURE 5.2
Splash screen design with layouts in mind

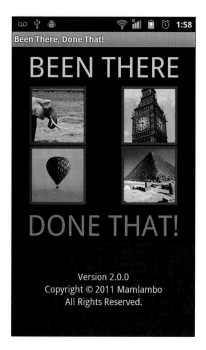

FIGURE 5.3
Final splash screen

More Layout Basics with LinearLayout

A `LinearLayout` positions views in either a column or a row. The `LinearLayout`'s orientation property determines the direction. If the orientation is vertical, the child views will be stacked in a column. If the orientation is horizontal, the child views will be placed in a row. Although many common attributes exist across layouts, the difference between different types of layouts is the order and rules they use for drawing widgets on the screen.

Common Attributes

Certain attributes are common across layouts and the child views within layouts. For example, all layouts share the attributes `android:layout_width` and `android:layout_height` for controlling how wide and high an item is. You can specify these attribute values in units such as density independent pixels (20dp) or as constant values that have a specific meaning. Possible values are `match_parent` and `wrap_content`.

Using `match_parent` instructs a layout to scale to the size of the parent layout, and using `wrap_content` wraps the child View control.

Changing LinearLayout Properties

Listing 5.1 defines a `LinearLayout` in XML. The layout includes a `TextView` and a `Button` as child views. Figure 5.4 shows this layout in Eclipse.

LISTING 5.1   LinearLayout in XML

```
1:    <?xml version="1.0" encoding="utf-8"?>
2:    <LinearLayout xmlns:android="http://schemas.android.com/apk/res/android"
3:        android:orientation="vertical"
4:        android:layout_width="fill_parent"
5:        android:layout_height="fill_parent">
6:        <TextView android:layout_width="fill_parent"
7:            android:layout_height="wrap_content"
8:            android:text="Hello Android"
9:            android:id="@+id/greeting"/>
10:       <Button android:text="Button"
11:           android:id="@+id/button1"
12:           android:layout_width="wrap_content"
13:           android:layout_height="wrap_content" />
14:   </LinearLayout>
```

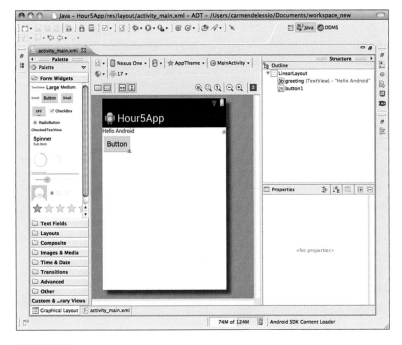

FIGURE 5.4
LinearLayout example

Line 8 of Listing 5.1 shows the text attribute for the `TextView` as `"Hello Android"`. You should define `"Hello Android"` in the res/values/strings.xml file and then refer to it as a resource. If you defined it as

```
<string name="hello_android">Hello Android </string>
```

then you would use it to replace line 8 with

```
android:text="@string/hello_android"
```

Changing things such as the background color and orientation is also easy. You can change the background color of the `LinearLayout` to gray by adding the following attribute:

```
android:background="#777777"
```

You might also set the alpha value for the color—that is, the first two values for the color that set the opaqueness of the color. Use 00 to make a transparent color. Use FF to create an opaque color. So, you can also use #FF777777. The alpha value is not required.

Let's also change the orientation from vertical to horizontal:

```
android:orientation="horizontal"
```

Something unexpected happens. The `Button` disappears completely.

The explanation lies in the details of the widgets. The `TextView` is set to a width of `"match_ parent"`. It fills the entire layout from left to right. Changing the orientation on the layout did not account for that. The `TextView` takes up the whole screen, and the `Button` is not in view. You can fix this by setting both the `TextView` and the `Button` to have a `layout_width` of `wrap_content`.

Laying Out Child Views

As you saw in Listing 5.1, changing the properties of the layout might affect where child views are placed on the screen. The following sections look at padding and margin properties and illustrate how they affect the display.

Padding

Padding is the amount of space that is added to a side of a UI element to give it more space on the screen. Padding often refers to the internal padding. For a standard `Button`, it is the space added between the button's text and sides of the button. You may set padding for the whole widget or set specifically for the top, bottom, left, and right sides.

The correct unit to use to set padding (and most UI elements) is a *device-independent pixel*, referred to as a dip or dp within the XML layout. Device-independent pixels factor in screen resolution when displayed.

Let's create a new layout file with three buttons to show the effect of padding.

The first button has no padding property specified. The second button has its padding set to 30dp by setting `android:padding="30dp"`. All sides of the button are padded with 30 device pixels. The third button has its padding set to 40dp for the right and left. The right padding is set using `android:paddingRight="30dp"`.

Figure 5.5 shows the result of using padding this way.

FIGURE 5.5
Using padding

Layout Margins

Layout margins define the amount of space between a child view and the side of a parent container. To "push" a button down and to the right, you set the margin from the top and the left side of the layout. By adding these two lines to the layout for the first `Button`, you can push the button down 40 pixels and to the right 120 pixels:

```
android:layout_marginTop="40dp"
android:layout_marginLeft="120dp"
```

Because this was done in a `LinearLayout` with vertical orientation, all the buttons are pushed down. You would get a different result if you used another kind of layout.

Gravity

The property `layout_gravity` applies to child views and is easy to use. You can set the `layout_gravity` property to values such as left, right, center, and so on. Figure 5.6 shows the options for setting `layout_gravity` on `button1` in this example. The button is currently set to right and is shown on the right side of the screen:

```
android:layout_gravity="right"
```

The `layout_gravity` property applies to the child views. Android gravity can apply to the entire layout. By setting gravity to right for the `LinearLayout`, all child views are moved to the right:

```
android:gravity="right"
```

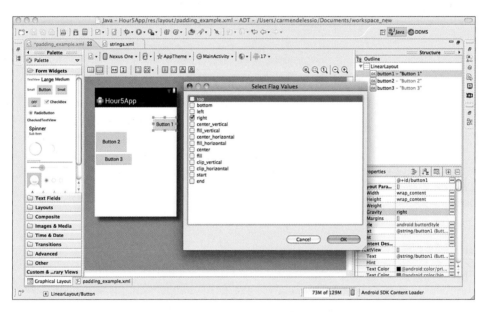

FIGURE 5.6
Adding gravity

Weight

The Android `layout_weight` property gives more space on the screen to the view with the higher weight. You can see this most easily when creating a `LinearLayout` with horizontal orientation.

Throwing Weight Around in a Layout

By following these steps, you can see a good example of how the `layout_weight` attribute works and can be used in your designs:

1. Create a new XML layout file called weight_example.xml in the res/layout folder.

2. Use a `LinearLayout` with the orientation set to `Horizontal` for the layout.

3. Add two `Buttons` to the layout. Their width should be set to `match_parent`.

4. Set the `layout_weight` attribute for both buttons to 1. They should share the available space.

5. Change the weight of only one of the buttons and check the result visually using Eclipse.

FrameLayout

A `FrameLayout` is a container that has no special rules for drawing widgets. By default, all widgets are drawn in the upper-left corner of the screen. That might not sound useful, but by using the layout margin, you can place widgets anywhere. The `FrameLayout` is helpful when two widgets should be drawn on top of each other. For example, you might put a `TextField` on top of an image or use several images to draw shadows and highlights within the UI.

You can use `layout_margins` wisely within a `FrameLayout` to create interesting and useful designs.

RelativeLayout

A `RelativeLayout` is similar to the `FrameLayout` in that you can place components on top of each other, but with the `RelativeLayout`, you can place views in relation to other views. In a `FrameLayout`, when you specify the `topMargin` for two buttons, you are indicating how far they are from the top of the parent. With a `RelativeLayout`, we can specify how far they are from each other.

For example, using `RelativeLayout`, you can place one button to the left, right, top, or bottom of another button. A `RelativeLayout` can be useful when creating complex user interfaces.

One way to use a `RelativeLayout` is to put a view in the middle of the design that references something above it and below it. Figure 5.7 shows a layout on Eclipse that has:

▶ A `Button` aligned with the bottom of the parent:
`android:layout_alignParentBottom="true"`

▶ A `TextView` that is in the top-left corner by default

▶ A `GridView` that is below the `TextView` and above the `Button`

To set the position of the `GridView`, these properties are used:

```
android:layout_below="@+id/textView1"
android:layout_above="@+id/loadPhotosButton"
```

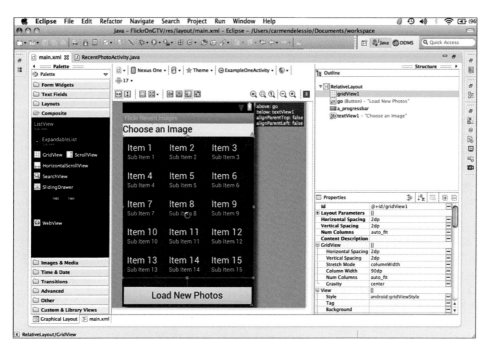

FIGURE 5.7
Eclipse view of a `RelativeLayout` design

You'll use this design as you develop a more sophisticated app in later chapters. You can access the most recent photos from Flickr using the API. Figure 5.8 shows the recent images displayed in the `GridView`.

FIGURE 5.8
The Flickr Recent Photo app

When you use `LinearLayouts` and `RelativeLayouts`, the Android operating system takes the physical screen dimension into consideration when rendering the user interface. Because these layouts use components that are relative to each other, more opportunity exists for the system to optimize the experience. For that reason, `LinearLayouts` and `RelativeLayouts` are generally recommended.

Summary

This hour reviewed what layouts are and how they work. It examined `LinearLayout` in more detail as a way to understand how layouts work. XML layouts are used to create user interfaces in Android by positioning child views on the screen. Using padding, margins, and other attributes gives you significant control over the user interface. Examples using `FrameLayout` and `RelativeLayout` showed the properties of those layouts and how they are different.

Q&A

Q. With layouts, what is meant by orientation?

A. Orientation defines the direction of the `LinearLayout`. Vertical creates a column, and horizontal creates a row. Orientation is not used in `FrameLayout`s or `RelativeLayout`. Different layouts have different rules for laying out child views, which means they might have different attributes.

Q. What is the difference between a `FrameLayout` and a `RelativeLayout`?

A. In a `RelativeLayout`, you can position widgets relative to one another. That cannot be done in `FrameLayout`.

Workshop

Quiz

1. What is the difference between setting a layout margin and layout padding?

2. What is the relationship between a `LinearLayout` and a `ViewGroup`?

3. How would you position a `Button` 100 pixels from the top of the device screen? Use density-independent pixels.

Answers

1. Layout margins define the distance between a component and the edge of the layout. Padding pads the size of the component. Depending on the component, this padding can have different effects.

2. A `LinearLayout` extends the `ViewGroup` class. A `ViewGroup` is a `View` in Android that contains other views.

3. Set the margin to be 100 device pixels from the top of the screen using `android:layout_marginTop="100 dp"`.

Exercises

1. Using `FrameLayout`, implement a user interface with a button in each corner of the screen. Do the same with a `RelativeLayout`.

   To do this using a `FrameLayout`, follow these steps:

   ▶ Create a layout file using `FrameLayout`.

   ▶ Create four `Button`s.

   ▶ Set the `topMargin` and `leftMargin` of each `Button` so that the `Button`s are placed in corners.

2. Try using one layout within another; specifically, create a `LinearLayout` with vertical orientation. Add a `FrameLayout` and a `Button`. Then add an `ImageView` to the `FrameLayout`.

3. Create an XML layout that uses `RelativeLayout`. Place an `ImageView` and `TextView` in the layout. Now, use that layout as an `include` in another layout.

Working with Basic UI Controls

What You'll Learn in This Hour:

▸ Using `TextViews`, `EditTexts`, and `Buttons`

▸ Creating controls with adapters

▸ Indicating progress with `ProgressBars`

▸ Showing an image with an `ImageView`

In this hour, you look at three common controls in detail. Using a `Button`, `EditText`, and `TextView` with different properties, in this hour you learn how to create a variety of user interfaces. The functionality and tone of the apps can change even when using the same views. This hour introduces the concept of data adapters and shows how adapters work with `Spinners` and `AutoCompleteTextViews`. The use of `ImageViews`, `ProgressBars`, and `SeekBars` is also covered.

Setting Up the Demo App

When you create a user interface using the visual editor in Eclipse, you select items from the palette. The palette organizes these items into categories that include Form Widgets and Text Fields. The Form Widget category includes `TextViews`, `Buttons`, `Spinners`, `ProgressBars`, and `Seekbars`. The Text Fields category includes `EditText` views and `AutoCompleteTextViews`. You'll examine these items individually and see how you can use them to create user interfaces with different functionality and styles. To do that, you'll create a demo app with five activities. The main activity handles simple navigation. Each of the other activities demonstrates how to use certain view controls.

For the demo app, you'll use a `LinearLayout` with a vertical orientation. Navigation will occur when the user clicks a button to go to another activity. Each button has the `layout_width` set to `match_parent`.

To get started, create an Android app called Hour6App. The XML layout file main_activity.xml will be created. Using Eclipse, remove the `TextView` that is automatically created. To change the layout from a `RelativeLayout` to a `LinearLayout`, right-click on the `RelativeLayout` and choose Change Layout.

Choose LinearLayout with vertical orientation (see Figure 6.1). After you change the layout, you can add buttons that will be used to launch other activities.

The Hour6App project that accompanies this book contains all the source code that accompanies this hour.

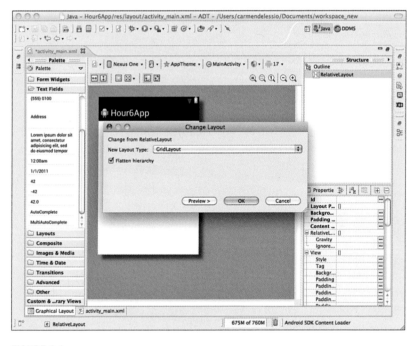

FIGURE 6.1
Change from `RelativeLayout` to `LinearLayout` using Eclipse

Using the Visual Editor

Right-clicking a control in the visual editor brings up a contextual menu of common tasks. You can perform tasks such as changing `text`, `id`, or `layout_width` in this way. Using the demo app is an easy way to change the text and `layout_width` of the buttons on the main_activity.xml layout.

Figure 6.2 shows the resulting layout for the demo app shown in the emulator.

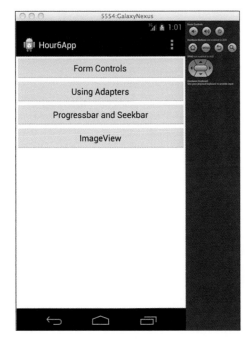

FIGURE 6.2
Start page for demo app in emulator

As you develop activities for various views, you'll "wire" them to the main page. On the `onClickListener()` for each button, the app launches the appropriate activity.

Using Input Controls

In many apps, there is a need to collect basic information from the user. The most basic data entry field to use on a layout is an `EditText`. You used an `EditText` in the sample app in Hour 1, "Getting Started: Creating a Simple App." As you design layouts, you can use `TextViews` as labels for clarity and perhaps to add instructions. You use `Buttons` to initiate an action.

Using TextView and EditText Views

A `TextView` displays text that the user cannot change. An `EditText` view is intended for user input. Like with other controls, you can change the size, color, and background properties of both a `TextView` and an `EditText` view.

This section considers two other properties of an `EditText` field: the hint property and the `inputType`. A hint displays in the contents of an unedited `EditText`. In Figure 6.3, the hint for `editText1` says "Enter a Name," and the hint for `editText2` says "Enter a Number." Figure 6.3 shows these in the Eclipse visual editor with the Edit Hint menu item selected.

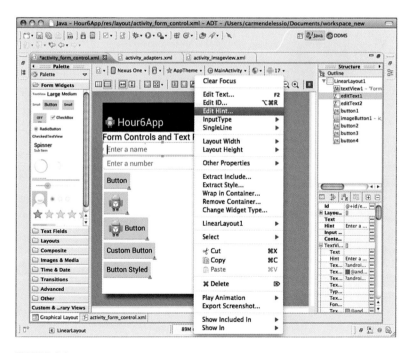

FIGURE 6.3
Showing hints in an `EditText` view

The `inputType` property has a long list of choices. The purpose of the `inputType` property is to show the appropriate keyboard layout for use with the `EditText` view. If the intended input is a number, then the keyboard will show numbers. If the input type should be an email address, then the keyboard shows text and an @ symbol. An `EditText` view has a method called `getText()` to access the current value in the view.

The demo app uses a default `inputType` and a number `inputType`. Figures 6.4 and 6.5 show the resulting keyboard for these `EditText` views.

FIGURE 6.4

`EditText` view with default `inputType` property

FIGURE 6.5
EditText view with number inputType property

To implement the FormControlActivity, create a FormControlActivity class and an XML
layout file that contains a TextView and two EditText views. The FormControlActivity
just uses setContentView() to show the layout file. To display the FormControlActivity,
MainActivity.java requires the creation of a showFormButton and a corresponding onClick-
Listener() with code that starts an activity. This is the same method used in Hour 2,
"Understanding an Android Activity," to launch an activity:

```
Button showFormButton =  (Button)findViewById(R.id.buttonFormControl);
showFormButton.setOnClickListener(new OnClickListener() {
        public void onClick(View v) {
Intent intent = new Intent(MainActivity.this, FormControlActivity.class);
startActivityForResult(intent, 0);
        }
    });
```

Using Different Kinds of Buttons

You used an unmodified button in Hour 1, "Getting Started: Creating a Simple App." You can
create buttons with a variety of styles and attributes.

Two controls are buttons: one is a Button (android.widget.Button) and the other is an ImageButton (android.widget.ImageButton). A Button contains a text label and an ImageButton contains an image. In the Eclipse visual editor, you access a Button via the Form Widgets section of the palette and an ImageButton in the Images and Media section.

You can also add a drawable image to a standard Button by providing a value for at least one of these properties: drawable_left, drawable_right, drawable_top, or drawable_bottom.

Listing 6.1 shows the XML layout for a Button, an ImageButton, and a Button with a value for drawable_left. For the drawables, use the ic_launcher.png file, which is the default image that is used for an app icon and provided when you create your activity.

NOTE

More About Button and ImageButtons

The Button class is extended from a TextView and an ImageButton is extended from an ImageView. A Button is a TextView that can have drawables placed around it. An ImageButton is an ImageView that acts like a button. An ImageButton displays a single image.

LISTING 6.1   Three Buttons Defined in an XML Layout

```
1:    <Button
2:            android:id="@+id/button1"
3:            android:layout_width="wrap_content"
4:            android:layout_height="wrap_content"
5:            android:text="Button" />
6:    <ImageButton
7:            android:id="@+id/imageButton1"
8:            android:layout_width="wrap_content"
9:            android:layout_height="wrap_content"
10:           android:src="@drawable/ic_launcher" />
11:   <Button
12:           android:id="@+id/button2"
13:           android:layout_width="wrap_content"
14:           android:layout_height="wrap_content"
15:           android:drawableLeft="@drawable/ic_launcher"
16:           android:text="Button" />
```

As with other views, you can programmatically change the contents and properties of a button. Swapping the image in an ImageButton or changing the drawable and text in a standard button might make sense.

Now add an `onClickListener()` for button2 that is defined in lines 11–16 of Listing 6.1. Clicking the button causes the image to be replaced and the text to be updated. To find out the current contents of the button, you must get the text being displayed.

Listing 6.2 shows the code to implement this. You use `getText()` and `setText()` to check the value and change contents. To change the image, use the method `setCompoundDrawablesWithIntrinsicBounds()`. The parameters to this method are the drawables to use in the button in this order: left, top, right, and bottom. Figure 6.6 shows the two buttons that you are switching between.

The skateboarding robot image needs to be imported into the drawables resource folder.

LISTING 6.2   Swapping Drawables in a Button

```
1:   mIcon = getResources().getDrawable( R.drawable.ic_launcher );
2:   mSkateboardIcon = getResources().getDrawable( R.drawable.robot_skateboarding );
3:   swapButton = (Button)findViewById(R.id.button2);
4:   swapButton.setOnClickListener(new OnClickListener() {
5:     public void onClick(View v) {
6:       if (swapButton.getText().equals("Button")){
7:         swapButton.setText("Skateboarder");
8:         swapButton.setCompoundDrawablesWithIntrinsicBounds(mSkateboardIcon,
9:                   null, null, null);
10:      }else{
11:        swapButton.setText("Button");;
12:        swapButton.setCompoundDrawablesWithIntrinsicBounds(mIcon, null, null,
null);
13:      }
14:    }
15: });
```

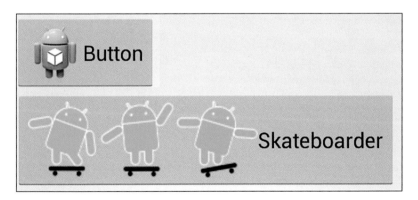

FIGURE 6.6
Switching between images: Only one at a time is shown in the app.

Several techniques are available for changing the look and feel of buttons. For example, you can change the style of the button or create a custom background for the button. You can also use an existing Android system style. This line sets the button to an existing Android system style:

```
style="@android:style/Widget.Button.Inset"
```

Creating a button with a custom background requires some additional work. You need a drawable image for each state of the button. A button can be displayed on a page, it can be the control on the page that has focus, and it can be pressed by the user. These three button states display differently. To handle each of these scenarios, you create an XML file in the drawable directory that references these three button states. That XML file is, in fact, a drawable.

Listing 6.3 shows the contents of the button_custom.xml. In this case, each drawable used in the XML file is a solid color image. This file is placed in a drawable resource folder. To use effects such as beveled edges, nine-patch images are recommended. You set the background property of the Button you want to customize to the button_custom.xml file by referring to the file as a drawable; for example:

```
android:background="@drawable/button_custom"
```

LISTING 6.3   **Defining a Drawable for a Custom Button**

```
1:   <?xml version="1.0" encoding="utf-8"?>
2:   <selector xmlns:android="http://schemas.android.com/apk/res/android">
3:       <item android:drawable="@drawable/button_pressed"
4:             android:state_pressed="true" />
5:       <item android:drawable="@drawable/button_focused"
6:             android:state_focused="true" />
7:       <item android:drawable="@drawable/button_default" />
8:   </selector>
```

Figure 6.7 shows all the views used in the FormControlActivity.

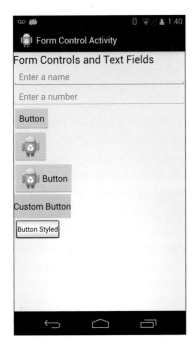

FIGURE 6.7
`EditText` and `Buttons` displayed in the `FormControlActivity`

Using Controls with Adapters

Many controls have a single text property. For example, a button might display "OK," or you can use a line of text as a label in a text view. Other controls require and must display more than one piece of data. For these, you use adapters to tie complex data to a control.

Adapters

An `Adapter(android.widget.Adapter)` binds data to a view. For example, a `Spinner` is a control that provides the user with a list of choices to select. The list of choices is the data required for the view to run. To make the handshake between the view and the data, you use an `adapter`. In this section, you'll use predefined adapters such as the `ArrayAdapter(android.widget.ArrayAdapter)` class. For more complex apps, creating custom adapters is common. You'll do that in later chapters that cover cursors and cursor adapters.

You will use an `ArrayAdapter` to show the same data in a `Spinner` control and in an `AutoCompleteTextView`.

In the examples, you use a `String` array that is programmatically defined. You can also define a `String` array as a resource. That method is appropriate for an unchanging list.

GO TO ▶ HOUR 15, "LOADERS, CURSORLOADERS, AND CUSTOMADAPTERS," for more information on creating custom adapters.

Using a Spinner Control

A spinner is essentially the Android platform's version of a drop-down list. Figure 6.8 shows an unselected spinner on the left and the same spinner on the right when focused with the "three" option selected in the dropdown.

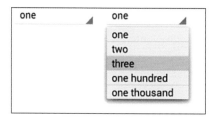

FIGURE 6.8
Spinner closed (left) and open (right)

Setting Up the Spinner

To show the spinner, you define it and then bind it to an adapter. The data for the adapter should be available when the spinner is set up. The data for this example is an array of string constants called `values`:

```
String[] values = {"one", "two", "three", "one hundred", "one thousand" };
```

To use this data, you create the spinner, use the data in an adapter, and tie the spinner to the adapter:

```
mSpinner = (Spinner)findViewById(R.id.spinner1);
ArrayAdapter<String> spinnerAdapter = new ArrayAdapter<String>
                    (this,android.R.layout.simple_spinner_item,values);
mSpinner.setAdapter(spinnerAdapter);
```

You create an `ArrayAdapter` called `spinnerAdapter` by tying the `values` array to a predefined system resource called `android.R.layout.simple_spinner_item`. You set the `spinnerAdapter` to be the adapter for the spinner. The adapter binds the data to the spinner and indicates how each item should be displayed.

Getting Data from a Spinner

You can do several things with the spinner. You can detect when an item is selected in the spinner by setting up an `OnItemSelectedListener()`. You can read the selected data from the spinner by using `getSelectedItem()` or `getSelectedItemPosition()`.

In this example, the items in the list are strings, so you would read the string value as follows:

```
String selected = (String) mSpinner.getSelectedItem();
```

Using an AutoCompleteTextView

An `AutoCompleteTextView` is an input field that provides a list of suggestions based on user input. The user may select one of the suggestions or make a new entry. Figure 6.9 shows several states of an `AutoCompleteTextView` based on the text entered. The list of possible values is the same that was used for the `Spinner`. The left image has no data entered. When "one" is entered, the words that begin with "one" appear. Note that when "th" is entered, both "three" and "one thousand" appear. Any word that begins with "th" makes the list.

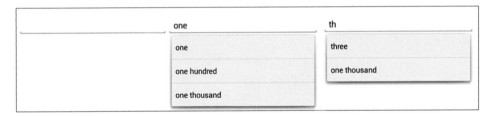

FIGURE 6.9
`AutoCompleteTextView` based on entered data

Setting up an `AutoCompleteTextView` is similar to setting up a spinner. You define an adapter and bind it to the view:

```
ArrayAdapter<String> textAdapter = new ArrayAdapter<String>
(this,android.R.layout.simple_spinner_dropdown_item,values);
mAutoCompleteTextView = (AutoCompleteTextView)findViewById(R.
id.autoCompleteTextView1);
mAutoCompleteTextView.setAdapter(textAdapter);
```

To retrieve data from an `AutoCompleteTextView`, you use the method `getText()`.

ProgressBars and SeekBars

A ProgressBar (android.widget.Progressbar) and SeekBar (android.widget.SeekBar) help tell the status of an event that is occurring. For example, you might want to show a ProgressBar in your user interface as an image file is downloading. A ProgressBar that is circular and indicates that something is occurring is known as an indeterminate progress bar. A horizontal ProgressBar can indicate how much of something is complete. A SeekBar is similar to a horizontal ProgressBar, but the user can set the SeekBar to a specific location. A SeekBar can be used to set the location within a VideoView, for example.

Before getting into ProgressBars and SeekBars, this section goes into the details of using an AsyncTask(android.os.AsyncTask). AsyncTasks are used for background processing. Moving intense tasks to background processes is important. This section shows how a background task can communicate with a ProgressBar in the UI thread. Updates from the AsyncTask will be reflected using a horizontal ProgressBar and a SeekBar.

Figure 6.10 shows a ProgressBar, a horizontal ProgressBar, and a SeekBar.

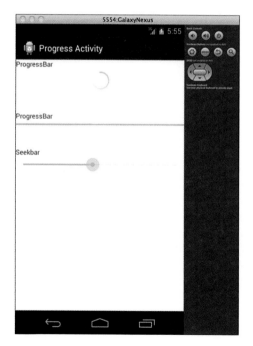

FIGURE 6.10
Showing progress

AsyncTask

You use the `AsyncTask` class to manage background operations that will eventually post back to the UI thread.

To use an `AsyncTask`, you must create a subclass of the `AsyncTask` class and implement the appropriate callback methods:

- ▶ `onPreExecute()`—Runs on the UI thread before background processing begins.

- ▶ `doInBackground()`—Runs in the background and is where all the real work is done.

- ▶ `publishProgress()`—This method, called from the `doInBackground()` method, periodically informs the UI thread about the background process progress. This method sends information to the UI process. Use this opportunity to send updated progress for a progress bar that the user can see.

- ▶ `onProgressUpdate()`—Runs on the UI thread whenever the `doInBackground()` method calls `publishProgress()`. This method receives information from the background process. Use this opportunity to update a `ProgressBar` control that the user can see.

  When launched with the `execute()` method, the `AsyncTask` class handles processing in a background thread without blocking the UI thread.

- ▶ `onPostExecute()`—Runs on the UI thread after the background processing is completed.

Three generic types are used with an `AsyncTask`. These represent the parameters passed to the task, the progress values used, and the final return value of the task. You define the class with these generic types as follows:

```
android.os.AsyncTask<Params, Progress, Result>
```

Using all the types is not required. `Void` indicates that the generic type is not used. The following defines `MyTask` with no parameters, progress types, or return values:

```
class MyTask extends AsyncTask<Void, Void, Void> { ... }
```

Listing 6.4 shows the complete code for an `AsyncTask` named `ShowProgressTask`.

In the `onPreExecute()` method, the visibility of an indeterminate `ProgressBar` is set to visible. In other words, on line 4, the app shows an indeterminate `ProgressBar`. The same `ProgressBar` is set to invisible in the `onPostExecute()` method on line 26. Tying the `ProgressBar` to these methods makes it visible while the background task is running.

In `ShowProgressTask`, the `doInBackround()` method increments an integer value and makes a call to `publishProgess()` with that value as a parameter. The `sleep()` method on line 10 is used to simulate the delay of some complex task. It is for demo purposes only. The onProgressUpdate() method accepts that value and updates a horizontal ProgressBar and SeekBar appropriately. You execute the ShowProgressTask as follows:

```
ShowProgressTask showTask = new ShowProgressTask();
showTask.execute();
```

LISTING 6.4   An AsyncTask That Updates the UserInterface

```
1:   private class ShowProgressTask extends AsyncTask<Void, Integer, Integer> {
2:   @Override
3:     protected  void onPreExecute (){
4:        mProgressBar.setVisibility(View.VISIBLE);
5:     }
6:   @Override
7:     protected Integer doInBackground(Void... params) {
8:     for (int i=0; i<=100; i++){
9:       try {
10:        Thread.sleep(100); // FOR DEMO ONLY!!!
11:        publishProgress(i);
12:      } catch (InterruptedException e) {
13:          return -1;
14:      }
15:     }
16:     return 100;
17:   }
18:   @Override
19:   protected void onProgressUpdate(Integer...progess) {
20:     Int progress = progess[0];
21:     mHorizontalProgressBar.setProgress(progress);
22:     mSeekBar.setProgress(progress);
23:   }
24:   @Override
25:   protected  void onPostExecute (Integer result){
26:     mProgressBar.setVisibility(View.INVISIBLE);
27:   }
28: }
```

ProgressBar

Listing 6.4 shows the work of the AsyncTask to update two different ProgressBars. In the onCreate() method for the ProgressActivity, you define the ProgressBars:

```
mProgressBar = (ProgressBar)findViewById(R.id.progressBar1);
mProgressBar.setVisibility(View.INVISIBLE);
mHorizontalProgressBar = (ProgressBar)findViewById(R.id.progressBar2);
```

In the layouts for the `ProgressBar`, the style setting gives `progressBar2` the horizontal style:

```
<ProgressBar
        android:id="@+id/progressBar1"
        android:layout_width="wrap_content"
        android:layout_height="wrap_content"
        android:layout_gravity="center" />


<ProgressBar
        android:id="@+id/progressBar2"
        style="?android:attr/progressBarStyleHorizontal"
        android:layout_width="fill_parent"
        android:layout_height="wrap_content"
        android:layout_gravity="center" />
```

SeekBar

The `SeekBar` is similar to the horizontal progress bar in this example. You can also set up a listener to listen and react to changes in a `SeekBar`.

In this case, the `SeekBar` is defined in the code and the max value is set to 100:

```
mSeekBar = (SeekBar)findViewById(R.id.seekBar1);
mSeekBar.setMax(100);
```

ImageViews

To complete this hour, we introduce a simple `ImageView(android.widget.ImageView)`. You use an `ImageView` to display an image. You can change different characteristics of the image including how the image scales and how opaque it is. Common attributes such as size and gravity apply to `ImageViews`. Hour 21, "Media Basics: Images, Audio, and Video," takes a look at `ImageViews` much more closely as you consider displaying media.

GO TO ▶ HOUR 21, "MEDIA BASICS: IMAGES, AUDIO, AND VIDEO," for more information on using `ImageViews`.

To show an image, you use an `ImageView` and the `layout_width` and `layout_height` to `match_parent`. The image will fill the available space:

```
<ImageView
        android:id="@+id/imageView1"
        android:layout_width="match_parent"
        android:layout_height="match_parent"
        android:src="@drawable/robot_skateboarding" />
```

Figure 6.11 shows the `ImageView` using the Eclipse visual editor.

FIGURE 6.11
ImageView set to match_parent for layout_width and layout_height

Summary

This hour examined several types of Android views. These views have common characteristics, such as width, height, and visibility. Using Buttons, you saw that you can customize the same view type to look different for a particular app. Adapters bind data to views. By using a Spinner and AutoCompleteTextView, you saw how views and adapters work together. An AsyncTask was introduced and used to show how to work with controls that show progress status for an app. A simple ImageView was also shown. This hour introduced views and showed basic methods on how to display them and retrieve data from them.

Q&A

Q. What are some differences between a Spinner and an AutoCompleteTextView?

A. Both of these things use an Adapter, display information to the user, and then collect information from the user. The main difference is that a Spinner shows a pre-set list to the user. The user must select an item from the list. With an AutoCompleteTextView, the list of words is only used as suggestions. The user can enter something completely new. With a `Spinner`, the data is accessed via methods that refer to the selected item. In an `AutoCompleteTextView`, the data is accessed using `getText()`.

Q. **Does this hour cover every type of view that can be used in an Android app?**

A. No, not at all. This hour introduced common controls and showed some ways to use them. Using different views is one way to understand them better.

Workshop

Quiz

1. What does a hint do in an `EditView`?

2. What must you do to implement a custom button?

3. What is the difference between an indeterminate `ProgressBar` and a determinate `ProgressBar`?

4. What does `publishProgess` mean when discussing an `AsyncTask`?

Answers

1. The hint is displayed in the `EditText` view as a prompt for the user. It is overwritten by user input.

2. To implement a custom button, an XML file is used as a drawable resource. The XML file defines which actual drawables to use based on button states.

3. An indeterminate `ProgressBar` is shown as a spinning circle and does not show the actual status of the current task. A determinate `ProgressBar`, like a horizontal `progressBar`, reflects the status of the background process. If the background task is 50 percent complete, the determinate `ProgressBar` will be at the halfway mark.

4. Using `publishProgress()` makes a call to `onProgressUpdate`, so you can use `publishProgress` as a mechanism to show the intermediate status of a task that is running in the background.

Exercise

Implement a sample app with an `EditView`, `Button`, and `AutoCompleteTextView`. Use the `EditView` and `Button` to populate a `String` array that is used by the `AutoCompleteView`. You will need to update the array and set the adapter with each update.

HOUR 7
ActionBar and Menu Navigation

What You'll Learn in This Hour:

▶ Understanding the Options Menu

▶ Using the Action Bar

▶ Strategies for Menu and ActionBar

So far, as you have worked with activities, the navigation in your apps has been based on moving from one activity to another. That navigation occurred via a button on the page. For persistent navigation and app functionality, you can add an `ActionBar`(`android.app.ActionBar`) to your apps. In this hour, you implement an action bar and learn several ways to use it. The action bar was introduced in Android 3.0. It is not part of the support package, but other options exist for navigation in earlier versions of the Android platform.

Understanding the Options Menu

Until version 3.0, all Android phones and devices included a hardware-based menu button. That assured that the option to click on Menu was persistent in apps. A Back and Home button were also present. A software infrastructure for handling the Menu button is supported in Android.

That same infrastructure is used to support the action bar in Android 3.0 and higher. The same application code can support two completely different interfaces. The advantage is that it provides a way to support older and newer devices with one code base.

This hour shows how to create an options menu that supports both older and newer Android versions and considers the variations on how items can be displayed in the action bar using just these methods.

To target both older and newer devices, you will use the support library that was covered in Hour 4, "Not Just Smartphones: Supporting Tablets, TVs, and More."

Displaying the Options Menu

You might have noticed that when you create a new Android project with an activity named MainActivity, a resource file named activity_main.xml is created in the menu folder. In the source for MainActivity.java, the following code is generated:

```
@Override
public boolean onCreateOptionsMenu(Menu menu) {
// Inflate the menu; this adds items to the action bar if it is present.
getMenuInflater().inflate(R.menu.activity_main, menu);
return true;
}
```

The onCreateOptionsMenu() method inflates the menu items defined in the menu resource file activity_main.xml. In devices that support the action bar, these items appear in the action bar. For devices that do not support the action bar, these items appear as menu items.

Create an Hour7App project now. The onCreateOptionsMenu() method will be generated and include in the code for the MainActivity. The contents of the menu resource fill will be as follows:

```
'<menuxmlns:android="http://schemas.android.com/apk/res/android"'>
'<item
android:id="@+id/menu_settings"
android:orderInCategory="100"
android:showAsAction="never"
android:title="@string/menu_settings"'/>
'</menu'>
```

A single item is defined with the attributes id, orderInCategory, showAsAction, and title. The title is a string that is defined as a resource with the value "Settings." OrderInCategory defines the order. In this case, showAsAction is set to "never."

When you run the app, you see an action bar as shown in Figure 7.1, which shows two states of the action bar. On the right image in Figure 7.1, the Settings menu item is selected.

The projects that accompany this book contain all the source code that accompanies this hour. The projects for Hour7 are Hour7App, Hour7ActionBarApp, and Hour7ActionBarTabApp.

FIGURE 7.1
The ActionBar showing the Settings menu option

The three vertical dots shown in both images in Figure 7.1 are known as the overflow menu. When menu items do not fit in the action bar, they are shown in the overflow menu. In this case, the Settings menu option value for `showAsAction` is never. Because it is not shown as an action, it appears in the overflow menu.

Understanding the showAsAction Attribute

You can specify how menu items are displayed in an action bar. Table 7.1 shows the possible values. If a menu item is displayed in the action bar, it is called an action item and can be clicked directly in the action bar. Menu items that are not action items appear like the Settings option in Figure 7.1.

TABLE 7.1   Values for showAsAction

Value	Definition
`always`	Always show in ActionBar.
`never`	Never show in ActionBar.
`ifRoom`	Show in the ActionBar if there is room.
`withText`	Show with `Text` from `android:Title`. Can be used with other values (`ifRoom|withText`).
`collapseActionView`	The `actionView` is collapsible (API level 14).

Let's add two more menu items to the action bar as action items. The `showAsAction` will be set to `ifRoom`. In general, using `always` should be avoided, because items could theoretically overlap in a user interface.

For the new items, use `Action 1` and `Action 2` for titles. The purpose of this example is to illustrate the concept of action items. A more common use of an action is to implement a share action. The XML for the first action item is as follows:

```
<item
android:id="@+id/menu_test"
android:orderInCategory="10"
android:showAsAction="ifRoom"
android:title="Action 1"/>
```

Figure 7.2 shows the action bar in the resulting app. The action items are available with Action 2 selected.

FIGURE 7.2
`ActionBar` with two action items

If you add more menu items with `showAsAction` set to `ifRoom`, the additional items appear as choices in the overflow menu, but you can see different results in portrait and landscape mode, as shown in Figure 7.3. There is more room in landscape mode, so more action items appear. The same is true when viewing this app on a tablet; if there is room, more action items appear.

FIGURE 7.3
`ActionBar` in portrait and landscape mode

Menu Items for Platforms with No ActionBar

The Hour7App with menu items defined as they are will run perfectly on earlier versions of Android that do not support action bars. Pressing the hardware menu button on these phones will result in a menu being displayed. Figure 7.4 shows the Hour7App with no menu shown and with the menu open. The frame of the phone is shown to illustrate the menu button.

FIGURE 7.4
Hour7App running on Android 2.3.3

Adding Icons to Menu Items

You can add an icon to any menu item. Icons are supported in both the action bar and older menu styles. Figure 7.5 shows the Hour7App with an icon provided for Action 1. The menu is shown on the left and the action bar is shown on the right. Note that the icons for Action 1 are different. This was accomplished by using alternate image resources based on the Android version.

FIGURE 7.5
Hour7App with an added icon

You can add the icon to the menu item XML with the single line:

```
android:icon="@+drawable/menu_share"
```

A drawable named `menu_share` must exist in the drawable resource folder.

In this case, two drawables were created. Both images are named menu_share.png. To support older versions of Android, you place one image in the /res/drawable-mdpi folder. To support versions of Android that include an ActionBar, you place the other menu_share.png image in the /res/drawable-mdpi-v11 folder. This latter image is used when the Android API version is 11 or greater; in other words, when there is an ActionBar.

Many suitable menu icons are defined as Android system resources. The Google guidelines for menus suggest that these *not* be used directly in your apps. You should use a local copy of the system resource to ensure that your app remains consistent. The possibility exists for these icons to change across platform versions. The `android.R.drawable` resources should not be used directly for menus.

NOTE

Finding System Drawable Resources

When you installed Eclipse and the Android Developer environment, at least one Android platform was installed. That platform includes all the menu icons used in Android. To find these images, go to the Preferences menu in Eclipse and choose Android. This tells you where the SDK is installed. In that folder, navigate to the /data/res/ folder and check the drawables. The directory will be something like adt-bundle-mac/sdk/platforms/android-4.2/data/res/drawable-mdpi. If you use a system menu icon, you should import all densities into your app (ldpi, mdpi, and so on).

You can also check out this helpful website: http://androiddrawables.com/.

You can find additional options for menu items at http://developer.android.com/guide/topics/resources/menu-resource.html.

Responding to the Options Menu

So far, you have only displayed the action bar or menu. Responding to a click on a menu item is straightforward. You created the menu with the onCreateMenuOptions() method. To respond to when a menu item is clicked, you use the onOptionsItemsSelected() method, as shown in Listing 7.1.

A Toast object is defined on line 2. A Toast provides a simple way to display a brief message on the screen. The onOptionsItemSelected() method is passed a MenuItem as a parameter. You use the item.getItemId() method in line 3 for a switch statement that determines which item to respond to. Note that you use the resource id for matching. When an item is clicked, a brief message displays using Toast.

LISTING 7.1   Using onOptionsItemSelected()

```
@Override
1:   public boolean onOptionsItemSelected(MenuItem item) {
2:     Toast toast = Toast.makeText(getApplicationContext(),"Option 1", Toast.
LENGTH_SHORT);
3:     switch (item.getItemId()) {
4:       case R.id.menu_item_1:
5:         toast.setText("Option 1");
6:         toast.show();
7:         return true;
8:       case R.id.menu_item_2:
9:         toast.setText("Option 2");
10:        toast.show();
11:        return true;
12:      case R.id.menu_item_3:
13:        toast.setText("Option 3");
14:        toast.show();
15:        return true;
```

```
16:  default:
17:      return super.onOptionsItemSelected(item);
18:    }
19:  }
```

Using the Action Bar

A number of additional features can appear on the action bar. These include tabs for navigation or drop-down navigation in the app. In these cases, you access the action bar directly in
the code. So far, you have used techniques that apply to both old-style Android menus and the
action bar. This section focuses on action bar–only features.

Drop-Down Navigation

In Hour 6, "Working with Basic UI Controls," you used a simple spinner control. The spinner acts
as a drop-down list and provides options for the user to select. Action bars include an option for
using similar drop-down style navigation.

To enable drop-down navigation, you must provide an adapter that includes the list of navigation options, and you must implement the `ActionBar` class's `OnNavigationListener`
interface.

You are familiar with creating an adapter from the work on spinners in Hour 6, in which you
used an array of string constants called values as the data:

```
String[] values = {"one", "two", "three", "one hundred", "one thousand" };
```

To use this data, you created an `ArrayAdapter` called `spinnerAdapter`, as follows:

```
ArrayAdapter<String> spinnerAdapter = new ArrayAdapter<String>
                    (this,android.R.layout.simple_spinner_item,values);
```

In that case, you used an existing Android layout named `android.R.layout.simple_`
`spinner_item` to tell the adapter how to show the contents of each item in the list.

In the case of the action bar, define your own layout to use for the adapter. The Android system
layouts use black text in the spinner layouts. Using those with a default action bar shows black
on black text. Fortunately, creating a custom layout is not difficult.

The following is a layout named navigation_item.xml that lives in the /res/layout folder:

```
<TextView xmlns:android="http://schemas.android.com/apk/res/android"
    android:id="@android:id/text1"
    style="?android:attr/dropDownItemStyle"
    android:layout_width="fill_parent"
    android:layout_height="?android:attr/listPreferredItemHeight"
    android:ellipsize="marquee"
    android:singleLine="true"
    android:textAppearance="?android:attr/textAppearanceLargeInverse"
    android:textColor="#eeeeee" />
```

The navigation_item.xml is used to define the spinnerAdapter:

```
mSpinnerAdapter = new ArrayAdapter<String>(this,R.layout.navigation_item, values);
```

That gives you the adapter. You must still implement the ActionBar.OnNavigationListener interface. The ActionBar.OnNavigationListener provides the position of the selected item in the drop-down list. From there, you can take whatever action you want. As in the previous example, you can show a simple Toast message. The goal at this point is to highlight the framework for navigation.

As shown in Listing 7.2, the NavigationListener class implements ActionBar. OnNavigationListener. It is created as a private inner class within the MainActivity class. On line 4, you use the values array and the position to get the text value of the selected dropdown item. It is then displayed in a Toast message. Figure 7.6 shows the drop-down navigation menu. Note that the drop-down menu is used in conjunction with action items.

LISTING 7.2   Implementing ActionBar.OnNavigationListener

```
1: private class NavigationListener implements ActionBar.OnNavigationListener{
2:    @Override
3:    public boolean onNavigationItemSelected(int position, long itemId) {
4:       String selected = values[position];
5:       Toast toast = Toast.makeText(getApplicationContext(), selected , Toast.
LENGTH_SHORT);
6:       toast.show();
7:       return false;
8:    }
9: }
```

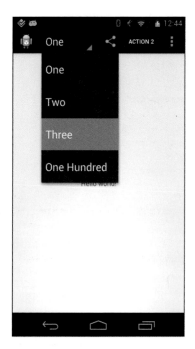

FIGURE 7.6
Drop-down navigation in the `ActionBar`

Tab Navigation

Tabs provide another navigation option for an action bar. Tabs take the user quickly from one mode to another in an app.

You implement tabbed navigation in a similar way to enabling the drop-down navigation. When the user chooses a tab, the appropriate `Toast` message appears.

Using tabs for navigation means that the action bar is set to a different navigation mode. You use the `NAVIGATION_MODE_TABS`. Tabs must be defined to display. Listen for a tab click; you define a class that implements `ActionBar.TabListener`.

A user can select, unselect, or reselect a tab. The `ActionBar.TabListener` covers all of those cases. For this example, you add code to the `onTabSelected()` method.

Listing 7.3 shows the action bar being created as before. The navigation mode is set in line 5, and lines 6 and 7 define two tab objects using the `actionBar.newTab()` method. This sets up two tabs to display. Note that icons are also supported in tabs.

LISTING 7.3   Displaying Tabs in the ActionBar

```
1:  protected void onCreate(Bundle savedInstanceState) {
2:     super.onCreate(savedInstanceState);
3:     setContentView(R.layout.activity_main);
4:     ActionBar actionBar = getActionBar();
5:     actionBar.setNavigationMode(ActionBar.NAVIGATION_MODE_TABS);
6:     mTab1= actionBar.newTab().setText("Tab 1").setTabListener(new
ExampleTabListener());
7:     mTab2= actionBar.newTab().setText("Tab 2").setTabListener(new
ExampleTabListener());
8:     actionBar.addTab(mTab1);
9:     actionBar.addTab(mTab2);
10: }
```

Listing 7.4 shows the methods onTabReselected(), onTabSelected(), and onTabUn-
selected() implemented. The onTabSelected() method contains the code to show a Toast
message when the tab is clicked.

Figure 7.7 shows the result.

LISTING 7.4   Implementing ActionBar.TabListener()

```
1:  private class ExampleTabListener implements ActionBar.TabListener {
2:     public ExampleTabListener() {
3:     }
4:     @Override
5:     public void onTabReselected(Tab tab, FragmentTransaction ft) {
6:     }
7:     @Override
8:     public void onTabSelected(Tab tab, FragmentTransaction ft) {
9:       Toast toast = Toast.makeText(getApplicationContext(), "tab" , Toast.LENGTH_
SHORT);
10:      if (tab.equals(mTab1)){
11:        toast.setText("Tab 1");
12:        toast.show();
13:      }else{
14:        toast.setText("Tab 2");
15:        toast.show();
16:      }
17:    }
18:    @Override
19:    public void onTabUnselected(Tab tab, FragmentTransaction ft) {
20:    }
21:}
```

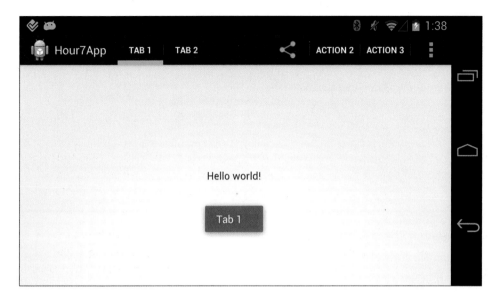

FIGURE 7.7
Tab navigation in the `ActionBar`

Two parameters are passed to the `TabListener`: One is the tab that was clicked on, and the other is a `FragmentTransaction`. Hour 8, "Activities and Fragments," covers fragments in detail. `FragmentTransactions` manage how fragments are used within an app. Android does not pre-define how a `FragmentTransaction` may be used with the `TabListener`. The parameter is provided for developers to take advantage of if needed.

Strategies for Using the ActionBar and Menus

This hour has not exhausted the possible options for using the action bar, but it has shown how to use menu items, drop-down navigation, and tab navigation within the action bar.

Of these, using menu items provides one opportunity to support older and newer versions of Android using the same code.

There are alternatives to consider for using advanced features of the `ActionBar` for newer Android versions while still supporting the old. Giving older versions of Android a look and feel that is similar to that of the action bar's is possible.

Let's consider four options:

▶ **Use menu options only:** Use `onCreateMenuOptions()` to create an app that will have an action bar on new versions and support a dedicated menu button on older versions. This method does not provide all action bar features, but could be a good solution for many apps.

▶ **Create an initial branching activity:** You learned in Hour 4 that you can check Android versions in your code. You can make an activity that checks for the Android version when the app starts. If the version is Honeycomb or higher, the app could show an activity that includes advanced action bar features. If it's not, the old-style menu would appear via a different activity. You can do a check like the following:

```
if (android.os.Build.VERSION.SDK_INT>=
android.os.Build.VERSION_CODES.HONEYCOMB) {}
```

▶ **Create a layout for versions lower than Honeycomb that mimics the functionality of an ActionBar:** Android provides a sample app called action bar compatibility that provides an example of this layout. To get it, follow the instructions at http://developer.android.com/tools/samples/index.html.

▶ **Use a third-party product called ActionBarSherlock:** This product implements the ActionBar API in older versions of Android and works with the support library. Hour 23, "Pro Tips, Finishing Touches, and Next Steps," includes an example app that uses ActionBarSherlock.

Summary

In this hour, you considered several ways to implement navigation on an ActionBar. You used menu items, drop-down navigation, and tab navigation. Drop-down navigation and tab navigation are supported in Android 3.0 and newer versions. You can create an app with menu items in which the same code will work on both older and newer versions of Android. Three basic strategies were considered to create apps for all versions of Android.

Q&A

Q. Are there design guidelines for using the ActionBar? There seem to be a lot of options.

A. Yes, the Android documentation on design guidelines is constantly improving. For information on the ActionBar specifically, check http://developer.android.com/design/patterns/actionbar.html.

Q. What problem does the ActionBar solve?

A. The ActionBar provides a prominent and consistent place for important actions within your app. It solves the problem of a user who is lost in navigation.

Workshop

Quiz

1. What does `getMenuInflater().inflate()` do?

2. What do `ActionBar.OnNavigationListener` and `ActionBar.TabListener` have in common?

Answers

1. When you create an app, you can include an XML file that defines a menu. The `getMenu-Inflater().inflate()` method inflates that XML file into an object that can be used in the app.

2. `ActionBar.OnNavigationListener` and `ActionBar.TabListener` are both interfaces of the `ActionBar` class that must be implemented to listen for and respond to specific `ActionBar` events. `ActionBar.OnNavigationListener` is used in drop-down navigation, and `ActionBar.TabListener` is used in tab navigation.

Exercises

1. Modify the code in this hour to display tabs that are meaningful to an app that you are thinking of creating.

2. Show the tabs you created in Exercise 1 as options for drop-down navigation.

3. Modify the code from this chapter to include more than five `MenuItems`. Add icons to two of those menu items and ensure that they always display in the app.

HOUR 8
Activities and Fragments

What You'll Learn in This Hour:

- ▶ What fragments are
- ▶ How to create and display fragments
- ▶ How to navigate with fragments
- ▶ How fragments and activities interact

In this hour, you will learn what fragments are and how to incorporate them into Android apps. Fragments make creating sophisticated user interfaces easier. In this hour, you learn how to display fragments, how fragments interact with an action bar, and how fragments interact with activities.

Using Fragments Across UIs

Fragments are sections of full user interface (UI) functionality on a device's screen. They were introduced in Android 3.0 Honeycomb, which was created to run on Android tablets. Before fragments, the user interface for an Android app was made up of activities, layouts, and controls such as buttons.

One reason fragments were introduced was to make an easier task of creating apps that worked well on small devices such as phones as well as on larger devices such as tablets and televisions. On a phone, you might use one fragment in an activity. On a tablet, you might combine several fragments in one layout to take advantage of the larger display area. You can use the same fragment on both a phone and a tablet. That same fragment can be displayed on its own in one user interface and with other fragments in another user interface.

Like activities, fragments have a lifecycle. They are started, paused, and destroyed. Fragments always live within an activity and whatever happens in the activity happens in the fragment. If an activity is destroyed, all the fragments within the activity are also destroyed.

As you saw in Hour 4, "Not Just Smartphones: Supporting Tablets, TVs, and More," the support package for Android provides backward compatibility of many new Android features to older versions of Android. Using the support package, fragments are available for commonly used Android platforms starting with API level 4 (Android 1.6).

The four projects in the source code that accompany this hour are the following:

- ▶ Hour8App.Intro
- ▶ Hour8App.Flip
- ▶ Hour8App.Tab
- ▶ Hour8App.Callback

Creating and Displaying Fragments

Like with an activity, you can create a fragment by using a layout file and a single class that defines the fragment and inflates the layout. You can use two techniques to display this fragment in an activity: either embed the fragment in an XML layout file or add it dynamically.

Using a Layout for Fragment Display

You can embed fragments directly into an XML layout for an activity. Using this approach, the fragment acts as a container for multiple controls. You use the fragment class name to identify the fragment. When the layout is inflated, the fragment class runs and the user interface displays.

Listing 8.1 defines a simple layout file for a fragment. On line 4 of Listing 8.1, a `TextView` is defined. Line 8 shows that the text in this `TextView` is set to `"Layout for fragment A"`. This example is contained in the project Hour8.intro.

LISTING 8.1 Layout for a Fragment (fragment_a.xml)

```
1: <RelativeLayout xmlns:android="http://schemas.android.com/apk/res/android"
2:      android:layout_width="match_parent"
3:      android:layout_height="match_parent" >
4:      <TextView
5:          android:id="@+id/textView1"
6:          android:layout_width="wrap_content"
7:          android:layout_height="wrap_content"
8:          android:text="Layout for fragment A"
9:          android:textAppearance="?android:attr/textAppearanceLarge" >
10:     </TextView>
11: </RelativeLayout>
```

The class that uses `fragment_a.xml` extends the `Fragment` class and implements one method called `onCreateView()`. `FragmentA` defined in Listing 8.2 inflates the layout and returns the resulting view.

LISTING 8.2   Creating a View for FragmentA (FragmentA.java)

```
1:import android.app.Fragment;
2:import android.os.Bundle;
3:import android.view.LayoutInflater;
4:import android.view.View;
5:import android.view.ViewGroup;
6:public class FragmentA extends Fragment   {
7:  @Override
8:  public View onCreateView(LayoutInflater
9:        inflater, ViewGroup container, Bundle savedInstanceState) {
10:   View v = inflater.inflate(R.layout.fragment_a, container, false);
11:   return v;
12: }
13:}
```

Listing 8.1 defines the layout for a simple fragment. Listing 8.2 shows the fragment class that inflates that view. In Listing 8.3, the fragment is added to the `activity_main.xml` layout. The result in this case is trivial. You've simply embedded a `TextView` in a fragment and displayed the fragment, but the process is the same for even complex fragments.

Line 6 defines the fragment using the class name. Line 7 gives the fragment an id.

LISTING 8.3   Activity Layout with Embedded Fragment

```
1:<RelativeLayout xmlns:android="http://schemas.android.com/apk/res/android"
2:    xmlns:tools="http://schemas.android.com/tools"
3:    android:layout_width="match_parent"
4:    android:layout_height="match_parent"
5:    tools:context=".MainActivity" >
6:<fragment android:name="com.bffmedia.hour8app.intro.FragmentA"
7:          android:id="@+id/fragment_a"
8:          android:layout_width="match_parent"
9:          android:layout_height="match_parent" />
10:</RelativeLayout>
```

Displaying Fragments Dynamically

You can add fragments to an activity dynamically. The idea is to have a layout, such as a `LinearLayout`, within the activity layout to hold the fragment.

In Listing 8.4, lines 6–10 define a `LinearLayout` and give it the id `layout_container`. You use that `LinearLayout` as the container for a fragment that is defined dynamically in code. That is, the dynamically created fragment will display within the `LinearLayout` with id `layout_container`. For this simple example, the `LinearLayout` is defined as the only element within the `RelativeLayout`; in practice, other controls or fragments could be defined in the `RelativeLayout`.

LISTING 8.4   Activity Layout with LinearLayout to Hold Fragments

```
1:<RelativeLayout xmlns:android="http://schemas.android.com/apk/res/android"
2:    xmlns:tools="http://schemas.android.com/tools"
3:    android:layout_width="match_parent"
4:    android:layout_height="match_parent"
5:    tools:context=".MainActivity" >
6:<LinearLayout
7:        android:id="@+id/layout_container"
8:        android:layout_width="wrap_content"
9:        android:layout_height="wrap_content">
10:</LinearLayout>
11:</RelativeLayout>
```

To tie the fragment to an activity's layout, you use a `FragmentTransaction` object, as shown in Listing 8.5.

In the `onCreate()` method of this activity, you create a new `FragmentA` object and a `FragmentTransaction` object. In line 3, you tie `FragmentA` to the layout using the `FragmentTransaction` `replace()` method. The contents of the `LinearLayout` associated with `R.id.layout_container` are replaced with the fragment that you created.

LISTING 8.5   Dynamically Adding a Fragment

```
1:FragmentA fragmentA = new FragmentA();
2:FragmentTransaction ft = getFragmentManager().beginTransaction();
3:ft.replace(R.id.layout_container, fragmentA);
4:ft.addToBackStack("example");
5:ft.setTransition(FragmentTransaction.TRANSIT_FRAGMENT_FADE);
6:ft.commit();
```

A `FragmentTransaction` object uses the following methods to manage fragments in a layout:

▶ `Add()`: Adds a fragment to a layout.

▶ `Replace()`: Replaces a fragment within a layout.

▶ `Remove()`: Removes a fragment from a layout.

▶ `AddToBackStack()`: Adds the set of commands in the transaction to the back stack. The fragment will not be destroyed when it is removed or replaced—it will be stopped. If the user navigates using the Back button, the fragment on the stack will redisplay.

▶ `SetTransition()`: Sets an animation for the `FragmentTransaction`.

▶ `Commit()`: Commits the transaction. This causes the transaction to take effect. The `AddToBackStack()` method is associated with all the commands that are committed.

Fragments and the Support Package

Fragments are available in all current versions of Android via the support package (which is also known as the compatibility library). Table 8.1 shows a comparison of the key differences between using fragments and the support package fragments. As you can see, the imports are different. Instead of an activity, you use a `FragmentActivity`, and instead of calling the `get-FragmentManager()` method, you use `getSupportFragmentManager()`.

If you use the support package, you will use the support package imports and methods. If your app targets Honeycomb and above, you can use the Android imports and methods.

TABLE 8.1 Fragments and Support Package Fragments

Fragments	Support Package Fragments
`importandroid.app.Activity;`	`importandroid.support.v4.app.` `FragmentActivity;`
`importandroid.app.` `FragmentTransaction;`	`importandroid.support.v4.app.` `FragmentTransaction;`
`importandroid.app.Fragment;`	`importandroid.support.v4.app.Fragment;`
`public class MainActivity extends Activity {`	`public class MainActivity extends FragmentActivity {`
`... getFragmentManager()`	`...getSupportFragmentManager()`

NOTE

Using Fragments for Phones and Tablets

Fragments make leveraging the same code in both tablet and phone apps easy. In a phone app, you might have two activities such as a list and a details page. Selecting from the list shows the entire details page. On a tablet, you can design the same app with the list and detail page side by side. In both cases, you should use the same fragment class for the list and for the detail page. For a detailed example of this method, see http://developer.android.com/guide/practices/tablets-and-handsets.html.

Using Fragments for Navigation

In this section, you learn two ways to navigate using fragments. In the first case, you use fragments that navigate to each other. When the user clicks a button on `FragmentA`, `FragmentB` appears and vice versa. Implementing that navigation technique shows how to navigate within a set of fragments. The back stack is supported in this case. To make this technique work efficiently and consistently, the methods used to show individual fragments are defined in the activity.

In the second way to navigate using fragments, you use an action bar to show a fragment when a tab is selected from the action bar. Each fragment that you want to display has a corresponding tab in the action bar. When the tab is selected, the fragment displays.

Navigating Between Fragments

Using one activity and two fragments, you can see how one fragment can navigate to another. Though you use two fragments in this example, you can implement a more complex navigation scheme with many fragments using the same method. Rather than having multiple activities to manage, you can work with just one activity and multiple fragments.

You need to define `FragmentA` and `FragmentB`. In each activity, a button is used to initiate navigation. The navigation always switches between fragments. Figure 8.1 shows the app with `FragmentA` displayed on the left and `FragmentB` displayed on the right. This example is contained in the project Hour8.Flip.

FIGURE 8.1
Switching between two fragments

The project contains three XML layout files and three java files. There is one layout for the activity and one for each fragment, so you have the following files:

- ▶ MainActivity.java
- ▶ FragmentA.java
- ▶ FragmentB.java
- ▶ activity_main.xml
- ▶ fragment_a.xml
- ▶ Fragment_b.xml

In MainActivity.java, you define two methods, showFragmentA() and showFragmentB(), to show each fragment. Listing 8.6 shows the complete code for the showFragmentA() method.

LISTING 8.6 Showing a Fragment with showFragmentA()

```
1:public void showFragmentA(){
2:FragmentA fragmentA = new FragmentA();
3:FragmentTransaction ft = getFragmentManager().beginTransaction();
4:ft.replace(R.id.layout_container, fragmentA);
5:ft.addToBackStack("fragment a");
6:ft.setTransition(FragmentTransaction.TRANSIT_FRAGMENT_FADE);
7:ft.commit();
8: }
```

The showFragmentA() method defined in Listing 8.6 is called in the onCreate() method of the MainActivity class, because you want to show FragmentA when the activity starts.

It is also called when the button in FragmentB is clicked. Fragments always live within an activity, and that activity is visible to the fragments. That means that a fragment can call a method defined in the activity. Listing 8.7 shows a snippet of FragmentB code that calls the showFragmentA() method.

On line 4 of Listing 8.7, the current activity is retrieved using the method getActivity(). The activity returned is cast to MainActivity, and the method showFragmentA() is called in line 5.

This example shows that the activity associated with the fragment is available via the getActivity() method. Getting the activity this way gives you access to methods within the activity. For simple examples like this one, calling methods that are defined in the activity can be handy.

LISTING 8.7 Calling showFragmentA() from FragmentB

```
1:Button button = (Button) v.findViewById(R.id.button1);
2:  button.setOnClickListener(new OnClickListener() {
3:    public void onClick(View v) {
4:      MainActivity currentActivity = (MainActivity) getActivity();
5:      currentActivity.showFragmentA();
6:    }
7: });
```

Using Fragments with an ActionBar

In Hour 7, "ActionBar and Menu Navigation," you created an action bar with two tabs and learned how to respond to the tab being selected by creating a class that implemented an ActionBar.TabListener. In this section, you use an action bar with tabs to display different fragments. The project that accompanies this example is Hour8.Tab.

Switching Between Fragments with Tabs

Listing 8.6 shows a method to display a fragment in a layout. You can call that method from within a tab listener to add tabs that can be used to navigate between fragments. The result is shown in Figure 8.2.

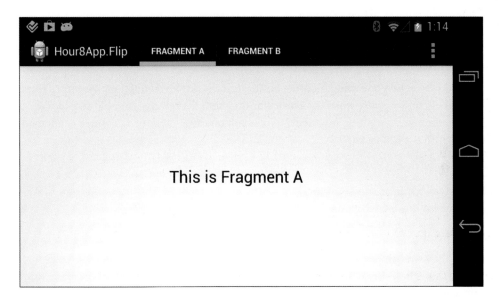

FIGURE 8.2
Using `ActionBar` tabs with fragments

To implement the interaction between fragments and the action bar, you create and display tabs as illustrated in Hour 7 in Listing 7.3. You implement a different tab listener, as shown in Listing 8.8.

LISTING 8.8 Implementing a Tab Listener

```
1:  private class NavTabListener implements ActionBar.TabListener {
2:      public NavTabListener() {}
3:      @Override
4:       public void onTabReselected(Tab tab, FragmentTransaction ft) {}
5:      @Override
6:       public void onTabSelected(Tab tab, FragmentTransaction ft) {
7:          if (tab.equals(mTab1)){
8:             showFragmentA();
9:          }else{
10:            showFragmentB();
11:          }
12:      }
```

```
13:        @Override
14:          public void onTabUnselected(Tab tab, FragmentTransaction ft) {}
15:          }
16:    }
```

When a tab is selected, the activity's `showFragmentA()` or `showFragmentB()` method will be called. The code is similar to Listing 7.4, but rather than show a message, you switch fragments.

Adding MenuItems from a Fragment

Adding items to the action bar when a particular fragment is displayed often makes sense. These menu items would only display when the particular fragment is showing. Android provides a concise mechanism for doing this. Fragments implement an `onCreateOptionsMenu()` method to append items to the action bar.

To add items to the action bar, the fragment must

▶ Call `setHasOptionsMenu()` during the `onCreate()` method. This is an indicator that the fragment has menu options.

▶ Implement an `onCreateOptionsMenu()` method.

▶ Handle the item being selected. This can be done in the activity's `onOptionsItemSelected()` method. The activity method can handle responses to all cases, even if the fragment added the menu item.

Fragment and Activity Interaction

You have seen that a fragment can call a method that is defined within an activity, as shown in Listings 8.6 and 8.7. In that case, you knew that the methods existed within the activity. You can take a further step when you create a fragment and require that a particular method be implemented in the calling activity. To do that, the fragment implements an interface for the activity to implement. The fragment enforces this requirement by checking on the existence of the implemented interface.

To see how a fragment can require an interface to be implemented within an activity, you will create `FragmentYesNo.java`. This fragment has two buttons: one for "yes" and one for "no." The fragment includes a `TextView` that you can populate with a question. Visually, this fragment can display a question and accept "yes" or "no" as possible responses. You define an interface within the fragment called `onAnswerSelectedListener()`. In order to be notified when a selection is made in `FragmentYesNo`, the activity must implement this method. The Hour 8. Callback project contains this example.

The following snippet shows a portion of the onCreateView() method for the fragment. A button is created. When the button is clicked, the fragment's onAnswerSelectedListener() method is passed "yes."

```
View v = inflater.inflate(R.layout.fragment_yes_no, container, false);
Button buttonYes = (Button) v.findViewById(R.id.buttonYes);
buttonYes.setOnClickListener(new OnClickListener() {
  public void onClick(View v) {
     mListener.OnAnswerSelected("yes");
  }
});
```

The code for the "no" button is identical except it passes "no" in the response.

The listener interface is defined as follows:

```
public interface OnAnswerSelectedListener {
public void OnAnswerSelected(String answer);
}
OnAnswerSelectedListener mListener;
```

The onAnswerSelectedListener interface is defined in the FragmentYesNo class and the member field mListener is defined.

You make it a requirement that the activity that uses FragmentYesNo must implement this call-back listener. You do that in the fragment's onAttach() method. The onAttach() method is called when the fragment is attached to the activity. It is also there that the listener that will be called in the fragment is assigned. Listing 8.9 shows the onAttach() method.

LISTING 8.9   The Fragment's onAttach() Method

```
1:  @Override
2:    public void onAttach(Activity activity) {
3:       super.onAttach(activity);
4:       try {
5:          mListener = (OnAnswerSelectedListener) activity;
6:       } catch (ClassCastException e) {
7:         throw new ClassCastException(activity.toString()
8:              + " must implement OnAnswerSelectedListener");
9:       }
10: }
```

The onAttach() method is passed the activity. On line 5 of Listing 8.9, the fragment's mListener is assigned to the activity cast as an OnAnswerSelectedListener. You are trying to get an OnAnswerSelectedListener from the activity. If the activity has not implemented the OnAnswerSelectedListener interface, this will fail. If the activity does not implement the interface, a `ClassCastException` is thrown. This forces any activity that wants to use this fragment to implement the callback.

On the activity side, the activity must implement the interface as follows:

```
public class MainActivity extends Activity
implements FragmentYesNo.OnAnswerSelectedListener {
...
@Override
public void OnAnswerSelected(String answer) {
    Toast.makeText(getApplicationContext(), answer, Toast.LENGTH_SHORT).show();
}
```

In this case, the `onAnswerSelected()` method just shows a toast message with the selected answer. Figure 8.3 shows the fragment and toast message.

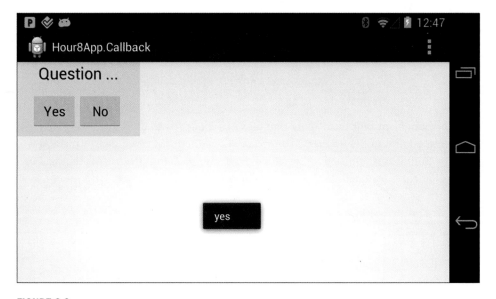

FIGURE 8.3
Activity shows the answer from the fragment via a listener

You can pass data to the fragment using a bundle as you did with an activity, as follows:

```
Bundle args = new Bundle();
args.putString("question", "Do you like fragments?");
FragmentYesNo yesNoFragment = new FragmentYesNo();
yesNoFragment.setArguments(args);
```

This data is read in the fragment by calling the fragment's `getArguments()` method.

Summary

This hour introduced fragments and demonstrated how you can display them dynamically or define them within the layout resource file of an activity. Fragments provide a convenient way to create and work with complex user interfaces. You saw several ways that an action bar can be used to work with fragments. Specifically, you implemented an action bar with two tabs to switch between fragments. You saw the ties between the activity that creates a fragment and the fragment itself. The fragment can call methods from that activity and can also require the activity to define specific methods.

Q&A

Q. What is the relationship between an activity and a fragment?

A. A fragment is always associated with an activity. An activity can include one or more fragments, so a fragment can be considered as a component within an activity.

Q. What are some advantages of using fragments?

A. Fragments make creating complex user interfaces easier and also make creating apps for tablets and phones that leverage the same code easier. Fragments allow you to design apps into visual and functional components and then implement these components as standalone units.

Workshop

Quiz

1. What is the `onAttach()` method?

2. What two techniques are used to display fragments?

3. What method is used to add items to the `ActionBar` from a fragment?

Answers

1. The `onAttach()` method is called when a fragment is attached to an activity. The activity is passed as a parameter. In this hour, you used the `onAttach()` method to ensure that the activity implemented a required callback.

2. Fragments can be created and displayed by using the XML layout for an activity or they can be dynamically created using `FragmentTransactions`.

3. Like an activity, the fragment has an `onCreateOptionsMenu()` method to add items to the `ActionBar`.

Exercises

1. Expand the `FragmentYesNo` example by implementing a dynamic display of questions. When the fragment is defined, a bundle should be passed with the question to display.

2. Expand the `FragmentYesNo` example by implementing navigation within the `onAnswerSelected()` callback. Implement two simple fragments. Navigate to one when "yes" is selected and to the other when "no" is selected.

3. Activities and fragments both go through a lifecycle. Using code such as the following snippet, log the methods for an activity and a fragment. The code uses the `Log` class to log the name of the method called. For the fragment, add a log statement for `onAttach()`, `onCreate()`, `onCreateView()`, and `onActivityCreated()`:

```
import android.util.Log;
public class MainActivity extends Activity {
  private static final String TAG = MainActivity.class.getName();
  @Override
  8protected void onCreate(Bundle savedInstanceState) {
    Log.d(TAG, "onCreate");
    super.onCreate(savedInstanceState);
    setContentView(R.layout.activity_main);
  }
```

HOUR 9
Alert! Working with Dialogs

What You'll Learn in This Hour:

▶ Understanding a dialog fragment
▶ Using date picker and time picker dialogs
▶ Working with an alert dialog

A dialog is a window that displays to the user. Dialogs might require a user to acknowledge information, make a decision, or enter additional information. Dialogs are typically used for modal windows, which means that they require a response from the user before they return to the main activity. In this hour, you use the DialogFragment class to create several types of dialogs.

Understanding a Dialog Fragment

Dialogs enable user interaction without losing context. When a dialog window displays, it usually contains a short message, or offers the user the ability to select a choice from a list, or make one or two other decisions.

Dialog fragments were introduced in the Honeycomb (API level 11, Android 3.0) release of Android but are also available in the support package. Via the support package, the DialogFragment class is backward compatible with earlier versions of Android.

Before the `DialogFragment` class was introduced, programmers used the `Dialog` class to create and display modal windows. With the availability now of the `DialogFragment` class, using dialogs directly in activities is not recommended. Rather, an activity should interact with a dialog fragment.

The Hour9App project contains the source code that accompanies this hour.

Displaying a Dialog

To demonstrate the basic use of a dialog fragment, you will create a window that requests that the user enter his or her first name. The window will display OK and Cancel buttons. You'll create an XML layout file and define the `DialogFragment` class. The accompanying source code is BasicDialogFragment.java.

You will create a basic dialog fragment by creating a layout and implementing the `onCreateView()` method. Subsequent examples in this hour will use the `onCreateDialog()` method.

The code for creating a basic dialog using this technique exhibits only minor differences from that for creating any other kind of fragment:

1. Rather than extend a fragment, you extend the `DialogFragment` class:

   ```
   public class BasicDialogFragment extends DialogFragment {
   ```

2. Because you are extending the `DialogFragment` class, you have access to a dialog window object. To access the underlying dialog, you make a call to `getDialog()`.

3. To set the title for the dialog, you call `getDialog()` and then set the title:

   ```
   getDialog().setTitle("First Name");
   ```

   You can also choose to show no title at all using the `requestWindowFeature()` method:

   ```
   getDialog().requestWindowFeature(Window.FEATURE_NO_TITLE);
   ```

Both `setTitle()` and `requestWindowFeature()` are methods of the `Dialog` class. Other methods are shown in the documentation for the class found at http://developer.android.com/reference/android/app/Dialog.html. Figure 9.1 shows the basic dialog. The title is set to "First Name."

FIGURE 9.1
Basic dialog

Besides extending the dialog fragment and adding the dialog title, no differences exist between this dialog fragment and other fragments that you have created. To retrieve data, you would implement a listener to see whether the name has been entered. The difference is in how the fragment displays. You do not load the fragment into a layout; rather, the dialog fragment is opened and closed.

To close the dialog, a call is made to the `dismiss()` method. The following shows the `onClick()` method for the Cancel button in the basic dialog:

```
mCancel = (Button)v.findViewById(R.id.buttonCancel);
mCancel.setOnClickListener(new OnClickListener() {
  public void onClick(View v) {
    BasicDialogFragment.this.dismiss();
  }
});
```

Opening and Closing a Dialog

Opening a dialog is similar to creating and showing a fragment. In an activity or fragment, you create the dialog and make a call to the show() method:

```
BasicDialogFragment basicDialog = new BasicDialogFragment();
basicDialog.show(getFragmentManager(), "basic");
```

Before the dialog is opened, an opportunity exists to set the style of the dialog. Predefined Android styles are available specifically for dialogs. You can also create custom styles.

Figure 9.2 shows a dialog that displays an image. The accompanying source code is ImageDialogFragment.java. The dialog on the left shows the image being displayed in a dialog with the default style. When displayed, this dialog includes a title and a background and dims the area behind the window. The dialog on the right shows no title, no frame, and no dimming of the background. This is the Theme.Dialog.NoFrame style, and you set it as follows for a dialog fragment named ImageDialogFragment:

```
ImageDialogFragment imageDialog = new ImageDialogFragment();
imageDialog.setStyle(DialogFragment.STYLE_NO_FRAME, 0);
imageDialog.show(getFragmentManager(), "image");
```

Listing 9.1 shows the style definition for Theme.Dialog.NoFrame.

These styles are defined in the Android source code, and you can access them at https://android.googlesource.com/platform/frameworks/base/+/refs/heads/master/core/res/res/values/themes.xml.

LISTING 9.1   Dialog NoFrame Theme

```
1:  <style name="Theme.Dialog.NoFrame">
2:          <item name="windowBackground">@android:color/transparent</item>
3:          <item name="android:windowFrame">@null</item>
4:          <item name="windowContentOverlay">@null</item>
5:          <item name="android:windowAnimationStyle">@null</item>
6:          <item name="android:backgroundDimEnabled">false</item>
7:          <item name="android:windowIsTranslucent">true</item>
8:          <item name="android:windowNoTitle">true</item>
9:          <item name="android:windowCloseOnTouchOutside">false</item>
10: </style>
```

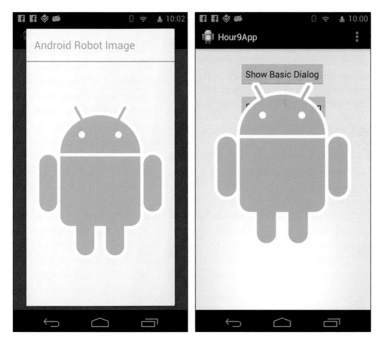

FIGURE 9.2
Dialog with style set to `NoFrame`

Dialogs for Picking Date and Time

The `Dialog` class predates the `DialogFragment` class. The `Fragment` class was introduced in Android 3.0. The basic dialog class and several specialty dialog classes were included in the API level 1 version of Android.

The recommended way to use a dialog class is to wrap it in a dialog fragment.

The types of dialogs include the following:

▶ `DatePicker`: User interface to select a date.

▶ `TimePicker`: User interface to select a time.

▶ `AlertDialog`: Can be used for many types of dialogs.

▶ `ProgressDialog`: See note. Not recommended!

NOTE

Avoid ProgressDialog

Android provides a `ProgressDialog` class that opens a small window that shows an indeterminate progress bar. This dialog is not recommended. Rather, incorporate a `ProgressBar` into your layout.

Using Date Picker

To use the date picker dialog, you wrap the dialog in a dialog fragment using the dialog fragment's `onCreateDialog()` method. A dialog is returned from this method. The accompanying source code is DatePickerDialogFragment.java.

Let's look at how to construct a `DatePickerDialog` instance. The constructor definition and parameters are as follows:

```
DatePickerDialog(Context context, DatePickerDialog.OnDateSetListener callBack, int
year, int monthOfYear, int dayOfMonth)
```

The constructor for the `DatePickerDialog` class includes a `DatePickerDialog.OnDateSetListener` callback parameter. You can use this parameter to provide an implementation of the `onDateSet()` method to handle when the user chooses a specific date within the picker. The year, month, and date are used to set an initial value for this dialog.

The following are the overall steps to use for creating the `DateDialogFragment` shown in Figure 9.3:

1. Create a `DateDialogFragment` class that extends `DialogFragment` and implements `DatePickerDialog.onDateSetListener()`.

2. Implement the `onDateSet()` method within the `DialogFragment`.

3. Create a `DatePickerDialog` in the `onCreateDialog()` method.

Let's do it. Create a `DateDialogFragment` that implements `DatePickerDialog.OnDateSetListener` as follows:

```
public class DatePickerDialogFragment extends DialogFragment implements
                DatePickerDialog.OnDateSetListener {
```

This is a stub for the `onDateSetMethod()`:

```
@Override
public void onDateSet(DatePicker view, int year, int monthOfYear,int dayOfMonth) {
    // TODO handle selected date
}
```

Because `DatePickerDialogFragment` implements `DatePickerDialog.OnDateSetListener`, you can use `this` as the second parameter when creating the `DatePickerDialog`. Listing 9.2 shows the `onCreateDialog()` method for the `DatePickerDialogFragment`. `DatePickerDialogdateDialog` is defined on lines 4–6 of Listing 9.2.

LISTING 9.2 DatePickerDialogFragment onCreateDialog()

```
1:  Calendar now = Calendar.getInstance();
2:  @Override
3:  public Dialog onCreateDialog(Bundle savedInstanceState) {
4:    DatePickerDialog dateDialog = new DatePickerDialog(this.getActivity(),
5:        this,
6:        now.get(Calendar.YEAR), now.get(Calendar.MONTH),now.get(Calendar.DAY_
OF_MONTH));
7:  return dateDialog;
8:  }
```

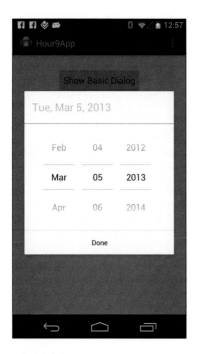

FIGURE 9.3
Displaying `DatePickerDialog`

You have used the onAttach() method and defined a listener interface in order for fragments to communicate with activities. You use the same method with the DatePickerDialogFragment. The onDateSet() method of the DatePickerDialog sets the value for the listener.

Listing 9.3 shows the full code for the DatePickerDialogFragment. The interface for communicating with the calling activity is defined in line 14. The onDateSet() method required by DatePickerDialog is created in line 31. In line 32, you use the onDateSet() method to call the OnDateEnteredListener.

LISTING 9.3   DatePickerDialogFragment Full Source

```
1:    package com.bffmedia.hour9app;
2:    import java.util.Calendar;
3:    import android.app.Activity;
4:    import android.app.DatePickerDialog;
5:    import android.app.Dialog;
6:    import android.app.DialogFragment;
7:    import android.os.Bundle;
8:    import android.widget.DatePicker;
9:
10:   public class DatePickerDialogFragment extends DialogFragment implements
11:                 DatePickerDialog.OnDateSetListener {
12:
13:     // OnDateEnteredListener is implemented by the calling Activity
14:     interface OnDateEnteredListener {
15:         public void OnDateEntered(int year, int monthOfYear, int dayOfMonth);
16:     }
17:     OnDateEnteredListener mListener;
18:
19:     // Get current date and create the DatePickerDialog
20:     Calendar now = Calendar.getInstance();
21:     @Override
22:     public Dialog onCreateDialog(Bundle savedInstanceState) {
23:         DatePickerDialog dateDialog = new DatePickerDialog(this.getActivity(),
24:         this,
25:         now.get(Calendar.YEAR), now.get(Calendar.MONTH),now.get(Calendar.DAY_OF_
MONTH));
26:         return dateDialog;
27:     }
28:
29:     // OnDateSet is required to implement DatePickerDialog.OnDateSetListener
30:     @Override
31:     public void onDateSet(DatePicker view, int year, int monthOfYear, int
dayOfMonth) {
32:         mListener.OnDateEntered(year, monthOfYear, dayOfMonth);
```

```
33:     }
34:     @Override
35:     public void onAttach(Activity activity) {
36:         super.onAttach(activity);
37:         try {
38:             mListener = (OnDateEnteredListener) activity;
39:         } catch (ClassCastException e) {
40:             throw new ClassCastException(activity.toString()
41:                     + " must implement OnDateEnteredListener");
42:         }
43:     }
44: }
```

To open `DatePickerDialogFragment`, you must implement the interface `onDateEn-teredListener`. So, the declaration for the calling activity looks like the following:

```
public class MainActivity extends Activity
            implements DatePickerDialogFragment.OnDateEnteredListener{
```

You then implement the required `OnDateSet()` method as follows:

```
@Override
public void OnDateEntered(int year, int monthOfYear, int dayOfMonth) {
    Toast.makeText(getApplicationContext(),
        dayOfMonth + "." + monthOfYear +"."+year,  Toast.LENGTH_SHORT).show();
}
```

A toast message displays the data returned.

Using Time Picker

You use `TimePickerDialog` in a dialog fragment similar to the technique used for the date picker dialog. Listing 9.4 shows the `onCreateDialog()` method for this fragment, and Figure 9.4 shows the resulting dialog. The accompanying source code is TimePickerDialogFragment. java.

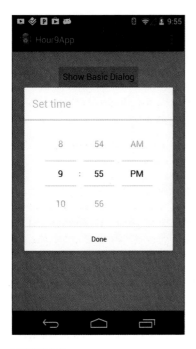

FIGURE 9.4
Displaying `TimePickerDialog`

LISTING 9.4   TimePickerDialog Fragment onCreateDialog() Method

```
1:  Calendar now = Calendar.getInstance();
2:  @Override
3:  public Dialog onCreateDialog(Bundle savedInstanceState) {
4:    final Calendar c = Calendar.getInstance();
5:    int hour = c.get(Calendar.HOUR_OF_DAY);
6:    int minute = c.get(Calendar.MINUTE);
7:    TimePickerDialog dateDialog = new TimePickerDialog(
8:      this.getActivity(),
9:      this,
10:     hour, minute, false);
11:   return dateDialog;
12: }
```

Using Alert Dialogs

An alert dialog uses the builder pattern to add features to a simple dialog. Each feature is added to the current dialog. To create dialog fragments for picking dates and times, you implemented the onCreateDialog() method and returned a dialog. Similarly, you will build an alert dialog in the onCreateDialog() class to create new dialog fragments. This section shows the typical components of an alert dialog and several examples.

You can use the techniques of creating listeners to interact with the calling activity and using the onAttach() method to ensure that the listener is defined with alert dialogs as well.

An alert dialog may include a title, content area, and up to three buttons that the user can select. For a simple dialog, a need might not exist for a separate content area. In that case, the title would ask the user a question and the buttons would handle the response. The buttons represent a positive response, a negative response, and a neutral response—for example, Yes, No, and Cancel.

Listing 9.5 shows the code for a simple alert dialog. The accompanying source code is BasicAlertDialogFragment.java. The dialog uses the builder pattern to add features to itself. In line 5, a message is added to the content area. Lines 6 and 10 add the positive and negative buttons. When they are selected, the buttons will just close the window. If you wanted to collect this data and return it to the activity that opened the dialog, you would add a listener interface. Figure 9.5 shows the resulting dialog. The positive button is set on line 6 and the negative button is set on line 10. There is no neutral button in this case.

LISTING 9.5   AlertDialog Basic Example

```
1:   public class BasicAlertDialogFragment extends DialogFragment{
2:      @Override
3:      public Dialog onCreateDialog(Bundle savedInstanceState) {
4:         AlertDialog.Builder builder = new AlertDialog.Builder(getActivity());
5:         builder.setMessage("Do you like Dialogs?")
6:                 .setPositiveButton("Yes", new DialogInterface.OnClickListener() {
7:                     public void onClick(DialogInterface dialog, int id) {
8:                     }
9:                 })
10:                .setNegativeButton("No", new DialogInterface.OnClickListener() {
11:                    public void onClick(DialogInterface dialog, int id) {
12:                    }
13:                });
14:   return builder.create();
15: }
16:}
```

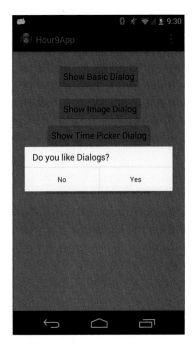

FIGURE 9.5
AlertDialog with a title and two buttons

You can build alert dialogs with different user interfaces using the same basic model.

The steps to create a dialog fragment using an alert dialog are as follows:

1. Create the dialog fragment.

2. Build and return an alert dialog in the onCreateDialog() method.

3. Provide a listener interface to pass the results of the dialog back to the activity.

By using various AlertDialog.Builder methods, you can create different user experiences.

Showing a List of Items

You can show a list of items in an alert dialog using the setItems() method. You can pass this method a resource that defines an array or an array of charSequence objects. Listing 9.6 shows the use of an array of String values to populate the item list. The title and a negative button are also added. In line 5, the onClick() method incudes the parameter which. It is the integer value corresponding to the position of the selected item. The accompanying source code is ListAlertDialogFragment.java.

LISTING 9.6   AlertDialog List Example

```
1:   String[] items ={"Beef", "Fish", "Chicken", "Pasta"};
2:   AlertDialog.Builder builder = new AlertDialog.Builder(getActivity());
3:   builder.setTitle("Your choices are:");
4:   builder.setItems(items, new DialogInterface.OnClickListener() {
5:     public void onClick(DialogInterface dialog, int which) {
6:     }
7:   })
8:   .setNegativeButton("Cancel", new DialogInterface.OnClickListener() {
9:     public void onClick(DialogInterface dialog, int id) {
10:    }
11:  });
```

You could define the array shown in line 1 of Listing 9.6 as an array resource. In the res/values/strings.xml, you would add the following:

```
<?xml version="1.0" encoding="utf-8"?>
<resources>
    <string-array name="food_array">
        <item>Beef</item>
        <item>Fish</item>
        <item>Chicken</item>
        <item>Pasta</item>
    </string-array>
</resources>
```

This resource array could then be passed as the first parameter to the setItems() method:

```
builder.setItems(R.array.food_array, new DialogInterface.OnClickListener()...
```

NOTE

Using setTitle() and setMessage()

setTitle() provides a title for an alert dialog. SetMessage() provides a message in the content area of an alert dialog. You cannot use setMessage() and setItems() together because both populate the content area of the window. Listing 9.6 used setTitle(). Listing 9.5 used setMessage().

Figure 9.6 shows the alert dialog created in Listing 9.6. The title, list of items, and Cancel button are displayed.

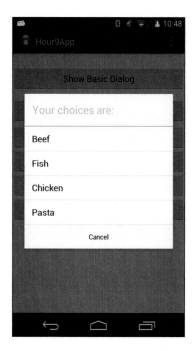

FIGURE 9.6
`AlertDialog` with title, list, and one button

Adding a Custom View

In the first example in this hour (BasicDialogFragment.java), which was shown in Figure 9.1, the custom layout included an `EditText` field and two buttons. You used the `onCreateView()` method rather than the `onCreateDialog()` method. You can change your approach and use a custom layout in an alert dialog to provide the same functionality. By creating a custom view within an alert dialog, you can create the precise user experience that you desire as a developer.

The custom layout for your new dialog will contain only an `EditText` field. The Cancel and OK buttons will be implemented as the negative and positive buttons using the builder methods.

Lines 3 and 4 of Listing 9.7 show how you get an inflater and inflate the layout into the view for this dialog. Line 8 shows that you are passing the entered name to a listener that you created. Figure 9.7 shows the dialog.

LISTING 9.7   AlertDialog with Custom Layout

```
1:    public Dialog onCreateDialog(Bundle savedInstanceState) {
2:        AlertDialog.Builder builder = new AlertDialog.Builder(getActivity());
3:        LayoutInflater inflater = getActivity().getLayoutInflater();
4:        builder.setView(inflater.inflate(R.layout.fragment_alert_dialog_name, null))
```

```
 5:              .setPositiveButton("OK", new DialogInterface.OnClickListener() {
 6:                  public void onClick(DialogInterface dialog, int id) {
 7:                      EditText nameText = (EditText) getDialog().findViewById(R.
id.editText1);
 8:                      mListener.OnNameEntered(nameText.getText().toString());
 9:                  }
10:              })
11:              .setNegativeButton("Cancel", new DialogInterface.OnClickListener() {
12:                  public void onClick(DialogInterface dialog, int id) {
13:                  }
14:              });
15:      return builder.create();
16: }
```

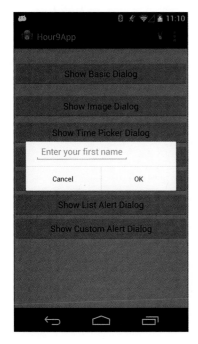

FIGURE 9.7
`AlertDialog` with a custom view

Summary

In this hour, you saw several ways to create dialogs. Dialogs provide small windows for user interaction within an app. Using dialogs, you can interact with the user and not lose overall context. You used the `DialogFragment` class and created dialogs for date and time. You saw how to create different kinds of dialogs by using the `AlertDialog` and `AlertDialog.Builder` classes. To pass data from dialogs back to the activities that opened them, you created listener interfaces in the dialogs.

Q&A

Q. **How is a dialog fragment different from a fragment?**

A. A dialog fragment is shown as an independent window. They are opened by calling `show()` and closed by calling `dismiss()`. A dialog fragment includes an `onCreateDialog()` method that can be overwritten as well as an `onCreateView()` method.

Q. **What is the purpose of creating a listener interface in a dialog fragment?**

A. The listener interface is a way for the dialog fragment to provide data back to the calling activity. The activity implements the listener. When the dialog fragment calls the listener, information can be passed back to the activity.

Workshop

Quiz

1. Name three kinds of dialogs.

2. When should the progress dialog be used?

3. When using an alert dialog with a positive button in a dialog fragment, how do you pass data back to the calling activity?

Answers

1. In this hour, you used dialog fragments and created dialogs within the `onCreateDialog()` method. There are four types of dialogs: `TimePickerDialog`, `DatePickerDialog`, `AlertDialog`, and `ProgessDialog`.

2. Never use a `ProgressDialog`.

3. A listener interface should be created and used to pass data to the activity.

Exercise

Use a `TimePickerDialog` and create a dialog fragment. In this dialog fragment, create a listener interface to pass the time back to the calling activity. Have the calling activity implement the listener.

Lists, Grids, Galleries, and Flippers

What You'll Learn in This Hour:

▶ Creating a `ListFragment`

▶ Customizing a `ListFragment`

▶ Using `GridView` and `Gallery`

▶ Using an `AdapterViewFlipper`

▶ Options for paging controls

In this hour, you will learn about the specific fragment known as the `ListFragment`. It is a convenient way to show a user a list of information. You'll implement a basic `ListFragment` and create a custom view for it. You'll then display the same data that was shown in the `ListFragment`, using a `GridView`, `Gallery`, and `ViewPageAdapter`. This demonstrates a common approach to displaying sets of data in different views.

ListFragments

A `ListFragment (android.app.ListFragment)` is a specialized fragment class that simplifies working with a list of items. In Hour 6, "Working with Basic UI Controls," you worked with basic user interface (UI) controls, including the spinner. The spinner acts as a drop-down menu and displays a list of information. When you implemented the spinner, you used an adapter to tie data to the display. You'll do the same in this hour.

You will create a simple data source that is used for all the examples in this hour. That data source will be a list of pie names. To store the pie names, you'll create a simple array as a resource.

In the Strings.xml file in the res/values/ folder, create an array called `pie_array`, as follows:

```
<string-array name="pie_array">
<item>apple</item>
<item>blueberry</item>
<item>cherry</item>
<item>coconut cream</item>
</string-array>
```

Creating a Simple ListFragment

You'll display the list of pies using a `ListFragment`. Throughout this hour, you will use one activity (MainActivity.java) with an action bar. The action bar has a set of tabs that display different fragments. The Hour10App project contains the source code that accompanies this hour.

To create a basic `ListFragment`, you do not need to create an XML layout. A `ListView(android.widget.ListView)` is inherent in the `ListFragment` class.

In other words, a `ListView` is created by the system each time you use a `ListFragment`. No need exists to explicitly create a `ListView` in the `onCreateView()` method.

Create a `ListFragment` class called `SimpleListFragment`. Listing 10.1 shows the entire class. Notice that there is no `onCreateView` method. The accompanying source code is SimpleListFragment.java.

Listing 10.1   Defining a ListFragment Class

```
1: package com.bffmedia.hour10app;
2: import android.app.ListFragment;
3: import android.content.res.Resources;
4: import android.os.Bundle;
5: import android.view.View;
6: import android.widget.ArrayAdapter;
7: import android.widget.ListView;
8: import android.widget.Toast;
9: public class SimpleListFragment extends ListFragment    {
10:String[] mPies;
11:@Override
12:public void onActivityCreated(Bundle savedInstanceState) {
13:super.onActivityCreated(savedInstanceState);
14:Resources resources = getResources();
15:mPies = resources.getStringArray(R.array.pie_array);
16:setListAdapter(new ArrayAdapter<String>(this.getActivity(),
17:android.R.layout.simple_list_item_1, mPies));
18:}
19:@Override
20:public void onListItemClick(ListView l, View v, int position, long id) {
21:Toast.makeText(this.getActivity().getApplicationContext(),
22:                mPies[position], Toast.LENGTH_SHORT).show();
23:}
24:}
```

In line 10, the string array `mPies` is defined. On lines 14–15, you associate `mPies` with the array that you defined in the resource file. The adapter is set in lines 16–17.

Note that an `ArrayAdapter<String>` is used to specify the type of data. The predefined layout `android.R.layout.simple_list_item1` is used to indicate how a single item should be displayed. It is a single `TextView`.

A `ListFragment` contains an `onListItemClick()` method. In this example, when an item is clicked, the position of the clicked item is used to get the name of the items and display it in a toast message. Lines 19–23 show the `onListItemClick()` method.

Figure 10.1 shows the resulting list.

FIGURE 10.1
Basic `ListFragment`

Customizing a ListFragment

The basic `ListFragment` implemented in Listing 10.1 did not include the `onCreateView()` method. The `ListView` that is inherent in the `ListFragment` was used.

You can use the `onCreateView()` method in a `ListFragment` to implement your own `ListView`. To use the `onCreateView()` method, create a custom XML layout file. When used with a `ListFragment`, that layout file must be defined precisely. It must include a `ListView` with the id set to `android:id="@id/android:list"` as it is in line 5 of Listing 10.2, which shows the entire XML file for the example custom `ListFragment`.

The accompanying source code is CustomListFragment.java.

Listing 10.2 ListFragment Custom Layout

```
1: <RelativeLayout xmlns:android="http://schemas.android.com/apk/res/android"
2:      android:layout_width="match_parent"
3:      android:layout_height="match_parent" >
4: <ListView
5:         android:id="@id/android:list"
6:         android:layout_width="match_parent"
7:         android:layout_height="match_parent"
8:         android:divider="@drawable/divider"
9:         android:listSelector="@drawable/selector" >
10: </ListView>
11: </RelativeLayout>
```

The `ListView` has the required id. For the custom `ListFragment`, you specify your own divider and selector. The divider divides the items in the list. The selector displays on the selected item.

In this case, you use shape drawables to define both the divider and the selector. These are XML files defined in the drawable resource folder.

The divider is defined as a rectangle that contains gradient coloring and has a height of 12dp:

```
<?xml version="1.0" encoding="utf-8"?>
<shape xmlns:android="http://schemas.android.com/apk/res/android"
    android:shape="rectangle">
<gradient android:startColor="#0000ff" android:endColor="#ffffff"
            android:angle="270"/>
<size  android:height="12dp" />
</shape>
```

The selector has a border defined by the stroke and a solid interior color. The interior color is slightly transparent. The alpha value for a color is defined in the first two characters. By specifying #330000ff, you can set the color to blue with the alpha set to hex 33. You can set the alpha value from 00, which is completely transparent, to FF, which is completely opaque:

```
<?xml version="1.0" encoding="utf-8"?>
<shape xmlns:android="http://schemas.android.com/apk/res/android"
  android:shape="rectangle">
<stroke android:width="2dp" android:color="#ff0000" />
<corners android:radius="12dp" />
<solid android:color="#330000ff"/>
</shape>
```

The onCreateView() method needs to return a view that contains a ListView with the speci-fied value. The id value is defined in the layout file. This is the entire onCreateView() method:

```
@Override
public View onCreateView(LayoutInflater inflater, ViewGroup container,
Bundle savedInstanceState) {
        View v   = inflater.inflate(R.layout.custom_list_fragment, container,
false);
return v;
}
```

Figure 10.2 shows the resulting custom ListFragment. Note the divider and the selector that were created as shape drawables.

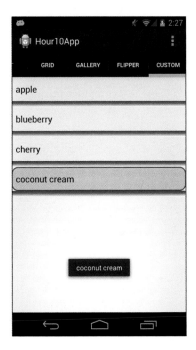

FIGURE 10.2
Custom ListFragment

Grids and Galleries

There are no specific classes like `ListFragment` for making `GridView(android.widget.GridView)` and `Gallery(android.widget.Gallery)` views, but you can create useful fragments with these components. When you use these views to create fragments, the code will be very similar to the code for a `ListFragment`.

In Listing 10.1, the `mPies` resource string array populates a `ListFragment` with data. You'll use the same method to display this data in a `Fragment` that contains a `GridView` and `Gallery`. This will show the same simple data in different views. Showing images and more elaborate views in gallery and grid views is a common practice. The examples in Hours 15, "Loaders, CursorLoaders, and CustomAdapters," and 16, "Developing a Complete App," show images displayed in a grid view.

Creating a Fragment with a GridView

A grid view displays data in a grid containing columns and rows. To create a fragment that displays the grid, you create a layout file that contains only a grid view. You can place this new fragment wherever you want in your design.

The fragment class uses the layout to define a `View` in the `onCreateView()` method. The data is populated and the adapter is set in the `onActivityCreated()` method. The grid view is populated in the same way that you populated a list in the `ListFragment`. Listing 10.3 defines the necessary layout.

LISTING 10.3   Layout for a GridView (grid_fragment.xml)

```
1: <?xml version="1.0" encoding="utf-8"?>
2: <GridView
3:    xmlns:android="http://schemas.android.com/apk/res/android"
4:    android:layout_width="match_parent"
5: android:layout_height="match_parent"
6: android:numColumns="2">
7: </GridView>
```

On line 5, the property for the number of columns to display is set. Use this grid view to create a new `SimpleGridFragment` class. Listing 10.4 defines a fragment using the layout from Listing 10.3. The accompanying source code is SimpleGridFragment.java.

LISTING 10.4   Creating a GridView Fragment

```
1: import android.app.Fragment;
2: public class SimpleGridFragment extends Fragment    {
3:     GridView mGrid;
4:     String[] mPies;
5:     @Override
6:       public void onActivityCreated(Bundle savedInstanceState) {
7:   super.onActivityCreated(savedInstanceState);
8:   Resources resources = getResources();
9:   mPies = resources.getStringArray(R.array.pie_array);
10:  mGrid.setAdapter(new ArrayAdapter<String>(getActivity(),
11:                     android.R.layout.simple_list_item_1, mPies));
12:       }
13:
14:    @Override
15:      public View onCreateView(LayoutInflater inflater, ViewGroup container,
16:         Bundle savedInstanceState) {
17:  mGrid  = (GridView) inflater.inflate(R.layout.grid_fragment, container,
false);
18:  mGrid.setOnItemClickListener(new OnItemClickListener() {
19:          public void onItemClick(AdapterView<?> parent,View v, int position,
long id){
20:             Toast.makeText(getActivity().getApplicationContext(),
21:                     mPies[position], Toast.LENGTH_SHORT).show();
22:          }
23:       });
24:       return mGrid;
25:    }
26: }
```

On line 3, you declare a variable called mGrid of type GridView. In the onCreateView() method on line 17, mGrid is populated by inflating the GridView layout. The view returned from the onCreateView() method is mGrid.

In the onActivityCreated() method, on lines 10 and 11, you set an ArrayAdapter for the GridView that you defined in the onCreateView() method. This part of the code is similar to the ListFragment code in Listing 10.1.

You display this fragment by selecting a tab in the action bar. A grid will appear.

Figure 10.3 shows the SimpleGridFragment defined in Listing 10.4.

FIGURE 10.3
Fragment with a `GridView`

Creating a Fragment with a Gallery

A `Gallery` displays data in a view that can be scrolled through horizontally. This is ideal for a photo gallery app where the goal is to show images and swipe through them. To set up a `Gallery` populated by the data in `mPies`, you use the code and layout similar to what you used for creating a `GridView` fragment.

The general approach is to use a `Gallery` widget instead of a `GridView` and then implement the same code for loading data. One reason for this example is to show how similar the code is. You are using the same data and displaying it in a different view. The accompanying source code is SimpleGalleryFragment.java.

Listing 10.5 is similar to Listing 10.3, but instead of using a `GridView`, you use a `Gallery`. In both cases, the idea is to create a layout with a single component. That layout will be used in the `onCreateView()` method of the fragment. The job of the fragment is to populate the view with data.

LISTING 10.5   Layout for a Gallery (gallery_fragment.xml)

```
1:  <?xml version="1.0" encoding="utf-8"?>
2:  <Gallery
3:      xmlns:android="http://schemas.android.com/apk/res/android"
4:      android:layout_width="fill_parent"
5:      android:layout_height="fill_parent" >
6:  </Gallery>
```

The code for the onCreateView() method for creating the SimpleGalleryFragment is nearly identical to that of the SimpleGridFragment. Rather than returning a GridView, the method returns a Gallery. Listing 10.6 shows the onCreateView() method.

LISTING 10.6   Gallery Fragment onCreateView()

```
1: @Override
2: public View onCreateView(LayoutInflater inflater, ViewGroup container,
3:                     Bundle savedInstanceState) {
4: mGallery  = (Gallery) inflater.inflate(R.layout.gallery_fragment, container,
false);
5: mGallery.setOnItemClickListener(new OnItemClickListener() {
6: public void onItemClick(AdapterView<?> parent, View v, int position, long id) {
7: Toast.makeText(getActivity().getApplicationContext(),
8:                     mPies[position], Toast.LENGTH_SHORT).show();
9: }
10:  });
11:  return mGallery;
12: }
```

Figure 10.4 shows the result of the SimpleGalleryFragment. The view slides from one string to another. In this case, the string cherry on the right side of the screen is being moved from right to left and is coming onto the screen. The string blueberry is mostly out of view. Using the same pie data for the gallery demonstrates how similar the code is that is used to display the same data in different views, but a much more common use of the gallery is to show images or complex views.

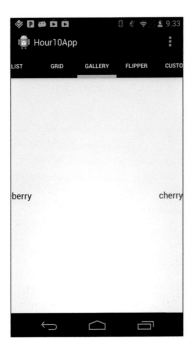

FIGURE 10.4
Fragment with a `Gallery`

NOTE

Gallery Deprecated

The Android platform is updated with regular releases. Those releases include the deprecation of certain features or methods. Typically, one method will replace another. The `Gallery` class was deprecated as of API level 16, which is the Android 4.1 or JellyBean release. Later this hour reviews the options for horizontal scrolling. Being deprecated does not mean the `Gallery` cannot be used, but you should be aware of the status when making implementation decisions. Suggested alternatives are `ViewPager` from the support package and `HorizontalScrollView`.

Using an AdapterViewFlipper

An `AdapterViewFlipper` (`android.widget.AdapterViewFlipper`) displays one view at a time and provides the ability to flip between views. You can use an `AdapterViewFlipper` in a fragment in the same way that you used a grid view and gallery. The `AdapterViewFlipper` has an option to flip between views automatically. Think of it as the ability to create a slideshow of views.

You implement the code to flip views automatically in the `onCreateView()` method. The `AdapterViewFlipper` was added in Android API level 11. Later in this hour, you learn about the available options for controls that handle page flipping and horizontal scrolling.

Listing 10.7 shows the layout used to create the `AdapterViewFlipper`.

LISTING 10.7   Layout for AdapterViewFlipper (view_flipper_fragment.xml)

```
1:  <AdapterViewFlipper xmlns:android="http://schemas.android.com/apk/res/android"
2:      android:id="@+id/flipper"
3:      android:layout_width="match_parent"
4:      android:layout_height="match_parent"
5:      android:layout_centerInParent="true">
6:  </AdapterViewFlipper>
```

Listing 10.8 shows the `onCreateView()` method for the `AdapterViewFlipper`. The accompanying source code is SimpleFlipperFragment.java. Lines 6 and 7 show the autostart set to true and the flipper time interval set in milliseconds. The view in this fragment changes every 2 seconds. You see the words *apple, blueberry, cherry,* and *coconut cream* repeated in the user interface.

Other useful methods available for the `AdapterViewFlipper` include `showNext()`, `showPrevious()`, `stopFlipping()`, and `startFlipping()`.

LISTING 10.8   AdapterViewFlipper Fragment onCreateView()

```
1:  @Override
2:  public View onCreateView(LayoutInflater inflater, ViewGroup container,
3:                      Bundle savedInstanceState) {
4:  mFlipper  = (AdapterViewFlipper) inflater.inflate(R.layout.view_flipper_
fragment,
5:                      container, false);
6:  mFlipper.setAutoStart(true);
7:  mFlipper.setFlipInterval (2000);
8:  return mFlipper;
9:  }
```

Options for Paging Controls

So far this hour, you've created a fragment that contains a `Gallery` and a fragment that contains an `AdapterViewFlipper`. There are additional options for handling content where you want horizontal scrolling or to flip between views. You've also learned how to take advantage of how the `Gallery` and the `AdapterViewFlipper` controls work with adapters. All the examples in this chapter use data provided via an adapter. Each of these classes extends the `AdapterView(android.widget.AdapterView)` class.

You can find more information on the `AdapterView` in the Android documentation at http://developer.android.com/reference/android/widget/AdapterView.html.

Other options include the `HorizontalScrollView`, `ViewFlipper`, and `ViewPager`.

Table 10.1 shows the available views with a description and API level listed.

TABLE 10.1   Options for Horizontal Scrolling or Paging.

View	Description	API Level/Availability
Gallery	Horizontal scrolling for views. Extends `AdapterView`.	Since API Level 1, deprecated API Level 16
AdapterViewFlipper	Flip between views. Extends `AdapterView`.	Since API Level 11
ViewFlipper	Flip between views.	Since API Level 1
ViewPager	Flip between views. Use a `PagerAdapter` to generate the pages to show.	Support package
HorizontalScrollView	A layout container for horizontal scrolling.	Since API Level 3

`ViewPager(android.support.v4.view.ViewPager)` is part of the support library, so it works with all versions of Android that are commonly used. Hour 23, "Pro Tips, Finishing Touches, and Next Steps," shows an example of `ViewPager`. `Gallery` has the advantage of extending `AdapterView`, but it is deprecated. If your goal is to target all common platforms, consider using `ViewPager`. If you can target Honeycomb (API level 11, Android 3.0), then `AdapterViewFlipper` is a good choice.

Summary

This hour began with the implementation of a simple `ListFragment`. You saw how to add an `onCreateView()` method to a `ListFragment` to customize it. You took the same data that you used for the `ListFragment` and displayed it in fragments that contained a `GridView`, `Gallery`, and `AdapterViewFlipper`. You saw that additional options exist for paging and horizontal scrolling.

Q&A

Q. What might be an advantage of embedding a single control such as a `GridView` in a fragment?

A. This hour began by examining the `ListFragment`. A `ListFragment` has an inherent `ListView`. You can use the `ListFragment` as a standalone fragment in different user interfaces. Creating a grid fragment with an embedded `GridView` serves the same purpose as a `ListFragment`. You can plug the same grid fragment into different user interfaces.

Q. What is the purpose of the `onCreateView()` method in a fragment?

A. The `onCreateView()` method supplies the view for the fragment to use. Think of it like the `setContentView()` method in an activity. The views that are created can be simple or complex. In these examples, you inflated a view from an XML layout.

Workshop

Quiz

1. In what view would you set the number of columns?

2. Which class from this hour did not require an `onCreateView()` method?

    A. `SimpleListFragment`

    B. `SimpleGridFragment`

    C. `SimpleGalleryFragment`

3. What is the purpose of the flip interval in an `AdapterViewFlipper` and how is it set?

Answers

1. A `GridView` has columns and the number of columns can be set in the XML layout.

2. The correct answer is A. The `SimpleListFragment` class that you created extended a `ListFragment`. A `ListFragment` has an inherent `ListView` and the `onCreate View()` method is not required. When you customized the `ListFragment`, you supplied your own view in the `onCreateView()` method.

3. The interval represents the length of time in milliseconds to display each view in the view flipper. You set it using the `setFlipInterval()` method.

Exercise

Create an activity with two layouts. In one, implement a `ListFragment`. When a user clicks an item in the `ListFragment`, change the fragment displayed in the second layout. Use any fragments created in previous chapters to help with this exercise.

App Setting: Managing Preferences

What You'll Learn in This Hour:

▶ Using `SharedPreferences` to store data

▶ Setting user preferences

▶ Creating a `PreferencesFragment`

▶ Generating a `PreferencesActivity`

`SharedPreferences` (`android.content.SharedPreferences`) is a class that provides the ability to store data in key-value pairs. This data can be set and retrieved in any activity. Android provides a robust Preferences API for user settings that use `SharedPreferences` as the underlying data store. In this hour, you learn how to use `SharedPreferences` for a simple app setting. You'll also develop a robust user interface for user settings in the app.

Using SharedPreferences

`SharedPreferences` provide a mechanism for storing and retrieving data as key-value pairs. In this hour, you create a single activity app to demonstrate how to use preferences. The Hour11App project that accompanies this hour contains this source code.

Setting Preferences

In this app, the goal is to show a message the first time the app is used. To do that, you need to know that the app has been run and you need to retain that information.

Logically, you can use a boolean value that is set to true the first time the user runs the app. After that, the value is false. Use the string `"firstUse"` as a key. Prefacing the key with the key with the package name for the app is common practice. If the package name is `com.example.app`, then the key would be `"com.example.app.firstUse"`. That string can be stored in a values resource file or in another definition file within the app. You define the key and the possible values are true and false.

The key-value pair you use must be retained across uses of the app. The data will be put into a file that is defined with a call to the `getSharedPreferences()` method. This method takes two parameters, name and `mode`. `name` is the filename where the key/value pairs are stored. It is a string and should be start with the package name. The mode parameters represent the type of file storage that should be used. This is typically `Context.MODE_PRIVATE` indicating that the settings are private. Others options are `Context.MODE_WORLD_READABLE` and `Context.MODE_WORLD_WRITABLE`, but these values were deprecated in API level 17. In standard use, app settings and shared preferences are private, and these settings were deprecated to help enforce that privacy.

Listing 11.1 shows a snippet of code that defines string constants for the SETTINGS and FIRST_USE.SETTINGS is used as the name parameter in the `getSharedPreferences()` method on line 3 and FIRST_USE is used for the key value on line 5.

On line 4, a `SharedPreferences.Editor` is instantiated. A `SharedPreferences.Editor` is used to insert or update values. On line 6, `commit()` is called to store the values.

LISTING 11.1   Setting a Value Using SharedPreferences

```
1:   public static final String SETTINGS = "com.bffmedia.hour11app.settings";
2:   public static final String FIRST_USE = "com.bffmedia.hour11app.firstUse";
3:   SharedPreferences preferences = getSharedPreferences(SETTINGS, MODE_PRIVATE);
4:   Editor edit = preferences.edit();
5:   edit.putBoolean(FIRST_USE, false);
6:   edit.commit();
```

Reading from SharedPreferences

On line 3 of Listing 11.1, a `SharedPreferences` object called `preferences` was created. To read `preferences`, you use the appropriate `get` method—in this case, `getBoolean()`. The first parameter is the key to read and the second parameter is a default value. If the key FIRST_USE has not been set, the returned value for the boolean `firstUse` would be true:

```
boolean firstUse = preferences.getBoolean(FIRST_USE, true);
```

Listing 11.2 shows how the `firstUse` variable is read and set within an activity's `onCreate()` method to display a message on the first time use of the app. On line 2, the method `preferences.getBoolean()` is called with the key FIRST_USE and a default setting of `true`. The first time this code runs, there will be no value associated with the key FIRST_USE, and the variable `firstUse` will be set to the default value of `true`. Lines 4–6 show a `Toast` message and lines 7–9 set the FIRST_USE value to `false`. This is the implementation for showing a message on the first use of the app.

LISTING 11.2 Reading and Setting Preferences

```
 1:  SharedPreferences preferences = getSharedPreferences(SETTINGS, MODE_PRIVATE);
 2:  boolean firstUse = preferences.getBoolean(FIRST_USE, true);
 3:  if (firstUse){
 4:  Toast helloMessage = Toast.makeText(getApplicationContext(),
 5:  "Hello First Time User",Toast.LENGTH_LONG);
 6:  helloMessage.show();
 7:  Editor editor = preferences.edit();
 8:  editor.putBoolean(FIRST_USE, false);
 9:  editor.commit();
10:  }
```

In the case of first-time use flag, `SharedPreferences` serves as a storage mechanism for key-value pairs. Nothing is directly entered by the user. You can also use `SharedPreferences` for timestamps or for simple tracking.

You can count the number of times a user takes a certain action in your app and store the value in `SharedPreferences`. At a certain threshold, you might prompt the user to rate your app or take some other action.

In another example, you can use the system time to set time stamps and then check for elapsed time. Note that if a timestamp is critical to your application, then do not use the system time because it can be changed in the Settings application. The following code saves the current time in milliseconds as a `long`. This can be read in the future and compared to the current time as one way to determine elapsed time since the value was saved:

```
public static final String TIMESTAMP = "com.bffmedia.hour11app.timeStamp";
long timeStamp = System.currentTimeMillis();
SharedPreferences.Editor editor = preferences.edit();
editor.putLong(TIMESTAMP, timeStamp);
editor.commit();
```

Data Types and Methods in SharedPreferences

Common types can be stored and retrieved from `SharedPreferences`. There are methods for `getBoolean()`, `getFloat()`, `getInt()`, `getLong()`, `getString()`, and `getStringSet()`.

In addition, there is a `getAll()` method and a `contains()` method. The `getAll()` method gets all key-value pairs as a `Map` where the key is a string and the value is whatever was put into `SharedPreferences`. The `contains()` method takes a string as a parameter. The string is the key to check. The `contains()` method returns true if the key is contained in `SharedPreferences`.

NOTE

Listening for Changes in SharedPreferences

SharedPreferences also includes a registerOnSharedPreferenceChangeListener() method. This allows your app to listen for changes to preferences and react if necessary. There is also a corresponding unregisterOnSharedPreferenceChangeListener() method.

Setting User Preferences

SharedPreferences implements a data store for key-value pairs. Android uses the SharedPreferences data store together with a set of Preference APIs to provide a robust way to implement user settings.

You can use either a PreferenceActivity(android.preference.PreferenceActivity) or a PreferenceFragment(android.preference.PreferenceFragment) as the user interface for settings. The user changes the settings, and the SharedPreferences data store updates.

The Preference class extends to provide subclasses to handle specific types of settings. Each subclass of Preference includes properties for the settings and a user interface for displaying the preference. For example, a CheckBoxPreference (android.preference. CheckBoxPreference) presents a checkbox and a message to the user. The user may check or uncheck the checkbox. The value associated with a CheckBoxPreference is a boolean with true indicating that the checkbox is checked.

Creating a PreferencesFragment

When creating a PreferenceFragment or PreferenceActivity, you use an XML file to define the preferences. This is not a res/layout XML file. Layout files define views. In this case, the XML file defines preferences. You put the preference XML file in a res/xml folder. Use the filename preferences.xml to create a PreferenceFragment.

Listing 11.3 shows the entire SettingsFragment class. SettingsFragment extends PreferenceFragment and implements onSharedPreferenceChangeListener. On line 12, within the onCreate() method, a call is made to addPreferencesFromResource(), which reads the data in the R.xml.preferences file and shows the appropriate user settings.

The onSharedPreferenceChangeListener is implemented. The registerOnSharedPreferenceChangeListener() method is called on lines 17–18 in the fragment's onResume() method. It is unregistered in the onPause() method on lines 23–24. When a change is detected in the onSharedPreferenceChanged() method, you just log the passed key. This allows you to see when a change occurs using LogCat.

LISTING 11.3 Extending PreferencesFragment

```
 1:  package com.bffmedia.hour11app;
 2:  import android.content.SharedPreferences;
 3:  import android.content.SharedPreferences.OnSharedPreferenceChangeListener;
 4:  import android.os.Bundle;
 5:  import android.preference.PreferenceFragment;
 6:  import android.util.Log;
 7:  public class SettingsFragment extends PreferenceFragment
 8:  implements OnSharedPreferenceChangeListener {
 9:  @Override
10:  public void onCreate(Bundle savedInstanceState) {
11:          super.onCreate(savedInstanceState);
12:          addPreferencesFromResource(R.xml.preferences);
13:      }
14:      @Override
15:  public void onResume() {
16:          super.onResume();
17:          getPreferenceScreen().getSharedPreferences().
18:                          registerOnSharedPreferenceChangeListener(this);
19:      }
20:      @Override
21:  public void onPause() {
22:          super.onPause();
23:          getPreferenceScreen().getSharedPreferences().
24:                          unregisterOnSharedPreferenceChangeListener(this);
25:      }
26:      @Override
27:      public void onSharedPreferenceChanged(SharedPreferences
28:                                  sharedPreferences, String key) {
29:          Log.d("Settings", key);
30:      }
31:  }
```

The contents of the preferences.xml file determine what the SettingsFragment looks like when displayed to the user.

CheckBoxPreference

Listing 11.4 shows a sample preferences.xml file. A PreferenceScreen contains a CheckBoxPreference. Lines 4–7 include the attributes for the preference. The key on line 4 stores the associated data. The title and summary on lines 5 and 6 are used when displaying this preference. The default value on line 7 indicates the initial setting for the preference. With a default value of false, the checkbox is not enabled.

Figure 11.1 shows the `SettingsFragment` when the preference.xml file defined in Listing 11.4 is used.

LISTING 11.4   CheckBoxPreference Definition

```
1:   <?xml version="1.0" encoding="utf-8"?>
2:   <PreferenceScreen xmlns:android="http://schemas.android.com/apk/res/android">
3:       <CheckBoxPreference
4:           android:key="hires"
5:           android:title="Hi-Res Images"
6:           android:summary="Show high quality images. These take longer to load"
7:           android:defaultValue="False" />
8:   </PreferenceScreen>
```

FIGURE 11.1

SettingsFragment with CheckBoxPreference

In the app, the `SettingsFragment` is used in a `SettingsActivity`. The `SettingsActivity` just uses `setContentView()` to display a layout that contains the `SettingsFragment`. The activity_settings.xml layout file is shown here:

```
<RelativeLayout xmlns:android="http://schemas.android.com/apk/res/android"
xmlns:tools="http://schemas.android.com/tools"
```

```
        android:layout_width="match_parent"
        android:layout_height="match_parent">
<fragment android:name="com.bffmedia.hour11app.SettingsFragment"
android:id="@+id/settings_fragment"
            android:layout_width="match_parent"
            android:layout_height="match_parent" />
</RelativeLayout>
```

The `onCreateMenuOptions()` and `onOptionsItemSelected()` were implemented in the `MainActivity` to show Settings in the overflow menu.

Preference types including the `CheckBoxPreference` are listed in Table 11.1.

TABLE 11.1 Preference Types

Preference Type	Stored Value	API Level	Description
CheckBoxPreference	Boolean	1	Shows a checkbox
EditTextPreference	String	1	Enter data in an `EditText`
ListPreference	String	1	Select from a list
MultiSelectListPreference	Set of strings	11	Show a dialog with multiple values
SwitchPreference	Boolean	14	An on/off toggle for boolean values

The following sections show additional simple preferences and then look at how you can handle implementing many preferences using titles and subscreens.

ListPreference

Listing 11.5 shows an additional `CheckBoxPreference` and a `ListPreference(android.preference.ListPreference)`. The `CheckBoxPreference` indicates whether or not the user likes pie. The `ListPreference` lets the user indicate which type of pie he or she likes. Perhaps the app will show hi-res images of pies.

In the `ListPreference` definition on lines 7–15, you should note several things. Line 8 indicates a dependency on `"pie"`, which is the `CheckBoxPreference` defined in lines 1–5. That means that the `ListPreference` will not be available if the `CheckBoxPreference` with the key `"pie"` is not selected. Figure 11.2 shows the two states for this. Line 15 specifies a `defaultValue`.

LISTING 11.5   ListPreference and Dependency

```
 1: <CheckBoxPreference
 2:        android:key="pie"
 3:        android:title="Pie"
 4:        android:summary="Like Pie"
 5:        android:defaultValue="true" />
 6:
 7: <ListPreference
 8:        android:dependency="pie"
 9:        android:key="pie_type"
10:        android:title="Pie Type"
11:        android:summary="Preferred pie type for eating"
12:        android:dialogTitle="Type of Pie"
13:        android:entries="@array/pie_array"
14:        android:entryValues="@array/pie_array"
15:        android:defaultValue="apple" />
```

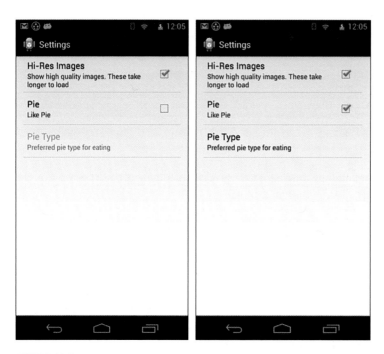

FIGURE 11.2

ListPreference depends on CheckBoxPreference

The `ListPreference` refers to the `@array/pie_array` that is defined in the res/values/Strings.xml file. `Entries` are what display to the user. `EntryValues` are the corresponding values. In this case, the name of the pies is both the `entries` and the `entryValues`. In other cases, the display name might be different than the `entryValue`. For example, a country code might be stored while a country name displays.

Figure 11.3 shows the `ListPreference` display.

FIGURE 11.3
`ListPreference` displaying options

EditTextPreference

The third basic type of preference is the `EditTextPreference` (`android.preference.EditTextPreference`). The `EditTextPreference` is for free-form entry from the user. The following XML snippet defines an `EditTextPreference`. Figure 11.4 shows the resulting display: the settings page and the dialog to accept additional data.

```
<EditTextPreference
android:key="more_info"
android:title="More Info"
android:summary="More about pies"
android:defaultValue="" />
```

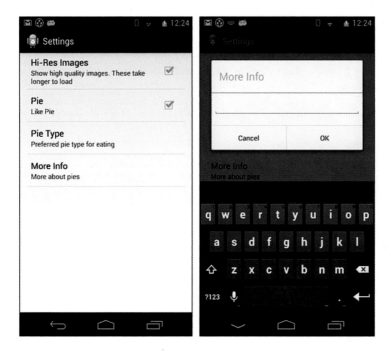

FIGURE 11.4
EditPreference example

Adding Titles

Adding titles to organize content for settings is easy. Each set of related content that appears under a title should be wrapped in the XML in a PreferenceCategory(android.pref-erence.PreferenceCategory) with a title. The following snippet shows a sample PreferenceCategory. The list of preferences is added to the PreferenceCategory. Figure 11.5 shows the result.

```
<PreferenceCategory android:title="Pie Info">

  ...add preferences here

</PreferenceCategory>
```

FIGURE 11.5
Titles for images and pie added

This example uses titles to organize the content on the preference screen. Another way to organize the content is to use subscreens. With a subscreen, a description of the preference is shown on the main preferences page, but the user selects options on a separate subscreen.

You define subscreens by nesting a PreferenceScreen(android.preference. PreferenceScreen) element in the XML. Listing 11.4 uses one PreferenceScreen to contain all the preferences. You can add one or more additional PreferenceScreens. Listing 11.6 shows a snippet of the preferences.xml file for a subscreen. The XML shown in Listing 11.6 is nested within another PreferenceScreenElement.

Figure 11.6 shows the resulting settings page. The title appears on the main settings page. Selecting that title makes the subscreen appear.

LISTING 11.6 Showing a Subscreen

```
1:  <PreferenceScreen
2:              android:key="second_preferencescreen"
3:              android:title="Second Screen of Settings">
4:          <EditTextPreference
5:          android:key="extraA"
6:          android:title="More Data"
```

```
 7:            android:summary="Another EditTextPreference"
 8:            android:defaultValue="" />
 9:       <EditTextPreference
10:            android:key="ExtraB"
11:            android:title="Even More Info"
12:            android:summary="What more can we say"
13:            android:defaultValue="" />
14:   </PreferenceScreen>
```

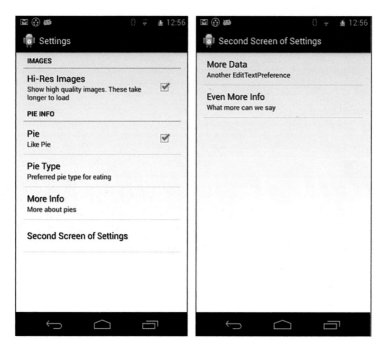

FIGURE 11.6
Using a subscreen to organize settings

Reading Preferences

Reading these preferences is like reading from `SharedPreferences`, but you use
`PreferenceManager` to get the default shared preferences:

```
SharedPreferences sharedPref =
PreferenceManager.getDefaultSharedPreferences(getActivity());
```

You can then retrieve data with `gets` from `SharedPreferences`; for example, `sharedPref.`
`getString("pie_type", "")`.

Generating a Preference Activity

A factor in using the `PreferenceFragment` is that some `PreferenceActivity` methods are being deprecated. Figure 11.7 shows the message from the online documentation regarding this issue.

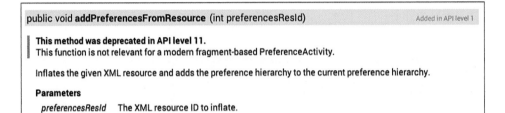

public void **addPreferencesFromResource** (int preferencesResId)   Added in API level 1

> **This method was deprecated in API level 11.**
> This function is not relevant for a modern fragment-based PreferenceActivity.

Inflates the given XML resource and adds the preference hierarchy to the current preference hierarchy.

Parameters

preferencesResId   The XML resource ID to inflate.

FIGURE 11.7
Deprecated methods for `PreferenceActivity`

On the other hand, Eclipse provides a convenient method for creating a `SettingsActivity`.

TRY IT YOURSELF ▼

Generate a SettingsActivity in Eclipse

To create a default project and add a `SettingsActivity`, follow these steps:

1. Create a new Android project with a `MainActivity`.

2. In that project, choose New, Other, Android Activity.

3. On the Activity selection screen, choose `SettingsActivity`. Click Next and click Finish to create this new activity (see Figure 11.8).

4. Use the new `SettingsActivity` by adding it to the overflow menu using the `onOptions ItemSelected()` method.

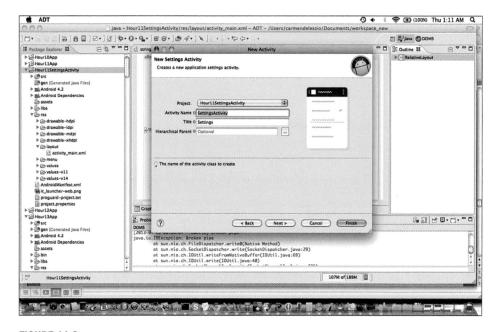

FIGURE 11.8
Generating a `SettingsActivity`

Figure 11.9 shows the generated `SettingsActivity`. You can modify it for your needs.

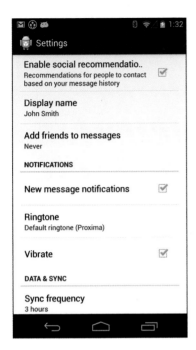

FIGURE 11.9
The generated `SettingsActivity`

Summary

In this hour, you used the `SharedPreference` data store to save key-value pairs. In the example, you used `SharedPreferences` to show a message only on the first-time app use. You learned about `Preferences` and how to make a settings page using XML to define preferences including `CheckBoxPreference`, `ListPreference`, and `EditTextPreference`. You saw how to add titles and subscreens to preferences. `SharedPreferences` enable simple data storage, and the Preferences API is a powerful way to implement user settings

Q&A

Q. Are settings required in an app?

A. No, but using them is often a good idea. The style guide for settings provides additional information on when you should add settings. The specific guidance is: *avoid the temptation to make everything a setting*. (See http://developer.android.com/design/patterns/settings. html.)

Workshop

Quiz

1. What are common types of preferences?

2. What does dependency mean in a preferences file?

3. If you are retrieving a boolean value from `sharedPreferences` and you want the value to be `false` if there was no value in `sharedPreferences`, how would you do that?

Answers

1. Common preferences are `CheckBoxPreference`, `ListPreference`, and `EditTextPreference`. Table 11.1 lists additional preferences.

2. When a dependency is included for a preference, the dependent preference will not be available unless the primary preference is set. You saw this in the pie example.

3. You indicate a default value on reading the data. For example, in this statement, the default value for `FIRST_USE` is `true`: `preferences.getBoolean(FIRST_USE, true);`.

Exercise

Settings depend on the app you are building. Consider an app that you are building or want to build and define a list of settings. Implement those settings in either a `PreferenceFragment` or a `PreferenceActivity`.

PART III

Data Access and Use

HOUR 12

Accessing the Cloud: Working with a Remote API

What You'll Learn in This Hour:

▶ How to fetch remote data

▶ How to parse JSON-formatted data

▶ How to put the pieces together to create a simple app

▶ How to check the online connection

In this hour, you discover how to access remote data. You'll develop an app that communicates with a remote API. The data from the API will be used and displayed in the app. You'll communicate with Flickr's API to get a list of recent public photos. You'll also learn to show the titles of available photos in a `ListFragment`. The next several chapters in this book cover more features, including displaying photos in a list and a grid and selecting a photo to display. To do this, you need to retrieve remote images and display them locally. You'll also use this app to learn about additional Android features such as a local database, using content providers, and using cursor loaders. The discussion starts with how to access and display remote data.

NOTE

What's an API?

API stands for Application Programming Interface. An API defines how separate software components communicate with each other. API is not a new term. Much of the data and content that is available on the Web is made available via APIs. Companies see the value in having developers use their APIs to create new API-based apps and products. The http://www.programmableweb.com/ site lists more 9,000 available APIs.

Fetching Remote Data

You might be developing for a phone, tablet, or even a TV. To fetch remote data, your device must be connected to the Internet. The app might connect over a wireless network or through a phone's mobile network. Android provides the ability to check to see whether a network connection is available. Your app should handle the lack of a network, and this hour shows you how to ensure that it does.

With a connected device, you can use existing APIs to retrieve data using the HTTP. HTTP (Hypertext Transport Protocol) is the data transfer protocol used on the Web.

Common data formats for these APIs are XML and JSON. Using the Flickr API, you'll focus on retrieving and parsing JSON data for the sample app. XML and JSON are both text-based standards for data exchange. XML is used internally for Android for layout files and other resource files. XML is often supported in HTTP-based APIs, but JSON is less verbose and is common.

For the app to access data over from the Internet, you must set the Internet permission in the manifest file (AndroidManifest.xml) as follows:

```
<uses-permission android:name="android.permission.INTERNET"></uses-permission>
```

The data source will be Flickr, the popular photo site from Yahoo!. Many Flickr API calls require the user to be logged in. In this, you use an API call that does not require authentication, which enables you to focus on retrieving and parsing the data. The Flickr API call for retrieving recent photos does not require authentication.

Making an API Call

Although this hour's example uses Flickr, many services provide interesting and useful APIs. Part of the work in using an API is to understand how to make a call to retrieve the data and what parameters to pass.

An *endpoint* for an API is the URL your app uses to communicate with the API. The endpoint for the Flickr API is http://api.flickr.com/services or https://secure.flickr.com/services. Using the Flickr API does require obtaining an API key, as follows:

```
http://www.flickr.com/services/apps/create/apply
```

Flickr has a feature called API Explorer that enables you to try an API call in a sandbox. The sandbox is a website where API calls can be entered and the results seen. If the API call is correct, data is returned and displayed on the web page. The sandbox is an area to safely test specific API calls and see the results.

By accessing the recent photo method via the API Explorer, you can see the data required for the call and the returned data. You can find the API Explorer at:

`http://www.flickr.com/services/api/explore/flickr.photos.getRecent`

Figure 12.1 shows the API Explorer page, and Figure 12.2 shows an example of the data returned in JSON format.

FIGURE 12.1
Flickr API Explorer page

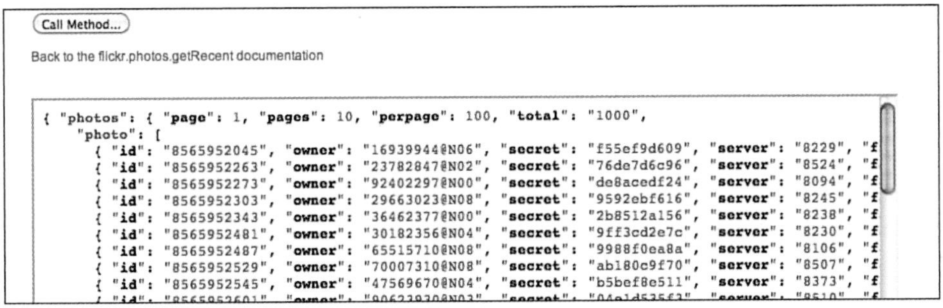

FIGURE 12.2
Flickr JSON results

Retrieving Data with HttpUrlConnection

Your first step is to make the data available at this URL available to your app. For that, use the `HttpUrlConnection`(`java.net.HttpURLConnection`) class. This class is used to access data on a remote URL. Google provides specific advice on what classes to use when retrieving data on Android. For Eclair and Froyo, Google recommends using Apache HTTP Client. For Gingerbread, use Honeycomb and Ice Cream Sandwich, and for future releases, use the `HttpUrlConnection` class. You might also consider source projects such as OkHttp (http://square.github.io/okhttp/).

We have all gone to a web page and received a 404 error to indicate that the page was not found on the server. 404 is the response code, and many possible response codes convey the failure or success of retrieving data. A 200 response indicates success.

The current goal of the app is to retrieve the data from the Flickr recent photo service and display the list of titles from those photos. To do that, you retrieve data from the following:

```
http://api.flickr.com/services/rest/?method=flickr.photos.getRecent
```

You must add additional parameters to indicate the API key, the number of photos to return, that you want to receive this in data format, and that there is no JSON callback. By using the Flickr API Explorer, those parameters are straightforward to determine.

You use the `HttpUrlConnection` class to create an `InputStream`. You check the response code and then read from the `InputStream` into a `String`. First look at the snippet of code to do this; then you can examine where it fits in with the activity and fragment structure.

The Hour12App project contains the source code that accompanies this hour. The API call is made in MainActivity.java. The source files used in this project are MainActivity.java, PhotoListFragment.java, and FlickrPhoto.java.

Listing 12.1 creates an `HttpUrlConnection` and connects to it in lines 1 to 9. In line 10, you get the response code, but for now just log it. Lines 12 to 20 get the data from the connection as an `InputStream` and converts it to a string. Each line is read and appended to a `StringBuilder`(`java.lang.StringBuilder`). Line 19 uses the `StringBuilder` `toString()` method to place the complete downloaded message on the string `photoData`.

LISTING 12.1   Making an HttpUrlConnection Request and Response

```
1:    HttpURLConnection connection = null;
2:    try {
3:      URL dataUrl = new URL(
4:          http://api.flickr.com/services/rest/?method=flickr.photos.
getRecent&api_key=
5:          + API_KEY
6:          + "&per_page=" = NUM_PHOTOS
7:          + "&format=json&nojsoncallback=1");
```

```
8:      connection = (HttpURLConnection) dataUrl.openConnection();
9:      connection.connect();
10:     int status = connection.getResponseCode();
11:     Log.d("connection", "status " + status);
12:     InputStream is = connection.getInputStream();
13:     BufferedReader reader = new BufferedReader(new InputStreamReader(is));
14:     String responseString;
15:     StringBuilder sb = new StringBuilder();
16:     while ((responseString = reader.readLine()) != null) {
17:       sb = sb.append(responseString);
18:     }
19:     String photoData = sb.toString();
20:     Log.d("connection", photoData);
21:   } catch (MalformedURLException e) {
```

The Structure of This App

This code appears in an `AsyncTask` in your activity. You get Flickr photo data in the background. Then next step is to parse the data. Retrieving and parsing Flickr data to display the titles of the photos in a list is the starting point for a more complex app you will build over the next several hours. Hour 6 introduced `AsyncTask`, during the demonstration of how progress bars work. You can do background processing in an `AsyncTask`. In this case, you want to do the intense work of downloading and parsing the JSON data in the background. By doing these tasks in the background, the user interface stays responsive.

GO TO ▶ **HOUR 6, "WORKING WITH BASIC UI CONTROLS,"** to review how `AsyncTask` works.

To review the structure of the app:

1. The activity will download the data in the background.

2. An object called `FlickrPhoto` is used to store the retrieved data.

3. `FlickrPhoto` has a method to parse the data and return an `ArrayList` of photo objects. These are `FlickrPhoto` objects that include the photo title.

4. When the data is available, the `ListFragment` will be displayed.

5. The `ListFragment` will get the data from the activity.

6. The list of titles will be displayed using a `StringAdapter`, as was done in Hour 10, "Lists, Grids, Galleries, and Flippers."

Using and Parsing JSON-Formatted Data

JavaScript Object Notation (JSON) began as a subset of the JavaScript language in the late 1990s, but it is a language-independent format for passing structured data in a human-readable format. Many web services offer JSON as their data format.

JSON data is based on name-value pairs. You see the name of a field paired with the value for that field.

Listing 12.2 shows a snippet of the data returned from the Flickr API. The curly brackets indicate the data for one object.

LISTING 12.2 JSON Snippet for a Flickr Photo

```
{
    "id": "8565953275",
    "owner": "46752538@N04",
    "secret": "5f5a2335f5",
    "server": "8093",
    "farm": 9,
    "title": "Stargazing",
    "ispublic": 1,
    "isfriend": 0,
    "isfamily": 0
}
```

Creating a JSONObject

The Android platform includes a class to work with JSON called `org.json.JSON`. If you start with a `String` of data in JSON format, you can create a new `JSONObject(org.json.JSONObject)` by using the `photoData` string as the parameter to the constructor:

```
JSONObject data = new JSONObject(photoData);
```

After you have a `JSONObject`, you can reference individual fields within the object using the name that you know. For example, in Listing 12.2, the "id" field has the value "8565953275". You can use the `getString()` or `optString()` method of a `JSONObject` to read this value. The benefits of `optString()` is that no exception is thrown if the name you are seeking is not in the object, because the `optString()` returns a default value and `getString()` does not. You have the option to specify a second parameter in `optString()` to set your own default value. Given a `JSONObject` called `data`, you would read the value of `id` into a `String` using:

```
String id=(String) data.optString("id");
```

NOTE

The JsonReader

In the API 11 Android release (HoneyComb), the `JsonReader` class was added. `JsonReader` makes parsing JSON objects easier. In this hour, you use methods that work on all platforms. The `JsonReader` class reference is at http://developer.android.com/reference/android/util/JsonReader.html.

Using a JSONArray

JSON is considered a human-readable format. It is structured text. In JSON, a JSON array consists of JSON objects. JSON arrays are surrounded by square brackets []. The Flickr photo data is returned as a single JSON object that contains a JSON array of JSON objects.

In Android, the class to use with a JSON array is JSONArray(org.json.JSONArray).

As an example of a simple structure, Listing 12.3 shows a JSON object that contains a JSON array called data. Lines 2 and 9 begin and end the array.

LISTING 12.3 JSONArray Structure

```
1:  {
2:  data: [
3:    {
4:      id: "1"
5:    }
6:    {
7:      id: "2"
8:    }
9:  ]
10: }
```

Assume you start out with a string called `photoData` that contains JSON-formatted data like that in Listing 12.3. Consider how to read this data into your Android app. Listing 12.4 loads the string into a JSONObject called `data`. In line 2, JSONArray photoArray is populated from the JSONObject. Lines 3 to 6 ready each object from the JSONArray into a JSONObject and log the id field for that object.

LISTING 12.4 Reading a JSONArray

```
1:  JSONObject data = new JSONObject(photoData);
2:  JSONArray photoArray = data.optJSONArray("data");
3:  for(int i = 0; i < photoArray.length(); i++) {
4:    JSONObject photo= (JSONObject) photoArray.get(i);
5:    Log.d(TAG, photo.optString("id"));
6:  }
```

Parsing JSON

You put together the info about the Flickr photo format, JSONObjects, and JSONArrays to create a new class called FlickrPhoto.java. The FlickrPhoto class contains the data that you care about from the Flickr photo data. You create a constructor that takes a JSONObject with photo data and loads your object. You also create a constructor that takes the full data that Flickr returns and creates an array list of FlickrPhoto objects for use in the app.

NOTE

Gson: Alternatives for Processing JSON Data

Gson is a library that converts Java objects to JSON. It also converts JSON Strings to Java objects. You can use it in projects that handle JSON data. For more info, see https://code.google.com/p/google-gson/.

Listing 12.5 creates the FlickrPhoto class with nine fields beginning with String id and ending with the Boolean isFamily.

Lines 12 to 22 define a constructor that creates a FlickrPhoto object from a JSONObject. Each field in the FlickrPhoto object is populated with a field from the JSONObject.

LISTING 12.5　Making FlickrPhoto Object from JSON

```
1:  public class FlickrPhoto extends Object{
2:      String id;
3:      String owner;
4:      String secret;
5:      String server;
6:      String farm;
7:      String title;
8:      Boolean isPublic;
9:      Boolean isFriend;
10: Boolean isFamily;
11:
12:    public FlickrPhoto(JSONObject jsonPhoto) throws JSONException{
13:      this.id=(String) jsonPhoto.optString("id");
14:      this.secret=(String) jsonPhoto.optString("secret");
15:      this.owner=(String) jsonPhoto.optString("owner");
16:      this.server=(String) jsonPhoto.optString("server");
17:      this.farm=(String) jsonPhoto.optString("farm");
18:      this.title=(String) jsonPhoto.optString("title");
19:      this.isPublic=(Boolean) jsonPhoto.optBoolean("ispublic");
20:      this.isFriend=(Boolean) jsonPhoto.optBoolean("isfriend");
21:      this.isFamily=(Boolean) jsonPhoto.optBoolean("isfamily");
22:  } ...
```

The Flickr data includes a JSONObject called photos. The photosJSONObject contains a JSONArray of photo data called photo. The JSON string for this structure looks like the following:

```
{ "photos": { "page": 1, "pages": 10, "perpage": 100, "total": "1000",
    "photo": [
      { ...
```

This is also shown in Figure 12.2.

The makePhotoList() method shown in Listing 12.6 is a method in the FlickrPhoto class. When passed a JSON String containing Flickr data, the makePhotoList() method returns an ArrayList of FlickrPhotoObjects.

LISTING 12.6   Making a FlickrPhoto ArrayList from a JSON String

```
 1:  public static ArrayList <FlickrPhoto> makePhotoList (String photoData )
 2:                          throws JSONException, NullPointerException {
 3:    ArrayList <FlickrPhoto> flickrPhotos = new ArrayList<FlickrPhoto>();
 4:    JSONObject data  = new JSONObject(photoData);
 5:    JSONObject photos = data.optJSONObject("photos");
 6:    JSONArray photoArray = photos.optJSONArray("photo");
 7:    for(int i = 0; i < photoArray.length(); i++) {
 8:      JSONObject photo=    (JSONObject) photoArray.get(i);
 9:      FlickrPhoto currentPhoto = new FlickrPhoto (photo);
10:      flickrPhotos.add(currentPhoto);
11:    }
12:    return flickrPhotos;
13:}
```

Line 8 reads a JSONObject from the JSONArray. In line 9, you use the JSONObject to create a new FlickrPhoto object called currentPhoto. In line 10, you add that to an ArrayList of FlickrPhotos that is declared earlier on line 3.

When you receive the data as a string from the Flickr API, you pass that String to the makePhotoList() method and get a list of objects back.

Putting the Pieces Together

The pieces to make your app are the activity, the FlickrPhoto object, and a ListFragment to show the list of photo titles returned from Flickr.

In the activity, you use an AsyncTask that retrieves data from Flickr. After you have the data, you show a ListFragment. For this example, you retrieve the data in the activity and display it in the fragment. To keep it simple, you add a method to the activity called getPhotos().

The fragment calls `getPhotos()` to access the data that was retrieved. The data will be an `ArrayList` of `FlickrPhoto` objects. To keep things even simpler, for now, you take the titles from the `FlickrPhoto` objects and load them into a string array. You can then display the titles using a simple `ArrayAdapter(android.widget.ArrayAdapter)`. Over the course of the next several hours in this book, you create a custom adapter and expand on this work.

The outline for the app functionality is as follows:

- ▶ Activity: MainActivity.java

  - ▶ Show progress bar.

  - ▶ In `OnCreate()` method, call `LoadPhotos AsyncTask` to load data.

- ▶ AsyncTask: `MainActivity.LoadPhotos`

- ▶ Retrieve data.

  - ▶ Hide the progress bar.

- ▶ Show the `ListFragment`.

- ▶ ListFragment: `PhotoListFragment`

  - ▶ Get the FlickrPhoto list from the activity.

  - ▶ Display titles only.

Download in the Background with AsyncTask

An `AsyncTask` includes a `doInBackground()` method for background processes and an `onPostExecute()` method to take action when the `doInBackground()` method completes. You download and parse Flickr photo data in the `doInBackground()` method and then show the `PhotoListFragment` by calling `showList()` in the `onPostExecute()` method.

You define the `LoadPhotos` class in MainActivity.java using the following:

```
private class LoadPhotos extends AsyncTask<String , String , Long > {
```

Listing 12.7 shows the `doInBackground()` method for the `LoadPhotos AsyncTask`. In lines 5–7, you build the URL to fetch Flickr data by creating a string. API_KEY and NUM_PHOTOS are static string variables that you define in the `MainActivity` class.

Lines 8–12 make a connection and retrieve the response code. If the response code is 200, indicating success, an `inputStream` is used to read data from the connections. In lines 13–20, the data is read using a `BufferedReader`. The data is read line by line and appended using the `append()` method of the `StringBuffer`.

On line 20, a string is created from the `StringBuffer`. That string contains the complete data from Flickr in JSON format. In line 21, you use that `photoData` string to create an `ArrayList` of `FlickrPhoto` objects by calling `FlickrPhoto.makePhotoList(photoData)`.

LISTING 12.7   LoadPhotos AsyncTask doInBackground()

```
1:   @Override
2:   protected Long doInBackground(String... params) {
3:   HttpURLConnection connection = null;
4:   try {
5:   URL dataUrl = new URL (
6:   "http://api.flickr.com/services/rest/?method=flickr.photos.getRecent&api_key="
7:   + API_KEY + "&per_page=" + NUM_PHOTOS +"&format=json&nojsoncallback=1");
8:   connection = (HttpURLConnection) dataUrl.openConnection();
9:   connection.connect();
10:  int status = connection.getResponseCode();
11:  Log.d("connection", "status " + status);
12:  if (status ==200){ //success
13:  InputStream is = connection.getInputStream();
14:  BufferedReader reader = new BufferedReader(new InputStreamReader(is));
15:  String responseString;
16:  StringBuilder sb = new StringBuilder();
17:  while ((responseString = reader.readLine()) != null) {
18:  sb = sb.append(responseString);
19:  }
20:  String photoData = sb.toString();
21:  mPhotos = FlickrPhoto.makePhotoList(photoData);
22:  Log.d("connection", photoData);
23:  return (0l);
24:  }else{
25:  return (1l);
26:  }
27:     } catch (MalformedURLException e) { ...
```

When data is successfully retrieved, a 200-response code is returned (see lines 10–12). In the success case, a 0 is returned from the `doInBackground()` method. A 1 is returned for all errors. That return value is used in the `onPostExecute()` method. Listing 12.8 shows the entire `onPostExecute()` method. If data is successfully retrieved, the `showList()` method is called.

LISTING 12.8   LoadPhotos AsyncTaskon PostExecute()

```
@Override
protected void onPostExecute(Long result) {
  if (result==0){
showList();
  }else{
Toast.makeText(MainActivity.this.getApplicationContext(),
    "Something went wrong",   Toast.LENGTH_SHORT).show();
  }
mProgressBar.setVisibility(View.GONE);
}
```

Displaying the List in a Fragment

The display of the list of titles from the Flickr data is straightforward, but several steps are involved:

▶ The onPostExecute() method calls the showList() method of MainActivity.

▶ ShowList() declares and displays a PhotoListFragment.

▶ The PhotoListFragment gets the ArrayList of FlickrPhoto objects from the activity.

▶ To keep things simple, the photo titles are loaded into a String array.

▶ The list of titles displays in the list.

The showList() method loads a PhotoListFragment using a FragmentTransaction. It is similar to the method that you used in Hour 10 to show a SimpleListFragment. The fragment is loaded for display.

The PhotoListFragment itself is similar to the SimpleListFragment that you created in Hour 10, where you read the data to display from an array that was defined as a resource. The PhotoListFragment calls the getPhotos() method from MainActivity. That method returns an ArrayList of FlickrPhoto objects. For now, you read those objects and load an array of strings. That string array is used for an ArrayAdapter and the list is displayed.

Listing 12.9 shows this code for the PhotoListFragment. Lines 6 and 7 get the current activity, cast it to MainActivity, and call the getPhotos(). That provides the Flickr data to work with. Lines 9–11 populate the string array mTitles. Now you can use that array to display the data using an ArrayAdapter. Figure 12.3 shows the result.

LISTING 12.9   PhotoListFragment

```
 1: public class PhotoListFragment extends ListFragment    {
 2: String[] mTitles;
 3: @Override
 4: public void onActivityCreated(Bundle savedInstanceState) {
 5: super.onActivityCreated(savedInstanceState);
 6: MainActivity currentActivity = (MainActivity) this.getActivity();
 7: ArrayList <FlickrPhoto> photos = currentActivity.getPhotos();
 8: mTitles = new String[photos.size()];
 9: for (int i=0; i < photos.size(); i++){
10: mTitles[i] =photos.get(i).title;
11: }
12: setListAdapter(new ArrayAdapter<String>(this.getActivity(),
13: android.R.layout.simple_list_item_1, mTitles));
14: }
15: @Override
16: public void onListItemClick(ListView l, View v, int position, long id) {
17: Toast.makeText(this.getActivity().getApplicationContext(),
18:         mTitles[position], Toast.LENGTH_SHORT).show();
19: }
20: }
```

FIGURE 12.3
Displaying titles of recent Flickr photos

Checking Connectivity

In an app that retrieves remote data, you want to ensure that you have a network connection. Android provides the `ConnectivityManager` (`android.net.ConnectivityManager`) class to provide information about the network. The `ConnectivityManager` has a method called `getActiveNetworkInfo()` that can tell you whether or not you are online.

Listing 12.10 defines a simple method for checking online status.

LISTING 12.10   **Checking for Connectivity**

```
1:  public boolean isOnline() {
2:      ConnectivityManager connectivityManager = (ConnectivityManager)
3:              getSystemService(Context.CONNECTIVITY_SERVICE);
4:      NetworkInfo networkInfo = connectivityManager.getActiveNetworkInfo();
5:      return (networkInfo != null && networkInfo.isConnected());
6:  }
```

You can use this code in the `MainActivity onCreate()` method to check for connectivity before you try to retrieve data. Listing 12.11 shows the online check. If you are online, the `LoadPhotos AsyncTask` executes; if not, a `Toast` message appears.

LISTING 12.11   **Using the Online Check**

```
1:  if (isOnline()){
2:    LoadPhotos task = new LoadPhotos();
3:    task.execute();
4:  }else{
5:    mProgressBar.setVisibility(View.GONE);
6:    Toast.makeText(MainActivity.this.getApplicationContext(),
7:        "Please connect to retrieve photos",
8:    Toast.LENGTH_SHORT).show();
9:  }
```

To check for online status, you must properly set the Android permission in the AndroidManifest. xml file. The permission required is ACCESS_NETWORK_STATE:

`<uses-permission android:name="android.permission.ACCESS_NETWORK_STATE" />`

NOTE

Working with XML

In this hour, you worked with JSON data. It is also common for remote data to be in XML format. Android provides several ways to parse XML data, including SAX and Dom parser. Android also provides an interface called XMLPullParser for working with XML. See http://developer.android.com/reference/org/xmlpull/v1/XmlPullParser.html.

Summary

To work with remote data, you built a simple app that retrieves data about recently posted photos on Flickr. In the app, you displayed the titles of the photos using techniques from earlier in the book. To create the app, you used the `HttpUrlConnection` class to retrieve the data. You understood the JSON data format and parsed the data returned from Flickr. You added a check for online status so that you would only retrieve the data if the device was connected.

Q&A

Q. In this hour, the titles that were displayed were moved from `FlickrPhoto` objects to strings for display. Is there a way to use those objects directly?

A. Yes, you will create custom adapters in upcoming chapters. Extending a `BaseAdapter` or `CursorAdapter` to handle the display of multiple objects is a common practice. To focus on retrieving data, this hour did not introduce those ideas.

Q. When working with an external API like Flickr, how do you know what objects to create?

A. APIs like Flickr might have helpful client libraries, sample code, and good documentation. Looking closely at the data returned is often helpful to determine precisely what to do. One reason that the Flickr recent photos method works well for this book is that no authentication is required. You can create an interesting app based on one URL for retrieving data.

Workshop

Quiz

1. If you have a snippet of a JSON `String`, how would you distinguish between whether the contents contained a `JSONObject` or a `JSONArray`?

2. How is an `InputStream` related to an `HttpUrlConnection`?

3. What two permissions are added to the AndroidManifest.xml in apps that check online status before retrieving data from a remote source?

Answers

1. The data that represents `JSONObject` is bounded by curly brackets { } and the data for a `JSONArray` is bounded by square brackets [].

2. After a connection is made using an `HttpUrlConnection`, the data can be retrieved as an `InputStream`. The example in this hour converted the `InputStream` to a `String`.

3. The `INTERNET` and `ACCESS_NETWORK_STATE` are required.

Exercise

Get an API key from Flickr or another back-end source for remote data. Using the code in Listing 12.7 as a guideline, make an API call with an `HTTPUrlConnection` and log the returned data. If the data is in JSON format, parse it and log the results. Often apps can create a clean separation between data retrieval and display. Retrieving data and logging results is a good first step for working with any API.

Using SQLite and File Storage

What You'll Learn in This Hour:

▸ Organizing data with tables

▸ Managing a database with `SQLiteOpenHelper`

▸ Adding, deleting, and updating data

▸ Using cursors to query data

▸ Using a database with your app

▸ Downloading and saving a remote image

SQLite is a small, fast, file-based database that is included with Android. In Hour 12, "Accessing the Cloud: Working with a Remote API," you retrieved data about Flickr photos in JSON format. You parsed the JSON and displayed a list of photo titles. In this hour, you will use an SQLite database to store that data. The code will read from the database to display the list of titles. In Hours 14–16, you'll use this code during the coverage of `ContentProviders` and `CursorLoaders` to develop a full app using this data. One advantage of having this data in the database is that it can be used even when the device is offline. After the initial database load, the app can retrieve the data from the database to support offline functionality.

Organizing a Database with Tables

At a basic level, a database stores information and provides a way to retrieve that data in a structured way. SQL stands for Structured Query Language and is the mechanism for data retrieval. You use queries to specify the data you want to retrieve. Data in a database is organized into tables.

A table is made up of items that form a logical group. In the photo data from Flickr, you used the returned JSON to create `FlickrPhoto` objects that included the fields for id, title, and so on. Starting with that data to define a table makes sense.

You can think of a table as having rows and columns. A column is similar to a heading on a spreadsheet. It defines the name of the data field. A row represents a data entry in the column. Multiple columns and rows comprise a table.

Listing 13.1 lists the specific fields that were used to define the `FlickrPhoto` object. An additional field has been added called `isFavorite`. As you continue to develop the app, you will add the ability to indicate that some photos are favorites. You'll use that field to perform database queries to select only favorite photos.

The `FlickrPhoto` object consists of string and boolean fields. You will use equivalent database values as columns to store and retrieve data.

The Hour13app project contains the source code that accompanies this hour. The database work is done in FlickrPhotoDbAdapter.java.

LISTING 13.1 Fields in the FlickrPhoto Object

```
 1:  public class FlickrPhoto extends Object{
String id;
String owner;
String secret;
String server;
String farm;
String title;
Boolean isPublic;
Boolean isFriend;
Boolean isFamily;
Boolean isFavorite=false;
```

Managing Data with SQLiteOpenHelper

Databases are opened and closed like files. To help manage the database, you can use the class `SQLiteOpenHelper`.

In Hour 12, you created the `FlickrPhoto` class for handling basic Flickr photo data. In that class, you created the method `makePhotoList()` to parse the JSON data provided by Flickr and to create an array of `FlickrPhoto` objects.

This section introduces a class to handle the database functionality for this app. The new class is `FlickrPhotoDbAdapter`. In `FlickrPhotoDbAdapter`, you use an `SQLiteDatabase` class to handle the database, and use an instance of the `SQLiteOpenHelper` class to take care of opening and closing the database. Listing 13.2 shows how to use the `SQLiteOpenHelper`.

LISTING 13.2   Using SQLiteOpenHelper

```
1:  private static final String DATABASE_NAME = "FLICKR_PHOTOS";
2:  private static final String DATABASE_TABLE = "flickrphoto";
3:  private static final int DATABASE_VERSION = 1;
4:
5:  private static class DatabaseHelper extends SQLiteOpenHelper {
6:    DatabaseHelper(Context context) {
7:      super(context, DATABASE_NAME, null, DATABASE_VERSION);
8:    }
9:    @Override
10:   public void onCreate(SQLiteDatabase db) {
11:     db.execSQL(DATABASE_CREATE);
12:   }
13:   @Override
14:   public void onUpgrade(SQLiteDatabase db, int oldVersion, int newVersion) {
15:     db.execSQL("DROP TABLE IF EXISTS " + DATABASE_TABLE );
16:     onCreate(db);
17:   }
18: }
```

In line 5 of Listing 13.2, the static class `DatabaseHelper` is defined as an inner class. It is an extension of the `SQLiteOpenHelper` (`android.database.sqlite.SQLiteOpenHelper`) class. The constructor for `DatabaseHelper` defined on line 6 calls the `super()` method with the parameters `context`, `DATABASE_NAME`, `null`, and `DATABASE_VERSION`. That means that the `SQLiteOpenHelper` class is being called with these parameters. `DATABASE_NAME` is the `String` defined on line 1 of this listing and `DATABASE_VERSION` is an `int` defined on line 3 of this listing.

`DATABASE_VERSION` represents the current version of the database. The version number starts at 1. If the `DATABASE_VERSION` in the constructor is larger than the current database version, the `onUpgrade()` method will be called. The `onUpgrade()` method on lines 14 to 17 drops the existing database table and makes a call to `onCreate()`. The table is dropped in the code on line 15 using the `SQLiteDatabase` method `db.execSQL()`. Any SQL passed to this method is executed on the database.

The `onCreate()` method defined on lines 10 to 12 defines the database with a call to `db.execSQL()`.

The `DATABASE_CREATE` field passed as a parameter in line 11 is a `String` that defines how to create the table in the database.

So overall, the purpose of Listing 13.2 is to create or upgrade an SQLite database. A database name and version number are required. Listing 13.3 shows the SQL executed to define the database.

LISTING 13.3   Creating the Flickr Photo Database

```
1: private static final String DATABASE_CREATE =
2:    "create table flickrphoto (_id INTEGER PRIMARY KEY AUTOINCREMENT,"
3:    + "flickr_id not null,"
4:    + "owner text,"
5:    + "secret text,"
6:    + "server text,"
7:    + "farm text,"
8:    + "title text,"
9:    + "isPublic INTEGER,"
10:   + "isFriend INTEGER,"
11:   + "isFamily INTEGER,"
12:   + "isFavorite INTEGER"
13:   +");";
```

Listing 13.3 shows the SQL used to create the table. In line 2, the table flickrphoto is created and the column _id is defined as an integer primary key that will autoincrement. Including a field called _id is not strictly required when using SQLite and Android, but it is required when working with certain other Android classes such as the CursorAdapter class. You use a CursorAdapter later in this hour.

You define DatabaseHelper as a static class for creating and upgrading the database. DatabaseHelper is defined in the FlickrPhotoDbAdapter class. Also in the FlickrPhotoDbAdapter class, you declare a field called mDbHelper of type DatabaseHelper. You use mDbHelper in three methods in your class: open(), upgrade(), and close(). Listing 13.4 shows them.

LISTING 13.4   Open, Close, and Upgrade

```
1:  public PhotoDBHelper open() throws SQLException {
2:     mDbHelper = new DatabaseHelper(mCtx);
3:     mDb = mDbHelper.getWritableDatabase();
4:     return this;
5:  }
6:  public void close() {
7:     if(mDbHelper!=null){
8:        mDbHelper.close();
9:     }
10: }
11: public void upgrade() throws SQLException {
12:    mDbHelper = new DatabaseHelper(mCtx); //open
13:    mDb = mDbHelper.getWritableDatabase();
14:    mDbHelper.onUpgrade(mDb, 1, 0);
15: }
```

When a call is made to the open() method, a new DatabaseHelper class is instantiated. As you saw in Listing 13.2, this creates a database if needed and upgrades the database if the version number has been increased. In line 3, a call is made to the getWritableDatabase() method of the SQLiteOpenHelper class. That returns a SQLiteDatabase object that is ready for reading and writing data. The database must be closed after it is opened, which happens on line 8 with a call to the close() method. You saw in Listing 13.2 that a Context is passed to the DatabaseHelper class. The variable mCtx passed in line 12 represents a value of type Context.

Adding, Updating, and Deleting Data

So far, this hour has focused on the structure of the database as well as defining a table and setting up a way to open and close the database. With that done, you now focus on getting FlickrPhoto objects into the database and learn how to update and delete entire rows.

Inserting a Photo

The goal of this section is to insert an existing FlickrPhoto object into the database. You must match fields in the object to columns in the database. The type of fields needs to match between the object and the database. Listing 13.5 shows the createPhoto() method. A FlickrPhoto object is passed as the only parameter. The createPhoto() method inserts data for a new photo into the database.

LISTING 13.5   Inserting a Photo into the Database

```
1:   public long createPhoto(FlickrPhoto photoToCreate) {
2:      ContentValues initialValues = new ContentValues();
3:      if (photoToCreate.id!=null)
4:        initialValues.put("flickr_id", photoToCreate.id);
5:      if (photoToCreate.owner!=null)
6:        initialValues.put("owner", photoToCreate.owner);
7:      if (photoToCreate.secret!=null)
8:        initialValues.put("secret", photoToCreate.secret);
9:      if (photoToCreate.server!=null)
10:       initialValues.put("server", photoToCreate.server);
11:     if (photoToCreate.farm!=null)
12:       initialValues.put("farm", photoToCreate.farm);
13:     if (photoToCreate.title!=null)
14:       initialValues.put("title", photoToCreate.title);
15:     if (photoToCreate.isPublic!=null)
16:       initialValues.put("isPublic", photoToCreate.isPublic);
17:     if (photoToCreate.isFriend!=null)
18:       initialValues.put("isFriend", photoToCreate.isFriend);
19:     if (photoToCreate.isFamily!=null)
20:       initialValues.put("isFamily", photoToCreate.isFamily);
```

```
21:    if (photoToCreate.isFavorite!=null)
22:      initialValues.put("isFavorite", photoToCreate.isFavorite);
23:    return mDb.insert(DATABASE_TABLE, null, initialValues);
24: }
```

You insert an existing FlickrPhoto object into the database in the createPhoto() method. That method takes a single FlickrPhotoObject as a parameter. You use the contents of this photo object to add a row to the database.

Data is read from the FlickrPhoto object and put into a ContentValues object as sets of name-value pairs. The ContentValues object initialValues is defined in line 2 of Listing 13.5.

In a SQLiteDatabase, the ContentValues names are the names of the columns in the database. In this case, the corresponding values come from the FlickrPhoto object. You do not pass in "_id" as a name. The value for that column will be set automatically.

Before you add a value, a check is made to see whether it is null. On line 23, the values in the initialValues ContentValues object are inserted into the database.

If the insert is successful, the returned value is the row id of the new photo record. If an error occurs, -1 is returned.

Updating a Photo

The method used to update photo data in the database is similar to inserting a photo, but with a key difference. For an update, you must identify the photo that you want to update. That is not required for an insert. An insert creates a completely new record in the database. An update updates an existing record. Listing 13.6 shows the code for an update.

LISTING 13.6   Updating a Photo in the Database

```
1:  public long updatePhoto(String id, FlickrPhoto photoToUpdate) {
2:    ContentValues updateValues = new ContentValues();
3:    if (photoToUpdate.id!=null)
4:      updateValues.put("flickr_id", photoToUpdate.id);
5:    if (photoToUpdate.owner!=null)
6:      updateValues.put("owner", photoToUpdate.owner);
7:    if (photoToUpdate.secret!=null)
8:      updateValues.put("secret", photoToUpdate.secret);
9:    if (photoToUpdate.server!=null)
10:     updateValues.put("server", photoToUpdate.server);
11:   if (photoToUpdate.farm!=null)
12:     updateValues.put("farm", photoToUpdate.farm);
13:   if (photoToUpdate.title!=null)
14:     updateValues.put("title", photoToUpdate.title);
15:   if (photoToUpdate.isPublic!=null)
```

```
16:        updateValues.put("isPublic", photoToUpdate.isPublic);
17:    if (photoToUpdate.isFriend!=null)
18:        updateValues.put("isFriend", photoToUpdate.isFriend);
19:    if (photoToUpdate.isFamily!=null)
20:        updateValues.put("isFamily", photoToUpdate.isFamily);
21:    if (photoToUpdate.isFavorite!=null)
22:        updateValues.put("isFavorite", photoToUpdate.isFavorite);
23:    return mDb.update(DATABASE_TABLE, updateValues, "flickr_id" + "=" + id, null)
> 0;
24: }
```

Two parameters are passed to the updatePhoto() method. The FlickrPhoto object passed contains the data to load. The String passed as the parameter id is the flickr_id of the photo in the database, and you use it to identify the photo to update.

Line 11 shows the update call. You pass a string representing the table, the ContentValues(android.content.ContentValues) with the new data, and a string to represent the query to identify the record. That query is known as a whereClause. The last parameter to the mDb.update() call is currently null. That parameter may contain an array of Strings that would be passed as arguments to the whereClause. It is called the whereArgs and would be declared as String[];.

In this case, to update a photo record in the database, you find the record by passing the flickr_id value as a parameter. If the passed parameter matches the id of a record in the database, an update occurs. The type returned from this method is a boolean. In Line 23, you see that the value returned is based on the result of the update statement being greater than 0. A result greater than 0 indicates that an update has occurred, and true will be returned, indicating success.

In line 23, you are trusting that the id value is properly formatted for a SQLite database. It should be "escaped." One way to do that is to use the DatabaseUtils.sqlEscapeString() method:

```
mDb.update(DATABASE_TABLE, "flickr_id='" + DatabaseUtils.sqlEscapeString(id) + "'")
```

An alternative is to use selection arguments. Selection arguments are covered during the querying data discussion later in this hour. This shows the query using selection arguments:

```
mDb.update(DATABASE_TABLE, updateValues, "flickr_id=?", new String[] {id})
```

Deleting a Photo

Deleting a photo is similar to updating a photo. You identify the row to delete and call the appropriate database method. The whereClause in this example is the same as in Listing 13.6. In Listing 13.7, you identify the row to delete based on the passed id matching the flickr_id in the table.

LISTING 13.7   Deleting a Photo from the Database

```
1:   public boolean deletePhoto(String photo_id) {
2:   return mDb.delete(DATABASE_TABLE, "flickr_id" + "=" + photo_id, null) > 0;
3:   }
```

Querying Data and Using Cursors

So far, you've used a whereClause to identify records to update or delete. The whereClause is key to constructing a SQL statement to retrieve data from a database.

After specifying the data to retrieve from the database, you need a way to work with the returned data. For example, if a query result includes 100 photos, you need a way to both iterate through the results and to work with a specific row of data. You use Cursors (android.database.Cursor) for this purpose. If you consider the result set of your query to be a list of data rows, the cursor acts a pointer to a specific row.

To be precise, the return value of a query is a cursor. You work with that cursor to get specific data.

Listing 13.8 shows the fetchFavorites method in the FlickrPhotoDbAdapter class. This method retrieves all the photos where isFavorite is equal to 1 and returns a Cursor.

LISTING 13.8   Getting Favorite Photos from the Database

```
1: public Cursor fetchFavorites() throws SQLException {
2:    Cursor cursor =
3:      mDb.query(true, DATABASE_TABLE, FLICKR_PHOTO_FIELDS, "isFavorite=1", null,
4:      null, null, null, null);
5:    if (cursor != null) {
6:       cursor.moveToFirst();
7:    }
8:    return cursor;
9: }
```

The query occurs on lines 2 to 4. Line 3 passes the first four parameters of the query method and leaves the remainder as nulls. The passed parameters are distinct, tables, columns, and selection. The distinct parameter is set to true and indicates that only unique rows should be returned. You set the Table parameter to DATABASE_TABLE and the Column parameter to FLICKR_PHOTO_FIELDS. These parameters specify the table to use and the columns that should be returned from that table. The selection parameter is a whereClause similar to what you used earlier. You want all the photos that have isFavorite set to 1.

Lines 3 and 4 contain five nulls for the remaining parameters to the query method. They are `selectionArgs`, `groupBy`, `having`, `orderBy`, and `limit`. These are all options supported in complex queries in SQLite databases.

When querying a database, you often want to specify the order in which the data is returned. If you have a database of people, you might want to order the data by last name. You use the `orderBy` parameter to specify a column in the database for ordering data. If you had a row with both a `firstName` column and a `lastName` column, you could set the order by `firstName` or `lastName` in ascending or descending order.

You can specify the order of the returned records. That means that you pick a column in the record and sort by the value in that column. If you had a person's first name and last name, you could sort by first or last and in ascending or descending order. To change to descending order, you use `DESC` and `specify a column`. To get favorite photos by the order of the photo titles in descending order, you would use this query:

```
mDb.query(true, DATABASE_TABLE, FLICKR_PHOTO_FIELDS, "isFavorite=1", null,
          null, null, "title DESC", null);
```

`Limit` specifies the limit on the number of rows to return. For complex queries, `selectionArgs` can be used as replacement values in the selection statement.

The `groupBy` and `having` parameters perform SQL `GROUP BY` and SQL `HAVING` clauses. A `GROUP BY` clause is useful when combining data. For example, you might have a database that includes multiple orders placed by customers. Customers can repeat in the rows in that database, so `GROUP BY` provides a way to group the orders by a customer. The `HAVING` clause acts like a `whereClause` for the `GROUP BY` clause. That is, the `HAVING` clause sets the criteria for the `GROUP BY`.

Listing 13.9 shows the definition of `FLICKR_PHOTO_FIELDS` that are used in line 3 of Listing 13.8. These are the fields that you want returned from the query. This is known as the projection. The case might be that you only want one or two fields from a record in the database. By limiting the fields returned, you can do that.

LISTING 13.9   Defining the Photo Columns

```
 1: public static final String KEY_ROWID = "_id";
 2: public static final String[] FLICKR_PHOTO_FIELDS = new String[] {
 3:   KEY_ROWID,
 4:   "flickr_id", // flickr id of the photo
 5:   "owner",
 6:   "secret",
 7:   "server",
 8:   "farm",
 9:   "title",
10:   "isPublic",
```

```
11:    "isFriend",
12:    "isFamily",
13:    "isFavorite"
14:};
```

The query in Listing 13.8 returns a `Cursor`. In that code, you check to see whether the cursor is null. If it is not, you move to the first position in the cursor. A cursor includes the methods `moveToFirst()`, `moveToNext()`, `moveToPrevious()`, `moveToPosition()`, and `moveTo-Last()`. These methods provide ways to move through the cursor to retrieve data.

You'll create a method to create a `FlickrPhoto` object from a `Cursor`, and then use an SQLite database to work with the remote data retrieval code from Hour 12.

In Listing 13.10, a `Cursor` is passed as a parameter to the `getPhotoFromCursor()` method. The method will return a `FlickrPhoto` object corresponding to the data where the `Cursor` is pointing. If the cursor is pointing at the first record in the result set, the `FlickrPhoto` object returned will consist of data from the first record.

LISTING 13.10 Getting a FlickrPhoto Object from a Cursor

```
1: public static FlickrPhoto getPhotoFromCursor(Cursor cursor){
2:    FlickrPhoto photo = new FlickrPhoto();
3:    photo.id = cursor.getString(cursor.getColumnIndex("flickr_id"));
4:    photo.owner = cursor.getString(cursor.getColumnIndex("owner"));
5:    photo.secret = cursor.getString(cursor.getColumnIndex("secret"));
6:    photo.server = cursor.getString(cursor.getColumnIndex("server"));
7:    photo.farm = cursor.getString(cursor.getColumnIndex("farm"));
8:    photo.title = cursor.getString(cursor.getColumnIndex("title"));
9:    photo.isPublic = (cursor.getInt(cursor.getColumnIndex("isPublic")) == 1);
10:   photo.isFriend = (cursor.getInt(cursor.getColumnIndex("isFriend")) == 1);
11:   photo.isFamily = (cursor.getInt(cursor.getColumnIndex("isFamily")) == 1);
12:   photo.isFavorite = (cursor.getInt(cursor.getColumnIndex("isFavorite")) == 1);
13:   return(photo);
14:}
```

To do this, two methods from the `Cursor` class are used in each line. The method `getColumn-Index()` is used to get a column number based on the name of the column. A call is then made to get the value associated with that column. On line 3, the call is `cursor.getString()`. On line 9, the call is `cursor.getInt()`. The fields to populate in lines 9–12 are booleans. In the database, a 1 represents true and 0 represents false. In lines 9–12, the boolean fields are populated by comparing the value in the database to 1 and returning the result. If the value in the database is 1, then true is returned.

This technique assumes you know the names of the columns in the database and how they correspond to the `FlickrPhoto` object class.

The `FlickrPhoto` object `photo` is defined in line 2. Each field in that object is populated from a value in the cursor. The `FlickrPhoto` object `photo` is returned so it can be used in the app.

Using a Database in the App

You'll build on the app created in Hour 12 by using the new `FlickrPhotoDbAdapter` class and creating a database of photo data. You'll load the database when you retrieve data from Flickr, and then use the database to show a list of photos in the `PhotoListFragment`.

In Hour 12, you used an `AsyncTask` to retrieve remote data in the background. After the data was retrieved, you parsed it and populated an array list of `FlickrPhoto` objects. See Listing 12.7 for the details.

Insert the Flickr Photo Data

To add a database to the app, do what you did in Hour 12 to retrieve photo data, and then load the `FlickrPhotos` from the array list directly into the database. Check to see whether a record exists in the database. If it does, update it; if not, create a new record. See Listing 13.11.

LISTING 13.11   Adding Records to the Database

```
1:   mPhotos = FlickrPhoto.makePhotoList(photoData);
2:   for (FlickrPhoto currentPhoto : mPhotos) {
3:     FlickrPhoto existingPhoto = photoDbAdapter.getPhotoByFlickrId(currentPhoto.
id);
4:     if (existingPhoto==null){
5:       Long dbId = photoDbAdapter.createPhoto(currentPhoto);
6:       Log.d(TAG,"Inserted " + dbId);
7:     } else{
8:       photoDbAdapter.updatePhoto(existingPhoto.id, currentPhoto);
9:       Log.d(TAG,"Updated " + exitingPhoto.id);
10:    }
11: }
```

In Hour 12, you loaded an array list of `FlickrPhotos` to use on the app. In Listing 13.11, you iterate through that array list to populate a database.

You use a variable called `photoDbAdapter` for database access. The `photoDbAdapter` object was instantiated as follows:

```
FlickrPhotoDbAdapter photoDbAdapter = new FlickrPhotoDbAdapter(MainActivity.this);
```

The `FlickrPhotoDbAdapter` constructor takes a `Context` (`android.content.Context`) as a parameter. An `Activity` is a subclass of `Context` and can be passed as the parameter. As mentioned, an `Application` is also a `Context`.

The `FlickrPhotoDbAdapter` object must be opened before you use it and then closed afterward.

Lines 2 to 10 iterate through each record in the array list of photos and try to retrieve the record from the database using the id of the photo. The id is the Flickr id. If the photo record does not exist in the database already, you add it using the `photoDbAdapter.createPhoto(currentPhoto)` method on line 5.

If the record exists, you update it in line 8 using `photoDbAdapter.updatePhoto(existingPhoto.id, currentPhoto)`.

This provides you with a database of photo objects to use in your app.

Read the Database to Display Photo Titles

With the photo data stored in SQLite, there is no need to pass data from the activity to the fragment. The activity shows the `PhotoListFragment` and all the work to display the titles is done there.

The next three listings show all the code for the `PhotoListFragment`. The `PhotoListFragment` uses a `Cursor`, a `PhotoDbAdapter`, and a `SimpleCursorAdapter`. A `SimpleCursorAdapter` associates data from the cursor with the display. The database is read and the display is done in the `onActivityCreated()` method. The `onPause()` method cleans up previously opened resources.

Listing 13.12 shows the package name, import statements, and class declaration for `PhotoListFragment`. On lines 10–12, the `Cursor`, `SimpleCursorAdapter`, and `FlickrPhotoDbAdapter` are defined.

LISTING 13.12 Declarations for PhotoListFragment

```
1:  package com.bffmedia.hour13app;
2:  import android.app.ListFragment;
3:  import android.database.Cursor;
4:  import android.os.Bundle;
5:  import android.app.SimpleCursorAdapter;
6:  import android.view.View;
7:  import android.widget.ListView;
8:  import android.widget.Toast;
9:  public class PhotoListFragment extends ListFragment    {
10:     Cursor mPhotoCursor;
11:     SimpleCursorAdapter mAdapter;
12:     FlickrPhotoDbAdapter mPhotoDbAdapter;
```

The bulk of the work for the `PhotoListFragment` occurs in the `onActivityCreated()` method. The steps are as follows:

1. Create a `PhotoDbAdapter` and open it.

2. Use a cursor to get the photos from the database.

3. Set up the `SimpleCursorAdapter` to display photo titles.

4. Use the `SimpleCursorAdapter` to display the photo titles in the list.

Listing 13.13 shows the `onActivityCreated()` method. Lines 3 and 4 declare and open the `PhotoDbAdapter`. The cursor `mPhotoCursor` is populated in line 6. The `fetchPhotos()` method gets all available photos.

Lines 7–11 define the `SimpleCursorAdapter mAdapter`. Line 8 uses a predefined Android layout for displaying the contents. The cursor that was created on line 6 is passed in line 9. Line 10 represents the columns from the cursor from which data should be retrieved. You want the `title` column. Line 11 passes the id of the resource that you are populating. That last parameter is a flag for how the `SimpleCursorAdapter` should behave. Leave this a `0` for now for no special functionality.

When you call the `setListAdapter()` method on line 12, the association is made between the cursor and the `ListView` that exists within a `ListFragment`. The titles for the photos are displayed.

LISTING 13.13 onActivityCreated() for PhotoListFragment

```
1:  @Override
2:  public void onActivityCreated(Bundle savedInstanceState) {
3:    super.onActivityCreated(savedInstanceState);
4:    mPhotoDbAdapter = new FlickrPhotoDbAdapter(getActivity());
5:    mPhotoDbAdapter.open();
6:    mPhotoCursor = mPhotoDbAdapter.fetchPhotos();
7:    mAdapter = new SimpleCursorAdapter(getActivity(),
8:      android.R.layout.simple_list_item_1,
9:      mPhotoCursor, //Cursor
10:     new String[] {"title"},
11:     new int[] { android.R.id.text1 }, 0);
12:   setListAdapter(mAdapter);
13: }
```

Listing 13.13 creates a cursor and calls `open()` for mPhotoDbAdapter. The `PhotoDbAdapter` and the cursor must be closed. That is done on the `onDestroy()` method, as shown in Listing 13.14.

LISTING 13.14   onDestroy() for PhotoListFragment

```
 1:  @Override
 2:  public void onDestroy() {
 3:    super.onDestroy();
 4:    if (mPhotoCursor!=null){
 5:      mPhotoCursor.close();
 6:    }
 7:    if (mPhotoDbAdapter!=null){
 8:      mPhotoDbAdapter.close();
 9:    }
10: }
```

You finish the PhotoListFragment by implementing a simple onListItemClick() method. This method is available as a convenience when using a ListFragment. The title for the photo is displayed as you did in Hour 12, but there is a difference. To get the FlickrPhoto object, you set the position of the cursor based on the position of the selected item in the list and then use the getPhotoFromCursor() method to retrieve the data. This happens on lines 3 and 4 of Listing 13.15.

LISTING 13.15   onListItemClick() for PhotoListFragment

```
 1:  @Override
 2:  public void onListItemClick(ListView l, View v, int position, long id) {
 3:    mPhotoCursor.moveToPosition(position);
 4:    FlickrPhoto selected = FlickrPhotoDbAdapter.getPhotoFromCursor(mPhotoCursor);
 5:    Toast.makeText(this.getActivity().getApplicationContext(),
 6:                   selected.title, Toast.LENGTH_SHORT).show();
 7:  }
```

Saving an Image File

In Hour 12, you retrieved data from Flickr to use in your app. In this hour, you loaded that data into a database. You can also retrieve and use remote media such as images and videos. With the data you have from Flickr, you can construct a URL that can be used to download and display these Flickr images.

As you prepare to develop a fully functional app though Hour 16, you will add the ability to download and display a photo. You'll modify the onListItemClick() in Listing 13.15 to change from displaying a Toast message to displaying a photo for the selected title. The steps to accomplish this are to:

1. Create a valid URL to retrieve for a Flickr photo.

2. Check to see whether you have a previously stored image available locally.

3. If not, retrieve the remote image data and save it locally.

4. Display the photo in an `ImageView`.

When you retrieve the data, you use an `AsyncTask` for background retrieval.

You show the photo in a new fragment called `ImageViewFragment`.

When you save the image locally, you use the method `getCacheDir()`. Android provides a cache directory for files that will be used in the app, but that can also be cleared by the system if needed.

Listing 13.16 shows a basic example of writing a file that can be used privately within your app. You use the `openFileOutput()` method to create a `FileOutputStream` for writing. The first parameter to `openFileOutput()` is the filename, and the second parameter is the mode to use to open the file. Using `MODE_PRIVATE` means this is set for app-only reading.

LISTING 13.16   Writing to a File

```
1: String FILENAME = "hello_file";
2: String string = "hello world!";
3: FileOutputStream outputStream = openFileOutput(FILENAME, Context.MODE_PRIVATE);
4: outputStream.write(string.getBytes());
5: outputStream.close();
```

To read the file created in Listing 13.16, you use the `openFileInput()` method. The filename to open would be passed as a `String`, and a `FileInputStream` would be returned for reading.

A number of options exist for file storage on Android. Table 13.1 shows some options for getting the path to a directory on the file system in Android. A description and the API level information are included.

TABLE 13.1   Methods to Get a File Directory

Class and Method	Description	Since API
`Context.getCacheDir()`	Directory for storing cached files.	8
`Environment.getExternalStorageDirectory ()`	Gets an external directory. This might be the SD card, but might be built-in device storage that is considered the external directory.	1

Class and Method	Description	Since API
Context.getExternalFilesDir (String type)	Gets an external directory for a specific type such as music or pictures. The parameter type is a String defined in the Environment class. For example, you can use Environment. DIRECTORY_PICTURES.	8
Context.getFilesDir ()	Returns a directory for files written to the app's private directory and opened with openFileOutput (String name, int mode).	1
Context.getExternalStoragePublicDirectory	Returns a public directory for files of a certain type such as Environment. DIRECTORY_PICTURES and Environment. DIRECTORY_MUSIC.	8

This example uses getCacheDir(), which is good for temporary files.

For long-term file storage, Context.getExternalFilesDir() is recommended. You can set the type parameter to null when calling this method. Any file type can be stored. The files placed in this directory are specific to the app and will be cleared up if the app is uninstalled. The directory of the file system will be the external location and then /Android/data/[your.package. name]. A file's being stored anywhere other than this is unlikely.

If you must develop for an API earlier than 8, then you can use these same conventions. You would use getExternalStorageDirectory(), add /Android/data/[your.package.name], and create any directories not already present. Do not store files in any directory outside of /Android/ data/[your.package.name].

TIP

Use the Right Methods for External Directories

Using Context.getExternalFilesDir(), Context.getCacheDir(), and Context.get ExternalStoragePublicDirectory() is highly recommended. These are all available in API Level 8 (Froyo). Few devices run earlier versions.

Retrieving an Image from Flickr

Flickr provides a formula for creating URLs to use for retrieving a specific photo. All the data necessary to get an image is contained in the `FlickrPhoto` object that you created.

Add a method to `FlickrPhoto` that will create the `String` you need. The method is called `getPhotoUrl()`; see Listing 13.17.

Flickr provides an option to get pictures in different sizes. The `boolean big` passed to the `getPhotoUrl()` method is used to determine whether a big photo should be used. Overall, the method creates a string according to the Flickr specifications.

LISTING 13.17 String to Retrieve a Photo from Flickr

```
1:   public String getPhotoUrl(Boolean big){
2:     String opt = "n";
3:     if (big)
4:       opt ="c";
5:     String photoUri =
6:     "http://farm"+this.farm + ".staticflickr.com/"+this.server+"/"
7:             + this.id+"_"+this.secret +"_" + opt +".jpg";
8:     return photoUri;
9:   }
```

You use the `getPhotoUrl()` method on the `PhotoListFragment.onListItemClick()` method. Instead of opening a `Toast` message, you get this `String` and pass it as a `Bundle` to a new fragment called `ImageViewFragment`.

Listing 13.18 shows the complete `onListItemClick()` method.

LISTING 13.18 Passing Data to ImageViewFragment

```
1:   @Override
2:   public void onListItemClick(ListView l, View v, int position, long id) {
3:   mPhotoCursor.moveToPosition(position);
4:   FlickrPhoto selected = FlickrPhotoDbAdapter.getPhotoFromCursor(mPhotoCursor);
5:   String photoUrl = selected.getPhotoUrl(true);
6:   ImageViewFragment flickrImageFragment = new ImageViewFragment();
7:   Bundle args = new Bundle();
8:   args.putString("URL", photoUrl);
9:   flickrImageFragment.setArguments(args);
10:    FragmentTransaction ft = getActivity().getFragmentManager().
beginTransaction();
11:    ft.replace(R.id.layout_container, flickrImageFragment);
12:    ft.addToBackStack("Image");
13:    ft.commit();
14:    Toast.makeText(this.getActivity().getApplicationContext(),
```

```
15:              selected.title,
16:   Toast.LENGTH_SHORT).show();
17: }
```

Using a Cached Image

The URL `String` for the image to retrieve is now available in the `ImageViewFragment`. You check to see whether you have already retrieved and saved the image to a file. If you have, you use the saved file to create a bitmap. If you have not, you retrieve the image data and save it to a file. By using a stored image, you avoid retrieving the image again and performance is improved.

This all occurs in an `AsyncTask` within the `ImageViewFragment`. You download the image in the background using an `AsyncTask`. You pass the `AsyncTask` a `String` representing the image to download and an `ImageView` to display the retrieved photo.

Listing 13.19 shows the constructor and the `onPostExecute()` method for the `LoadImage()` `AsyncTask`.

An `ImageView` called `mImageView` and a `String` called `mImageString` are defined as fields and assigned in the constructor. There is also a field called `mBitmap` of type `Bitmap`. When you have successfully created a `Bitmap`, it is assigned to `mBitmap`. In the `onPostExecute()` method, `mBitmap` is shown in `mImageView`.

LISTING 13.19   Displaying a Bitmap in an ImageView

```
1:   public LoadImage (ImageView v, String imageString){
2:      mImageView =v;
3:      mImageString = imageString;
4:   }
5:   @Override
6:   protected void onPostExecute(Long result) {
7:      if (result==0){
8:        mImageView.setImageBitmap(mBitmap);
9:      }
10: }
```

The bulk of the work to retrieve the image occurs in the `doInBackground()` method. Listing 13.20 shows that entire method.

LISTING 13.20   Getting the Image Using doInBackground()

```
1:   @Override
2:   protected Long doInBackground(String... params) {
3:   String imageFileName = mImageString.replace(":", "");
4:   imageFileName =imageFileName.replace("/", "");
5:   imageFileName =imageFileName.replace(".", "");
6:   File imageFile = new File(getActivity().getCacheDir(), imageFileName);
7:   OutputStream imageOS;
8:   if (imageFile.exists()){
9:   mBitmap = BitmapFactory.decodeFile(imageFile.getAbsolutePath());
10: return (0l);
11:   }
12: try {
13: imageFile.createNewFile();
14: URL imageUrl = new URL(mImageString);
15: URLConnection connection = imageUrl.openConnection();
16: connection.connect();
17: InputStream is = connection.getInputStream();
18: mBitmap = BitmapFactory.decodeStream(is);
19: imageOS = new BufferedOutputStream(new FileOutputStream(imageFile));
20: mBitmap.compress(Bitmap.CompressFormat.JPEG, 100, imageOS);
21: imageOS.flush();
22: imageOS.close();
23: return (0l);
24: } catch (MalformedURLException e) {
25: e.printStackTrace();
26: return (1l);
27: }
28: catch (IOException e) {
29: e.printStackTrace();
30: return (1l);
31: }
32: }
```

You can think about the logic of Listing 13.20 in two parts: One is to retrieve the image from a file if it exists, and the other is to download the image and write it to a file if that is not the case. In both instances, a bitmap is created and used to display the image.

Lines 3–5 of Listing 13.20 do some cleanup of the filename. The imageName passed is the full URL of where to retrieve the image. The dots, slashes, and colons are removed.

Line 6 is an attempt to access the file. Line 8 checks to whether the file exists. If it does, the file is read into a bitmap on line 9. The BitmapFactory.decodeFile() method takes a filename with a full path and creates a Bitmap.

If the file does not exist, the remote file is retrieved and made into a `Bitmap` in lines 14–18. The method `BitmapFactory.decodeStream()` creates a `Bitmap` from an `InputStream`.

The `Bitmap` is saved to a file in line 20 using the `Bitmap.compress()` method. This method saves a `Bitmap` to a file. To do that, you create an `OutputStream` for writing data and handle all file open and close functionality.

Summary

This hour covered the basic functionality of a SQLite database. Using the same Flickr photo data used in Hour 12, you inserted and updated records into an SQLite database. To accomplish that, you created the `FlickrPhotoDBAdapter` class to handle the opening and closing of the database and common queries. You gained an understanding of `Cursors` and how to use them in your apps.

You also learned about retrieval and display of remote images. In doing so, you worked with the `URLConnection`, `Bitmap`, and `BitmapFactory` classes to retrieve images and create `Bitmaps`. You also cached bitmap files locally so that they could be retrieved without being downloaded, which improves performance in the app.

Q&A

Q. What is `SQLiteOpenHelper` **used for?**

A. `SQLiteOpenHelper` handles creating and opening SQLite databases. It contains methods to upgrade the database when needed.

Q. Within a database, you can insert, update, and delete data. How are updates and deletes different from inserts?

A. With both deletes and updates, a record or records must already exist in the database. You select the records to act on and then perform the update or delete action. To select the records, you form a query with a `whereClause`. For an insert, a new record is inserted. There is no need to find an existing record.

Q. How is a cursor used?

A. A cursor is what is returned from a query. You can think of a cursor as a pointer to the list of results. You can iterate through the entire list of results, and you can get the data for a specific result.

Q. Can a fragment use an `AsyncTask` **for background processing?**

A. Yes, the `ImageViewFragment` in this hour used an `AsyncTask` to download an image in the background and display it.

Workshop

Quiz

1. How is DESC used?

2. What type of objects are returned by queries?

3. Is the field _id required to define a table?

Answers

1. DESC is used in an ORDER BY clause to indicate descending order.

2. Cursors are returned by queries.

3. The field _id is not required to define a table, but it is needed when working with other Android classes such as CursorAdapter, so it is recommended to use _id as your table's unique identifier.

Exercises

1. Implement an ORDER BY clause in a query in the app. Verify the results by seeing the order of the titles in the PhotoListFragment change. Change the order by direction from DESC to ASC and verify that the opposite result is achieved.

2. Add a new field to the database. Make note of all the places that must change and upgrade the database version.

Creating a Content Provider

What You'll Learn in This Hour:

▶ Retrieving data with a URI
▶ Building a content provider
▶ Using a content provider in your app

Hour 13, "Using SQLite and File Storage," introduced SQLite, and you used cursors in your app to access data from the database. You can think of content providers as a bridge between the database and the app. Content providers work with any type of structured data. One reason to use a content provider is that it provides a way for other apps to access the data. That is what makes it a *content* provider. Another reason, covered in detail in Hour 15, "Loaders, CursorLoaders, and CustomAdapters," is that you can use content providers with the `CursorLoader` class to make updating data in fragments and activities easy. Content providers simplify providing data to the Android UI in your app.

The focus of this hour is to create your own `ContentProvider(android.content.ContentProvider)` class for the Flickr photo SQLite database that you created in Hour 13. In this hour, you use a content provider to populate the `PhotoListFragment` and to get the selected image to display. Content providers can return cursors for data or streams that can contain a file.

Using a URI for Data Retrieval

Content providers use Uniform Resource Identifiers (URIs) to identify the data resources that they provide. We are all familiar with URLs of the format http://www.amazon.com. A URL, or Uniform Resource Locator, is an example of a URI that defines the network location of a specific resource.

The format of the URI should represent the data being returned. Content providers return cursors that may point to a single item or to a list of items.

URIs for Android content providers start with *content://*. To create the full URI, you add the *authority* and a meaningful path. The *authority* is the creator of the content provider, and the Android package name and class should be used here. That will ensure uniqueness. In this chapter's example, the package name is `com.bffmedia.hour14App`. By convention, to create the full authority name, `provider` is appended, so you get an authority of `com.bffmedia.hour14App.provider`. In this hour, you work with Flickr photos, so in your base path, you will use `flickrphoto`. When you put it all together, you get the following:

```
content://com.bffmedia.hour14App.provider/flickrphoto/
```

You can also create a URI to access an individual photo that you identify by the Flickr photo id:

```
content://com.bffmedia.hour14App.provider/flickrphoto/12345.
```

In this case, `12345` represents the id of a particular Flickr photo.

Building a Content Provider

You have defined the URIs to use in our content provider. In this section, you examine the process to build a content provider in detail. You then use the new content provider in your app to get a cursor to a list of photo records. You'll create the new class `FlickrPhotoProvider` as an extension of `ContentProvider` and build on it in Hours 15 and 16.

The Hour14app project contains the source code that accompanies this hour. The content provider work is done in FlickrPhotoProvider.java.

Methods Required in a Content Provider

When you define a new class as an extension of `ContentProvider`, you are required to implement six methods. Four methods interact with the data managed by the content provider: `insert()`, `update()`, `delete()`, and `query()`. All must be implemented, but creating a provider without providing full functionality to these methods is possible. That is, you can have stub methods if that fits your purpose. The two other methods are `onCreate()` and `getType()`. The `onCreate()` method is used to initialize the content provider. That initialization often means opening a database. The `getType()` method indicates the type of data that the content provider returns.

Listing 14.1 shows an empty content provider that is not useful, but implements a stub for all required methods.

LISTING 14.1   Shell of a Content Provider

```
1: package com.bffmedia.example;
2: import android.content.ContentProvider;
3: import android.content.ContentValues;
4: import android.database.Cursor;
```

```
5: import android.net.Uri;
6: public class EmptyProvider extends ContentProvider {
7:    @Override
8:    public int delete(Uri uri, String selection, String[] selectionArgs) {
9:      return 0;
10:   }
11:   @Override
12:   public String getType(Uri uri) {
13:     return null;
14:   }
15:   @Override
16:   public Uri insert(Uri uri, ContentValues values) {
17:    return null;
18:   }
19:   @Override
20:     public boolean onCreate() {
21:    return false;
22:   }
23:   @Override
24:   public Cursor query(Uri uri, String[] projection, String selection,
25:                       String[] selectionArgs, String sortOrder) {
26:     return null;
27:   }
28:   @Override
29:   public int update(Uri uri, ContentValues values,
30:                     String selection,String[] selectionArgs) {
31:     return 0;
32:   }
33: }
```

Declaring the Content Provider

You will examine each section of the `FlickrPhotoProvider` class. Often, field definitions are self-explanatory, but in the case of `FlickrPhotoProvider`, it is beneficial to examine the declarations and definitions carefully. There are static fields that correspond to the parts of the URI definition. There are static fields that will be used in the `getType()` method and elsewhere to make the code more readable.

A static `UriMatcher` will be declared. The job of the `UriMatcher` is to match the string pattern of a URI to a specific constant value as a convenience for development. Instead of string and pattern-matching logic to determine what action should be taken with a URI, you can use the `UriMatcher` and a switch statement to simplify the code. The `UriMatcher` is a convenience class created for this purpose.

When you create a content provider, you'll see that there are many interconnected pieces. Listing 14.2 shows the `FlickrPhotoProvider` declarations and definitions.

LISTING 14.2 FlickrPhotoProvider Declarations

```
1:  public class FlickrPhotoProvider extends ContentProvider {
2:  private FlickrPhotoDbAdapter mPhotoDbAdapter;
3:  private static final UriMatcher sUriMatcher = new UriMatcher(UriMatcher.NO_
MATCH);
4:  static {
5:      sUriMatcher.addURI("com.bffmedia.hour14app.provider", "flickrphoto", 1);
6:      sUriMatcher.addURI("com.bffmedia.hour14app.provider", "flickrphoto/#", 2);
7:  }
8:  public static final Uri CONTENT_URI =
9:                      Uri.parse("content://com.bffmedia.hour14app.provider/
flickrphoto");
```

Lines 3 through 7 define the `UriMatcher`. In lines 5 and 6, the URIs for the content are represented along with an integer value to return when there is a matching URI. Line 5 represents
getting all Flickr photos and line 6 represents getting a single Flickr photo that is specified by
passing a number as an appended id. The # indicates that.

Line 8 creates a static variable called `CONTENT_URI` that will be used by apps that use the
`FlickrPhotoProvider`.

Given a URI, the `UriMatcher` returns the integer code that you associated with the URI. This
example has URIs for getting a single photo based on id, and a URI for getting a list of photos
based on page id. Lines 5 and 6 add these URIs to the `UriMatcher` and specify the integer values to return when a match is found.

You'll use the `UriMatcher` for two of the methods that you are required to implement when creating a content provider.

The `getType()` method returns a string representing the type of data you are returning. In that
case, you will use the `UriMatcher` to determine whether the request for the content type is for a
single photo based on a Flickr photo id or for a list of photos.

You will also use the `UriMatcher` for the `query()` method. In this `query()` method, you either
return a cursor to all the photos or a single photo. The URI passed determines that.

The string constants like `"flickrphoto"` in Listing 14.2 help make the example clear. Using
static variables to define these strings is recommended. For example, if you used:

```
private static final String AUTHORITY = "com.bffmedia.hour14app.provider";
private static final String BASE_PATH = "flickrphoto";
public static final int PHOTOS = 1;
public static final int PHOTO_ID = 2;
```

Then you would create the `UriMatcher` using:

```
sUriMatcher.addURI(AUTHORITY, BASE_PATH, PHOTOS );
sUriMatcher.addURI(AUTHORITY, BASE_PATH+"/#", PHOTO_ID);
```

Updating the Android Manifest

Adding content provider information to the AndroidManifest.xml file is critical because the app will not work if this is not done. The following snippet shows the definition for this provider. The authority is provided. The `android:name` attribute is the name of the class that defined the provider. The `android:exported` attribute specifies whether or not third-party apps can use this content provider. When set to `false`, it indicates that only the current app can use the provider.

The name and authorities values must be set. You should make a decision on whether the data should be exported. If you are not sure, set `exported` to `"false"`; not exporting data is better than exporting it by mistake. Leaving `multiprocess` set to `"true"` is fine:

```
<provider
            android:authorities="com.bffmedia.hour14app.provider"
            android:multiprocess="true"
            android:exported="false"
            android:name="com.bffmedia.hour14app.FlickrPhotoProvider">
</provider>
```

For additional details and other options, see http://developer.android.com/guide/topics/manifest/provider-element.html.

Content Provider Query Method

The plan is to support two URIs in the `FlickrPhotoProvider` content provider. When requested from `FlickrPhotoProvider`, these URIs will be fulfilled from the `query()` method. You learn how to implement the specific response required by these URIs. This section then covers the parameters that are passed to this method and considers alternative implementations.

Listing 14.3 implements the `query()` method for `FlickrPhotoProvider`. It checks the URI that was passed and fulfills the request based on the URI. If the URI is not recognized, an exception is thrown.

LISTING 14.3 FlickrPhotoProvider Query Method

```
1:  @Override
2:  public Cursor query(Uri uri, String[] projection, String selection,
3:  String[] selectionArgs, String sortOrder) {
4:  Cursor cursor;
5:  int uriType = sUriMatcher.match(uri);
6:  switch (uriType) {
7:  case 1:
8:  cursor = mPhotoDbAdapter.mDb.query(true, FlickrPhotoDbAdapter.DATABASE_TABLE,
9:          projection, selection, selectionArgs, null,null,sortOrder, null);
10: cursor.setNotificationUri(getContext().getContentResolver(), uri);
11: break;
12: case 2:
```

```
13:   cursor = mPhotoDbAdapter.fetchByFlickrId(uri.getLastPathSegment());
14:   cursor.setNotificationUri(getContext().getContentResolver(), uri);
15:   break;
16:   default:
17:   throw new IllegalArgumentException("Unknown URI");
18:   }
19:   return cursor;
20: }
```

Three tasks are being handled in Listing 14.3:

▶ Identify the URI to handle using `UriMatcher`.

▶ Create a `Cursor` that fulfills the request for data.

▶ Set a notification URI for the cursor.

Lines 10 and 14 set the notification URI for the cursor. The URI will be watched for changes. The `ContentResolver` associated with the context will be notified when a change occurs. That means that the `ContentResolver` associated with the activity is observing this URI and will be notified of changes. This hour covers this topic more later.

This implementation of `FlickrPhotoProvider` handles two URIs. The `uriType` specifies whether to return a single photo or a list of photos. When retrieving a single photo, the call to `uri.getLastPath()` segment returns the value of the specific photo id to use.

The cursor for returning a single photo is created on line 13 and the cursor for fulfilling a list of photos occurs on line 8. You use the `FlickrPhotoDbAdapter` class to do this for a single photo. To get a list of photos, you create the query directly in the content provider.

By examining the parameters passed to the `query` method, you can see how to do a database query. Lines 2 and 3 of Listing 14.3 show these parameters. We'll define each one:

`String[] projection, String selection, String[] selectionArgs, String sortOrder`

The `projection` parameter identifies the columns in a database table that should be returned. A `null` projection means to return all columns. To create a SQL query, you would use `selection` and optionally `selectionArgs` parameters. The `sortOrder` parameter defines the order of the data being returned.

These are the parameters that you would pass to a `SQLDatabase query()` method. See Hour 13 to see how to use a query in the `FlickrPhotoDBAdapter` class.

The parameters from the query method in the content provider will be passed to a `SQLiteDatabase query()` method. That method is available to use because the `SQLiteDatabase` is available through `FlickrPhotoDbAdapter`. The parameters form a query and return a cursor.

The parameters passed determine the data returned. If you wanted to put more restrictions on the data that can be returned, you could define URIs that *only* return data from a hardcoded query in the `query()` method. That is, all the passed parameters would be ignored and a specific query would be performed. To make that more flexible for apps using the content provider, defining multiple URIs to call would make sense.

Using the FlickrPhotoProvider Query

As a review, this hour implements support for two URIs in the `ContentProvider query()` method. The URIs are used to get a list of photos and get an individual photo.

When called from an activity, you use the content provider via a `managedQuery`. This calls the content provider's query method with the parameters discussed earlier.

To get a single photo, you need to create a URI with an appended path of the `flickr_id`. The URI is

```
content://com.bffmedia.hour14app.provider/flickrphoto/12345
```

where `12345` is the id. To call this from an `Activity` with a `managedQuery`, you use the following:

```
managedQuery(Uri.withAppendedPath(FlickrPhotoProvider.CONTENT_URI ,"12345"), null,
null, null, null);
```

You can access content providers using `getContentResolver()`, `managedQuery()`, or `CursorLoaders`. The benefit of using `managedQuery()` is that the `Activity` takes care of maintaining the cursor. Hour 15 covers the advantages in using `CursorLoaders`.

GO TO ▶ **HOUR 15, "LOADERS, CURSORLOADERS, AND CUSTOMADAPTERS,"** to learn about using content providers with `CursorLoaders`.

To retrieve multiple photos, you would create a query as follows:

```
Cursor photoCursor = managedQuery(FlickrPhotoProvider.CONTENT_URI, null, null,
null, null);
```

That would get all photos. To get just favorites, you could use:

```
Cursor photoCursor = managedQuery(FlickrPhotoProvider.CONTENT_URI, null,
"isFavorite='1'", null, null);
```

To get the favorite photos using this URI, you add a selection parameter in the call to `manageQuery`.

Implementing the GetType() Method

The purpose of the `getType()` method is to show the type of data that will be returned from the content provider. The `ContentResolver` class offers two Android MIME types to use for this purpose. One MIME type represents a cursor that can have multiple objects, and the other MIME type is used for when a single item is returned in the cursor. You use `ContentResolver.CURSOR_DIR_BASE_TYPE` for multiple items and `ContentResolver.CURSOR_ITEM_BASE_TYPE` for a single item.

Because this example uses `FlickrPhoto` objects, the types will be a string, like this:

`ContentResolver.CURSOR_DIR_BASE_TYPE + "/com.bffmedia.hour15app.FlickrPhoto"`

Listing 14.4 shows the full `getType()` method.

On lines 5 and 6, the type for a list of items is returned, and on lines 7 and 8, the type for a single item is returned. Recall that type for the URI was defined in the `UriMatcher`. Refer to Listing 14.2 for review.

LISTING 14.4 Return Type of Data in GetType()

```
1: @Override
2: public String getType(Uri uri) {
3:    int uriType = sUriMatcher.match(uri);
4:    switch (uriType) {
5:      case 1:
6:        return ContentResolver.CURSOR_DIR_BASE_TYPE+"/com.bffmedia.hour15app.
FlickrPhoto";
7:      case 2:
8:        return ContentResolver.CURSOR_ITEM_BASE_TYPE+"/com.bffmedia.hour15app.
FlickrPhoto";
9:      default:
10:      return null;
11:  }
12: }
```

Implement Insert, Update, and Delete Methods

To create a content provider, you must implement `insert()`, `update()`, and `delete()` methods. This provides a consistent way to keep the app in synch and aware of updates as they happen.

These methods must exist in the content provider, but making a read-only content provider is possible as well. To create a read-only content provider, the query methods would be fully implemented to return results. The `insert()`, `update()`, and `delete()` methods would exist, but would not actually change the underlying data.

Listing 14.5 shows a complete `insert()` method.

Listing 14.5 inserts the passed `ContentValues` into the database by directly accessing the `mDb` field in the `FlickrPhotoDbAdapter` class.

LISTING 14.5   Content Provider insert() Method

```
1: @Override
2: public Uri insert(Uri uri, ContentValues values) {
3:   long newID=mPhotoDbAdapter.mDb.insert(FlickrPhotoDBHelper.DATABASE_
TABLE,null,values);
4:   if (newID > 0) {
5:     Uri newUri = ContentUris.withAppendedId(uri, newID);
6:     getContext().getContentResolver().notifyChange(uri, null);
7:     return newUri;
8:   } else {
9:     throw new SQLException("Failed to insert row into " + uri);
10:  }
11: }
```

Listing 14.6 shows the database update. With an update, the selection criteria are passed to the argument so that the rows to be updated can be identified.

LISTING 14.6   Content Provider update() Method

```
1: @Override
2: public int update(Uri uri, ContentValues values, String selection,
3:                   String[] selectionArgs) {
4: return mPhotoDbAdapter.mDb.update(FlickrPhotoDBHelper.DATABASE_TABLE,
5:        values, selection, selectionArgs);
6: }
```

Listing 14.7 shows the `delete()` method. Like the `update()` method, it takes selection criteria as parameters. When updating or deleting, you must specify the rows to act upon via these parameters.

LISTING 14.7   Content Provider delete() Method

```
1: @Override
2: public int delete(Uri uri, String selection, String[] selectionArgs) {
3:   return mPhotoDbAdapter.mDb.delete(PhotoDBHelper.DATABASE_TABLE,
4:        selection, selectionArgs);
5: }
```

Using FlickrPhotoProvider in the App

Hour 13 showed a `Cursor` and `SimpleCursorAdapter` in the `PhotoListFragment` used to display the list of titles. The `Cursor` was created by making direct database calls via `FlickrPhotoDbAdapter`. Modifying this code in `PhotoListFragment` to use in the new content provider is possible and has several advantages. By using a `managedQuery`, you do not have to use the `FlickrPhotoDbAdapter` class directly or have to manage the cursor. That means you can completely remove the `onDestroy()` method that you were using to close the cursor.

Listing 14.8 shows the new `onActivityCreated()` method for `PhotoListFragment`.

LISTING 14.8   Using a Content Provider in PhotoListFragment

```
 1: @Override
 2: public void onActivityCreated(Bundle savedInstanceState) {
 3:    super.onActivityCreated(savedInstanceState);
 4:    mPhotoCursor = getActivity().managedQuery(FlickrPhotoProvider.CONTENT_URI,
 5:        null, null, null, null);
 6:    mAdapter = new SimpleCursorAdapter(getActivity(),
 7:       android.R.layout.simple_list_item_1,
 8:       mPhotoCursor, //Cursor
 9:       new String[] {"title"},
10:       new int[] { android.R.id.text1 }, 0);
11:    setListAdapter(mAdapter);
12:}
```

The `FlickrPhotoProvider` is also used to insert records in the `MainActivity` class.

Listing 14.9 revises the portion of the `doInBackground()` method where you currently insert or update photo objects with `FlickrPhotoDbAdapter`. You use the `FlickrPhotoProvider` `insert()` and `update()` methods. You take an available `FlickrPhoto` object and populate a `ContentValues` object with name/value pairs as required by the `insert()` and `update()` methods.

You query the database to determine whether a record already exists for the photo. If it does exist, it is updated. If it does not exist, it is inserted. The query to check the database is on lines 8–10. If you can do a `moveToFirst()` on the cursor it means that the record exists. The `update()` and `insert()` methods occur on lines 11–18. Note that the full set of name/value pairs for the `ContentValues` object defined on line 2 is not included.

LISTING 14.9   Inserting and Updating Using a Content Provider

```
1:  for (FlickrPhoto currentPhoto : mPhotos) {
2:     ContentValues newValues = new ContentValues();
3:        if (currentPhoto.id!=null)
```

```
4:       newValues.put("flickr_id", currentPhoto.id);
5:       ...
6:       if (currentPhoto.isFavorite!=null)
7:         newValues.put("isFavorite", currentPhoto.isFavorite);
8:       Cursor photoCursor = managedQuery(Uri.withAppendedPath(
9:             FlickrPhotoProvider.CONTENT_URI,currentPhoto.id), null, null, null,
null);
10:   if (photoCursor.moveToFirst()){
11:   FlickrPhoto existingPhoto = FlickrPhotoDbAdapter.getPhotoFromCursor(photoCurs
or);
12:   photoDbAdapter.updatePhoto(existingPhoto.id, currentPhoto);
13:    Log.d(TAG,"Updated " + existingPhoto.id);
14:   }else{
15:   Uri newUri = getContentResolver().insert(
16:   FlickrPhotoProvider.CONTENT_URI,
17:   newValues);
18:   }
19:   }
```

Requesting a File from a Content Provider

You have learned to update an app to retrieve, insert, and update data using a content provider. You can take an additional step and incorporate the retrieval of an image file into the FlickrPhotoProvider class. That will cleanly separate all content retrieval in the app from presentation and logic.

The job of the content provider is to retrieve content. That content may be data returned in a Cursor or an inputStream. The logic of the app and the visual presentation of the app are independent from the content provider.

Currently, the code to retrieve the image is in the ImageViewFragment class. Hour 13 showed how to pass a full image URL to the ImageViewFragment. You modify that to pass the id instead. When you retrieve a file from a content provider, you are retrieving a file that is associated with a single item. The URI to use is the same as for retrieving the data for a single item from that database.

It will look like the following:

```
content://com.bffmedia.hour14App.provider/flickrphoto/12345
```

The request to the content provider will be for the file associated with the record specified by this URI. The return value is actually an InputStream that points to the file.

You can use the logic covered in Hour 13 for retrieving an image. You can retrieve the image contents from Flickr and write the image to the cache file system for faster retrieval on subsequent calls.

The following sections introduce the concept of a content observer. The class `ContentObserver` watches for changes in a given URI. This is important because you might request an image that has not yet been written as a file. In that case, you set a content observer to display the image file when it becomes available.

Listings 14.10 to 14.14 show the process of retrieving data from a file and using a `ContentObserver` to track whether the file has been written.

How to Return a File from a Content Provider

Start with the changes to the `FlickrPhotoProvider` class. You implement the `openFile` method. The `FlickrPhotoProvider`'s `openFile` method is called when you request an `InputStream` from the provider. That is, a request in your app to open an `InputStream` from `FlickrPhotoProvider` like the following results in a call to the `openFile` method in your `FlickrPhotoProvider` class:

```
InputStream is=getActivity().getContentResolver(.
openInputStream(Uri.withAppendedPath(PhotoProvider.CONTENT_URI ,mPhotoId));
```

The URI to use to grab the file is the `CONTENT_URI` with an appended photo id:

```
content://com.bffmedia.hour14App.provider/flickrphoto/12345
```

Listing 14.10 shows the implementation of the `openFile` method within the `FlickrPhotoProvider` class.

LISTING 14.10   Implementing File Support in FlickrPhotoProvider

```
1: @Override
2: public ParcelFileDescriptor openFile(Uri uri, String mode)
3:                                 throws FileNotFoundException {
4:    File root = new File(getContext().getApplicationContext().getCacheDir(),
5:    uri.getEncodedPath());
6:    root.mkdirs();
7:    File imageFile = new File(root,  "image.jpg");
8:    final OutputStream imageOS;
9:    final int imode = ParcelFileDescriptor.MODE_READ_ONLY;
10:   if (imageFile.exists()) {
11:     return ParcelFileDescriptor.open(imageFile, imode);
12:  }
13:   Cursor photoCursor = query(uri, null, null, null, null);
14:   if (photoCursor == null) return null;
15:   if (photoCursor.getCount()==0) return null;
16:   FlickrPhoto currentPhoto = FlickrPhotoDbAdapter.getPhotoFromCursor(photoCursor);
17:   final String imageString = currentPhoto.getPhotoUrl(true);
18:   imageOS = new BufferedOutputStream(new FileOutputStream(imageFile));
19:   RetrieveImage ri = new RetrieveImage (uri, imageString, imageOS);
```

```
20:   ri.execute();
21:   throw ( new FileNotFoundException());
22: }
```

Listing 14.10 does two things. If the requested file exists, it is returned as a `ParcelFileDescriptor`.

If the file does not exist several things happen. The codes begins retrieving the image in the background and, in the meantime, throws a `FileNotFoundException` so that the requesting activity can show something else. In a subsequent refresh, after the image has been downloaded, the content provider returns the file descriptor for the file.

The activity that requests the file you need to handle the exception when the file is not present.

Lines 4 to 7 of Listing 14.10 create a directory for the file based on the URI and then access a file called image.jpg in that directory. If the file exists, it is used to create a `ParcelFileDescriptor` that is returned. `ParcelFileDescriptors` provide a way to work on the original file. On line 9, the `ParcelFileDescriptor` is set to read-only. It is returned on line 11.

The underlying logic is to create a folder for each image and to include a file called image.jpg in that folder.

Retrieving an Image from a File or Remotely

If the file is not found, the code gets a `FlickrPhoto` object based on the photo id. You use the `query()` method of the provider to get the `FlickrPhoto` object. With the `FlickrPhoto` object, you can create a photo URL to retrieve the image from Flickr. You use the `AsyncTask` `RetrieveImage` shown in Listing 14.11.

LISTING 14.11   Retrieving an Image in FlickrPhotoProvider

```
1:private class RetrieveImage extends AsyncTask<String , String , Long > {
2:   String  mImageString;
3:   OutputStream mImageOS;
4:   Uri mUri;
5:   public RetrieveImage ( Uri uri, String imageString, OutputStream imageOS){
6:     mImageString = imageString;
7:     mImageOS = imageOS;
8:     mUri = uri;
9:   }
10: @Override
11:   protected Long doInBackground(String... params) {
12:   try {
13:     URL imageUrl = new URL(mImageString);
14:     URLConnection connection = imageUrl.openConnection();
15:     connection.connect();
```

```
16:        InputStream is = connection.getInputStream();
17:        Bitmap mBitmap = BitmapFactory.decodeStream(is);
18:        mBitmap.compress(Bitmap.CompressFormat.JPEG, 100, mImageOS);
19:        mImageOS.flush();
20:        mImageOS.close();
21:        getContext().getContentResolver().notifyChange(mUri, null);
22:        return (0l);
23:    } catch (MalformedURLException e) {
24:        e.printStackTrace();
25:        return (1l);
26:    }
27:    catch (IOException e) {
28:        e.printStackTrace();
29:        return (1l);
30:    }
31: }
32:}
```

The image is retrieved from the URL as you have done previously, but instead of creating a bitmap to return, you write the URL to the file that you created in the openFile() method. You pass the RetrieveImage class a URI, a string containing the Flickr photo URL, and the OutputStream for writing the file.

Line 21 calls the notifyChange method of ContentResolver. A notification is sent to any observers of the URI that a change has occurred. You must set up an observer in the ImageViewFragment class to act on this notification.

Let's review the logic for the case where the file does not exist. The ImageViewFragment requests the file. Because the file does not exist at that moment, the FlickrPhotoProvider throws a FileNotFoundException. On getting that exception, the ImageViewFragment sets an observer to wait for the URI associated with the file to change. From the perspective of the ImageViewFragment, there is no file, but if it becomes available, a notification occurs.

Meanwhile, in addition to throwing the FileNotFoundException, the FlickrPhotoProvider is retrieving the image from Flickr. After the image is received and it is written to file, a notification occurs. The ImageViewFragment receives that notification, opens the file, and creates a bitmap.

Listing 14.12 shows the onActivityCreated method of ImageViewFragment.

LISTING 14.12   Creating a Bitmap Using the Content Provider

```
1:   @Override
2:   public void onActivityCreated(Bundle savedInstanceState) {
3:       super.onActivityCreated(savedInstanceState);
4:       Bundle b = this.getArguments();
5:       if (b!=null){
```

```
 6:        mPhotoId=b.getString("PHOTO_ID");
 7:      }
 8:      Handler handler = new Handler();
 9:      InputStream is;
10:      try {
11:        is = getActivity().getContentResolver().openInputStream
12:                    (Uri.withAppendedPath(FlickrPhotoProvider.CONTENT_URI
,mPhotoId));
13:        mBitmap =  BitmapFactory.decodeStream(is);
14:        mImageView.setImageBitmap(mBitmap);
15:      } catch (FileNotFoundException e) {
16:         getActivity().getContentResolver().registerContentObserver(
17:                    Uri.withAppendedPath(FlickrPhotoProvider.CONTENT_URI
,mPhotoId),
18:                    false, new PhotoContentObserver(handler));
19:      }
20: }
```

Instead of passing the contents of the source field in the bundle, you are now passing the id of the photo. You use that ID to form a URI and use that URI on lines 11 and 12 when you call openInputStream. Calling openInputStream will call the FlickrPhotoProvider's open-File method. If no exception is thrown, lines 13 and 14 execute, creating a bitmap and displaying that bitmap in an ImageView.

If an exception is thrown, you register a content observer called PhotoContentObserver to watch the specified URI for changes.

Using a ContentObserver When Content Changes

Listing 14.13 defines a class called PhotoContentObserver of type ContentObserver. The purpose of this class is to perform an action when the content being observed changes. In this case, the content being observed is the file you are trying to use.

LISTING 14.13 **ContentObserver Defined in ImageViewFragment**

```
 1:  class PhotoContentObserver extends ContentObserver {
 2:     public PhotoContentObserver(Handler handler) {
 3:       super(handler);
 4:     }
 5:     @Override
 6:     public void onChange(boolean selfChange) {
 7:       InputStream is;
 8:       try {
 9:         if (ImageViewFragment.this.isAdded()){
10:           is = getActivity().getContentResolver().openInputStream
11:               Uri.withAppendedPath(FlickrPhotoProvider.CONTENT_URI ,mPhotoId));
12:           mBitmap =  BitmapFactory.decodeStream(is);
```

```
13:            mImageView.setImageBitmap(mBitmap);
14:        }
15:      } catch (FileNotFoundException e) {
16:      }
17:    }
18: }
```

The `PhotoContentObserver` is notified when a new file is created. Line 21 of Listing 14.11 sends that notification. When that occurs, the `onChange()` method of the `ContentObserver` is called. Line 9 of Listing 14.13 checks to see whether the fragment is still attached to the activity.

This possibility exists that the notification of file availability will occur at a point when the `ImageViewFragment` is no longer in the current activity. In that case, a call to `getActivity()` returns `null`. This check prevents that issue. Lines 10 to 12 get the `InputStream` for the file, create a `Bitmap`, and display it.

You have now created and used a content provider for both data retrieval for a `Cursor` representing a database and to get an image represented by a file.

Summary

In this hour, you created your own content provider by implementing `insert()`, `query()`, `update()`, and `delete()` methods. You saw how to use a `UriMatcher` to examine a URI and direct you to an action. After the `FlickrPhotoProvider` was in place, you used it in the app for both data and file retrieval.

Q&A

Q. What kinds of content can be returned from a content provider?

A. A content provider can return data from a database in a `Cursor`, and it can return a file via the `openFile()` method.

Q. How do content providers use URIs?

A. In content providers, URIs are used to identify the data to return. In this hour, you used URIs to get data for a single item, results from a query, and an input stream.

Q. What is the purpose of a read-only content provider?

A. Content providers must include `insert()`, `update()`, and `delete()` methods, but those methods are not required to change the underlying data. The purpose of a read-only content provider is to make data from an app available to third-party apps, but to restrict those apps from changing the underlying data.

Workshop

Quiz

1. What method is used to call a content provider's query method from an app?

2. What is a `ContentObserver`?

3. What method is called from an app to trigger a call to a content provider's `openFile` method?

Answers

1. An activity contains a `managedQuery` method for this purpose.

2. A `ContentObserver` is a class that responds to changes in a given URI. When the URI changes, the `onChange` method of the `ContentObserver` fires.

3. A call to `openInputStream` does this:

getActivity().getContentResolver().openInputStream

Exercises

1. The example in this hour retrieves a list of photos. Change the `PhotoListFragment` to retrieve a list of favorite images. Continue to display the titles, but sort the results by putting the titles in alphabetical order. Optionally, create a new URI for retrieving the list of favorites. To do that, you need to extend the content provider infrastructure by defining a new URI and using the `UriMatcher`. To test this, you must set some images as favorites.

2. Create a `GridView` of image titles using the content provider created in this hour. Note that you will be doing this in Hour 15.

Loaders, CursorLoaders, and CustomAdapters

What You'll Learn in This Hour:

▶ Learning how loaders work

▶ Seeing what loader classes are available

▶ Initializing, creating, and resetting a loader

▶ Incorporating loaders into the Flickr photo app

▶ Creating a `CustomAdapter`

In Hour 14, "Creating a Content Provider," you created your own `ContentProvider`. `FlickrPhotoProvider` provides content about Flickr photos and returns an image file when requested. One reason to develop your own `ContentProvider` is to take advantage of how well `ContentProviders` work with `CursorLoaders`. In this hour, you change the app to take advantage of a `CursorLoader(android.content.CursorLoader)`. `CursorLoaders` are an implementation of the `Loader(android.content.Loader)` class.

How Loaders Work

Loaders were introduced in Android 3.0. They are also available in the support library. Loaders help to asynchronously load data in a fragment or activity, something you have been working on since Hour 12. So far, the book has covered downloading data, writing to a SQLite database, and creating a content provider. You'll use all that work to create and use a `CursorLoader` in your `FlickrPhotoListFragment`.

Loaders provide the functionality of a `ContentObserver` by monitoring the source of their data and providing updates when the data changes. Much of the work that is commonly done in a data-driven app is done in a streamlined way using loaders.

Loaders retain their data after being stopped. That means that if an activity or fragment that uses a loader is stopped, the data in the loader is retained. When the fragment starts again, the data is available and the fragment does not need to wait for the data to reload.

Loader Classes

When implementing loaders, you'll use a number of classes and interfaces:

▶ Loader—A Loader is an abstract class to asynchronously load data.

▶ AsyncTaskLoader—An AsyncTaskLoader is an abstract class that is a subclass of Loader. It uses an AsyncTask to do the work of loading data.

▶ CursorLoader—A CursorLoader is a subclass of AsyncTaskLoader. Typically, you'll use a CursorLoader when implementing a Loader. A CursorLoader queries a ContentResolver and returns a cursor that can be used in the activity or fragment. CursorLoaders and ContentProviders work well together.

▶ LoaderManager—A LoaderManager is associated with each activity or fragment. There is a single LoaderManager for each activity or fragment, but a LoaderManager can manage more than one loader.

▶ LoaderManagerCallbacks—LoaderManagerCallbacks is an interface for an activity or fragment to interact with the LoaderManager. A fragment will implement a LoaderCallbacks interface:

```
public class ImageViewFragment extends Fragment implements
LoaderCallbacks<Cursor>
```

To implement LoaderManagerCallbacks, you must use the methods onCreateLoader(), onLoadFinished(), and onLoaderReset().

You will use a CursorLoader in your app. The CursorLoader is your loader.

To manage the connection between the loader and a fragment or activity, you use the LoaderManager class. A LoaderManager includes the interface LoaderManager. LoaderCallbacks to communicate between the LoaderManager and the fragment or activity.

Understanding Loader States

You can use loaders in an activity or in a fragment. Loaders must be initialized. In an activity, a loader is initialized in the onCreate() method. In a fragment, a loader is initialized in the onActivityCreated() method. For the rest of the examples, assume that a fragment is using the loader.

After initialization, a loader is created if it does not already exist. If it does exist, it is used immediately. When data is available from a loader, the fragment is notified via the LoaderManager.Callback method onLoadFinished(). If initLoader() is called and data is available, onLoadFinished() is called immediately.

Initializing a Loader

A loader is initialized with a call to the `initLoader()` method of the `LoaderManager`. It looks like this:

```
getLoaderManager().initLoader(LOADER_ID, null, this);
```

The `getLoaderManager()` method returns the `LoaderManager` for the current fragment. `LOADER_ID` is a unique id integer value that identifies the loader. That is important if more than one loader exists. The id is used to distinguish which loader is being used in the `LoaderManager.Callback` method `onCreateLoader()`.

The second parameter is a `Bundle` for passing any optional parameters to the loader constructor. In this case, that parameter is `null`.

The last parameter is a class that implements `LoaderManager.Callbacks`. Because you will be implementing `LoaderManager.Callbacks` in your fragment, you use `this` to reference your fragment.

Creating a Loader

When the `initLoader()` method is called, if the loader does not exist, a call to the `LoaderManager.Callback`'s on `CreateLoader()` method is called. The loader is created using this method.

When creating a `CursorLoader`, you use the parameters of a query on a `ContentProvider`. Specifically, as you saw in Hour 14, the query requires a `uri`, `projection`, `selection`, `selectionArgs`, and `sortOrder`. The `CursorLoader` is created using these parameters and is returned in `onCreateLoader()`.

Taking Action When Data Is Available

The `LoaderManager.Callback` method `onLoadFinished()` is called when data is available. In the case of `CursorLoader` implementation, the `onLoadFinished()` method is passed a `Cursor` to use.

When working with a `CursorAdapter`, you use the `onLoadFinished()` method to swap in new data with a call to the adapter's `swapCursor()` method.

Figure 15.1 shows a simplified version of these relationships.

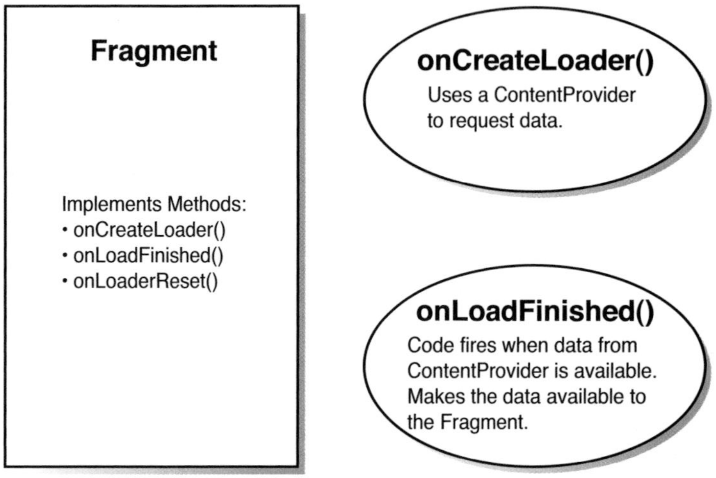

FIGURE 15.1
Relationship of a fragment to `LoaderManagerCallback` methods

Resetting a Loader

When the application determines that the loader no longer has any associated data, the `onLoaderReset()` method fires. This is an opportunity to remove any references to the data.

With a `CursorLoader`, this is the point where the cursor associated with the loader is about to be closed. If more than one cursor is associated with the loader, the `onLoaderReset()` method fires when the last cursor is about to be closed.

When you're using a `CursorAdapter` with a `CursorLoader`, this is the opportunity to reset the cursor to `null` with a call to the adapter's `swapCursor()` method:

```
MyAdapter.swapCursor(null);
```

Using a CursorLoader with a CursorAdapter

Using a `CursorLoader` with a `CursorAdapter` is powerful. The `CursorAdapter` uses the data from the loader to show the data. The `CursorLoader` keeps the data up to date. As the data changes, the display changes.

In Listings 15.1–15.5, examine the updated `PhotoListFragment` and learn how `CursorLoaders` are used.

Listing 15.1 lists the required import statements; the class is defined on lines 9 and 10. The `PhotoListFragment` extends `Fragment` and implements `LoaderCallbacks`.

Line 11 defines a `SimpleCursorAdapter` named `mAdapter`. You initialize this cursor adapter by setting the cursor value to `null`. When data is available in a new cursor, you update `mAdapter`.

LISTING 15.1   PhotoListFragment Definition

```
1:   package com.bffmedia.hour15app;
2:   import android.app.ListFragment;
3:   import android.app.LoaderManager.LoaderCallbacks;
4:   import android.content.CursorLoader;
5:   import android.content.Loader;
6:   import android.database.Cursor;
7:   import android.os.Bundle;
8:   import android.widget.SimpleCursorAdapter;
9:   public class PhotoListFragment extends ListFragment implements
10:             LoaderCallbacks<Cursor>     {
11:   SimpleCursorAdapter mAdapter;
```

Listing 15.2 shows the `onActivityCreated()` method. Line 4 shows the `initLoader()` method. The id of this loader is 0. The second parameter is `null`. That is where a bundle could be used to pass data when creating the loader.

Lines 5–9 define the `SimpleCursorAdapter mAdapter`. Note that on line 7, the cursor for the adapter is set to `null`. When data is available, this will be updated.

LISTING 15.2   PhotoListFragment onActivityCreated() Method

```
1:   @Override
2:   public void onActivityCreated(Bundle savedInstanceState) {
3:       super.onActivityCreated(savedInstanceState);
4:       getLoaderManager().initLoader(0, null, this);
5:       mAdapter = new SimpleCursorAdapter(getActivity(),
6:               android.R.layout.simple_list_item_1,
7:               null, //cursor
8:               new String[] {"title"},
9:               new int[] { android.R.id.text1 }, 0);
10:      setListAdapter(mAdapter);
11: }
```

Listing 15.3 shows the `onCreateLoader()` method. In line 2, the `id` of the loader is passed along with a bundle. These values were set with the call to `initLoader()` in Listing 15.2 on line 4. Because you use only one loader, the id is not important and a bundle is not passed. Lines 3 and 4 define a new `CursorLoader` based on querying the `ContentProvider` `FlickrPhotoProvider`. The new `CursorLoader` is returned.

LISTING 15.3 PhotoListFragment onCreateLoader() Method

```
1:  @Override
2:  public Loader<Cursor> onCreateLoader(int id, Bundle args) {
3:      CursorLoader cursorLoader = new CursorLoader(getActivity(),
4:      FlickrPhotoProvider.CONTENT_URI, null, null, null, null);
5:      return cursorLoader;
6:  }
```

Listing 15.4 shows the onLoadFinished() method. The cursor that is passed to this method is used to update the adapter with a call to swapCursor(). At this point, the data is available in the cursor and is available for display in by setting the adapter. Recall that the originally set value for cursor in the adapter was null. See line 7 of Listing 15.2.

LISTING 15.4 PhotoListFragment onLoadFinished() Method

```
1:  @ @Override
2:  public void onLoadFinished(Loader<Cursor> loader, Cursor cursor) {
3:          mAdapter.swapCursor(cursor);
4:  }
```

When the loader has no associated data, the onLoaderReset() method is called. Listing 15.5 shows this method. On line 3, a call is made to swapCursor() with null as the parameter.

LISTING 15.5 PhotoListFragment onLoaderReset() Method

```
1:  @Override
2:  public void onLoaderReset(Loader<Cursor> loader) {
3:          mAdapter.swapCursor(null);
4:  }
```

Listings 15.1–15.5 comprise all the code in the PhotoListFragment. The process to use a CursorLoader to provide data is as follows:

1. Initialize the loader.

2. Create the loader by querying the content provider.

3. Use the data on the fragment when the loader finished.

Figure 15.2 shows a simplified diagram of how a fragment uses a CursorLoader and CursorAdapter.

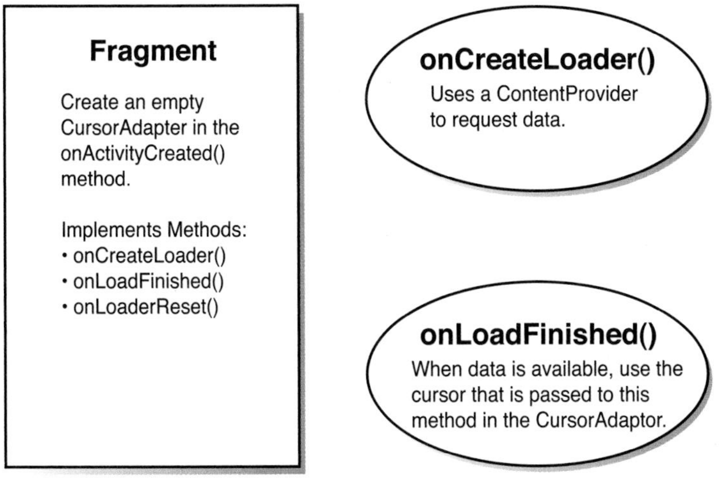

FIGURE 15.2
Fragment using a `CursorLoader` and `CursorAdapter`

Using a similar technique as creating a `PhotoListFragment`, you can create a fragment that displays data in a `GridView`. By creating a `GridView` layout as you did in Hour 10, you can populate a new `PhotoGridFragment` with code that is nearly identical to the `PhotoListFragment` code.

To create the `PhotoGridFragment`, you must create a layout, implement the `onCreateView()` method in the fragment, and set the adapter on the new `GridView`.

Listing 15.6 shows the definition and `onActivityCreated()` method for the new class called `PhotoGridFragment`. Listing 15.6 is nearly identical to Listing 15.2 except a `GridView` is used.

LISTING 15.6 PhotoGridFragment onActivityCreated()

```
1:  public class PhotoGridFragment extends Fragment implements
LoaderCallbacks<Cursor>    {
2:  GridView mGrid;
3:  SimpleCursorAdapter mAdapter;
4:  @Override
5:  public void onActivityCreated(Bundle savedInstanceState) {
6:  super.onActivityCreated(savedInstanceState);
7:  getLoaderManager().initLoader(0, null, this);
8:  mAdapter = new SimpleCursorAdapter(getActivity(),
9:  android.R.layout.simple_list_item_1,
10:  null,
11:  new String[] {"title"},
12:  new int[] { android.R.id.text1 }, 0);
13:  mGrid.setAdapter(mAdapter);
14:  }
```

Listing 15.7 shows the `onCreateView()` method for the `PhotoGridFragment`.

The `CursorLoader` methods `onCreateLoader()`, `onLoadFinished()`, and `onLoader-Reset()` for the `PhotoGridFragment` are identical to those in the `PhotoListFragment` in Listings 15.3–15.5.

LISTING 15.7   PhotoGridFragment onCreateView()

```
1:  public View onCreateView(LayoutInflater inflater, ViewGroup container,
2:               Bundle savedInstanceState) {
3:    mGrid = (GridView) inflater.inflate(R.layout.grid_fragment, container,
false);
4:    return mGrid;
5:  }
```

Using your knowledge of the action bar, you can use two tabs in the example app: one to show the `PhotoListFragment` and the other to show the `PhotoGridFragment`. Figure 15.3 shows the two views side by side.

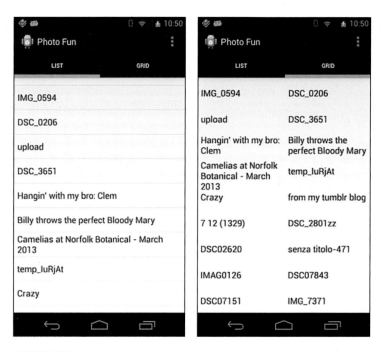

FIGURE 15.3
`PhotoListFragment` and `PhotoGridFragment`

Creating Custom Adapters

You have used `SimpleCursorAdapters` in this hour. In Hour 10, you used an `ArrayAdapter` to create fragments that displayed data in lists, grids, and galleries. To create robust apps, custom adapters are often used.

The following sections show you how to create a simple custom adapter, by extending the `BaseAdapter` to perform the same function as the `ArrayAdapter`. In the next hour, you will create a custom cursor adapter to use in the Flickr photo app.

Using BaseAdapter

To use a `BaseAdapter(android.widget.BaseAdapter)`, you must implement four methods: `getCount()`, `getItem()`, `getItemId()`, and `getView()`. With a `BaseAdapter`, you work with a set of items. In the case of the simple `PieAdapter`, the set is a string array with the names of pies. The `getCount()` method provides the number of items. The other methods work with a single item to provide the item, the item id, and a view for the item. By creating the view you desire, you can customize how the item displays.

Listing 15.8 is a simple version of a `BaseAdapter` that illustrates these methods.

The `Hour15AppCustomAdapter` project contains the source code that accompanies this hour. The custom adapter work is done in SimpleListFragment.java.

LISTING 15.8   Extending BaseAdapter

```
 1:   public class PieAdapter extends BaseAdapter {
 2:       Context mContext;
 3:       String mPies[];
 4:       LayoutInflater mInflater;
 5:       public PieAdapter(Context c, String[] pies) {
 6:           mContext = c;
 7:           mPies = pies;
 8:           mInflater = (LayoutInflater) mContext.getSystemService
 9:                                   (Context.LAYOUT_INFLATER_SERVICE);
10:       }
11:       public int getCount() {
12:            return  mPies.length;
13:       }
14:       public Object getItem(int position) {
15:            return mPies[position];
16:       }
17:       public long getItemId(int position) {
18:            return position;
19:       }
20:       public View getView(int position, View convertView, ViewGroup parent) {
21:         View view = mInflater.inflate(R.layout.list_item, null);
22:         TextView textView = (TextView) view.findViewById(R.id.pieTextView);
23:         textView.setText(mPies[position]);
```

```
24:        return view;
25:     }
26:  }
```

The `PieAdapter` in Listing 16.1 uses a string array as the set of items. The `getCount()` method of line 11 uses the length of the array to determine the number of available items. The `getItem()` and `getItemId()` methods are both passed the position in the list that can be used. For `getItem()`, `position` is used to get the item in that position in the array. For `getItemId()`, `position` itself is used as the id.

In the `getView()` method on lines 20 and 21, a `View` is inflated with the layout defined by `R.id.list_item`. That XML layout contains a `RelativeLayout` that holds a `TextView` with the id `pieTextView`. On line 22, you use `findViewById()` to get the `TextView`, and on line 23, you set the text of the `TextView` with the string value from the `mPies` array. The `Viewview` is returned.

To use the `PieAdapter` in the `onActivityCreated()` method in a `ListFragment`, you would instantiate the `PieAdapter` and set the list adapter as follows:

```
PieAdapter adapter = new PieAdapter(getActivity(), mPies);
setListAdapter(adapter);
```

Figure 15.4 shows the `list_item.xml` layout in the visual editor in Eclipse. The `TextView` uses large, bold, blue text. Figure 15.5 shows the resulting app with the names of the pies shown in a list.

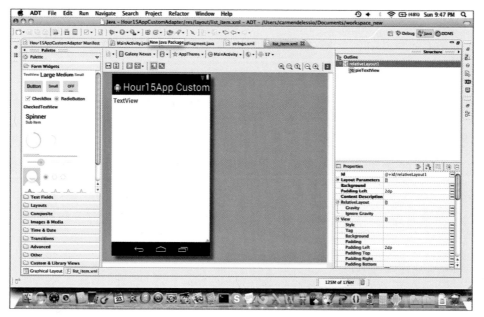

FIGURE 15.4
Layout for a single item

FIGURE 15.5
Displaying pies via the `PieAdapter`

Introducing the View Holder Pattern

Implementing a `BaseAdapter` like the `PieAdapter` of Listing 15.8 is fairly straightforward. You have a set of items and the `BaseAdapter` is the mechanism for tying the data in those items to a particular view.

There is a way to make a `BaseAdapter` more efficient. You can implement the view holder pattern with the `PieAdapter`. Doing so can also help you understand how Android deals with views when they are used in a list.

Android reuses views that have been shown in the list. In line 20 of Listing 15.8, the `getView()` method is passed a `View` named `convertView`. If `convertView` is not `null`, then it is being reused. You can use it directly. The expensive operations in Android are creating a new `View` and finding the view by id. Avoiding those operations can make your adapter more efficient. The pattern to implement this technique is known as the *view holder pattern*.

Listing 15.9 shows the changes to the `getView()` method to implement the view holder pattern.

Lines 15–17 define a new class called `ViewHolder` that contains a field of type `TextView`. To avoid inflating views, you can reuse the `ViewHolder` class.

The logic for reuse begins on line 3. Remember that `convertView` may be `null` or it may contain a `View` that can be reused. Line 3 checks to see whether it is `null`.

If `convertView` is `null`, you need to create a new `View`. Line 4 creates a new `View` by inflating the XML layout. The inflated `View` is assigned to `convertView`. On line 5, you create a new `ViewHolder`, and on line 6, you use `findViewById()` to assign the `textView` field within `viewHolder`.

Line 7 takes the `View convertView` and associates it to the `viewHolder` via the `setTag()` method. Using `setTag()` is powerful. It allows you to associate any object with a view. In this case, the `View convertView` uses `setTag()` to create a reference to `viewHolder` and hence the `textView` field with `viewHolder`.

Continuing this case where `convertView` is `null`, after setting the tag on line 7, the text value for `textView` is set on line 11 and the `convertView` is returned on line 12.

If the `getView()` method runs and `convertView` is not `null`, then the embedded `ViewHolder` object is retrieving using a call to `getTag()` on line 9. The retrieved `viewHolder` that was previously attached to the `View` with `setTag()`. Because you have a `ViewHolder` object, you have a `TextView` that you can use. Lines 11 and 12 perform the same functions whether the `viewHolder` was just created or retrieved from the `convertView`.

LISTING 15.9   Using the View Holder Pattern

```
1:     public View getView(int position, View convertView, ViewGroup parent) {
2:        ViewHolder viewHolder;
3:        if (convertView == null) {
4:           convertView = mInflater.inflate(R.layout.list_item, null);
5:           viewHolder = new ViewHolder();
6:           viewHolder.textView = (TextView) convertView.findViewById(R.
id.pieTextView);
7:           convertView.setTag(viewHolder);
8:        } else {
9:           viewHolder = (ViewHolder) convertView.getTag();
10:       }
11:       viewHolder.textView.setText(mPies[position]);
12:       return convertView;
13:       }
14:    }
15:
16:    private static class ViewHolder {
17:        public TextView textView;
18:       }
```

Introducing Custom Cursor Adapters

A `CursorAdapter` uses data from a `Cursor` to populate a `View`. You have used a `SimpleCursorAdapter` to show data from a `Cursor` in both a grid and a list. See Listing 15.2 for an example.

To create a custom `CursorAdapter`, you must implement two methods: `newView()` and `bindView()`. In the `newView()` method, a new view is defined and returned. In the `bindView()` method, the data from `cursor` is used in the `View`.

Hour 16 covers this topic in detail.

GO TO ▶ **HOUR 16, "DEVELOPING A COMPLETE APP,"** to see how to create and use a custom cursor adapter.

Summary

This hour covered loaders at a conceptual level, and you implemented two examples using a `CursorLoader`. To accomplish this, you used the `FlickrPhotoProvider` content provider that you developed in Hour 14. You saw how a `CursorLoader` and `CursorAdapter` can work together in fragments that implemented `LoaderManager.LoaderCallbacks`. You also created a custom adapter by extending `BaseAdapter`.

Q&A

Q. How do `onCreateLoader()` **and** `onLoadFinished()` **work together?**

A. The `onCreateLoader()` method requests data using a content provider and returns a `CursorLoader`. The `onLoadFinished()` method fires when the data from the content provider is available, so the `onCreateLoader()` creates the `CursorLoader` and the `onLoadFinished()` uses the data.

Q. What is the advantage of using a `CursorAdapter` **with loaders?**

A. A `CursorAdapter` maps data from a cursor to the user interface. Because `onLoadFinished()` returns a cursor, you can use a `CursorAdapter` in the `onLoadFinished()` method to display the data that is available from the loader. The `CursorAdapter` is created in the `onActivityCreated()` method, and in the `onLoadFinished()` method, a new `Cursor` is swapped in.

Q. What is the relationship between an `AsyncTaskLoader` **and a** `CursorLoader`**?**

A. A `CursorLoader` is a subclass of `AsyncTaskLoader`. `AsyncTaskLoader` is a subclass of `Loader`.

Q. Can loaders be used on Android 2.x devices?

A. Loaders were introduced in Android 3.0 (HoneyComb), but they are available via the support library for older versions of Android.

Workshop

Quiz

1. What methods would typically call an adapter's `swapCursor()` method?

2. What method fires when data is available?

3. What is the first parameter of the `initLoader()` method and why is it important?

Answers

1. The `onLoadFinished()` and `onLoaderReset()` methods use `swapCursor`.

2. `onLoadFinished()` fires when data is available.

3. The first parameter to `initLoader()` is an id. It is important because it identifies the loader if more than one loader exists in the fragment or activity. It is passed to the `LoaderManager.Callbacks` methods.

Exercise

Implement a gallery view to show titles. Base it on the `PhotoGridFragment` class. Review Hour 10 for the implementation of a fragment that displays data in a gallery view. The exercise requires implementing a `CursorLoader` with a fragment that uses a gallery.

HOUR 16
Developing a Complete App

What You'll Learn in This Hour:

▶ Determining app functionality
▶ Planning the app
▶ Developing the app
▶ Creating a custom adapter
▶ Loading images in a list

This book covers many aspects of developing an Android app. In the past four hours, you learned about retrieving remote data, using `ContentProviders`, `Cursors`, and `CursorLoaders`. In this hour, you create a complete app that takes advantage of these features. You'll continue to use the Flickr photo app in this hour. To create a full and robust app, you learn to create a custom `CursorAdapter` for displaying items in a list and grid. You also learn how to efficiently load remote images into a list or grid.

Determining App Functionality

One design concept in regard to creating an app is that it should do one thing and do it well.

For this hour, you must first decide what the app will do. Deciding what the app does and what features to keep in and which features to take out might be the most important decisions made in any app project.

Starting with Flickr Photos

You've worked with Flickr photos in an earlier hour, so that is a good place to start. You know how to get a set of recently posted photos and how to save and display these photos. You also know how to store and retrieve data about these photos. You can apply this knowledge to incorporating various features in a potential app.

For an app that shows lots of publicly available Flickr photos, enabling the user of the app to designate some photos as favorites seems like a reasonable idea. Favorite photos would be easy to retrieve and view.

At some point, users would probably want to get rid of photos that they don't care about, so you need a way to delete all photos that are not favorites.

The goal is to make a simple, yet complete and functional app. The Hour16App project contains the source code that accompanies this hour.

An inventory of the proposed functionality for the app would include the following:

▶ Display recent photos from Flickr

▶ Pick some photos as favorites

▶ View favorite photos

▶ Delete non-favorites

You know how to do most of these things. To make a complete app, you must address creating custom cursor adapters and consider how to display many images in a list.

Consider giving the user choices on how to display the data. You can offer a `ListView` and a `GridView`. You must decide on navigation. How will the user indicate that he or she wants to see favorite photos? How do you show an individual photo? Does a dialog window make sense? How should you indicate a favorite?

This chapter helps you consider your app's functionality and shows how to create a simple wireframe for the app as well as discusses what decisions make can help keep the app simple. One of the goals is to make an application that you can use as a starting point for your own apps.

Creating a Wireframe for the App

Figures 16.1 and 16.2 show four simple wireframe diagrams used to describe the app. Wireframes help when considering the layout and data required for an app.

Figure 16.1 shows the app displaying a list of images and an action bar with two tabs and an overflow menu indicator. The second image in Figure 16.1 shows the overflow menu expanded with the choices to "Show as List," "Show as Grid," and "Delete non-favorites."

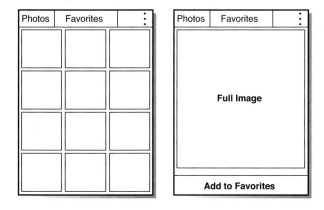

FIGURE 16.1
App list view and menu

Figure 16.2 shows the app with images displayed in a grid. The second image in Figure 16.2 shows a single image being displayed. It also shows an option to "Add to Favorites."

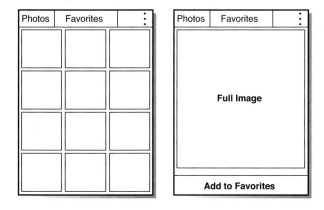

FIGURE 16.2
App grid and detail view

These simple wireframes can help you plan the app and take inventory of what is required for implementation. You have already created a FlickrPhoto object and included a field to indicate that a photo was a favorite. You know how to retrieve and save FlickrPhoto data. As you begin to turn what you've learned into an app, the wireframe will help with planning.

NOTE

Great Design Resources

The Android developer site includes a design section at http://developer.android.com/design/index.html. You can find an active professional Android designer group on Google+ at https://plus.google.com/communities/113499773637471211070. The blog for the company opoloo is amazing. In particular, check out the raw material and process for designing a complete app found in this post: http://blog.opoloo.com/articles/redesigning-the-topgear-app.

Planning the App: Taking Inventory

The wireframes are helpful in determining the visual and layout needs for the app. With them, you can see that you need to create the following:

▶ ActionBar with two tabs and an overflow menu

▶ Overflow menu on action bar with three choices

▶ Activity, for swapping in fragments

▶ List fragment to show photos and titles

▶ Grid fragment to show photos in a grid

▶ Detail fragment to show a single photo

You can leverage your work from previous hours by using a:

▶ `FlickrPhoto` object to describe Flickr photo data

▶ `DatabaseAdapter`, the database for Flickr photos

▶ `ContentProvider` to provide the ability to get photo data and images for use in the app

You need several more things to create this app. So far in this book, you have used `SimpleCursorAdapters` to display data in lists or grids. For this app, you must develop two simple custom cursor adapters, one for the list and one for the grid. The list shows the title and the image. The grid shows just the image.

To create a custom cursor adapter, you tie the `FlickrPhoto` data from the app to a specific layout that you create; in this case, two layouts to go with the two adapters. So, to complete the app inventory, you need a:

▶ List adapter to tie the FlickrPhoto title and image to the layout

▶ List item layout for showing one FlickrPhoto in a list

▶ Grid adapter to tie the FlickrPhoto image to the layout

▶ Grid item layout for showing one FlickrPhoto in a grid

Developing the App

A key part of the app is how the data for a `FlickrPhoto` object appears in the list, so you need to continue with the development of the `ListCursorAdapter`. For example, you must create the navigation including the action bar, handle showing all photos and just favorites, create a detail page to show one photo and make it a favorite, and delete all non-favorite photos.

Using a Custom CursorAdapter

To create a custom `CursorAdapter`, you implement the `newView()` and `bindView()` methods. The `newView()` method defines and returns a new `View`. In the `bindView()` method, the data from cursor is used in the `View`.

The app will display `FlickrPhoto` data, so you use the `Cursors` and `CursorLoaders` as you did in Hour 15.

Listing 16.1 shows the `newView()` method for the `ListCursorAdapter` class that you will create and use in this app. Line 3 creates a `LayoutInflater`. Line 5 uses the `LayoutInflater` to inflate a layout from the XML layout file `R.layout.list_item`. That layout file contains a `RelativeLayout` with an `ImageView` and a `TextView`. The view holder concept (see the next section) is in use here. Each time the `newView()` method is called, a `ListViewHolder` class is instantiated to hold the `ImageView` and `TextView` that the layout contains. You tie the `ListViewHolder` to the view using `setTag()`.

LISTING 16.1   CursorAdapter newView()

```
 1:  @Override
 2:  public View newView(Context context, Cursor cursor, ViewGroup parent) {
 3:      LayoutInflater li = (LayoutInflater) mContext.getSystemService(
 4:                          Context.LAYOUT_INFLATER_SERVICE);
 5:      View v = li.inflate(R.layout.list_item, parent, false);
 6:      ListViewHolder viewHolder = new ListViewHolder();
 7:      viewHolder.photoImageView =  (ImageView) v.findViewById(R.
id.photoImageView);
 8:      viewHolder.titleTextView = (TextView) v.findViewById(R.id.titleTextView);
 9:      v.setTag(viewHolder);
10:      return (v);
11:  }
```

To complete this `CursorAdapter`, you must implement the `bindView()` method.

Implementing BindView for ListCursorAdapter

The basics of using the `bindView()` method are fairly straightforward—you tie the data from a cursor with a view to display.

Efficiently displaying images can be a challenge. In the `ListCursorAdapter`, you show an image for each `FlickrPhoto`. You must consider how to do it without hindering performance. A particular challenge when retrieving data in the background is tying the retrieved image to a particular `ImageView` in the list. This process is sometimes called *lazy loading*.

If a user flings the list, then updating individual list items does not make sense. Updating items that are not in view can be a painfully slow experience for the user. In the `bindView()`, you will not update items if the user flings the list. The occurrence of the fling is determined by a gesture that occurs on the `ListView` or `GridView`.

Basic Implementation of bindView()

The basic implementation of `bindView()` is simple. The `bindView()` method is passed a `View`, a `Context`, and a `Cursor`. You use data from the `Cursor` to populate the `View`:

```
public void bindView(View v, Context context, Cursor c) {
```

You can use the method `getPhotoFromCursor()` to get a `FlickrPhoto` object from the passed `Cursor`:

```
FlickrPhoto currentPhoto = FlickrPhotoDbAdapter.getPhotoFromCursor(c);
```

The `View` that is created in the `newView()` method is passed. In this case, the `View` is a `RelativeLayout` that includes a `TextView` and an `ImageView`. So, you could use that view to display the title for `currentPhoto`:

```
TextView titleTextView = (TextView) v.findViewById(R.id.titleTextView);
titleTextView.setText(currentPhoto.title);
```

Full Implementation of bindView()

The full implementation of `bindView()` contains references to flinging the list and to lazy-loading images. The `bindView()` method is the core functionality that ties cursor data to the `View`. After you see how that is done, you learn how to address performance and image loading.

Listing 16.2 shows the entire `bindView()` method. Because a `ListViewHolder` is added as a tag to the `View` in the `newView()` method, you know that you can retrieve that `ListViewHolder` using `getTag()`, which occurs in line 3.

LISTING 16.2   CursorAdapter bindView() BaseAdapter

```
1:  @Override
2:  public void bindView(View v, Context context, Cursor c) {
3:  ListViewHolder vh = (ListViewHolder) v.getTag();
4:  FlickrPhoto currentPhoto = FlickrPhotoDbAdapter.getPhotoFromCursor(c);
5:  vh.titleTextView.setText(currentPhoto.title);
6:  if (!flinging){
7:  vh.photoImageView.setImageResource(R.drawable.imageholder);
8:  vh.id = currentPhoto.id;
9:  v.setTag(vh);
10: vh.photoImageView.setTag(currentPhoto.id);
11: LoadBitmapTask task = new LoadBitmapTask(mContext, mViewGroup, currentPhoto);
12: task.execute();
13: }else{
14: vh.photoImageView.setImageResource(R.drawable.imageholder);
15: }
16: }
```

A cursor is available, and it is used in line 4 to obtain a `FlickrPhoto` object that you can use in the `View`. On line 5, you set the title of the photo.

Line 6 makes a check to see whether the user is flinging the list where the data is being presented. You see how to detect that next, but for now you want to know what to do when the list is being flung and when it is not. If it is not, you populate the `ImageView` on the list page with a resource called `R.drawable.imageholder`, a placeholder image that contains a light gray square. When the user is flinging the list, you do not want to display anything and, more importantly, you do not want to grab a remote image for a view that is not in the current display. Getting images for views that are not displayed can be painfully slow for the user, who is looking at his or her phone waiting for image 250 to appear, and the app is downloading images 40 through 250. The better idea is to jump to image 250, retrieve it, and display it.

Lines 7–12 show what happens in the case where the list is not being flung: The `ImageView` is temporarily set to the placeholder image.

Lines 8–10 do several things. The `ListViewHolder` contains data as well as `Views`. On line 8, you set the id value of the `ListViewHolder` to the id of the `currentPhoto`, which enables you to associate a view in the list with a particular `FlickrPhoto` object. You can take advantage of the fact that you have the `FlickrPhoto` object when someone clicks on the view. The data from the object is immediately available to act on.

Line 10 associates the id of the photo with the `ImageView`. You use that information when lazy-loading to display an image in the `ImageView`.

Lines 11 and 12 kick off an `AsyncTask` that retrieves and displays the image.

Later, this hour looks at loading images in more detail. Images should be cached for efficiency. You'll use the simple technique of caching to disk. More complex techniques can be used to improve efficiency.

TIP

Consider Picasso

Picasso is an open source library from the company Square. Picasso makes loading images easy. In Hour 23, you use Picasso to load images in an app that uses a number of open source projects. To learn more about Picasso, see http://square.github.io/picasso/.

Detecting Flinging

In Listing 16.2, a check of the variable `flinging` determines what to display. You set the variable with a getter and setter in the `ListCursorAdapter` class:

```
public Boolean getFlinging() {
  return flinging;
}
public void setFlinging(Boolean flinging) {
  this.flinging = flinging;
}
```

The state of flinging is detected in the `ListFragment`. Both `ListView` and a `GridView` have a method called `setOnScrollListener()`. By using an `onScrollListener`, you can detect the states of the `ListView` including whether flinging is occurring.

Listing 16.3 shows how to use the `OnScrollListener` within a `ListFragment`. Scrolling is associated with the `ListView` within the `ListFragment`, so on line 1, you get the `ListView` using `getListView()`. The method `setOnScrollListener()` is called.

When creating an `OnScrollListener()`, you must implement two methods. The `OnScroll()` method and `onScrollStateChanged()` methods are required. The work to detect flinging is contained in the `onScrollStateChanged()` method.

The parameter `scrollState` indicates the status of scrolling. The three possible states indicated by constants in the `OnScrollListener` class are the following:

▶ SCROLL_STATE_IDLE: The view is not scrolling.

▶ SCROLL_STATE_TOUCH_SCROLL: The user is touching the screen to scroll.

▶ SCROLL_STATE_FLING: The user has performed a fling.

The logic for detecting flinging and setting the value for flinging in the `ListCursorAdapter` is to set flinging to `true` when the state is `SCROLL_STATE_FLING`. When the state is `SCROLL_STATE_IDLE`, you make a check to see whether flinging is `true`. If it is, then the `View` was flinging and has now come to a stop. That is when you set flinging to `false`. You also tell the adapter to update the `ListView` by calling `notifyDataSetChanged()`.

Listing 16.3 shows the fling status set in lines 19–22. Lines 9–15 handle the idle status.

LISTING 16.3 Detecting Flinging in a ListFragment

```
1:   getListView().setOnScrollListener(new OnScrollListener() {
2:   @Override
3:   public void onScroll(AbsListView view, int firstVisibleItem,
4:                        int visibleItemCount, int totalItemCount) {
5:   }
6:   @Override
7:   public void onScrollStateChanged(AbsListView view, int scrollState) {
8:     switch (scrollState) {
9:       case OnScrollListener.SCROLL_STATE_IDLE:
10:         if (mAdapter!=null){
11:           if (mAdapter.getFlinging()){
12:             mAdapter.setFlinging(false);
13:             mAdapter.notifyDataSetChanged();
14:           }
15:         }
16:       break;
17:       case OnScrollListener.SCROLL_STATE_TOUCH_SCROLL:
18:         break;
19:       case OnScrollListener.SCROLL_STATE_FLING:
20:         if (mAdapter!=null)
21:           mAdapter.setFlinging(true);
22:       break;
23:     }
24:   }
25:   });
```

Loading Images

You have seen the `bindView()` method in action and seen how to detect flinging in a `ListView`. The `bindView()` method also handles associating images with the `ImageView` in the item layout. This is done with a call to the `AsyncTask` `LoadBitmapTask`:

```
LoadBitmapTask task = new LoadBitmapTask(mContext, mViewGroup, currentPhoto);
task.execute();
```

Recall that you add the id of the `FlickrPhoto` as a tag to the `ImageView`. See line 10 of Listing 16.2:

```
vh.photoImageView.setTag(currentPhoto.id);
```

You use that tag within the `LoadBitmapTask` to ensure that the proper `ImageView` is updated.

Three parameters are passed to the `LoadBitmapTask`. They are the current context, the current `ViewGroup`, and the current `FlickrPhoto` object. The `ViewGroup`, in the case of the `ListCursorAdapter`, is the `ListView`.

The constructor for `ListCursorAdapter` is passed a `ViewGroup`:

```
public ListCursorAdapter(Context context, Cursor c, int flags, ViewGroup viewGroup)
{
  super(context, c, flags);
  mContext = context;
  mViewGroup = viewGroup;
}
```

The `ListView` associated with the `ListFragment` is passed to the `ListCursorAdapter` constructor as the `ViewGroup`:

```
mAdapter = new ListCursorAdapter(getActivity(), null,0, getListView());
```

So, you have the `ListView` as the `ViewGroup` and `ImageViews` within the `ListView` that are tagged with the id of the associated `FlickrPhoto`.

Using that information, you can find the `ImageView` within the `ListView` that is associated with a particular `FlickrPhoto` via the `findViewWithTag()` method:

```
ImageView imageViewByTag = (ImageView) mViewGroup.findViewWithTag(mPhoto.id);
```

Given the `FlickrPhoto` and the `ViewGroup`, the `LoadBitmapTask`:

▶ Retrieves the image for the photo in the `doInBackground()` method

▶ Displays the retrieved image in the `ImageView` in the on `PostExecute()` method

Listing 16.4 shows both the `doInBackground()` and `onPostExecute()` methods.

LISTING 16.4   Displaying a Retrieved Image in an ImageView

```
1:  // Decode image in background.
2:  @Override
3:  protected Object doInBackground(Object... params) {
4:  InputStream is;
5:  try {
6:  is =  mContext.getContentResolver().openInputStream(Uri.withAppendedPath
```

```
 7:  (FlickrPhotoProvider.CONTENT_URI ,mPhoto.id));
 8:  Bitmap bitmap =  BitmapFactory.decodeStream(is);
 9:  return(bitmap);
10:  } catch (FileNotFoundException e) {
11:  mContext.getContentResolver().registerContentObserver
12:  (Uri.withAppendedPath(FlickrPhotoProvider.CONTENT_URI ,mPhoto.id),
13:  false,
14:  new PhotoContentObserver(mContext, mViewGroup, mHandler, mPhoto.id));
15:  return null;
16:  }
17:  }
18:  @Override
19:  protected void onPostExecute(Object bitmap) {
20:  if ( bitmap != null) {
21:  ImageView imageViewByTag = (ImageView)
22:  mViewGroup.findViewWithTag(mPhoto.id);
23:  if (imageViewByTag != null) {
24:  imageViewByTag.setImageBitmap((Bitmap) bitmap);
25:  }
26:  }
27:  }
```

Handling onClick() for the ListFragment

Listing 16.2 shows the id of the `FlickrPhoto` tied to the current `View` by using the `setTag()` method. The variable `vh.id` is the `ViewHolder` id field and the variable `v` is the `View` to display within the list:

```
vh.id = currentPhoto.id;
v.setTag(vh);
```

By making this association in the `bindView()` method, you have access to the `ViewHolder` when someone clicks on an item in the `ListView`. You can retrieve the `ViewHolder` by using the `getTag()` method.

Listing 16.5 shows the `onListItemClick()` method. This method is passed the `View` that was clicked. That `View` contains a tag with a `ViewHolder` object. Using that `ViewHolder` object, you obtain the id of the `FlickrPhoto` associated with this `View`. That id is passed to the `ImageViewFragment` and is used to display the full image.

LISTING 16.5   Handling onListItemClick()

```
1:  @Override
2:  public void onListItemClick(ListView l, View v, int position, long id) {
3:      ListViewHolder vh = (ListViewHolder) v.getTag();
4:      ImageViewFragment flickrImageFragment = new ImageViewFragment();
```

```
5:    Bundle args = new Bundle();
6:    args.putString("PHOTO_ID", vh.id);
7:    flickrImageFragment.setArguments(args);
8:    FragmentTransaction ft = getActivity().getFragmentManager().
beginTransaction();
9:    ft.replace(R.id.layout_container, flickrImageFragment);
10:   ft.addToBackStack("Image");
11:   ft.commit();
12: }
```

Summarizing bindView()

The `bindView()` method of a `CursorAdapter` ties data from a cursor to a specific `View`. Serving as the hub between data and display, this method is tied to several other areas within the app. In the primary function of tying data to display, data is populated into a `View` that was created by inflating an item layout file. The data from the passed cursor is displayed in that `View`.

In the `bindView()` method, you associate the id of a photo with both an `ImageView` and the entire item view that will displayed within a `ListView`. The data for the `ImageView` is used to support the lazy-loading of images. The data for the item view is used to handle a click on the `View`.

The state of the `ListView` indicates whether to handle flinging within the `bindView()` method.

Creating the Photo and Favorite Photo Fragments

The wireframe diagram shown earlier in Figure 16.1 shows tabs for "Photos" and "Favorites" within the action bar for the app. You will create the action bar and add tabs in the `onCreate()` method of the activity. Listing 16.6 shows the tab definition. This creates the tabs in the action bar, as shown in Figure 16.3.

LISTING 16.6   ActionBar Tabs for Photos and Favorites

```
1:  @ActionBar actionBar = getActionBar();
2:  actionBar.setNavigationMode(ActionBar.NAVIGATION_MODE_TABS);
3:  mPhotosTab= actionBar.newTab().setText("Photos").setTabListener(new
NavTabListener());
4:  actionBar.addTab(mPhotosTab);
5:  mFavoritesTab= actionBar.newTab().setText("Favorites")
6:                              .setTabListener(new NavTabListener());
7:  actionBar.addTab(mFavoritesTab);
```

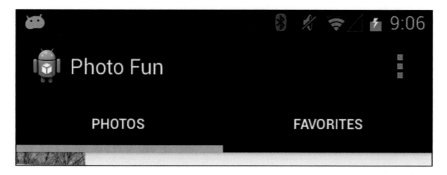

FIGURE 16.3
`ActionBar` tabs

You set up the navigation in the `NavTabListener` class.

How you display `FlickrPhotos` is identical whether the user displays all photos or just favorites. The difference is in the data to display. That means you can create a single `ListFragment` that displays either all photos or favorite photos based on a value passed in arguments to the fragment.

In this case, you can use a `Boolean` called `all` to pass to the `ListFragment`. When `all` is `true`, all photos display, and when `all` is `false`, only favorites display. In the activity, you can use a method called `showList()` to show the `ListFragment`. If the user selects the Photos tab, the call to `showList()` will be `showList(true)` to indicate to display all photos. Listing 16.7 contains the `showList()` method.

LISTING 16.7 Method to Show ListFragment with Arguments

```
1:  public void showList(Boolean all){
2:     Bundle args = new Bundle();
3:     if (all){
4:        args.putBoolean("ALL", true);
5:     }else{
6:        args.putBoolean("ALL", false);
7:     }
8:     PhotoListFragment photoListFragment = new PhotoListFragment();
9:     photoListFragment.setArguments(args);
10:    FragmentTransaction ft = getFragmentManager().beginTransaction();
11:    ft.replace(R.id.layout_container, photoListFragment);
12:    ft.setTransition(FragmentTransaction.TRANSIT_FRAGMENT_FADE);
13:    ft.commit();
14: }
```

As you can see from Listing 16.7, the `PhotoListFragment` will be passed a `Bundle` that contains a boolean variable indicating whether to show all photos or favorites.

The `PhotoListFragment` class implements `LoaderCallbacks` and uses `Cursors` and `Loaders` as you have done previously. Recall that both the `initLoader()` method and the `onCreateLoader()` method take a bundle as a parameter. In this case, you pass the bundle that was received by the fragment and that contains the boolean for whether to show all photos.

The `initLoader()` is passed the bundle:

```
Bundle b = this.getArguments();
getLoaderManager().initLoader(0, b, this);
```

Listing 16.8 shows the `onCreateLoader()` method that determines whether to show all photos or just favorites. Looking at lines 9–10 and lines 14–15, you can see that the only difference between showing all photos and favorites is how the `cursorLoader` is defined. By using the `FlickrPhotoProvider ContentProvider` in this way, you can display different data in an easy way. A clean separation exists between the data retrieval and the presentation. (This is a common concept of separating data access from the presentation of the data—Content Providers make that separation clear.)

LISTING 16.8   Showing All Photos or Favorites in onCreateLoader()

```
 1:  @Override
 2:  public Loader<Cursor> onCreateLoader(int id, Bundle args) {
 3:    boolean showAll = true;
 4:    CursorLoader cursorLoader;
 5:    if (args!=null){
 6:      showAll = args.getBoolean("ALL", true);
 7:    }
 8:    if (showAll){
 9:      cursorLoader = new CursorLoader(getActivity(),
10:      FlickrPhotoProvider.CONTENT_URI,
11:      null, null, null, null);
12:    }else{
13: cursorLoader = new CursorLoader(getActivity(),
14:      FlickrPhotoProvider.CONTENT_URI,
15:                 null, "isFavorite=1", null, null);
16:    }
17:    return cursorLoader;
19: }
```

Showing Data in a List or Grid

You now know how to display data in a `ListFragment` and how to implement `bindView()`.

Per the wireframe diagrams in Figures 16.1 and 16.2, you should also implement a `GridView`. The options for whether to show a grid or a list appear in the overflow menu in the action bar. As you know, to create the menu, you must:

▶ Create the menu resource XML file

▶ Implement the `onCreateOptionsMenu()` method

▶ Implement the `onOptionsItemSelected()` method

These actions result in the overflow menu shown in Figure 16.4.

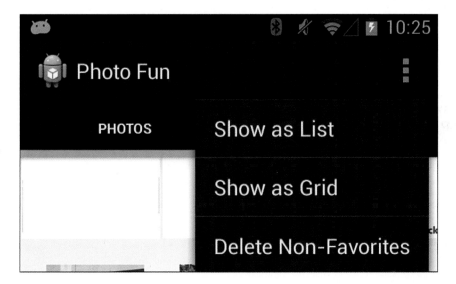

FIGURE 16.4
Overflow menu

At a high level, when the user selects either Show as List or Show as Grid from the overflow menu, a check occurs on the selected tab on the action bar and either the list or grid is shown.

This code nipped shows the case to handle the list option being selected. The `showList()` method is called with `true` and `false` to indicate whether to display all photos or just favorites:

```
case R.id.menu_show_as_list:
showList=true;
if (getActionBar().getSelectedTab() == mPhotosTab){
    showList(true);
}else{
    showList(false);
}
```

You use `showList()` to show the `ListFragment` and a method called `showGrid()` to show a fragment called `PhotoGridFragment`. `PhotoGridFragment` uses the same logic as `PhotoListFragment`, but displays the data in a `GridView` instead of a `ListView`.

If you recall, to develop the `PhotoListFragment`, you:

▶ Create an XML layout for an item in the list called `list_item.xml`

▶ Create a custom `CursorAdapter` called `ListCursorAdapter`

▶ Implement `PhotoListFragment` with a `LoaderCallback`

▶ Handle the `onScrollListener` in `PhotoListFragment`

▶ Implement the `onListItemClick()` method in `PhotoListFragment`

As you saw beginning in Hour 10, many similarities exist when creating a `ListFragment` and a fragment that implements a `GridView`. One difference is that the fragment that implements a `GridView` must implement an `onCreateView()` method. Another difference is that, rather than implementing the `ListFragment`'s `onListItemClick()` method, in a fragment with a `GridView`, you must implement the `setOnItemClickListener()` of the `GridView`. Though it may be challenging, the pieces are in place to implement the `GridView` fragment described in the following Try It Yourself.

▼ TRY IT YOURSELF

Implementing PhotoGridFragment

The new concepts in this hour include creating a custom `CursorAdapter`, handling fling, and lazy-loading images. You can use the `LoadBitmapTask` class precisely the way you did for the `PhotoListFragment`:

1. Create an XML layout for a single grid item called `grid_item.xml`. It should contain a `RelativeLayout` and a single `ImageView`.

2. Create a custom `CursorAdapter` called `GridCursorAdapter`. This should be virtually identical to `ListCursorAdapter` except it will populate the image into the `ImageView` created in step 1. Create an inner class called `GridViewHolder` class that contains an id and `ImageView`.

3. Create the `PhotoGridFragment` with `LoaderCallbacks`. It will be similar to `PhotoListFragment`, but includes an `onCreateView()` method where the `GridView` is created. The `GridView` can be inflated from an XML layout that contains only a `GridView`.

4. Handle the `onScrollListener` in the `onCreateView()` method. If you create a `GridView` called `mGrid`, you can do this with `mGrid.setOnScrollListener(new OnScrollListener()`.

5. Handle a click on the `GridView` in the `onActivityCreated()` method. If you create a `GridView` called `mGrid`, you can do this with `mGrid.setOnItemClickListener(new OnItemClickListener()`.

Figure 16.5 shows the app showing the same data in both a list and a grid.

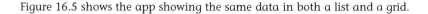

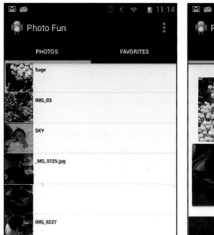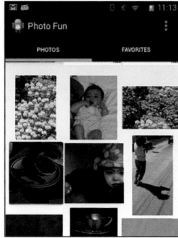

FIGURE 16.5
Display in `ListView` and `GridView`

Displaying the Selected Image

When the user selects an image, whether from a list or a grid, you want to display that single image. To do that, you use a fragment called `ImageViewFragment` and pass a single photo id to the fragment.

Even though you are getting a single item, you can take advantage of your content provider and even the `LoaderCallbacks` to handle this case.

In the `onCreateLoader()` method, you use the single photo id that was passed to the fragment. The cursor loader is created with the `FlickPhotoProvider` content provider. The method `Uri.withAppendedPath()` is used to append the id of the selected photo to `FlickrPhotoProvider.CONTENT_URI`. That means that a single `FlickrPhoto` object will be returned:

```
@Override
public Loader<Cursor> onCreateLoader(int id, Bundle args) {
if (args!=null){
    mPhotoId=args.getString("PHOTO_ID");
    CursorLoader cursorLoader = new CursorLoader(getActivity(),
        Uri.withAppendedPath(FlickrPhotoProvider.CONTENT_URI ,mPhotoId),
        null, null, null, null);
    return cursorLoader;
}
    return null;
}
```

In the `onLoadFinished()` method, you can retrieve the single FlickrPhoto object from the cursor. At that point, you have the information that you need to display it. You can also determine whether it is a favorite or not.

Figure 16.6 shows the display of a single image.

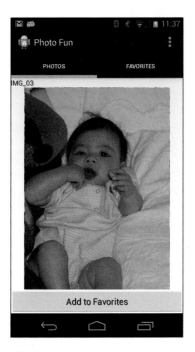

FIGURE 16.6
Displaying a single image

Handling Favorites

You've learned how to list favorite images, but not how to create them. Looking back at Figure 16.2, the wireframe indicates that you show a single image and have an option to make that image a favorite. Figure 16.5 shows this option implemented.

In the `onLoadFinished()` method in `ImageViewFragment`, you can obtain a `FlickrPhoto` object from the cursor. Using that, you check the `isFavorite` value to determine whether the photo is a favorite or not. The display updates to reflect that quality:

```
mCurrentPhoto = FlickrPhotoDbAdapter.getPhotoFromCursor(cursor);
if (mCurrentPhoto.isFavorite){
   mFavoriteButton.setText("Remove from Favorites");
}else{
   mFavoriteButton.setText("Add to Favorites");
}
```

When the favorite button is clicked, the values for the current `FlickrPhoto` object update in the database. Recall that you do this by setting `ContentValues` and calling the update method of the `ContentProvider`. Listing 16.9 shows a portion of the code to accomplish this. For a `FlickrPhoto` that is already a favorite, you set the value for `isFavorite` set to 0. To make a photo a favorite, you set the value of `isFavorite` to 1. The button label is also updated.

LISTING 16.9 Setting Favorites in ImageViewFragment

```
1:  if (mCurrentPhoto.isFavorite){
2:      newValues.put("isFavorite", 0);
3:      mFavoriteButton.setText("Add to Favorites");
4:  }else{
5:      newValues.put("isFavorite", 1);
6:      mFavoriteButton.setText("Remove from Favorites");
7:  }
8:  int id = getActivity().getContentResolver().update(
9:          FlickrPhotoProvider.CONTENT_URI,
10:         newValues, "flickr_id='"+mCurrentPhoto.id+"'", null);
```

The menu option to delete all non-favorites also uses the content provider. To select all non-favorites and delete them, you use the following:

```
getContentResolver().delete( FlickrPhotoProvider.CONTENT_URI,   "isFavorite='0'",
null );
```

Final App Inventory

With the app complete, taking an inventory of what you created to support an app of this scope makes sense. Consolidating some functionality might have been possible, but this seems fairly typical. You used the following:

- ▶ 1 activity: `MainActivity`
- ▶ 3 fragments: `PhotoGridFragment`, `PhotoListFragment`, and `ImageFragment`
- ▶ 2 adapters: `GridAdapter` and `ListAdapter` to work with their respective fragments
- ▶ 2 layouts for items: `list_item.xml` and `grid_item.xml`
- ▶ 1 AsyncTask to load images: `BitmapLoadTask`
- ▶ 1 data object: `FlickrPhoto`
- ▶ 1 database adapter: `FlickrPhotoDbAdapter`
- ▶ 1 content provider: `FlickrPhotoProvider`
- ▶ 1 menu resource

▶ 2 layouts for fragments

▶ 1 layout for the activity

Summary

In this hour, you implemented a full app. In Hour 12, you began to work with data retrieved from the Flickr API. You learned how to retrieve that data, store it in a SQLite database, and use it through a content provider. You created the complete app using cursors and `LoaderCallbacks`. This hour introduced a custom `CursorAdapter`, showed how to handle flinging, and showed how to display images in a `ListView` and `GridView`. By using content providers, cursors, `CursorLoaders`, and `CursorAdapters`, you learned to show the same data in different views.

Q&A

Q. What is the purpose of a `CursorAdapter`**?**

A. A `CursorAdapter` populates a `View` from data provided in a cursor. It maps the data to specific UI components.

Q. Why are two layout XML files needed to show images in the `GridFragment`**?**

A. One defines the `GridView` for the `GridFragment`. Another defines the items displayed in the `GridView`. You can think of one view defining the container and another view defining the contents of the container. The `GridView` is used for the container. A `CursorAdapter` maps data from the cursor to the content items within the container.

Workshop

Quiz

1. What methods must a `CursorAdapter` implement?

2. When you're implementing a `BaseAdapter`, how does the view holder pattern improve performance?

Answers

1. A `CursorAdapter` must implement the methods `newView()` and `bindView()`.

2. Implementing the view holder pattern in a `BaseAdapter` avoids the costly methods associated with inflating new views.

Exercise

1. Change the layout for items in the `GridView` fragment to display include a `TextView` with the `Title` displayed.

2. Implement a gallery instead of a `GridView` to display the set of images. You saw in Hour 10 that you can switch between a gallery and `GridView` with minor changes to the fragments that are defined. The fragment's `onCreateView()` method would need to return a gallery, and other changes would be required throughout the fragment definition.

PART IV
Special Topics

Contacts and Calendar: Accessing Device Data

What You'll Learn in This Hour:

▶ Understanding calendar data

▶ Using the calendar content provider

▶ Using a calendar intent

▶ Understanding contacts

▶ Using the contact content provider

▶ Using a contact `intent`

Android ships with a set of core applications that include calendar and contact applications. When these applications have publicly documented APIs, they are considered part of the Android Application Framework. Apps that are part of the Android Application Framework include test cases that appear in the *Compatibility Test Suite* that Google makes available to Android hardware partners. The idea is that these APIs will work the same way across devices. Unlike private undocumented APIs, they are much less likely to change or be removed in the future. A contacts API has existed in Android since API level 1. The calendar public API became available with Ice Cream Sandwich (API Level 14). In this hour, you learn to use the calendar and contact APIs to retrieve calendar events and contacts. This hour also shows how to make simple applications to display the data and how to use intents to insert and update this data.

All About the Calendar

Most people know that a calendar divides time into specific periods of days, weeks, months, and years. People have personal calendars to schedule events in their lives. A calendar app, like Apple's iCal and Google Calendar, enables calendar owners to add and track events on their calendar. An event might be a meeting with an agenda and attendees or it might be a personal event such as "soccer game tonight." In either case, events on the calendar include a time period and a description. Events may include a list of attendees, and many calendar apps use reminders, warnings that a meeting is about to start in 5 minutes, for example.

Calendar apps can include a recurring event, which occurs at specific intervals and is scheduled into the future. A recurring event might be a weekly status meeting at work that occurs 2 p.m. each Monday or a drama class that occurs each Saturday at 10 a.m.

The calendar app in the Android Framework includes a database that provides for all of this information. That data is made available through the calendar content provider.

Calendar Data on Android

Understanding the structure of calendar data for Android is important to being able to query the data and successfully use the calendar content provider.

More than one calendar might be available. You might have a personal calendar and have access to view another person's calendar. In that case, two calendars are available for viewing when using the calendar content provider.

The calendar API is basically a data model, with tables, columns, and relations specified so you can use them through content provider queries. You implement the calendar content provider in the `android.provider.CalendarContract` class. The class refers to five tables containing calendar data comprised of `CalendarContract.Calendar`, `CalendarContract.Events`, `CalendarContacts.Attendees`, `CalendarContacts.Instances`, and `CalendarContacts.Reminders`.

The following list describes the tables in `CalendarContract` `(android.provider.CalendarContract)`:

▶ **Calendar:** Details for a single calendar including the account type, account name, calendar id, and calendar display name.

▶ **Events:** Event-specific information including the event title, description, start date, and end date.

▶ **Attendees:** Event guests and whether they have responded to indicate that they are attending the event.

▶ **Instances:** Each row in the instance table represents one occurrence of an event. For recurring events, multiple entries are in this table. For non-recurring events, there is one entry.

▶ **Reminders:** Reminder information for an event. An event might have multiple reminders.

Figure 17.1 shows the relationships between these tables. Calendars have events, and events have attendees, instances, and reminders.

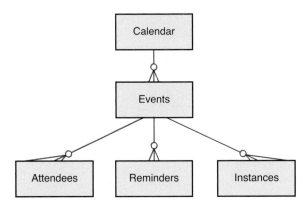

FIGURE 17.1
Calendar data diagram

Calendar Data via the Calendar Content Provider

Calendar data is available to use via the `CalendarContract` content provider. In Hours 14–16, you saw how to develop a content provider to work with Flickr photo data and take advantage of `LoaderCallbacks` to display that data in fragments. You can use the same approach to query and display calendar data.

This hour shows how to create a simple application to read calendar data. You'll also see how to interact with calendar data via intents. The third way to interact with calendar or contact data is via a sync adapter. A sync adapter syncs remote data with a local content provider, which could be the calendar or contacts provider.

Permissions are required in the Android manifest XML file in order to use the calendar content provider. The read and write permissions are as follows:

```
<uses-permission android:name="android.permission.READ_CALENDAR" />
<uses-permission android:name="android.permission.WRITE_CALENDAR" />
```

NOTE

Sync Adapter and Calendar Content Provider

A sync adapter has write access to more columns than an application. An app can change a calendar name, display name, and whether the calendar is synced. A sync adapter can change these and in addition can update the account name, account type, maximum number of reminders, and many other columns. For the full list, see http://developer.android.com/reference/android/provider/CalendarContract.Calendars.html.

This section shows how to create a `ListFragment` called `CalendarListFragment` to list available calendars. The goal is to list all available calendars on the device. You use a `SimpleCursorAdapter` to display calendar data in a list. To display the account name and display name, you use the `Calendars.ACCOUNT_NAME` and `Calendars.CALENDAR_DISPLAY_NAME` columns.

The four projects that accompany this hour are the following:

▶ Hour17AppCalendar, the basic calendar app

▶ Hour17CalendarIntent, for using intents with the calendar

▶ Hour17AppContacts, the basic contact app

▶ Hour17AppContactIntent, for using intents with contacts

Listing 17.1 shows the `CalendarListFragment` definition and `onActivityCreated()` method. The `SimpleCursorAdapter` `mAdapter` is instantiated in the `onActivityCreated()` method. The Hour17AppCalendar project contains this source code.

LISTING 17.1   CalendarListFragment Using a SimpleCursorAdapter

```
1:   public class CalendarListFragment extends ListFragment
2:               implements LoaderCallbacks<Cursor>    {
3:     SimpleCursorAdapter mAdapter;
4:     @Override
5:     public void onActivityCreated(Bundle savedInstanceState) {
6:       super.onActivityCreated(savedInstanceState);
7:       getLoaderManager().initLoader(0, null, this);
8:       mAdapter = new SimpleCursorAdapter(getActivity(),
9:           android.R.layout.simple_list_item_2,
10:          null, //cursor
11:          new String[] {Calendars.ACCOUNT_NAME, Calendars.CALENDAR_DISPLAY_NAME},
12:          new int[] { android.R.id.text1,  android.R.id.text2,}, 0);
13:      setListAdapter(mAdapter);
14:  }
```

Listing 17.1 is similar to Listings 15.1 and 15.2. Hour 15 showed you how to create a simple `ListFragment` to display Flickr photo data. Listing 17.1 also uses a `ListFragment`, but with the goal of displaying calendar data. On line 2, you see that this code implements `LoaderCallbacks`. Line 7 calls `initLoader()`. A `SimpleCursorAdapter` is instantiated in lines 8–12. Line 11 specifies the calendar columns that should be used to retrieve data; in this case, the `Calendars.ACCOUNT_NAME` and `Calendars.CALENDAR_DISPLAY_NAME`.

Because you implement `LoaderCallbacks`, you must add the three required methods: `onCrea-teLoader()`, `onLoadFinished()`, and `onLoaderReset()`, as shown in Listing 17.2.

LISTING 17.2 LoaderCallback Methods

```
1:  @Override
2:  public Loader<Cursor> onCreateLoader(int id, Bundle args) {
3:    CursorLoader cursorLoader = new CursorLoader(getActivity(),
4:        Calendars.CONTENT_URI,
5:        null, null, null, null);
6:    return cursorLoader;
7:  }
8:  @Override
9:  public void onLoadFinished(Loader<Cursor> loader, Cursor cursor) {
10:    mAdapter.swapCursor(cursor);
11: }
12: @Override
13: public void onLoaderReset(Loader<Cursor> loader) {
14:     mAdapter.swapCursor(null);
15: }
```

The `onLoadFinished()` and `onLoaderReset()` methods call the `swapCursor()` method, as you have seen previously. The work in Listing 17.2 occurs in the `onCreateLoader()` method. A `cursorLoader` is created using the `Calendars.CONTENT_URI` on line 4. You are adding no additional parameters, thereby retrieving all data for the calendar.

When the data from the `Calendars.CONTENT_URI` is available, the `onLoadFinished()` method runs and the cursor becomes available to the `SimpleCursorAdapter` `mAdapter`. As specified in Listing 17.1, data from two fields in the cursor will be displayed.

Figure 17.2 shows the result. Two calendars are available: the main account calendar and a calendar that was made visible to the main account.

FIGURE 17.2
CalendarListFragment display

Now that a list of calendars is on the device, you can consider displaying available events
for a specific calendar. To do that, you implement the onListItemClick() method of the
CalendarListFragment. Listing 17.3 shows the onListItemClick() method and Listings
17.1–17.3 include the code for all the CalendarListFragment.

LISTING 17.3   Clicking on a Calendar Item

```
1:  @Override
2:  public void onListItemClick(ListView l, View v, int position, long id) {
3:      EventListFragment eventListFragment = new EventListFragment();
4:      Bundle args = new Bundle();
5:      args.putLong("calendarId", id);
6:      eventListFragment.setArguments(args);
7:      FragmentTransaction ft = getFragmentManager().beginTransaction();
8:      ft.replace(R.id.layout_container, eventListFragment);
9:      ft.setTransition(FragmentTransaction.TRANSIT_FRAGMENT_FADE);
10:     ft.commit();
11: }
```

In Listing 17.3, the parameter id of the onListItemClick() method is put into a bundle and
made available to the new fragment EventListFragment. The id is used to retrieve the data
for a particular calendar.

Listing Calendar Events

A calendar event includes important data such as title, description, attendees, time, and location to help you be where you need to be for an event.

Names for some common fields are `CALENDAR_ID`, `ORGANIZER`, `TITLE`, `EVENT_LOCATION`, `DESCRIPTION`, `EVENT_COLOR`, `DTSTART`, `DTEND`, `EVENT_TIMEZONE`, `EVENT_END_TIMEZONE`, `DURATION`, `ALL_DAY`, `RRULE`, and `RDATE`.

`DTSTART` and `DTEND` are the columns for start and end dates. `RRULE` and `RDATE` contain information about recurring events.

Additional columns are available for events. The full list is on the `CalendarContract.Events` page at http://developer.android.com/reference/android/provider/CalendarContract.Events.html.

Your goal is to list all future events, but first look at how an event is defined on the Google Calendar web app and how that event looks on an Android device. Because the underlying data is the same, you can make a connection between what is displayed on the Web and in the app and what is available via the content provider. Figure 17.3 shows a simple event defined in a web browser. Figure 17.4 shows the same event in the Android calendar on a device running Jelly Bean.

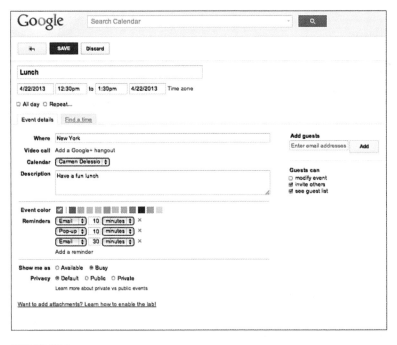

FIGURE 17.3
Calendar event defined in a web browser

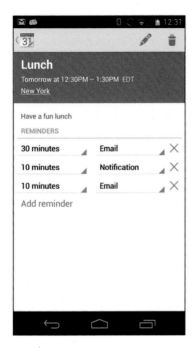

FIGURE 17.4
Calendar event on an Android device

Figures 17.3 and 17.4 show event details that you can edit that match the columns from the calendar content provider.

To use this data in your own app, let's keep things simple and create another ListFragment that uses a SimpleCursorAdapter. The ListFragment is called EventListFragment.

Listing 17.4 shows the onActivityCreated() method for the EventListFragment.

LISTING 17.4   EventListFragment onActivityCreated()

```
1:  public void onActivityCreated(Bundle savedInstanceState) {
2:      super.onActivityCreated(savedInstanceState);
3:      Bundle b = this.getArguments();
4:      getLoaderManager().initLoader(0, b, this);
5:      mAdapter = new SimpleCursorAdapter(getActivity(),
6:        android.R.layout.simple_list_item_2,
7:        null, //cursor
8:        new String[] {CalendarContract.Events.TITLE, CalendarContract.Events.
RRULE},
9:        new int[] { android.R.id.text1,  android.R.id.text2,}, 0);
10: setListAdapter(mAdapter);
11: }
```

Listing 17.4 uses a `SimpleCursorAdapter` and line 8 specifies that it should display the `TITLE` and `RRULE` for the event. Note that in lines 3 and 4, the bundle passed to this fragment is retrieved and passed a parameter to `initLoader()`.

Listing 17.5 shows the `onCreateLoader()` method for `EventListFragment`. The bulk of the work for the fragment happens here. The bundle that was passed in `initLoader()` is accessed and the calendar id is retrieved. That calendar id is used to query the events table.

The query occurs on lines 7–10. You're looking for two things in this query:

▶ All calendar events that have an end date greater than the current date and time

▶ All calendar events that have an `RRULE` defined

LISTING 17.5   EventListFragment onCreateLoader()

```
1:  @Override
2:  public Loader<Cursor> onCreateLoader(int id, Bundle args) {
3:  long calendarId = args.getLong("calendarId");
4:  CursorLoader cursorLoader = new CursorLoader(getActivity(),
5:  Events.CONTENT_URI,
6:  null,
7:      Events.CALENDAR_ID +"= '" + calendarId +"' AND " +
8:      Events.DTEND + "> " + new Date().getTime() +
9:      " OR " + Events.CALENDAR_ID +"= '" + calendarId +
10:     "' AND " + Events.RRULE + " NOT NULL", null, null);
11: return cursorLoader;
12: }
```

This simple application illustrates getting all future events and all recurring events. The `RRULE` contains rules for recurring events. Using it in this way ensures that you capture recurring events in the query.

This example does a specific query based on the dates of future events. Line 8 compares the end date of the event to the current date.

This listing also checks for recurring events via line 10, which checks the `RRULE` value. If this value is not `null`, then the event is returned in the query.

NOTE

Recurring Event Definitions

The RRULE is one component of defining a recurring event. Recurrence relies on the start date, the recurrent rules, and exceptions to recurrence rules. RFC 5545 contains a detailed definition of RRULE. See http://tools.ietf.org/html/rfc5545#section-3.8.5.3.

Figure 17.5 shows the `EventListFragment`. You can see a recurring event that is a reminder to check bank statements, an event to work on Hour 17, and the lunch meeting that is referred to in Figures 17.3 and 17.4.

FIGURE 17.5
`EventListFragment` showing three events

Drilling Further into Calendar Data

Given the calendar id, you can retrieve a list of events as shown earlier. You can access attendees, instances, and reminders for a particular event in a similar way.

▼ **TRY IT YOURSELF**

Get a List of Event Attendees

The steps to get a list of attendees for an event mirror the steps to get a list of events for a calendar:

1. Implement the `onListItemClick()` method for the `EventListFragment`.

2. Create an `AttendeeListFragment` and pass it the id of an event in a bundle.

3. Create a `SimpleCursorLoader` to display the data and the proper query to access the attendees for an event.

One option to get all additional event data would be to create a single fragment with multiple cursor loaders. Multiple `initLoader()` methods would be called with different identifiers for different types of data.

Using Intents to Update a Calendar

You can use the calendar provider to insert and update new data into a calendar. The calendar application provides a set of intents that can be used to view, update, and insert calendar data.

Doing these tasks does not require any additional permissions for the app. Listing 17.6 shows an example of using an `INSERT` intent on the calendar to schedule a New Year's Eve party. The code is in the `onCreate()` method of an activity. When the activity runs, the calendar app appears with this data pre-populated, as shown in Figure 17.6. The Hour17CalendarIntent project contains this source code.

LISTING 17.6   Inserting an Event Using an Insert Intent

```
1: @Override
2: protected void onCreate(Bundle savedInstanceState) {
3: super.onCreate(savedInstanceState);
4: setContentView(R.layout.activity_main);
5: Calendar beginTime = Calendar.getInstance();
6: beginTime.set(2013, 11, 31, 10, 30);
7: Calendar endTime = Calendar.getInstance();
8: endTime.set(2014, 0, 1, 2, 30);
9: Intent intent = new Intent(Intent.ACTION_INSERT)
10: .setData(Events.CONTENT_URI)
11:       .putExtra(CalendarContract.EXTRA_EVENT_BEGIN_TIME, beginTime.
getTimeInMillis())
12:       .putExtra(CalendarContract.EXTRA_EVENT_END_TIME, endTime.
getTimeInMillis())
13:       .putExtra(Events.TITLE, "New Years Party")
14:        .putExtra(Events.DESCRIPTION, "Have fun")
15:.putExtra(Events.EVENT_LOCATION, "Our house")
16:       .putExtra(Events.AVAILABILITY, Events.AVAILABILITY_BUSY)
17:        .putExtra(Intent.EXTRA_EMAIL, "carmendelessio@gmail.com");
18:startActivity(intent);
19:}
```

The event is defined on line 9 with additional data being added in lines 10–17 using the `putExtra()` method.

The result that the calendar app opens with this data pre-filled, as shown in Figure 17.6.

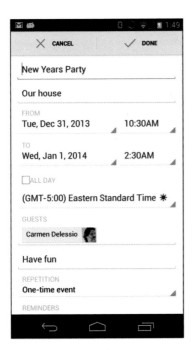

FIGURE 17.6
Inserting an event via a calendar `Intent`

Understanding Contacts

Contacts are easy to understand conceptually. Contacts represent a list of people you know and how to reach them. You might know details about a person such as where he or she works. You might have multiple ways of reaching a person such as through email, work phone, or cell phone. People might also have multiple email addresses that include personal and work. You might also contact them on different types of services or accounts such as Facebook and Twitter.

On Android, you handle these distinctions regarding data and people using a three-tiered data model. A raw contact represents a person's data coming from a single account type and account name. Gmail is an example of account type. The Gmail address of the contact is the account name. You can have more than one raw contact for a single individual. A Facebook account and user name would represent an account type and account name.

Raw contacts exist in the `ContactsContract.RawContacts` table.

When one or more raw contacts are aggregated and presumed to be for the same person, the result is an entry in the `ContactsContract.Contacts` table.

The `ContactsContract.Data` table holds specific data such as telephone number or email address for a raw contact.

Additional tables of the `ContactsContract` class include groups, status updates, and phone lookups.

The following list describes the tables in `ContactsContract`:

- ▶ `Contacts`: People who can be contacted.

- ▶ `RawContacts`: Individual accounts for people (for example, a specific Gmail account).

- ▶ `Data`: Specific contact data such as telephone numbers.

- ▶ `Groups`: Contact groups such as a Gmail group.

- ▶ `StatusUpdates`: Social status updates, including IM availability.

- ▶ `PhoneLookups`: Use for caller id, which can identify a contact by phone number.

Querying Contacts

You can again use a `ListFragment` to show some simple contact queries. You can see the columns available for the contacts at http://developer.android.com/reference/android/provider/ContactsContract.ContactsColumns.html.

You use the `DISPLAY_NAME` and `HAS_PHONE_NUMBER` columns to get data to display in a list using a `SimpleCursorAdapter` as shown here. The Hour17AppContacts project contains this source code:

```
mAdapter = new SimpleCursorAdapter(getActivity(),
    android.R.layout.simple_list_item_2,
    null, //cursor
    new String[] {Contacts.DISPLAY_NAME, Contacts.HAS_PHONE_NUMBER},
    new int[] { android.R.id.text1,  android.R.id.text2,}, 0);
setListAdapter(mAdapter);
```

To get all available contacts, you would use the `Contact.CONTENT_URI` in the `onCreate-Loader()` method.

With all parameters set to `null`, all contacts are retrieved and used:

```
@Override
public Loader<Cursor> onCreateLoader(int id, Bundle args) {
  CursorLoader cursorLoader = new CursorLoader(getActivity(),
  Contacts.CONTENT_URI, null, null, null, null);
  return cursorLoader;
}
```

The `ContactListFragment` displays the `DISPLAY_NAME` for the contact and a 0 or 1 to represent the `HAS_PHONE_NUMBER` column.

You can use the `Contacts.CONTENT_FILTER_URI` to filter the results by specifying a full or partial name to filter on. You append the name to the `CONTENT_FILTER_URI`. You can use this to filter contacts that contain "Scott."

```
Uri.withAppendedPath(Contacts.CONTENT_FILTER_URI, "Scott"),  null, null, null,
null);
```

Getting additional details for contacts requires using the retrieved data and drilling into the other contact tables.

Permissions are required in the Android manifest XML file in order to use the contact content provider. The read and write permissions are as follows:

```
<uses-permission android:name="android.permission.READ_CONTACTS" />
<uses-permission android:name="android.permission.WRITE_CONTACTS" />
```

Using Contact Intents

A number of actions are available via intents for contact data. You can pick a contact, insert a contact, edit a contact, or display a contact picker that also provides for adding a contact.

The specific intents available are as follows:

▶ `ACTION_PICK`: Pick from a list of contacts.

▶ `ACTION_INSERT_OR_EDIT`: Pick an existing contact or add a new one.

▶ `ACTION_EDIT`: Edit a contact.

▶ `ACTION_INSERT`: Insert a new contact.

To define an intent to pick from a list of contacts, you must set the data for contacts in the intent. The Hour17AppContactIntentproject contains this source code:

```
//PICK A CONTACT
Intent intent = new Intent(Intent.ACTION_PICK);
intent.setData(Contacts.CONTENT_URI);
startActivity(intent);
```

To define an intent to insert or edit a contact, you must set the `mimeType` to the `contacts` type:

```
//PICK OR INSERT A CONTACT
Intent intent = new Intent(Intent.ACTION_INSERT_OR_EDIT);
intent.setType(Contacts.CONTENT_ITEM_TYPE);
```

Figure 17.7 shows the result of the intent to pick a contact and the intent to insert or edit a contact.

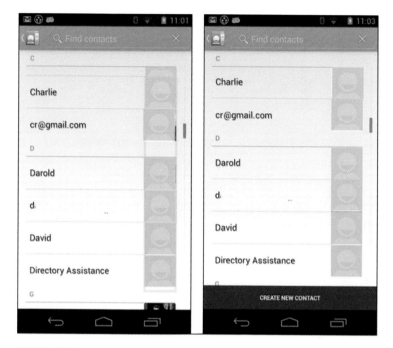

FIGURE 17.7
Results of contact intents

Summary

In this hour, you relied on your knowledge of ListFragments, CursorLoaders, and SimpleCursorAdapters to explore the data provided by the calendar and contact content providers. Calendar and contact data are accessible via content providers. You can also use intents within your apps to read and update this data.

Q&A

Q. Does accessing calendar and contact data from a content provider or an intent make more sense?

A. One answer is that it depends on your app. Intents are useful and show the user a familiar interface for performing a common task. If your app needs to occasionally interact with the calendar or contacts app, then using intents is a good idea.

Workshop

Quiz

1. What is the INSTANCES table used for?

2. What is RRULE?

3. When working with contacts, how do you use the CONTENT_FILTER_URI?

Answers

1. You use the INSTANCES table in the calendar to handle recurring events.

2. RRULE is a column in the calendar data. It represents rules for recurring events.

3. You use the CONTENT_FILTER_URI with an appended path to filter data from the content provider. You can include a name or phone number as a part of an appended path. That appended value is used to filter the returned data.

Exercise

Create a fragment to display additional data about an event. Experiment by using multiple loaders to load data from different tables. You may use a DialogFragment.

HOUR 18

Where Are We? Working with Location-Based Services

What You'll Learn in This Hour:

▶ Determining location
▶ Using geolocation
▶ Mapping a location
▶ Additional location features
▶ Using Google Play services

This hour covers what location-based services are and how to use them in Android. From Foursquare to GPS navigation to tagging places in Facebook posts, location can be a core feature for an app or a great enhancement. You'll use several features for location-based support in Android. Most are included in the `LocationManager` class. Location-based services include determining your location with longitude and latitude, determining the address of your location, and mapping your location. In this hour, you learn to implement a location-based services solution using core Android libraries and using Google Play services.

Determining Location

An Android device can obtain your current location in several ways. A global positioning system (GPS) uses satellite data to determine location. The underlying technique is triangulation. If you know your distance from three points, then you can determine where you are. GPS relies on triangulating satellite data. If you are connected to a cellular network, the id of the cell tower that the device is connected to provides your location. The Wi-Fi network that the device is attached to can also be used as the source of location information. Multiple companies, including Google, can tie a specific Wi-Fi network to a specific location.

Each method has advantages and disadvantages. Generally, you must balance the accuracy of GPS with the lower power consumption of the other methods:

▶ GPS is very accurate but might not work inside or with an obstructed view of the sky. It consumes a significant amount of power and causes battery drain.

▶ Cell id is less accurate than GPS but consumes little power.

▶ Wi-Fi might be very accurate depending on whether a network is recognized. It also consumes little power.

Using cell tower and Wi-Fi data together gives a more accurate location than either method alone, and Android has built-in support for this technique.

Android permissions for location-based services include a coarse location and a fine location. You must set these permissions to use location in your app:

▶ `android.permission.ACCESS_FINE_LOCATION`—The permission to use GPS.

▶ `android.permission.ACCESS_ COARSE_LOCATION`—The permission to use the Android network provider. It uses both Wi-Fi and cell id for location.

Using LocationManager to Determine Location

`LocationManager` (`android.location.LocationManager`) is used to access to system location services on the device and to request location updates. Location-based services rely heavily on the use of `LocationManager`.

To begin using `LocationManager`, let's start with a simple example that detects changes in location using GPS.

To do this, you need to:

▶ Set `android.permission.ACCESS_FINE_LOCATION`

▶ Instantiate `LocationManager`

▶ Request location updates via GPS

▶ Listen for location changes

Listing 18.1 shows how to listen for location changes using GPS. It demonstrates several aspects of using the `LocationManager`. In Listing 18.1, changes in location are detected and acted on by an `onLocationChanged()` listener. By checking small distances and checking frequently, the current location is determined and made available to the app.

LISTING 18.1   Detecting Changes in Location Using GPS

```
1:   public class MainActivity extends Activity {
2:   TextView mDisplayTextView;
3:   @Override
4:   protected void onCreate(Bundle savedInstanceState) {
5:   super.onCreate(savedInstanceState);
6:   setContentView(R.layout.activity_main);
7:   LocationManager locationManager = (LocationManager)
8:   this.getSystemService(Context.LOCATION_SERVICE);
9:   locationManager.requestLocationUpdates(LocationManager.GPS_PROVIDER,
10:  0, 0, locationListener);
11:  mDisplayTextView = (TextView) findViewById(R.id.displayTextView);
12:     }
13:  LocationListener locationListener = new LocationListener() {
14:  @Override
15:  public void onLocationChanged(Location location) {
16:  mDisplayTextView.setText(location.getLatitude() + ","
17:  + location.getLongitude());
18:  }
19:             @Override
20:  public void onProviderDisabled(String provider) {}
21:  @Override
22:             public void onProviderEnabled(String provider) {}
23:             @Override
24:             public void onStatusChanged(String provider, int status, Bundle
extras){}
25:  };
26:  }
```

In the onCreate() method on lines 7–8, the LocationManager is defined. Lines 9–10 make a request to begin receiving updates from the LocationManager.GPS_PROVIDER. Those updates will be sent to the LocationListener defined on lines 13–25.

You must implement four methods in the LocationListener, but you only have running code for the onLocationChanged() method that is on lines 15–17. When the location changes, you get the Location object that was passed as a parameter and display the latitude and longitude of the detected location. The parameters to onLocationChanged() include the minimum time in milliseconds between location updates and the minimum distance in meters between update changes. In this case, these are both set to 0. Figure 18.1 shows the result. Note the notification icon indicating location.

FIGURE 18.1
Showing latitude and longitude

The Location Object

Listing 18.1 showed how to use the `Location` object that was passed the `onLocation-Changed()` method to get the latitude and longitude of the location. Together, latitude and longitude provide a coordinate system for specifying any point on earth. Latitude describes the north-south position and is represented in degrees, ranging from the equator at zero degrees to the poles at 90 degrees. Longitude describes the east-west position. Greenwich, England is designated as the Prime Meridian with a longitude of zero degrees. The longitude for other locations is defined by the degree of difference east or west from the Prime Meridian, ranging from 180 degrees to –180 degrees.

Latitude and longitude specify a single point on earth. The `Location` object contains additional data including altitude, speed, accuracy, and the provider used. The `Location` object can also be used to determine the distance between two points or the distance to a specific location.

Using Criteria with Location Providers

Listing 18.1 used `LocationManager.GPS_PROVIDER` to detect changes in location. To use Wi-Fi and cell tower data, you can use `LocationManager.NETWORK_PROVIDER` in the same way.

An alternative to setting a specific provider is to set criteria for the provider to be used and request that the best provider be used. To do that, you use the `Criteria` class. You set the `Criteria` class to specific requirements for the location provider to get the best provider that meets the criteria. Listing 18.2 shows an example method for getting a provider by setting criteria. If no provider is available, the `GPS_PROVIDER` is used.

LISTING 18.2 Using Criteria to Set Location Providers

```
1:   public String getProvider(){
2:      Criteria criteria = new Criteria();
3:      criteria.setAccuracy(Criteria.ACCURACY_FINE);
4:      criteria.setSpeedRequired(true);
5:      String providerName = mLocationManager.getBestProvider(criteria, true);
6:      if (providerName != null) {
7:        return providerName;
8:      }else{
9:        return LocationManager.GPS_PROVIDER;
10:     }
11: }
```

To use the `getProvider()` method of Listing 18.2, the call to `requestLocationUpdates()` method would not specify a particular provider. Instead, it would call the `getProvider()` method:

`mLocationManager.requestLocationUpdates(getProvider(), 0, 0, locationListener);`

Getting the Last Known Location

Given a provider, you can use `LocationManager` to get the last known location specified by that provider. This is often the best starting point for determining location. To get the last known location specified by GPS, you would use the following:

`mLocationManager.getLastKnownLocation(LocationManager.GPS_PROVIDER);`

This method returns the last known location as a `Location` object. With the `Location` object, you can get the time that this location was specified as the last known location as well as the accuracy, provider, and other information.

Consider the case where GPS is disabled, but the user of the device is in a known Wi-Fi location. Getting the last known location for GPS is not helpful. To get the most accurate and up-to-date last known location, you can call `getLastKnownLocation()` for each location provider and check for the best results.

Listing 18.3 shows a basic example for this approach. In this case, all providers are retrieved on line 4. An iteration over the list of providers checks for the location that was used for the most recent update. A `Location` object is returned for the location that has the most recent date. The `location.getTime()` method used on line 8 returns the time as milliseconds since January 1, 1970 (UTC Time). A higher value returned by `getTime()` means a more recent update.

You can then check this location to see whether it was obtained within an acceptable time period. That is, the possibility exists that the last location time for all providers is more than an hour old, which might not meet your app's criteria for being useful. The location might be stale.

If the location returned is fresh, you can use the provider for that location for updates. To get the provider, you use the `Location` method `getProvider()`.

LISTING 18.3   Get Recent Locations for All Providers

```
1:  public Location getRecentLocation() {
2:      Location recentLocation = null;
3:      long bestTime = 0;
4:      List<String> matchingProviders = mLocationManager.getAllProviders();
5:      for (String provider: matchingProviders) {
6:        Location location = mLocationManager.getLastKnownLocation(provider);
7:        if (location != null) {
8:          long time = location.getTime();
9:          if (time > bestTime) {
10:             bestTime = time;
11:             recentLocation = location;
12:          }
13:        }
14:      }
15:      return recentLocation;
16:  }
```

The following is a sample result of logging the time of the last known GPS location and the most recent location update:

```
04-28 21:12:05.935: D/Location(23894): last: 41.255505247972906,-73.56329055503011
from gps at 18:49

04-28 21:12:05.943: D/Location(23894): last: 41.2553161,-73.5633479 from network at
21:12
```

The last GPS time was at 6:49 p.m. and the last network time was at 9:12 p.m. The log shows that 9:12 p.m. was the current time. Using the `LocationManager.NETWORK_PROVIDER` in this case gave more up-to-date locations.

Looking back at Listing 18.1, note the methods `onProviderDisabled()`, `onProviderEn-abled()`, `onStatusChanged()` implemented in the `onLocationChange()` have to do with provider availability. To get the best location and to use the best available provider, you can implement these methods.

NOTE

Deep Dive into Location

A post on the Android Developer blog called a "Deep Dive in Location" provides tips, code, and detailed techniques and examples on getting an up-to-date and accurate location for your app. Listing 18.3 is a simplified version of one of the techniques used in this post. See http://android-developers.blogspot.com/2011/06/deep-dive-into-location.html.

Taking Care of Loose Ends

You must take care to clean up some items when checking for location.

When you request location updates, you should stop listening when the updates are no longer needed. To do that, use the `LocationManager removeUpdates()` method and pass in the current listener:

```
protected void onStop() {
    super.onStop();
    mLocationManager.removeUpdates(locationListener);
}
```

The `requestLocationUpdates()` method takes time and distance parameters to determine the criteria for a location. Listing 18.1 used 0 time and 0 distance as examples. Define these parameters as appropriate for your app. For certain apps, 10 seconds and 10 meters might be accurate. One minute and 1000 meters might be appropriate for another app. The larger the numbers, the fewer system resources are used. If you are getting a location for a moment in time, then you can get the location using a high degree of time and accuracy, but then immediately stop listening for updates.

Before using a provider, you should check to see whether it is enabled. You do this using the `isProviderEnabled()` method in `LocationManager`. The provider is passed to this method and a boolean is returned:

```
if (mLocationManager.isProviderEnabled(LocationManager.GPS_PROVIDER)){
    mLocationManager.requestLocationUpdates(LocationManager.GPS_PROVIDER, 0, 0,
                                    locationListener);
}
```

You enable and disable location providers in the Settings app, as shown in Figure 18.2.

FIGURE 18.2
Location settings

Using Geocoding Services

Geocoding is the process of translating a description of a location into GPS coordinates (latitude, longitude, and sometimes altitude). Geocoding enables you to enter a place name, such as Eiffel Tower, into Google Maps (http://maps.google.com) and get the appropriate spot on the map. Many geocoding services also have reverse-geocoding abilities, which can translate raw coordinates into some form of address (usually a partial address).

Android devices might or might not have geocoding services available, and geocoding requires a back-end network service, so the device must have network connectivity to function. Different geocoding services support different types of descriptions, but the following are some of the most common ones:

- ▶ Names of towns, states, and countries
- ▶ Various forms of postal-style addresses (full and partial)
- ▶ Postal codes

▶ Airport codes (for example, LAX, LHR, JFK)

▶ Famous landmarks

Many geocoding services also allow input of raw coordinates (latitude and longitude). Finally, geocoding services are often localized. An address in the United States will not follow the same format as an address in Canada or another country.

Geocoded addresses are often ambiguous, so a geocoding service might return multiple records. For example, if you were to try to resolve the address "Springfield," you would likely get quite a few results because a town called Springfield is in 35 of the states in the United States and even more Springfields are outside of the U.S. You might also get results for places called "East Springfield" or "Springfield by the Sea," for example. For the best results, choose a geocoding label, or address, that is the most specific. For example, use the zip code for your Springfield of choice instead of its name to resolve the coordinates.

Android Support for Geocoding

The Android SDK includes the `Geocoder` (`android.location.Geocoder`) class to provide geocoding and reverse-geocoding services. Instantiating the `Geocoder` class is a straightforward task:

```
Geocoder coder = new Geocoder(getApplicationContext());
```

Geocoding: Translating Addresses into Coordinates

You can use the `getFromLocationName()` method of the `Geocoder` class to resolve a location into coordinates. This method takes two parameters: the string containing the location information and the number of results you want returned. For example, the code in Listing 18.4 looks up a location for"White Plains, NY" and limits the number of results to 3.

LISTING 18.4   Get Recent Locations for All Providers

```
1:  Geocoder coder = new Geocoder(getApplicationContext());
2:  String locationToFind = "White Plains, NY";
3:  List<Address> geocodeResults;
4:  try {
5:  geocodeResults = coder.getFromLocationName(locationToFind, 3);
6:  for (Address address: geocodeResults){
7:  Log.d("Location", locationToFind + " "
8:          + address.getLatitude() +"," + address.getLongitude());
9:  }
10:  } catch (IOException e) {
11:  // TODO Auto-generated catch block
12:  e.printStackTrace();
13:  }
```

Each resulting `Address` object (in this case, there are up to three) contains information about the location. You can use the `getLatitude()` and `getLongitude()` methods of the `Address` class to access the location's coordinates. Depending on your implementation, you might want to give the user the option to choose the right location, or simply take the first `Address` and use it.

In this case, we just log all the results. The output in the log file for this snippet of code is as follows:

```
White Plains, NY 41.0339862,-73.7629097
```

Reverse-Geocoding: Translating Coordinates into Addresses

Using the `Geocoder getFromLocation()` method, you can translate raw latitude and longitude coordinates into address information. The parameters for the `getFromLocation()` method are the coordinates and the number of results to be returned. You can have some fun with this by enhancing the code in Listing 18.1. Rather than just displaying the latitude and longitude, you can pass that location data to the `Geocoder getFromLocation()` method. Listing 18.5 shows the modified `onLocationChanged()` for the `LocationListener` that was originally defined in Listing 18.1.

LISTING 18.5 Looking Up Locality by Coordinates

```
1:  public void onLocationChanged(Location location) {
2:  Geocoder coder = new Geocoder(getApplicationContext());
3:  List<Address> geocodeResults;
4:  try {
5:  geocodeResults = coder.getFromLocation(location.getLatitude(),
6:                      location.getLongitude(), 1);
7:  for (Address address: geocodeResults){
8:  Log.d("Location", location.getLatitude()+"," + location.getLongitude()
9:                              +" : " +address.getLocality());
10:  mDisplayTextView.setText(location.getLatitude()+"," + location.getLongitude()
11:                              +" : " +address.
getLocality());
12:  }
13:  } catch (IOException e) {
14:  e.printStackTrace();
15:  }
16: }
```

Listing 18.5 takes the latitude and longitude that was detected in the `onLocationChanged()` listener and uses those values to determine a locality. The `Geocoder getFromLocation()` method is used on line 5. The latitude, longitude, and number of results to retrieve are passed as parameters—in this case, one result. Lines 7–10 show to iterate through the results, log the data, and display it in the `TextView` in the activity. You can obtain additional data using the `Address getLocality()` method. Other `Address` data is available.

The result in the log is as follows:

```
41.2553163,-73.5633481 : Pound Ridge
```

Using the Geo Intent

Where are we? You have seen how to determine the location specified by latitude and longitude. You use that information to determine your locality by using reverse geocoding. The last location-based task to do is to map your location. Actually, you will use an `ACTION_VIEW` intent with location data. Any apps that handle a latitude and longitude will respond—typically a map application.

Location applications handle the `ACTION_VIEW` intent when supplied with a URI with geographic coordinates. This URI has a special format. You can launch the Maps application to a specific set of coordinates using the following URI format string:

```
geo:latitude,longitude
```

Here's an example of how to create this URI string using the latitude and longitude from a location object:

```
String geoURI = "geo:" + location.getLatitude() +"," + location.getLongitude() ;
```

This special URI also includes a zoom level, which is a number between 1 and 23, where zoom level 1 shows the whole earth, level 2 shows a quarter of the earth, and each larger number shows a closer view. You use the following URI format string for zoom:

```
geo:latitude,longitude?z=level
```

Here's how to format a URI string with the zoom level set to 8:

```
String geoURI = "geo:" + location.getLatitude() +"," + location.getLongitude() +
"?z="";
```

You use the `String` in this format and pass it to the `parse()` method of the `Uri` class to create the required `Uri`. You then use that `Uri` with the `ACTION_VIEW` intent, as follows:

```
Uri geo = Uri.parse(geoURI);
Intent geoMap = new Intent(Intent.ACTION_VIEW, geo);
startActivity(geoMap);
```

Any application that can handle URIs in this format will respond to the `Intent`. This will typically be the Google Maps implementation, but other apps might be available. Figures 18.3 and 18.4 show the user experience when both Google Maps and Google Earth are available. Both use the retrieved location data and display the appropriate location.

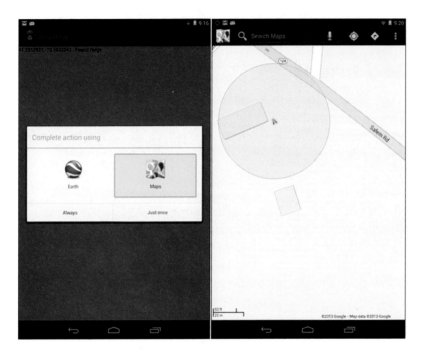

FIGURE 18.3
Geo Intent with Maps app

In addition using the geo URI, support for Google Street View is also available. The basic URI for Google Street View is as follows:

```
google.streetview:cbll=lat,lng
```

A number of additional parameters are available for Street View. For details, go to http://developer.android.com/guide/appendix/g-app-intents.htm.

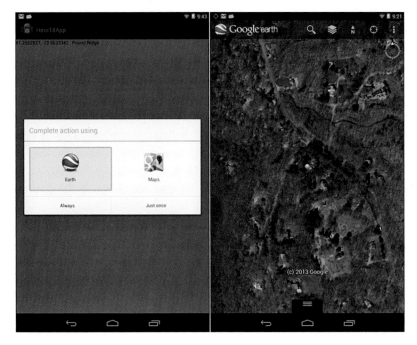

FIGURE 18.4
Geo `Intent` with Google Earth

Additional Location Features

You've seen how to use an `ACTION_VIEW` `Intent` to display a map. Another approach to maps is to use Google Maps Android API v2. The Maps API provides the ability to add icons, lines, and bitmaps to a map using a `MapView` or `MapFragment` objects. More information on how to download and use the API is available at https://developers.google.com/maps/documentation/android/.

The `ProximityAlert` that is available in the `LocationManager` class might also be useful for certain location-based services. It can help support the concept of geofencing, which is specifying a certain geographic location and having an app take an action when it is in that area. You add a `ProximityAlert` with the `addProximityAlert()` method of `LocationManager`. You specify a latitude, longitude, and radius to define the fenced-in area. The area is defined by a circle with the latitude and longitude as the center point. You can specify an expiration period. Using -1 indicates that there is no expiration. The final parameter to add is a `PendingIntent`, which fires an `Intent` when the device has entered or exited the specified area.

The Maps API and `ProximityAlerts` are additional tools to use in location-based services. The location features to use in an app are driven by the application needs. The ability to track a run or bike ride with GPS is different from the need to find a movie theater. Both apps might need location-based services, but the factors of accuracy, battery life, and the length that the location-based service is needed are different. If you have an app that tracks a bike ride, you don't want it to miss part of the ride. If you need the address of the nearest movie theater, you don't need to stay connected to GPS for that. The needs of your app determine the location-based services that are required.

Using Google Play Services

Google Play services allow your app to take advantage of Google services such as Maps, Google+, and now some location-based services. Google Play is not part of the Android OS. Google Play is a library that you can include in your project.

You can find more information on Google Play at http://developer.android.com/google/play-services/index.html.

The advantages of using Google Play location services are ease of use and accuracy. You do not need to specify Wi-Fi or GPS use or check all the providers for their last location. To use Google Play location services, you specify the desired accuracy of the location and frequency of the location checks.

The JellyBean release of Android 4.3 includes optimization for the Google Play location services. The API is the same, but if there is hardware support for geofencing, the Android 4.3 will use it. In addition, it is possible to scan a Wi-Fi network for location even if not connected to Wi-Fi. Both changes will extend the battery life of a device.

Not all devices have Google Play available, so checking is necessary. If Google Play services are not available, you can use the Android location features discussed earlier in this hour.

To install Google Play, use the SDK Manager in Eclipse. Choose Window, SDK Manager. Find the Google Play services package and install it. Figure 18.5 shows the SDK Manager with Google Play services selected.

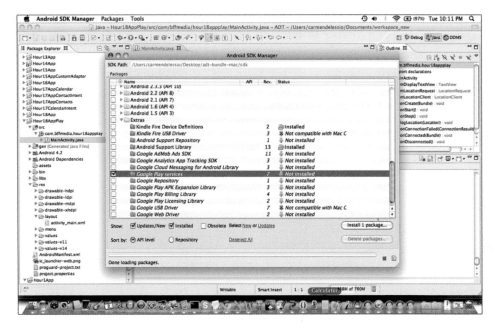

FIGURE 18.5
Adding Google Play services

After the Google Play installation, a library project is created in the directory where your android-sdk is installed. This is the directory that the Eclipse ADT installed to. In that directory is a subdirectory called sdk and another called eclipse. After installing Google Play services, the path in the sdk directory to the Google Play library is:

```
extras/google/google_play_services/libproject/google-play-services_lib/
```

Install this library project using Eclipse by choosing File, Import, Android, Existing Android Code into Workspace.

To use this library, you must refer to it from your current project. The Hour18AppPlay project that accompanies this hour contains the source code that uses this library.

To add the library, choose Properties, Android and add the library as shown in Figure 18.6.

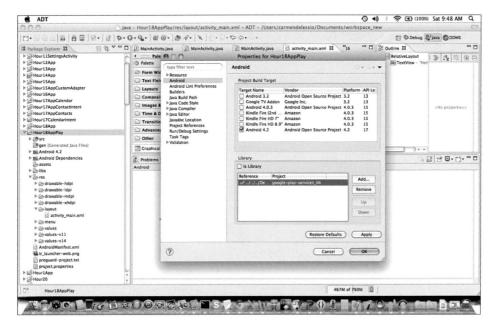

FIGURE 18.6
Adding the Google Play library to a project

With the library set up, you can use the simplified location-based services. The Hour18AppPlay project includes MainActivity.java. The activity is similar to the earlier examples in this hour. The current location is determined and displayed.

To determine location, you use `LocationListener`, `LocationRequest`, and `LocationClient` classes. All are part of the Google Play library and are in the package `com.google.android.gms.location`. The full class name for `LocationListener` is `com.google.android.gms.location.LocationListener`.

In the `onCreate()` method in `MainActivity`, you instantiate a `LocationClient` and a `LocationRequest`. In the `LocationRequest`, set the priority to `PRIORITY_HIGH_ACCURACY`:

```
mLocationRequest = LocationRequest.create();
mLocationRequest.setPriority(LocationRequest.PRIORITY_HIGH_ACCURACY);
```

In the `onStart()` method, a check is made to see whether Google Play services are available. If they are available, then the `LocationClient` connects. If not, a `Toast` message appears:

```
int googlePayResult = GooglePlayServicesUtil.isGooglePlayServicesAvailable(this);
if (googlePayResult == ConnectionResult.SUCCESS ) {
    mLocationClient.connect();
else{
    Toast.makeText(this, "Google Play is not Available", Toast.LENGTH_LONG).show();
}
```

`MainActivity` implements `LocationListener`, at which time, one of the required methods, `onLocationChanged()`, is passed the current location. That location is used to update the display in the app.

Using Google Play services provides an accurate and easy-to-implement solution for location-based services. The result of the Hour18AppPlay project is the same as the Hour18App project. Both display the current location. Less code and complexity are involved when using Google Play services to implement location services.

Figure 18.7 shows a location being displayed in the Hour18AppPlay app.

FIGURE 18.7
Showing location using Google Play services

Summary

In this hour, you learned the basics of how an Android device determines location. You saw how to build a simple app to demonstrate location features including getting the last known location and listening for location changes. This hour also discussed strategies for getting an accurate and current location. You saw how after determining a location, you can use reverse geocoding to retrieve information about the location and use an `Intent` to map the location.

Q&A

Q. What are some of the things that the Maps V2 API can do?

A. With the Maps API, you can place markers on a map to identify a location on a map. Markers respond to click events, so you can add more functionality. With the API, you can draw on the map and use map-specific UI features.

Q. What are some techniques for advanced location-based applications?

A. This hour covered listening for location changes and offered a basic strategy for getting the most recent known location. Additional techniques for getting accurate locations and using intent services and broadcast receivers for location changes are covered in the location Deep Dive blog post on the Android developers blog at http://android-developers.blogspot. com/2011/06/deep-dive-into-location.html.

Workshop

Quiz

1. Which is more accurate at determining location: `LocationManager.NETWORK_PROVIDER` or `LocationManager.GPS_PROVIDER`?

2. Given a latitude and longitude, what additional information can an app retrieve?

3. Is it true that when you retrieve the last known location for the GPS provider that you are guaranteed to receive up-to-the-minute information?

Answers

1. Typically, we would say that the `LocationManager.GPS_PROVIDER` is more accurate, but that just means if both the `NETWORK_PROVIDER` and `GPS_PROVIDER` are available, the `GPS_PROVIDER` will likely give a more accurate result. The problem is that the `GPS_PROVIDER` might not be available in certain situations in which case the `NETWORK_PROVIDER` will give better results.

2. Given a latitude and longitude, an `Address` object can be retrieved using reverse geocoding. The `Address` object gives us locale, country, and address information.

3. No; the last known location for any provider might be stale and out of date.

Exercise

Modify the app in this hour to retrieve data at 5-minute intervals with an accuracy of 100 meters. Display the full address of the location that you receive.

Optionally, create a `ProximityAlert` to detect that you are entering or leaving a specific area.

HOUR 19
Bonjour, World! Localizing Your Apps

What You'll Learn in This Hour:

▶ Android as a global marketplace
▶ Supporting multiple languages
▶ Calendar, currency, and other localization concerns
▶ Localization checklist

The Android marketplace is global—serving many countries and locales. The global market provides an opportunity to bring your app to more people. You might also find that your app is a catching on in a particular country. So being international can expand both the number of people who use your app and increase the possibility of your app catching on in a particular locale. This hour covers localization features on the Android platform and strategies for localization.

General Internationalization Principles

With a global marketplace, developers can maximize profits and grow their user base by supporting a variety of different languages and locales. Let's make a distinction between languages and locales. You understand what a language is. Languages may include a number of different locales commonly called dialects. For example, the Spanish spoken in Spain is different from that spoken in the Americas; the French spoken in Canada differs from that spoken in Europe and Africa; and the English spoken in the United States differs from that spoken in Britain. English is a language, while English (United States), English (United Kingdom), and English (Australia) are locales. The Android platform provides support at the locale level.

Applications are made up of data and functionality. For most applications, the functionality is the same, regardless of the locale. However, the data must be localized. This is one of the key reasons resource files exist—to externalize application data. Locale and language differences include different word spellings, meanings, slang, and format of regional data such as date and time and primary currency. The most common type of application data that requires localization is the strings of text used by the application. For example, a string of data might represent a user's name, but the text label for that value on an application screen needs to be shown in the proper language (for example, Name, Nom, Nombre).

Development platforms that support internationalization typically allow for string tables, which can be swapped around so that the same application can target different languages. The Android platform is no exception.

Do not hard code localizable data such as string information into the application source files, particularly in Java and layout resource files. Doing so hinders internationalization efforts. (Note that for simplicity and clarity of code examples, the authors have not followed this practice in earlier examples in this book.)

Working with Localization with Android

The Android SDK provides extensive support for internationalization through the use of locales.

Android localization considerations fall into three main categories:

▶ The languages and locales supported by the Android platform (an extensive list—the superset of all available languages)

▶ The languages and locales supported by a specific Android device (a list that varies—a subset of languages chosen by a device manufacturer or operator)

▶ The countries, languages, and locales supported by the Android Market application (the countries and locales where Google can sell legally; this list grows continuously)

At a high level, a locale is specified by language code and country code. For example, the constants en_US, en_GB, and en_AU represent the English language as spoken in the United States, Great Britain, and Australia, respectively.

The only locale that is guaranteed to be available is en_US locale. Not all devices will have all locales. A device sold in the US will likely support en_US and es_US (English and Spanish for the U.S.), but will not necessarily support en_GB (English Great Britain).

NOTE

Language Codes and Country Codes

Languages codes and country codes are defined by ISO standards. Language codes are defined in ISO 639-1 and country codes are defined in ISO 3166-1.

Handling Locales with Android

Much like other operating systems, the Android platform has a system setting for locale. This setting has a default setting that the mobile operator can modify. For example, a German mobile operator might make the default locale Deutsch (Deutschland) for its shipping devices. An American mobile operator would likely set the default locale to English (American) and include an option for the locale Español (Estados Unidos)—thus supporting American English and Spanish of the Americas.

A user can change the systemwide setting for locale in the Settings application. The locale setting affects the behavior of all applications installed on the device. Some apps might support the selected language and others might not. If the app does not support the selected language, the default language for that app will be used.

Figure 19.1 shows the Settings application.

TRY IT YOURSELF ▼

Changing Locale on a Device

To change the locale on a device, perform the following steps. *Be sure to remember the steps (or related icons),* because you have to navigate back to the locale settings in the foreign language you chose:

1. Open the Settings app.

2. From the Settings menu, select the Language & Input option.

3. Choose Language and select a language. The Android platform immediately changes the locale on the system. For example, if you choose Español, you see that many of the menus on the Android platform are now in Spanish.

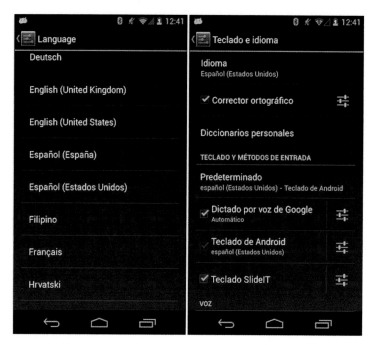

FIGURE 19.1
Language settings in English and switched to Spanish (U.S.)

Using Applications to Handle Locales

Now take a look at how the systemwide locale setting affects an Android application. When an Android application uses a project resource, the Android operating system attempts to match the best possible resource for the job at runtime. In many cases, this means checking for a resource in the specific language or regional locale. If no resource matches the required locale, the system falls back on the default resource.

Developers can include language and locale resources by providing resources in specially named resource directories of the project. You can localize any application resource, whether it is a string resource file, a drawable, an animation sequence, or some other type. Considering setting locales for layout is important resources. Layouts that are carefully reviewed in English might need to change for other languages. A short word in one language might be a long word in another language. If your buttons just fit in a layout, you might need to change them for other locales.

Specifying Default Resources

Hour 3 introduced using a resource file, and in Hour 4, you saw how to use resource qualifiers such as `layout-land` to specify alternative resources for different conditions.

A default resource is a resource that has no resource qualifiers.

Default resources are the most important resources because they are the fallback for any situation when a specific, tailored resource does not exist (which happens more often than not).

Specifying Language-Specific Resources

To specify strings for a specific language, you must supply the resource under a specially named directory that includes the two-letter language code provided in ISO 639-1. For example, English is en, French is fr, and German is de. Let's look at an example of how this works.

Say that you want an application to support English, German, and French strings. To do so, take the following steps:

1. Create a strings.xml resource file for each language. Each string that is to be localized must appear in each resource file with the same name, so it can be programmatically loaded correctly. Any strings you don't want to localize can be left in the default (English) / res/values/strings.xml file.

2. Save the French strings.xml resource file to the /res/values-fr/ directory.

3. Save the German strings.xml resource file to the /res/values-de/ directory.

Android can now grab the appropriate string, based on the system locale. However, if no match exists, the system falls back on whatever is defined in the /res/values/ directory. This means that if English (or Arabic, or Chinese, or Japanese, or an unexpected locale) is chosen, the default (fallback) English strings are used.

Similarly, you could provide German-specific drawable resources to override the default graphics in the /res/drawable/ directory by supplying versions (each with the same name) in the /res/drawable-de/ directory.

TIP

Limit Text in Image Resources

Your app might require different images for different locales, but using most images in all locales is ideal. Changing a text file is easier and relatively less time consuming than changing an image. So, try to minimize, or ideally eliminate, all text in image resources.

Specifying Region-Specific Resources

You might have noticed that the previous example specifies high-level language settings only (English, but not American English versus British English versus Australian English). Adding the region or locale as part of the resource directory name is a straightforward process as well.

To specify strings for a specific language and locale, you must store the localized resource under a specially named directory that includes the two-letter language code provided in ISO 639-1 followed by a dash, then a lowercase *r*, and finally the ISO 3166-1-alpha-2 region code. For example, American English is en-rUS, British English is en-rGB, and Australian English is en-rAU. Let's look at an example of how this works.

To support these three versions of English, do the following:

1. Create a strings.xml resource file for each language. You can leave any strings you don't want to localize in the default (American English) /res/values/strings.xml file.

2. Save the British English strings.xml resource file to the /res/values-en-rGB/ directory.

3. Save the Australian English strings.xml resource file to the /res/values-en-rAU/directory.

To summarize, start with a default set of resources, which should be in the most common language your application will rely on. Then, add exceptions—such as separate language and region string values—where needed. This way, you can optimize your application so it runs on a variety of platforms.

Reviewing Apps in Multiple Languages

In the earlier Try It Yourself section, you saw how to change the locale on the phone. Changing locales is an easy way to review apps that you are familiar with in another language. It can be helpful for doing simple translations. You might be able to see the words for *OK, Cancel, Settings,* and *playlist* in another language. The best way to translate an app is to work with a native speaker, but for a simple app, looking at other apps in the target language can be helpful.

Figure 19.2 shows the Google+ menu in Spanish. It provides a hint about the words for *profile* and *photos* among others.

Translation services are also available for websites and apps. As part of the Android publishing process in Google Play, you have the option to get a professional translation. It is a paid service, but one that might be worthwhile for your app.

Open-source Android projects might include language resource files that can be helpful to start translating an app.

FIGURE 19.2
Google+ menu in Spanish

Android Internationalization Strategies

Internationalization might be important to your project or a nice enhancement, or it might not be particularly important. Therefore, give some thought to how important internationalization is to your application during the design phase of your project. Develop a strategy that suits your specific needs and follow through on that strategy.

You might "discover" a strategy as you develop your app and see how it is used.

A typical sequence for internationalizing an app would be to

▸ Create a prototype in your target locale. You might have some hard-coded text values as you develop the product.

▸ Externalize your strings—move any hard-coded text resources into resource files.

▸ Add one language for a market where your app is doing well by adding a language-specific resource file.

▶ Add more customizations for your new market by customizing the graphics and layouts as needed.

▶ Add another language and continue on through this process.

Work through the new issues that come up as you perform these steps, but realize that Android has a robust way of handling internationalization.

No single rule exists for internationalization, but you can consider three approaches:

▶ No internationalization

▶ Limited internationalization

▶ Implement robust internationalization for target audiences

The following sections consider each of these strategies in more detail.

Forgoing Application Internationalization

Whenever possible, save your development and testing teams a lot of work—don't bother to internationalize your application. This is the "one size fits most" approach to mobile development, and using it is often possible with simple, graphic-intensive applications such as games that do not have a lot of text to display. If your application is simple enough to work smoothly with internationally recognized graphical icons (such as play, pause, stop, and so on) instead of text labels, then you might be able to forgo internationalization entirely. Games such as tic-tac-toe and chess are games that require little, if any, text resources.

TIP

Always Put Strings in Resource Files

Even if you are not planning on internationalizing your app, externalizing strings is a best practice. When a text value is in the res/values resource folder in the strings.xml file, it is a single point of reference for the value. You can use them in multiple source files and then if you need to change it, you make the change in one place.

Some of the pros of this strategy are the following:

▶ Simplified development and testing

▶ Smallest application size (only one set of resources)

Some of the cons of this strategy are the following:

▶ For text- or culture-dependent applications, this approach greatly reduces the value of the application. It is simply too generic.

▶ This strategy automatically alienates certain audiences and limits your application's potential marketplaces.

▶ This technique works only for a subset of applications. If your application requires a help screen, for example, you're likely going to need at least some localization for your application to work well all over the world.

Limiting Application Internationalization

Most applications require only some light internationalization. This often means internationalizing string resources only, but other resources, such as layouts and graphics, remain the same for all languages and locales.

Some of the pros of this strategy are the following:

▶ Modest development and testing requirements

▶ Streamlined application size (specialized resources kept to a minimum)

Some of the cons of this strategy are the following:

▶ This strategy might still be too generic for certain types of applications. Overall design (especially screen design) might suffer from needing to support multiple target languages. For example, text fields might need to be large enough to support verbose languages such as German but look odd and waste valuable screen real estate in less verbose languages.

▶ Because you've headed down the road of providing language-specific resources, your users are more likely to expect other languages you haven't supported. In other words, you're more likely to start getting requests for your app to support more languages if you've supported some. That said, you've already built and tested your application on a variety of languages, so adding new ones should be a straightforward process.

Implementing Robust Application Internationalization

Some types of applications require complete internationalization. Providing custom resources for each supported language and locale is a time-intensive endeavor. This approach often necessitates breaking the individual languages into separate APK files for publication, resulting in more complex configuration management. However, this allows a developer to tailor an application for each specific marketplace to a fine degree.

Some of the pros of this strategy are the following:

▶ The application is fully tailored and customized to individual audiences; this strategy allows for tweaks to individual locales.

▶ It builds user loyalty by providing users with the best, most customized experience. (This is also a technique used by Google.)

Some of the cons of this strategy are the following:

▶ It is the most lengthy and complicated strategy to develop.

▶ Each internationalized version of the application must be fully tested as if it were a completely different application (which it might well be, if you are forced to split it into different APK files due to application size).

Using Localization Utilities

The Android SDK includes support for handling locale information. For example, the `Locale` (`java.util.Locale`) class encapsulates locale information.

Determining System Locale

If you need to modify application behavior based on locale information, you must be able to access information about the Android operating system. You can do this by using the `getConfiguration()` method of the `Context` object, as follows:

```
Configuration sysConfig = getResources().getConfiguration();
```

One of the settings available in the `Configuration` object is the locale:

```
Locale curLocale = sysConfig.locale;
```

You can use this locale information to vary application behavior programmatically, as needed.

Formatting Date and Time Strings

Another aspect of internationalization is displaying data in the appropriate way. For example, U.S. dates are formatted MM/DD/YY and October 26, 2013, whereas much of the rest of the world uses the formats DD/MM/YY and 26 October 2013. The Android SDK includes a number of locale-specific utilities. For example, you can use the `DateFormat` (`android.text.format.DateFormat`) class to generate date and time strings in the current locale, or you can customize date and time information as needed for your application.

Handling Currencies

Much like dates and times, currencies and how they are formatted differ by locale. You can use the standard Java `Currency` (`java.util.Currency`) class to encapsulate currency information. Use the `NumberFormat` (`java.text.NumberFormat`) class to format and parse numbers based on locale information.

Summary

This hour covered basic internationalization principles such as externalizing project resources. You learned how the Android platform handles different countries, languages, and locales. Finally, it covered several strategies for internationalization.

Q&A

Q. Which languages and locales should I target in my Android applications?

A. The answer to this question depends on a variety of factors and is particular to your app and your business plan for the app. The short answer is this: The fewest you can get away with. The answer boils down to knowing your user audience and target markets.

Q. What languages should I use for default resources such as strings?

A. Your default resources should be in the language/locale used by your largest target audience—the most generic and likely values that appeal to the most users. If you're targeting the world at large, the choice is often English, but it need not be. For example, if your application allows turn-based directions anywhere in China, then you probably want your default language/locale to be one of the Chinese options.

Q. I changed the locale to Spanish. Why do some applications still display in English?

A. If an application has its default strings in English and has no Spanish resources available, then the defaults are used, regardless of the language chosen.

Workshop

Quiz

1. True or false: An Android application can support multiple languages within a single APK file.

2. What language should your default resources be?

   A. English

   B. The language that most appeals to your target audience

   C. En_US

Answers

1. True. An application can be compiled with resources in several different languages. The Android platform can switch between these resources on-the-fly, based upon the locale settings of the device.

2. The correct answer is B. Your default resources should be the ones that are most likely to load and be used. Therefore, designing these resources to be in the language and locale that appeals to the most number of users makes sense.

Exercises

1. Add a new set of string resource values to an app from a previous hour in the language or locale of your choice.

2. Change any app from a previous chapter so that it loads a custom drawable or color resource for a specific language or locale.

3. Review Hour 3 and Hour 4 with a focus on how to use resource files and resource qualifiers for localization. In particular, review the qualifier types listed in Table 4.1 (refer to Hour 4).

HOUR 20

Say Cheese! Working with Cameras

What You'll Learn in This Hour:

▶ Capturing media

▶ Using intents to take photos and videos

▶ Creating a custom camera app

As you have seen, Android devices come in different sizes and have different features. Most Android phones and many Android tablets include a camera. Some have two cameras. A front-facing camera faces the user and enables apps for video chatting as well as self-portraits. Cameras on Android devices take both photos and videos. In this hour, you learn how to take photos and videos easily using the built-in camera app and how to control the camera directly.

Capturing Media

Whether you use the built-in camera app or write code to control the camera directly, you follow some common procedures to handle the media. Videos and full-size photos contain a significant amount of data. Typically, the media data is stored in a file. This section goes through the details of defining a file for use in media storage.

NOTE

Capturing a Photo in Memory

Android provides an intent for capturing photos. That intent can be used to capture a photo in memory or to a file. The catch with capturing an image to memory is that only a thumbnail-sized photo is captured. In practice, photos are captured to files.

Android has a mechanism called the *media scanner service* that makes media-like photos available via a content provider. Apps such as the Gallery app access the MediaStore (android. provider.MediaStore) content provider to obtain available images and videos. When an app creates a new image, the media scanner discovers that image and makes the image available in the `MediaStore` content provider. After you create a new photo or video, you can make it immediately available to the media scanner by adding a few lines of code.

The Hour 20 App project contains this source code.

Common Steps When Capturing Media

Whenever you capture media in this hour, you:

▶ Create a file for storage using a timestamp and proper extension

▶ Create a URI from the file

▶ Use the URI to invoke media scanner

Specifying a File for Media Storage

The first step to take when capturing a photo or video is to specify the file that will hold the captured content. Since API version 8, a specific directory is available for storing public pictures. If you have an app that creates pictures, an app user might want the pictures even if he or she deletes the app. Placing the pictures in the public pictures directory ensures that they are accessible and will be retained even if the user deletes the app.

Each media file will be given a unique name. You can use a naming scheme for photos and videos that adds a timestamp. Photos are stored as JPGs, and videos are stored as MP4s.

In Listing 20.1, a directory named Hour 20 is created within the public pictures directory, and the current date and time are used to create a unique filename.

The sample application uses the code from Listing 20.1 in several places. It is used each time you want to capture an image or video.

To save files to external storage, you must set the `android.permission.WRITE_EXTERNAL_STORAGE` in the AndroidManifest.xml file.

LISTING 20.1 Snippet to Create Picture File

```
 1: File mediaStorageDir = new File(Environment.getExternalStoragePublicDirectory(
 2:                             Environment.DIRECTORY_PICTURES), "Hour20");
 3: if (!mediaStorageDir.exists()){
 4:     mediaStorageDir.mkdirs();
 5: }
 6: String timeStamp = new SimpleDateFormat("yyyyMMdd_HHmmss").format(new Date());
 7: mDisplayFolder = "Pictures" + File.separator +"Hour20"
 8:                 + File.separator +"IMG_"+ timeStamp + ".jpg";
 9: mPhotoFile = new File(mediaStorageDir.getPath() + File.separator +"IMG_"
10:                 + timeStamp + ".jpg");
```

Lines 1 and 2 use the `Environment.getExternalStoragePublicDirectory()` method to define the app's Hour 20 directory within the public pictures directory. The first parameter to this method, `Environment.DIRECTORY_PICTURES`, specifies to use the pictures directory. Other available public directories in the `Environment` class are `DIRECTORY_DOWNLOADS`, `DIRECTORY_MOVIES`, `DIRECTORY_MUSIC`, `DIRECTORY_NOTIFICATIONS`, `DIRECTORY_PODCASTS`, and `DIRECTORY_RINGTONES`.

Lines 3–5 create this directory if it does not exist.

On line 6, the Java `SimpleDateFormat (java.text.SimpleDateFormat)` class is used in conjunction with the `Date (java.util.Date)` class to create a timestamp string. `SimpleDateFormat` provides many options for transforming `Date` objects. In this case, the result is specified by the string `"yyyyMMdd_HHmmss"` where `y` refers to year, `M` to month, `d` to day, and so on for hours, minutes, and seconds.

On lines 7 and 9, the variable `mDisplayFolder` is populated. It is a string that displays to the user.

Lines 9 and 10 populate the `File` variable `mPhotoFile`. This `File` object contains the name of the file where the photo will actually be stored. To create the `File`, you pass the directory path, the name of the file specified by `IMG` and the timestamp, and the `.jpg` file extension. For a video, you would specify the file using `VID`, the timestamp, and the `.mp4` file extension.

At this point, you have learned to define a `File` in which to save a captured photo. The process for defining a `File` for capturing a video is similar.

Creating the URI and Invoking the Media Scanner

The following sections cover several ways to capture photos and videos. In each case, you want to make the captured media available to the `MediaStore` and apps such as the Gallery app that display this content.

You invoke the media scanner via an `Intent`. The key piece of information that is required is the name of the file where the media is stored.

Listing 20.1 showed how to create the variable `mPhotoFile` for storing a photo. Assuming the file now contains a captured photo, you create a `Uri` from the `mPhotoFile` variable using the `Uri.fromFile()` method. When you create the file, you'll also create a URI:

```
mPhotoFileUri=Uri.fromFile(mPhotoFile);
```

You then use this URI to invoke the media scanner via an `Intent`:

```
Intent mediaScanIntent = new Intent(Intent.ACTION_MEDIA_SCANNER_SCAN_FILE);
mediaScanIntent.setData(mPhotoFileUri);
this.sendBroadcast(mediaScanIntent);
```

The ACTION_MEDIA_SCANNER_SCAN_FILE Intent scans the media file. The setData() method is used to specify the URI to scan. You use the sendBroadcast() method to invoke the media scanner.

Each time you capture a photo or video, you invoke the media scanner in this way.

NOTE

Hiding Images from Media Scanner

The media scanner will eventually discover media files even if it is not directly called as it is in Listing 20.3. That means that images written to the external file system in the app will be made available in the gallery app. To prevent images from being discovered, do not use a public folder such as Environment.DIRECTORY_PICTURES and include a file in your private folder called .nomedia. Note the dot in the filename.

The recommended approach for storing media files and using the media scanner is as follows:

▶ If your app takes photos the user might want to save, put them in DIRECTORY_PICTURES and invoke the media scanner.

▶ If those photos are for other purposes (for example, an attachment for a message, or to change the user profile), then it should go into the app's private data directory and that directory should have a .nomedia file to prevent the media scanner from indexing it.

▶ Any other image file the app might include, or save, or download, or generate, should be in a directory with a .nomedia file unless you're certain the user might want to browse it in the gallery, in which case it should be in one of the standard locations provided by Environment.

Using Intents to Take Photos and Videos

In this hour, you learn to capture photos and videos in two ways. First, you see how to use the built-in camera app to capture images and videos by using intents. You then learn to create your own simple camera activities to capture photos and videos.

The example app launches an activity called MainActivity.java. That activity displays four buttons. The first two buttons use intents to capture photos and videos. That intent code is in the onClickListener() methods for the buttons in MainActivity.java. The last two buttons launch your custom camera activities.

You invoke these intents using the StartActivityForResult() method. You used the StartActivityForResult() method in Hour 2 when you started an Activity and then handled the result in the `onActivityResult()` method. When you capture a photo or video, the captured media is made available in the `onActivityResult()` method. Figure 20.1 shows the app when it launches.

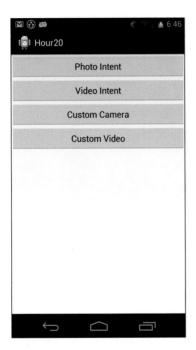

FIGURE 20.1
The Hour 20 App at launch

Taking a Photo Using an Intent

When you launch an activity with the `startActivityForResult()` method, you handle the result in the `onActivityResult()` method. These two methods are linked by the use of a common request code parameter. You include the request code provided to `startActivity-ForResult()` as a parameter to the `onActivityResult()` method. Use `CAPTURE_IMAGE_REQUEST_CODE` as your request code variable for photo capture. It is defined in MainActivity. java:

```
private static final int CAPTURE_IMAGE_REQUEST_CODE = 1;
```

Launching the Camera with an Intent

The first button defined in MainActivity.java is the `takePhotoButton`. In the `OnClickListener()` method for `takePhotoButton`, you define an intent for capturing a photo and call the `StartActivityForResult()` method.

Listing 20.2 shows the entire `onClickListener()` method for the `takePhotoButton`. To create this intent, you use `MediaStore.ACTION_IMAGE_CAPTURE` (see line 4).

Lines 5–14 include the code for defining a file for media capture. This code is the same as in Listing 20.1. With the intent and the filename, you can put together the image capture request. Line 16 sets the media file as an extra value for the intent, and on line 17, the `startActivityForResult()` begins the image capture. It is there that the `CAPTURE_IMAGE_REQUEST_CODE` is used.

In line 15, you set `mPhotoFileUri`. This field is used later for the media scanner.

LISTING 20.2 Capturing a Photo via an Intent

```
 1:   Button takePhotoButton = (Button) findViewById(R.id.photoIntentButton);
 2:   takePhotoButton.setOnClickListener(new OnClickListener() {
 3:       public void onClick(View v) {
 4:           Intent intent = new Intent(MediaStore.ACTION_IMAGE_CAPTURE);
 5:           File mediaStorageDir = new File(Environment.
getExternalStoragePublicDirectory(
 6:           Environment.DIRECTORY_PICTURES), "Hour20");
 7:           if (! mediaStorageDir.exists()){
 8:               mediaStorageDir.mkdirs();
 9:           }
10:           String timeStamp = new SimpleDateFormat("yyyyMMdd_HHmmss").format(new
Date());
11:           mDisplayFolder = "Pictures" + File.separator +"Hour20"
12:                           + File.separator +"IMG_"+ timeStamp + ".jpg";
13:           mPhotoFile = new File(mediaStorageDir.getPath()
14:                           + File.separator +"IMG_"+ timeStamp + ".jpg");
15:           mPhotoFileUri=Uri.fromFile(mPhotoFile);
16:           intent.putExtra(MediaStore.EXTRA_OUTPUT,mPhotoFileUri );
17:           startActivityForResult(intent, CAPTURE_IMAGE_REQUEST_CODE);
18:       }
19:   });
```

When the `ACTION_IMAGE_CAPTURE` intent fires, the built-in camera app appears.

The user can take a picture and either accept or reject the picture for use. If the picture is rejected, the user can take another picture (see Figure 20.2).

FIGURE 20.2
Taking and accepting a picture with the camera app

Handle the Resulting Image in onActivityResult()

You saw how to use the onActivityResult() method in Hour 2 in a basic example to handle data returned from an activity. The parameters for onActivityResult() are for request-Code, resultCode, and data. You use the requestCode to match the activity result that you are handling to the original request. The resultCode indicates a result with RESULT_OK or that the user cancelled the request with RESULT_CANCELLED.

For a photo capture, if RESULT_OK is returned in onActivityResult(), you can rely on the filename and URI that was set up when you made the request to get the photo data.

In MainActivity.java, you defined the field mDisplayFolder as a String. Listing 20.2 shows that during the Intent creation, mDisplayFolder was populated with the name of the folder and file for the image. The field mPhotoFileUri was also defined and assigned the URI that corresponds to the file.

The onActivityResult() method shown in Listing 20.3 uses both of these fields.

Line 3 compares the requestCode to the CAPTURE_IMAGE_REQUEST_CODE value. A match means that this is the capture image event. Line 4 checks to see whether the resultCode matches RESULT_OK. If this is the result of an image capture event and the result is OK, two things happen:

▶ Lines 5 and 6 use the previously defined `mDisplayFolder` `String` to display a `Toast`.

▶ Lines 7–10 invoke the media scanner. Line 7 defines an `Intent` for media scanning using the previously defined `mPhotoFileUri` for the data, and calls the `sendBroadcast` method. This immediately makes the image data available to the media scanner.

LISTING 20.3   Handle the Captured Photo in onActivityResult()

```
 1:  @Override
 2:  protected void onActivityResult(int requestCode, int resultCode, Intent data)
{
 3:      if (requestCode == CAPTURE_IMAGE_REQUEST_CODE) {
 4:        if (resultCode == RESULT_OK) {
 5:            Toast.makeText(this, "Image saved to:\n" +
 6:                          mDisplayFolder, Toast.LENGTH_LONG).show();
 7:            Intent mediaScanIntent = new Intent(Intent.ACTION_MEDIA_SCANNER_SCAN_
FILE);
 8:            mediaScanIntent.setData(mPhotoFileUri);
 9:            this.sendBroadcast(mediaScanIntent);
10:        } else if (resultCode == RESULT_CANCELED) {
11:        } else {
12:  Toast.makeText(this, "Something went wrong", Toast.LENGTH_LONG).show();
13:        }
14:      } . . .
```

Listings 20.2 and 20.3 show the steps in using an intent to capture a photo:

▶ Create a `File` object with a unique filename to hold the captured image

▶ Create a URI pointing at that unique filename

▶ Create an intent using `MediaStore.ACTION_IMAGE_CAPTURE`

▶ Use `StartActivityForResult()` to launch the intent

▶ Use `onActivityForResult()` to handle the results of the intent

▶ Check to see whether the result is for the image capture intent

▶ Check to see whether the result is successful

▶ Invoke the media scanner intent by passing the URI for the image

Taking a Video Using an Intent

The structure of the code for taking a video using an intent is just like that for taking a photo. The steps are the same. The differences are that you use a different filename, file extension, and intent to capture video.

Listing 20.4 shows the onClickListener() code for the shootVideoButton from MainActivity.java. The intent to capture video is MediaStore.ACTION_VIDEO_CAPTURE (see line 4). You use the same directory for storing videos as for storing photos, but the filename begins with VID and the file extension is .mp4.

LISTING 20.4 Capturing a Video Using an Intent

```
1:   Button shootVideoButton = (Button) findViewById(R.id.videoIntentButton);
2:   shootVideoButton.setOnClickListener(new OnClickListener() {
3:    public void onClick(View v) {
4:       Intent intent = new Intent(MediaStore.ACTION_VIDEO_CAPTURE);
5:       File mediaStorageDir = new File(Environment.
getExternalStoragePublicDirectory(
6:                               Environment.DIRECTORY_PICTURES), "Hour20");
7:       if (! mediaStorageDir.exists()){
8:           mediaStorageDir.mkdirs();
9:       }
10:      String timeStamp = new SimpleDateFormat("yyyyMMdd_HHmmss").format(new
Date());
11:      mDisplayFolder = "Pictures" + File.separator +"Hour20"
12:                       + File.separator +"VID_"+ timeStamp + ".mp4";
13:      mVideoFile = new File(mediaStorageDir.getPath()
14:                       + File.separator +"VID_"+ timeStamp + ".mp4");
15:      mVideoFileUri=Uri.fromFile(mVideoFile);
16:      intent.putExtra(MediaStore.EXTRA_OUTPUT, mVideoFileUri);
17:      startActivityForResult(intent, CAPTURE_VIDEO_REQUEST_CODE);
18:     }
19:   });
```

Handling the result from capturing a video is also similar to capturing a photo. Listing 20.5 shows this. The check is made for the requestCode CAPTURE_VIDEO_REQUEST_CODE. If the result is RESULT_OK, a Toast appears and the video becomes available to the media scanner. The intent for the media scanner, shown on line 5, is the same for images and videos.

LISTING 20.5 Handle the Captured Video in onActivityResult()

```
1:    if (requestCode == CAPTURE_VIDEO_REQUEST_CODE) {
2:        if (resultCode == RESULT_OK) {
3:    Toast.makeText(this, "Video saved to:\n" +
4:                        mDisplayFolder, Toast.LENGTH_LONG).show();
5:    Intent mediaScanIntent = new Intent(Intent.ACTION_MEDIA_SCANNER_SCAN_FILE);
6:           mediaScanIntent.setData(mVideoFileUri);
7:           this.sendBroadcast(mediaScanIntent);
8:    } else if (resultCode == RESULT_CANCELED) {
9:    } else {
10:          Toast.makeText(this, "Something went wrong", Toast.LENGTH_LONG).
show();1:  11:   }
```

```
11:        }
12:      }
```

Advantages of Using Intents for Capturing Media

Using an intent is much easier than creating a custom camera application. Using an intent allows a developer to minimize the number of permissions that are required for the app.

When using an `Intent`, the camera apps on the device will be used. A user who has more than one camera app will be given the choice to use the one he prefers. The user does not need to learn about a new app. In many cases, the user will choose the default camera app.

The default camera app will likely take advantage of all the features for a particular API level. More camera features are available in Ice Cream Sandwich and Jelly Bean than in Froyo.

Developing a Camera App

You might have a creative or novel idea for an app that goes beyond using an intent to capture an image or a video. This section shows basic examples of activities that do this. Figure 20.1 shows Custom Camera and Custom Video buttons. These buttons both launch activities. The first button launches CustomCameraActivity.java and the second button launches CustomVideo.java.

Some common elements exist between these two activities. Permissions are required when using the camera and in both cases, you need to support a preview feature for the image or video. This section covers these common elements and then examines the individual activities.

Permissions for Capturing Media

When saving media to external storage, you need the `WRITE_EXTERNAL_STORAGE` permission. To use the camera directly, you must include the `CAMERA` permission. That is not the case when you use an intent to launch the camera. Video capture requires the `RECORD_AUDIO` permission.

These permissions are set as follows in the AndroidManifest.xml file:

```
<uses-permission android:name="android.permission.WRITE_EXTERNAL_STORAGE" />
<uses-permission android:name="android.permission.CAMERA"/>
<uses-permission android:name="android.permission.RECORD_AUDIO" />
```

Creating a Camera Preview Class

In a physical camera, a photographer looks through a viewfinder to determine what picture to take. When you create a camera app, your job is to provide the viewfinder, which you do via the `CameraPreview.java` class. `CameraPreview`'s job is to show the scene as the photographer sees it.

You use the `CameraPreview` class in the `CustomCameraActivity` and the `CustomVideoActivity`. The preview function works the same in both.

The `CameraPreview` class extends a `SurfaceView` (`android.view.SurfaceView`). A `SurfaceView` provides a surface for drawing. When you use it with the camera, the `SurfaceView` displays what the camera sees.

Figure 20.3 shows the `CustomCameraActivity`. The `CameraPreview` class shows the display.

FIGURE 20.3
`CameraPreview` shows the scene.

Associate a Camera with the SurfaceView

You want the `CameraPreview` class to have the device's camera show a preview. `CameraPreview` extends a `SurfaceView` that you use for displaying the content. You must associate the device's camera with the view, which you do in the constructor for `CameraPreview`. Listing 20.6 shows the constructor.

LISTING 20.6 Constructor for CameraPreview

```
1:  public CameraPreview(Context context, Camera camera) {
2:     super(context);
3:     mCamera = camera;
4:     mHolder = getHolder();
5:     mHolder.addCallback(this);
6:  }
```

In Listing 20.6, a `Camera` object is passed as a parameter. On Line 3, that camera object is assigned to the `mCamera` field in the `CameraPreview` class. `CameraPreview` extends `SurfaceView`. To actually enable drawing on the `SurfaceView`, you must access the `SurfaceHolder` interface that is provided via the `getHolder()` method. That is done on line 4 and the `SurfaceHolder`.

You can monitor changes to the `SurfaceHolder` via a callback. Line 5 tells the `SurfaceHolder` `mHolder` to use the `CameraPreview` class itself for callbacks.

Implementing SurfaceHolder.Callback

The `CameraPreview` class implements `SurfaceHolder.Callback`. The declaration for the class is as follows:

```
public class CameraPreview extends SurfaceView implements SurfaceHolder.Callback {
```

With the `SurfaceHolder.Callback`, you must implement methods that handle different states of the `SurfaceHolder`, which are `surfaceCreated()`, `surfaceDestroyed()`, and `surfaceChanged()`.

In `surfaceCreated()`, you begin the camera preview and display it on the `SurfaceHolder`. In the `surfaceChanged()` method, you stop and then restart the `Camera` preview. You must implement the `surfaceDestroyed()` method, but nothing is done in the method.

Listing 20.7 shows the `surfaceCreated()` method from CameraPreview.java. Line 3 associates the preview display of the `Camera` with the `SurfaceHolder` that is passed as a parameter. Line 4 starts the `Camera` preview.

LISTING 20.7   SurfaceHolder.Callback onSurfaceCreated()

```
1:  public void surfaceCreated(SurfaceHolder holder) {
2:     try {
3:        mCamera.setPreviewDisplay(holder);
4:        mCamera.startPreview();
5:     } catch (IOException e) {
6:         Log.d(TAG, "Error setting camera preview: " + e.getMessage());
7:     }
8:  }
```

At this point, you have a class that you can use for previewing. `CameraPreview` is a `SurfaceView` that is created by passing a `Camera` object. The preview of that `Camera` is shown in the view.

Now you can use this class for both the `CustomCameraActivity` and `CustomVideoActivity`. `CameraPreview` is the same whether you take a picture or shoot a video.

Creating a Custom Camera Activity

You use the CameraPreview class when you create the activity CustomCameraActivity. java.

The layout file associated with CustomCameraActivity.java is activity_custom_ camera.xml. The layout includes a FrameLayout with the id previewFrameLayout and a Button with the id takePictureButton. In CustomCameraActivity, you display the CameraPreview within previewFrameLayout.

The following steps occur in CustomCameraActivity:

1. Open the camera.

2. Create the camera preview.

3. Show the camera preview in the FrameLayout.

4. Get a list of possible sizes for the camera preview.

5. Determine the appropriate preview size and update the layout.

6. Take a picture when the user clicks the Take Picture button.

7. Save the picture.

The Camera object includes a set of parameters that you can access. Those parameters include a list of possible sizes for the preview. By using one of these preview sizes, you can be assured that the preview displays appropriately.

Displaying a Preview

The code shown in Listings 20.8–20.10 appears in this same order in the onCreate() method of CustomCameraActivity.java.

In Listing 20.8, you call Camera.open() to access the camera on the device. This method can return null if no back-facing camera is available. After you obtain a Camera object, you use the CameraPreview class that you created earlier in this hour. On line 3 of Listing 20.8, the CameraPreview object is created. In line 4, you create a FrameLayout with the findView-ById() method using the id previewFrameLayout from activity_custom_camera.xml.

After you initialize the Camera, CameraPreview, and FrameLayout and the objects on lines 2 and 4, you add the CameraPreview object to the layout (see line 5). The method preview. addView() adds the CameraPreview class mPreview to the FrameLayout preview that was defined in line 4.

This ties the Camera object to the CameraPreview class and places it within a layout for the activity.

LISTING 20.8   SurfaceHolder.Callback onSurfaceCreated()

```
1:  //open the Camera and display the Preview in the FrameLayout preview
2:  mCamera = Camera.open();
3:  mPreview = new CameraPreview(this, mCamera);
4:  FrameLayout preview = (FrameLayout) findViewById(R.id.previewFrameLayout);
5:  preview.addView(mPreview);
```

You can set the size of the preview by changing the width and height of the `FrameLayout` named `preview`. To get the best size for the preview for the display, you get a list of possible preview sizes from the camera and select the one that fits the screen display best.

Listing 20.9 shows how this is done. Line 2 retrieves the camera's current parameters with a call to `Camera.getParameters()`. The `Camera.Parameters` object allows you to get and set many camera features including zoom level, white balance, and many others. For now, focus on the possible sizes that you can use for preview.

You get that list of sizes on line 3 by calling the `Camera.Parameters` method `getSupport-PreviewSizes()`. A list of `Camera.Size` objects is returned. `Camera.Size` objects include a width and height value. The values in the list are returned in no particular order. On line 5 of Listing 20.9, the list is sorted. The class `OrderByHeight` is defined in CustomCameraActivity.java. It compares two `Camera.Size` objects to sort in ascending order by height. That is important because you must compare the possible preview sizes to the current display size to get the best fit for the preview display.

Lines 9–11 get the current display width and height.

Lines 12–16 iterate through the possible preview sizes and set the best fit. In this logic, the best size is the largest height and width that fits in the display. Looking at line 15, the check is whether the current `size.height` is less than the display height and greater than the current best size. If the current `size.width` and `size.height` are greater than the current best size and are not bigger than the whole display, then you use those values for the best size.

LISTING 20.9   Determine Preview Size

```
 1:  //Get the possible sizes for preview
 2:  Camera.Parameters currentParameters = mCamera.getParameters();
 3:  List<Camera.Size> sizes =    currentParameters.getSupportedPreviewSizes();
 4:  //Sort size by ascending Height
 5:  Collections.sort(sizes, new OrderByHeight());
 6:  //Set bestSize to the smallest
 7:  Camera.Size bestSize = sizes.get(0);
 8:  //Get size of the display
 9:  Display display = getWindowManager().getDefaultDisplay();
10:  int width = display.getWidth();
11:  int height = display.getHeight();
12:  // Make the best size the largest one whose height appears in the display
```

```
13: for (Camera.Size size: sizes){
14: System.out.println("size is " + size.width+"," +size.height);
15: if (size.height< height && size.height > bestSize.height
16:     && size.width < width && size.width > bestSize.width){
17: bestSize = size;
18: }
19: }
```

Having determined the best size for the display, you use the width and height to programmatically set the width and height of the FrameLayout that is displaying the camera preview. You do this on lines 3 and 4 of Listing 20.10 where you instantiate a RelativeLayout.Params object using bestSize.width and bestSize.height as parameters. You can add rules to a RelativeLayout.Params object. In line 5, you make the layout CENTER_VERTICAL and on line 6, you make the layout to the LEFT_OF the picture button. That is how to get the layout shown in Figure 20.3.

LISTING 20.10   Set Preview Size

```
1: //Get the possible sizes for preview
2: // Set the layout parameters
3: RelativeLayout.LayoutParams layoutParams = new RelativeLayout.LayoutParams
4: (bestSize.width, bestSize.height);
5: layoutParams.addRule(RelativeLayout.CENTER_VERTICAL);
6: layoutParams.addRule(RelativeLayout.LEFT_OF, R.id.takePicture);
7: preview.setLayoutParams(layoutParams);
```

You've done a lot of work to obtain the Camera object and associate the preview of the Camera with a view in your activity. You created a CameraPreview object that extended SurfaceView and added that CameraPreview object to a FrameLayout within the activity.

The Camera and preview are available in the activity. Now you can concentrate on taking a photo.

Taking a Picture

The two parts to taking a photo are to call Camera's takePicture() method and to create a callback for handling the picture. Taking a picture is a straightforward process. This code creates a takePictureButton and calls mCamera.takePicture() method when the button is clicked. The mPicture field is the callback function. When the picture becomes available, mPicture runs as the callback method:

```
Button takePictureButton = (Button) findViewById(R.id.takePicture);
takePictureButton.setOnClickListener(new OnClickListener() {
  public void onClick(View v) {
    mCamera.takePicture(null, null, mPicture);
  }
});
```

Listing 20.11 shows how `mPicture` is defined. On line 3, you see that the picture's data is passed as a byte array parameter. You define a file as you have previously, and on lines 16–18, you write the picture data to the file. As done previously, you initiate the media scanner by invoking an `Intent` on lines 21–23.

LISTING 20.11   Implementing Camera.PictureCallback()

```
1: mPicture= new Camera.PictureCallback() {
2: @Override
3: public void onPictureTaken(byte[] data, Camera camera) {
4: File mediaStorageDir = new File(Environment.getExternalStoragePublicDirectory(
5: Environment.DIRECTORY_PICTURES), "Hour20");
6: if (! mediaStorageDir.exists()){
7: mediaStorageDir.mkdirs();
8: }
9: String timeStamp = new SimpleDateFormat("yyyyMMdd_HHmmss").format(new Date());
10: String displayFolder = "Pictures" + File.separator +"Hour20"
11: + File.separator +"IMG_"+ timeStamp + ".jpg";
12: File photoFile = new File(mediaStorageDir.getPath()
13: + File.separator +"IMG_"+ timeStamp + ".jpg");
14: Uri photoFileUri=Uri.fromFile(photoFile);
15: try {
16: FileOutputStream fos = new FileOutputStream(photoFile);
17: fos.write(data);
18: fos.close();
19: Toast.makeText(CustomCameraActivity.this, "Image saved to:\n" +
20: displayFolder, Toast.LENGTH_LONG).show();
21: Intent mediaScanIntent = new Intent(Intent.ACTION_MEDIA_SCANNER_SCAN_FILE);
22: mediaScanIntent.setData(photoFileUri);
23: CustomCameraActivity.this.sendBroadcast(mediaScanIntent);
24: mCamera.startPreview();
25: } catch (FileNotFoundException e) {
26: Toast.makeText(CustomCameraActivity.this, "Something went wrong",
27: Toast.LENGTH_LONG).show();
28: } catch (IOException e) {
29: Toast.makeText(CustomCameraActivity.this, "Something went wrong",
30:Toast.LENGTH_LONG).show();
31: }
32: }
33: };
```

You have now created a simple, but useful custom camera application. You've taken into consideration the size and aspect ratio of the preview and shown that you can take a picture. This introduces the necessary concepts for building a camera app.

To make this app more robust, you can check for specific camera features, availability, and the number of cameras. If only a front-facing camera were available, you could use it. In that case, the call to `Camera.open()` would specify the front-facing camera. By default, `Camera.open()` does not include a front-facing camera.

Creating a Custom Video Activity

MainActivity.java includes a `Button` to initiate an `Activity` called CustomVideoActivity. java, which shows a camera and a `Start Recording` button. When the user chooses the Start Recording button, video recording is initiated and the button text changes to Stop Recording.

In many ways, CustomVideoActivity.java is similar to CustomCameraActivty.java. The differences are with recording video rather than taking a picture.

When recording video, a `MediaRecorder` object is created. You must control `MediaRecorder` in a specific way to record videos.

You use the `MediaRecorder` object with the `Camera` object. The `Camera` object is locked and unlocked for use with the `MediaRecorder`. The following code shows the `MediaRecorder` instantiated, the `Camera` associated with the `MediaRecorder`, and the key `MediaRecorder` settings initialized:

```
mMediaRecorder = new MediaRecorder();
mCamera.unlock();
mMediaRecorder.setCamera(mCamera);
mMediaRecorder.setAudioSource(MediaRecorder.AudioSource.DEFAULT);
mMediaRecorder.setVideoSource(MediaRecorder.VideoSource.CAMERA);
mMediaRecorder.setProfile(CamcorderProfile.get(CamcorderProfile.QUALITY_HIGH));
```

You create a file for storing the video as you did previously. You set that file as the output file for the `MediaRecorder` using `setOutputFile()`:

```
mMediaRecorder.setOutputFile(mVideoFile.toString());
```

To show the preview of what is being recorded, you use the `MediaRecorder`'s `setPreviewDisplay()` method:

```
mMediaRecorder.setPreviewDisplay(mPreview.getHolder().getSurface());
```

Much of the remainder of the `CustomVideoActivity` code handles the state of starting and stopping a video.

Summary

This hour showed you how to take a photo and record a video using intents. These intents are easy to use and take full advantage of the camera's features. You created an activity to control the camera and take a picture. A key component of taking a picture is creating a preview for the display. You did that by creating a `CameraPreview` class that extended a

SurfaceView. You used the `CameraPreview` class on both the `CustomCameraActivity` and the `CustomVideoActivity`.

Q&A

Q. In what cases does controlling the camera directly and not using an intent for capturing media make sense?

A. Some great apps control the camera directly. There is no rule of thumb, but if taking a picture or shooting a video is not the core functionality of your app using an intent makes.

Q. What other features can be added in a camera app?

A. Camera updates have been included in many recent Android updates. Ice Cream Sandwich added continuous focus, image zoom, and the ability to capture still images during video play. Faces can be detected and tracked in preview. For Jelly Bean, support for detecting whether the shutter sound can be disabled, providing an alternate shutter sound, and for High Dynamic Range (HDR) images was added.

Workshop

Quiz

1. After an image has been scanned by the media scanner, where can it be seen?

2. Why is the `EXTERNAL_WRITE_PERMISSION` needed in custom camera apps?

Answers

1. The image can be seen in the Gallery app. Technically, the image is being made available via the `MediaStore` content provider.

2. When you create photos and videos in a custom camera app, you save the media content to the file system. To do that, you need permission to write to the file system. `EXTERNAL_WRITE_PERMISSION` means you can write to the external file system.

Exercise

Create a new Android project with the goal of creating a standalone camera app. Use the `CameraPreview` and `CustomCameraActivity` classes from this hour as a starting point. At a minimum, launch the `CustomCameraActivity` as the main activity for the app. Look at the documentation for camera parameters and try setting various features.

Media Basics: Images, Audio, and Video

What You'll Learn in This Hour:

▶ Examining the `ImageView` control

▶ Using bitmaps and canvas

▶ Playing audio

▶ Playing video

▶ Checking out more media options

Images and media can play an important role in creating an exceptional Android app. This chapter takes a closer look at the details of handling images and bitmaps including creating bitmaps, using drawing commands, and handling very large images. It also covers audio, video, and other media options.

Examining the ImageView Control

Hour 6 showed how to use a simple `ImageView`. In that case, you saw how to display a drawable resource in the `ImageView`. An `ImageView` can display any drawable image. The source of the image can be a resource, a drawable, or a bitmap.

The source code for basic `ImageView` examples are in the accompanying Hour21ImageView project.

The four projects that contain the source code for this hour are the following:

▶ Hour21ImageView

▶ Hour21LargeImage

▶ Hour21VideoView

▶ Hour21Audio

Displaying an Image

Four methods are available for setting an image in an `ImageView`. They differ by how the image passed is defined. The image can be a bitmap, drawable, URI, or resource id. The methods are as follows:

▶ `setImageDrawable()`: Set a drawable as the content of the `ImageView`.

▶ `setImageBitmap()`: Set a bitmap as the content of the `ImageView`.

▶ `setImageResource()`: Use a resource id to set the content of the `ImageView`.

▶ `setImageUri()`: Use a URI to set the content of the `ImageView`.

To set an `ImageView` to an image resource defined by `R.Drawable.mainImage`, you would use the following:

```
ImageView mainImage = (ImageView) findViewById(R.id.imageView1);
mainImage.setImageResource(R.drawable.mainImage)
```

In this hour, you take a closer look at using bitmaps with `ImageViews`.

In Hour 3, you used a `ShapeDrawable` that had been defined as a resource. If you were working with a `ShapeDrawable` in code, you would use the `setImageDrawable()` method.

To populate a `Drawable` object from a resource, use the `getResources.getDrawable()` method:

```
Drawable myDrawable = getResources().getDrawable(R.drawable.ic_launcher);
```

You'll populate an `ImageView` using a resource id to explore some the available features in an `ImageView`.

Using ScaleTypes in ImageView

`ImageViews` include a `ScaleType` property. The `ScaleType` defines how an image displays within the `ImageView`. Using `ScaleType`, you can have an image fill the entire `ImageView`, be centered in the `ImageView`, or be cropped and centered in the `ImageView`.

The options for `ScaleType` are defined in `ImageView.ScaleType`. For example, `ImageView.ScaleType.CENTER` refers to a scale type in which the image is centered in the `ImageView`.

All scale types except for `FIT_XY` and `FIT_MATRIX` maintain the aspect ratio.

The complete set of `ScaleTypes` includes the following:

- ▶ `ImageView.ScaleType.CENTER`: Center the image with no scaling. The image dimensions are unchanged.

- ▶ `ImageView.ScaleType.CENTER_CROP`: Scales the image and keeps the aspect ratio until either the width of height of the image is the same as the width or height of the ImageView. For a small image, this will have the effect of enlarging the entire image. For a large image, this will have the effect of showing the center of the image.

- ▶ `ImageView.ScaleType.CENTER_INSIDE`: Scale the image and maintain aspect ratio. The width and height of the image fit within the `ImageView`.

- ▶ `ImageView.ScaleType.FIT_CENTER`: Fit the image in the center of the `ImageView`.

- ▶ `ImageView.ScaleType.FIT_START`: Fit the image in the left and top edge of the `ImageView`.

- ▶ `ImageView.ScaleType.FIT_END`: Fit the image in the right and bottom edge of the `ImageView`.

- ▶ `ImageView.ScaleType.FIT_XY`: Fit into the length and width of the `ImageView`. Does not maintain the aspect ratio.

- ▶ `ImageView.ScaleType.MATRIX`: Scale using a matrix. This allows for more complex translations of the image and is described later this hour.

The app created in the Hour21ImageView project illustrates the effects of setting different values for `ScaleType`. The layout file for this app includes an `ImageView` that fills the layout and a set of radio buttons for setting the `ScaleType`. MainActivity.java is set up in a simple way. With the `ImageView` and `RadioButtons` defined, when a button is clicked, the `ScaleType` value is set in the `ImageView`. Listing 21.1 shows the `onCheckChangeListener()` method for the `RadioButton` named `centerCrop`. If this `RadioButton` is checked, the `ScaleType` for `ImageView` is updated.

LISTING 21.1 Changing ScaleType Programatically

```
1:  centerCrop.setOnCheckedChangeListener(new OnCheckedChangeListener() {
2:  @Override
3:  public void onCheckedChanged(CompoundButton buttonView, booleani sChecked) {
4:  if (isChecked){
5:  imageView.setScaleType(ImageView.ScaleType.CENTER_CROP);
6:  }
7:  }
8:  });
```

The Hour21Image app uses the image shown in Figure 21.1 as the image for the `ImageView`.
The image is 900 pixels wide and 200 pixels high.

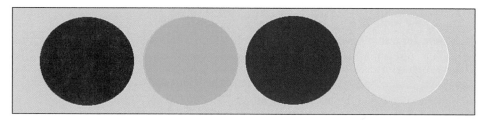

FIGURE 21.1
Base image for showing `ScaleType` (scaletest.png)

By using this simple image with four circles of different colors, you can easily see the effect of the
changing `ScaleType`.

Figure 21.2 shows the base image using the `ScaleTypes` CENTER, CENTER_CROP, and CENTER_
INSIDE. Using CENTER shows the image in actual size. Because the size of the image is larger
than the `ImageView`, the green and blue circles in the center display. CENTER_CROP shows half
of the green and half of the blue circles. The height of the image fills the `ImageView`. CENTER_
INSIDE shows the entire image centered in the `ImageView`.

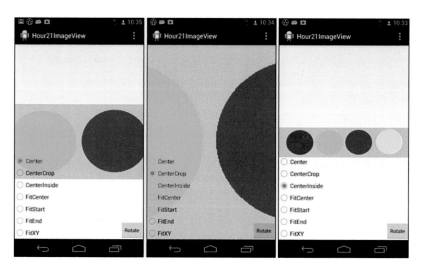

FIGURE 21.2
ScaleTypes CENTER, CENTER_CROP, and CENTER_INSIDE

Figure 21.3 shows the base image using the ScaleTypes FIT_CENTER, FIT_START, FIT_END, and FIT_XY. The aspect ratio is maintained in the first three options, but when you use FIT_XY, the image fills the ImageView and "stretches" the image to fit.

FIGURE 21.3
ScaleTypes FIT_CENTER, FIT_START, FIT_END, and FIT_XY

Rotating an Image with Matrix

In graphics programming, a matrix is used to transform an image. Simple transformations include scaling, translating, or rotating an image. Android includes a Matrix class (android.graphics.Matrix) to support these graphic transformations.

You might have noticed the Rotate button in the earlier images. As a simple example of using a Matrix, the Hour21ImageView app implements a Button that rotates the image in the ImageView by 30 degrees.

Listing 21.2 shows the OnClickListener() method for the rotate Button. On line 3, the Matrix associated with the ImageView is obtained. On line 4, you use the setScaleType() method to set the ScaleType to MATRIX. You must set ImageView.ScaleType.MATRIX in order to use a modified matrix on the ImageView. Line 5 is a matrix instruction to rotate the image 30 degrees around the point that is the center of the ImageView. Line 6 shows the matrix set for the ImageView. You must set ImageView ScaleType to MATRIX for this to take effect.

Figure 21.4 shows the rotated image.

LISTING 21.2 Rotating an Image

```
1:  rotate.setOnClickListener(new OnClickListener() {
2:  public void onClick(View v) {
3:  Matrix matrix = imageView.getImageMatrix();
4:  imageView.setScaleType(ImageView.ScaleType.MATRIX);
5:  matrix.postRotate(30, imageView.getWidth()/2, imageView.getHeight()/2);
6:  imageView.setImageMatrix(matrix);
7:  }
8:  });
```

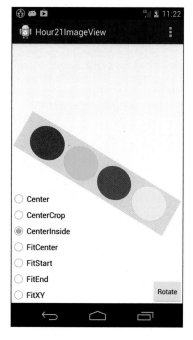

FIGURE 21.4
Rotated image

You can create complex transformations using `Matrix`. This app is a simple introduction to using a `Matrix` and the `MATRIX ScaleType`.

NOTE

Rotation in Honeycomb

Since API Level 11 (Honeycomb), the `View` class includes support for rotation. The methods `set-PivotX()`, `setPivotY()`, and `setRotation()` are supported. The `Matrix` class supports more complex transformations.

Setting Alpha

Alpha level indicates the opacity of an image. An image can be completely transparent, completely opaque, or somewhere in the middle. You can set the alpha level on an `ImageView` using the `setAlpha()` method or, since API level 11, by using the `setImageAlpha()` method. These methods take an integer parameter. A parameter of `0` indicates complete transparency and `255` indicates complete opacity.

Bitmaps and Canvas

The `Bitmap` (`android.graphics.Bitmap`) class represents a bitmap image. You create bitmaps via the `BitmapFactory` (`android.graphics.BitmapFactory`) class.

Using a `BitmapFactory`, you can create bitmaps in three common ways: from a resource, a file, or an `InputStream`. To create a bitmap from a resource, you use the `BitmapFactory` method `decodeResource()`:

```
Bitmap bitmap = BitmapFactory.decodeResource(getResources(), R.drawable.someImage);
```

To create a bitmap from a file or `InputStream`, you use the `decodeFile()` and `decodeStream()` methods, respectively.

Handling Large Images

There are techniques for avoiding the dreaded OOM (out of memory) exception. Large images can have a significant impact on memory use in your app. To demonstrate this, in this section, you create an unrealistically large image to display in an `ImageView`. When the image is just loaded into the `ImageView`, the app fails with an out-of-memory error. A `java.lang.OutOfMemory` exception occurs. You'll learn to fix the memory error for this case.

You want to display the image at an appropriate size and resolution for the device. No point exists in showing a 10-foot mural in a 6-inch frame. Similarly, no point exists in showing a 20-inch image on a 3-inch phone screen. You can manipulate the image to display well and save memory.

The details of your app will influence your memory usage and the techniques that will work best in your case. This example shows how to handle a single large image.

As a demonstration, start with an image and increase it to an unrealistic size. This example uses a photo that is 72 inches x 54 inches and that has a 28Mb file size.

The image is in the `drawable` resource folder and has the id `R.drawable.largeimage`.

You can cause the app to fail with an out-of-memory error by trying to set an `ImageView` to this resource. You have an `ImageView` named `largeImage`. This line of code causes the app to fail:

```
largeImage.setImageResource(R.drawable.largeimage);
```

Some work is required to fix this, but handling an image this large is possible. In all cases, working with appropriately sized images would be ideal, but that does not always happen.

The goal is to get the dimensions of the underlying bitmap without actually rendering it. Getting those dimensions is not a memory-intensive activity. After you have the bitmap, you can determine an appropriate size for the bitmap that will fit in your display. If you have a 20-inch image and a 4-inch display, you request that the bitmap that is created in memory be created at a size and resolution that is appropriate for the 4-inch display.

Using BitmapFactory.Options

You use the `BitmapFactory.Options` class with the `BitmapFactory` class; it is essential to how you handle large `Bitmaps`.

You use the following options from the `BitmapFactoryOptions` class:

▶ `inJustDecodeBounds`: If set to `true`, this option indicates that the bitmap dimensions should be determined by the `BitmapFactory`, but that the bitmap itself should not be created. This is the key to getting the bitmap dimensions without the memory overhead of creating the bitmap.

▶ `outWidth`: The width of the image set when you use `inJustDecodeBounds`.

▶ `outHeight`: The height of the image set when you use `inJustDecodeBounds`.

▶ `inSampleSize`: This integer indicates how much the dimensions of the bitmap should be reduced. Given an image of 1000x400, an `inSampleSize` of 4 will result in a bitmap of 250x100. The dimensions are reduced by a factor of 4.

Listing 21.3 shows the code to address handling large images. We'll step through the approach and the code. The code is in the Hour21LargeImage project in MainActivity.java.

LISTING 21.3   Displaying a Large Image

```
 1:  ImageView largeImage = (ImageView) findViewById(R.id.imageView1);
 2:  Display display = getWindowManager().getDefaultDisplay();
 3:  int displayWidth = display.getWidth();
 4:  BitmapFactory.Options options = new BitmapFactory.Options();
 5:  options.inJustDecodeBounds = true;
 6:  BitmapFactory.decodeResource(getResources(), R.drawable.largeimage, options);
 7:  int width = options.outWidth;
 8:  if (width > displayWidth) {
 9:    int widthRatio = Math.round((float) width / (float) displayWidth);
10:    options.inSampleSize = widthRatio;
11:  }
```

```
12:   options.inJustDecodeBounds = false;
13:   Bitmap scaledBitmap = BitmapFactory.decodeResource(getResources(),
14:   R.drawable.largeimage, options);
15:   largeImage.setImageBitmap(scaledBitmap);
```

Lines 2 and 3 get the size of the device display. You use this as the target size for reducing the image size.

In lines 4–7, you determine the size of the current bitmap. You do that by creating a `BitmapFactory.Options` class and setting the `inJustDecodeBounds` value to `true`. On line 6, the bitmap is decoded to get the dimensions. This is where you get the dimensions without the memory overhead of creating the bitmap. The result is available in `options.outWidth`. On line 7, you assign `options.outWidth` to the `int` variable `width`.

This example uses a simple test for the size of the image. Line 8 checks whether the width of the bitmap is greater than the size of the display. If that is the case, you determine the `inSample-Size` to use. You do that on lines 9 and 10. If the width of the bitmap is 1000 pixels and the size of the display is 250 pixels, you get an `inSampleSize` of 4 by dividing the width of the bitmap by the width of the display. For simplicity, this example does not check the height, which could theoretically leave you exposed to a bitmap that was 20 inches tall and 2 inches wide.

With the `imSampleSize` set to an appropriate value, you can render the image.

On line 12, the `inJustDecodeBounds` value is set to `false`. You want to decode the image and create the `Bitmap` object.

Lines 13 and 14 use the `BitmapFactory.decodeResource()` method to create a `Bitmap` and assign it to the variable `scaledBitmap`. Note that in this call, the `BitmapFactory.Options` variable `options` is passed as a parameter. That is how you indicate to the `BitmapFactory` what `inSampleSize` to use.

Displaying a 72-inch image on a phone is certainly not recommended, but Figure 21.5 shows that it can be done.

FIGURE 21.5
Very large photo displayed on device

Drawing Directly on a Canvas

You can do one more thing with an `ImageView` and bitmap. You can create a bitmap and draw directly on the `Canvas(android.graphics.Canvas)` that is associated with the bitmap. A `Canvas` is an object that you can draw on by calling drawing commands.

To see this, add another `Button` to the MainActivity activity from the Hour21ImageView project. Listing 21.4 shows the `onClickListener()` method for the draw button. The code creates a bitmap, gets the canvas, and draws the word "Hello" on the canvas. The resulting bitmap appears in the `ImageView`.

You create a new `Bitmap` on lines 3 and 4 by using the method `Bitmap.createBitmap()`. You set the width and height of the bitmap to that of the `ImageView` and use the `Bitmap.Config` (`android.graphics.Bitmap.Config`) set to `Bitmap.Config.ARGB_8888`.

The documentation for the `Bitmap` class offers a number of `createBitmap()` methods that take different parameters. These methods may return a mutable or an immutable `Bitmap`, but only a mutable `Bitmap` can be used for drawing.

On line 5, a `Canvas` is instantiated based on the bitmap that you created.

You apply simple drawing commands to the `Canvas` on lines 6–10. You create a `Paint` object, set the `Color` to blue, and set the text size. Line 6 gets the density of the display, which is used to get the text size you want. Hour 4 covered converting density independent pixels to pixels. Line 10 draws the word "Hello" in the center of the `ImageView`.

Line 11 updates the `ImageView` to show the generated bitmap.

LISTING 21.4   Drawing on a Canvas

```
1: draw.setOnClickListener(new OnClickListener() {
2:     public void onClick(View v) {
3:         Bitmap imageBitmap = Bitmap.createBitmap(imageView.getWidth(),
4:         imageView.getHeight(), Bitmap.Config.ARGB_8888);
5:         Canvas canvas = new Canvas(imageBitmap);
6:         float scale = getResources().getDisplayMetrics().density;
7:         Paint p = new Paint();
8:         p.setColor(Color.BLUE);
9:         p.setTextSize(24*scale);
10:         canvas.drawText("Hello", imageView.getWidth()/2,imageView.getHeight()/2,
p);
11:         imageView.setImageBitmap(imageBitmap);
12:     }
13: });
```

Using VideoViews

You use `VideoViews` (`android.widget.VideoView`) to play videos. In this section, you create a simple app in which a video is served from a web URL and shown in a `VideoView`. You have the option to control the video with controls that you create or with a `MediaController` (`android.widget.MediaController`). The example app uses both methods. First we'll look at the basics.

A `VideoView` layout is often simple. Listing 21.5 shows a typical example. The desire to show a full screen video is common. The Hour21VideoView project contains this source code.

LISTING 21.5   VideoView Layout

```
1: <VideoView android:id="@+id/VideoView01"
2:     android:layout_height="match_parent"
3:     android:layout_width="match_parent">
4: </VideoView>
```

Loading a Video

After you declare the `VideoView`, you need to give the view a video to play and start the video. A video may be read from a local file or from a remote server. In both cases, you can use the `setVideoUri()` method of `VideoView`. That method takes a URI as a parameter. Creating a URI from a string is typical. Listing 21.6 shows a `Uri` class being defined from a `String` and the resulting `Uri` being set to the `VideoView` in line 3.

LISTING 21.6 Assigning a Video to a VideoView

```
1: String videoToPlay = "http://bffmedia.com/bigbunny.mp4";
2: Uri videoUri = Uri.parse(videoToPlay);
3: videoView.setVideoURI(videoUri);
```

You could use the same code in Listing 21.6 for reading a file from the SD card. Line 1 would change to include the location of a file:

```
String videoToPlay= Environment.getExternalStorageDirectory()+ "/Android/data/com.
bffmedia/videos/bigbunny.mp4";
```

`Environment.getExternalStorageDirectory()` refers to the location of the SD card.

Starting, Pausing, and Positioning a Video

For controlling a video, the `VideoView` includes methods called `start()`, `pause()`, and `seekTo()`. The `start()` and `pause()` methods start and stop the video. The `seekTo()` method positions the video at a specific location and is based on milliseconds. Calling `seekTo()` with 10,000 positions the video at the tenth second. You can get the current position and duration of the video with the methods `getCurrentPosition()` and `getDuration()`. To skip ahead 10 seconds in the video, you use the following:

```
mVideoView.seekTo(mVideo.getCurrentPosition + 10000);
```

Listening for the States of a VideoView

Two listeners are unique to a `VideoView`: `onPreparedListener()` and `OnCompletionListener()`. Videos do not start playing immediately. First, they are downloaded and buffered. That is where the `onPreparedListener()` comes in. You can do something in your user interface before the video begins. When it is ready, you can do something else. For example, you can show a progress bar before the video starts and then hide it in the `onPreparedListener()`.

The onCompletionListener() triggers when the video is done playing. It is an opportunity to repeat the video, start a new video, or change the user interface to prompt the user about what to do next.

To demonstrate the use of VideoViews, in this section you create an app with two activities. In MainActivity.java, there is a VideoView, a pause/play button, and a full screen button. The play/pause button controls the video. The full screen button opens the second activity. That activity, VideoActivity.java, plays the video in full screen and attaches a MediaController that provides native controls. Both MainActivity.java and VideoActivity.java are in the Hour21VideoView project.

You'll use the OnPreparedListener() to know when the video is ready to play. Until that time, you'll show a progress bar.

Listing 21.7 shows how to show a video. The OnPreparedListener() code begins on line 6. If the video is ready, the progress bar is hidden and the video plays. This occurs on lines 8–10.

LISTING 21.7 Showing a Video

```
 1: final VideoView videoView = (VideoView) findViewById(R.id.videoView);
 2: final ProgressBar progressBar = (ProgressBar) findViewById(R.id.progressBar);
 3: String videoToPlay = "http://bffmedia.com/bigbunny.mp4";
 4: Uri video = Uri.parse(videoToPlay);
 5: videoView.setVideoURI(video);
 6: videoView.setOnPreparedListener(new MediaPlayer.OnPreparedListener(){
 7:    public void onPrepared(MediaPlayer mp) {
 8: progressBar.setVisibility(View.GONE);
 9: videoView.requestFocus();
10: videoView.start();
11:    }
12: });
```

In MainActivity.java, you can implement a play/pause button. To control the video, you use the start() and pause() methods of the VideoView.

The full screen button opens the VideoActivity. The code for VideoActivity is similar to the MainActivity code, but a MediaController is implemented.

Listing 21.8 shows the onCreate() method of VideoActivity(). A MediaController is defined in line 5. On line 6, that MediaController is set as the anchor of the VideoView, and on line 9, the VideoView sets its MediaController to the defined MediaController. This code creates and shows the VideoView with a MediaController attached.

See Figures 21.6 and 21.7 to see how these two activities show videos.

LISTING 21.8 Showing a Video with MediaController

```
 1: protected void onCreate(Bundle savedInstanceState) {
 2: super.onCreate(savedInstanceState);
 3: setContentView(R.layout.activity_video);
 4: VideoView videoView = (VideoView) findViewById(R.id.videoView);
 5: MediaController mediaController = new MediaController(this);
 6: mediaController.setAnchorView(videoView);
 7:   String videoToPlay = "http://bffmedia.com/bigbunny.mp4";
 8:   Uri video = Uri.parse(videoToPlay);
 9: videoView.setMediaController(mediaController);
10: videoView.setVideoURI(video);
11: videoView.start();
12: }
```

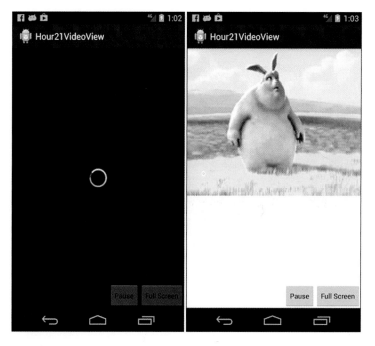

FIGURE 21.6
VideoView with a custom pause button

FIGURE 21.7
`VideoView` with `MediaController`

Playing Audio with MediaPlayer

Now consider a simple example of playing an `.MP3` audio file using a `MediaPlayer` (`android.media.MediaPlayer`). When you do this, you are responsible for the state of the `MediaPlayer`. A `MediaPlayer` can be `reset()` and must be released when you are done using it.

The code for this example is in the Hour21Audio project in MainActivity.java. In the example, you read a file called `helloworld.mp3` from the assets directory. You do this in the `onResume()` method. The `MediaPlayer` is released in the `onPause()` method.

Listing 21.9 shows the `onResume()` method of MainActivity.java. The audio file is read from the assets folder and played using a `MediaPlayer`.

LISTING 21.9   Playing an MP3 Audio File

```
1: protected void onResume() {
2: super.onResume();
3: try {
4: audioFileDescriptor = getAssets().openFd("helloworld.mp3");
5: mediaPlayer.setDataSource(audioFileDescriptor.getFileDescriptor(),
6: audioFileDescriptor.getStartOffset(),audioFileDescriptor.getLength());
7: mediaPlayer.prepare();
8: mediaPlayer.start();
9: } catch (IOException e) {
10: e.printStackTrace();
11: }
12: }
```

Exploring More Media Options

This hour considered `ImageViews`, `Bitmaps`, `VideoViews`, and `MediaPlayer` and covered these components at a basic level. If you are creating complex media apps, you will want to dig deeper.

In addition, you might want to explore other media-related topics, including the following classes in Android:

▶ AudioManager: android.media.AudioManager

▶ AudioFocus: android.media.AudioManager.OnAudioFocusChangeListener

▶ SoundPool: android.media.SoundPool

▶ AudioTrack: android.media.AudioTrack

▶ MediaPlayer: android.media.MediaPlayer

▶ Presentation: android.app.Presentation

Summary

This hour took a close look at `ImageViews` and bitmaps, including how to handle large images, and offered a basic approach to drawing directly on a canvas. The hour covered how to use `ScaleType` in detail and introduced the `Matrix` class to show a simple rotation of an image in an `ImageView`. This hour also introduced video and audio concepts using `VideoView` and `MediaPlayer`. Android provides significant ability to record and play various media types. This hour showed the basics and introduced the next steps to take to make great media-based apps.

Q&A

Q. If I am developing an app that places images in a `ListView` or `GridView`, should I use `BitmapFactory.Options` to check the image size for each image?

A. If you do not have control of the size of the images coming from the server, then checking size is important. If you do have control over the images, then the ideal scenario is to have appropriately sized images. You can also check out open source projects such as Thumbor for resizing images from a server and Picasso for handling images in code. See https://github.com/globocom/thumbor/wiki and https://github.com/square/picasso.

Q. Is `VideoView` the only way to play a video on Android?

A. No, `VideoView` is one of the easier ways to play a video. You can also play a video via an `ActionView` intent or by using `MediaPlayer`. To show a video using an intent, create a `Uri` and an `Intent` as follows:

```
Intent intent = new Intent();
intent.setAction(Intent.ACTION_VIEW);
intent.setDataAndType(videoUri, "video/mp4");
startActivity(intent);
```

Workshop

Quiz

1. What is the purpose of `inJustDecodeBounds`?

2. How is `onPreparedListener()` used?

3. What does *mutable* mean?

Answers

1. In `BitmapFactory.Options`, you use `inJustDecodeBounds` to decode a `Bitmap` to get the dimension, but not actually create a `Bitmap` in memory.

2. In a `VideoView`, `onPreparedListener()` listens for when a video is ready to play. The example in this hour showed a progress bar until the video was prepared and then displayed the video.

3. *Mutable* means *changeable*, which is important when you create `Bitmaps`. Some methods return mutable `Bitmaps` and others return immutable `Bitmaps`.

Exercise

Add a `Button` in the Hour21ImageView project to set the alpha level. It will be like the rotation example. When the user clicks on the button, the alpha level should change.

You can use the other examples in this hour as starting points for what you would like to do in media.

Using the Facebook SDK

What You'll Learn in This Hour:

▶ Getting an introduction to Facebook development

▶ Setting up for Facebook Android development

▶ Using the Facebook SDK

▶ Uploading a photo to Facebook

▶ Creating your own libraries

Incorporating Facebook into your app or creating an app just for Facebook offers benefits. This hour covers those benefits and shows how to implement a Facebook app for Android. In doing so, it also shows you how to integrate an existing third-party library into an app and considers the benefits of creating your own libraries.

About Facebook

If you are a Facebook user, then you are familiar with Facebook as a social utility or social platform. As a Facebook user, you create a Facebook profile and connect with your friends. This set of connections between Facebook users is what makes programming for social platforms different. This set of connections is known as the social graph. By connecting people to each other, your apps can become more engaging.

Facebook is one way to introduce the "network effect" into apps. The network effect is the idea that an app is more valuable when more people use it. That is not a new concept. A telephone is not very valuable to a user when 10 people have telephones, but it is incredibly valuable when everyone has a telephone.

There can be even smaller positive effects with users within a social network. Most games have leaderboards that display high scores. The high score for a game might seem unobtainable when you are one of 100,000 players and just starting out. But, if you were able to compare your game scores to only your friends' scores, you might find that you are actually pretty good at the game. As an individual user, you are encouraged to continue and to pass your friend who has the next highest score.

One of the key things that Facebook did as a company was to open its platform to developers. That platform has changed much since the early days. Developing on Facebook is easier than before and the concepts behind developing for Facebook are clear and well documented.

In 2010, Facebook released its first Android SDK. The SDK supports Facebook's Graph API. It has been updated regularly with new and more robust features.

Setting Up for Facebook Development

The three key steps to get set up for Facebook Development on Android are to:

▶ Create a new Facebook app on https://developers.facebook.com/apps

▶ Get the latest version of the Facebook Android SDK

▶ Install the Facebook Android SDK

If you do not have a Facebook account, you need to create one. To create an app, you need to become a Facebook developer by agreeing to Facebook's terms of service.

The following are the relevant Facebook websites:

▶ **http://www.facebook.com**—The Facebook consumer-facing site.

▶ **https://developers.facebook.com/**—The main developer page.

▶ **https://developers.facebook.com/android/**—Android developer page.

▶ **https://developers.facebook.com/apps**—Facebook Developer Dashboard.

▶ **https://github.com/facebook/facebook-android-sdk**—Open source Facebook Android library, including samples.

▶ **https://github.com/fbsamples/android-3.0-howtos**—Open source Facebook Android How-tos.

Creating a New Facebook App

You need to create a new Facebook app in the Facebook Developer Dashboard. This is where you will give the app a name and choose other settings. Facebook will generate a Facebook app id and secret key, which you use for Facebook to identify your app.

Go to https://developers.facebook.com/apps and choose the Create New App button. The window shown in Figure 22.1 appears. Enter an app name and click Continue. If you have not already registered as a Facebook developer, you will be asked to register.

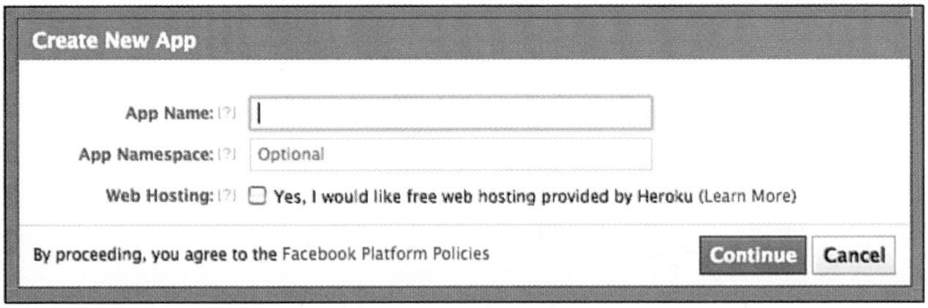

FIGURE 22.1
Create a Facebook app

You then choose to create a native Android app. Enter a package name and a class name, as shown in Figure 22.2.

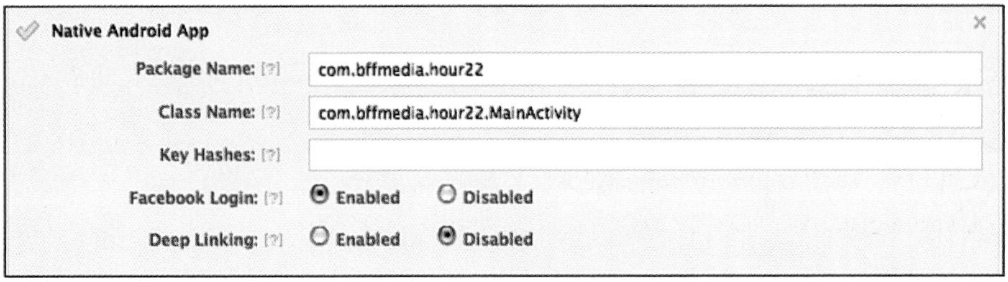

FIGURE 22.2
Add Android native app settings

A key hash is required as part of the security check that Facebook will run before authorizing your app. Hour 24 covers creating keys in more detail. You can use the following instructions to get your debug key on either a Macintosh or Windows computer that has your Android development environment.

For Macintosh, enter the following in the terminal app:

```
keytool -exportcert -alias androiddebugkey -keystore ~/.android/debug.keystore |
openssl sha1 -binary | openssl base64
```

On Windows, run this as a command prompt:

```
keytool -exportcert -alias androiddebugkey -keystore %HOMEPATH%\.android\debug.
keystore | openssl sha1 -binary | openssl base64
```

You can find information on the Facebook developer website at https://developers.facebook.com/docs/getting-started/facebook-sdk-for-android/3.0/.

Troubleshooting login errors on Facebook can be difficult. Often, the issue is related to an incorrect key hash. The troubleshooting tips found on the developer website listed earlier can be useful. In particular, you can put code snippet in an `Activity onCreate()` method that will log the key hash. *This can be used if login fails, but never include that code in a release!*

For reference, the troubleshooting code is included in the MainActivity.java example from this hour.

Downloading the Facebook SDK

Download the Facebook Android SDK from https://developers.facebook.com/android/.

The downloaded file is a zip file with a name like `facebook-android-sdk-3.0.1.zip`.

Unzip the file. A folder will be created with a similar name like `facebook-android-sdk-3.0.1`.

If you examine the contents of the folder, you will see subfolders called `bin`, `docs`, `Facebook`, and `samples`. The samples subfolder contains sample Android projects. The Facebook subfolder is the Facebook SDK itself.

Installing the Facebook SDK

The Facebook SDK is an Android Library project. First, import the library using Eclipse and then take a look at what makes it a library project.

To import the SDK library project, go to Eclipse's File, Import menu. Select General, Existing Projects into Workspace, as shown in Figure 22.3.

FIGURE 22.3
Importing an existing project

For now, select just the Facebook SDK, but you can also import all the sample projects. When you select the Facebook folder, your import window will look like Figure 22.4.

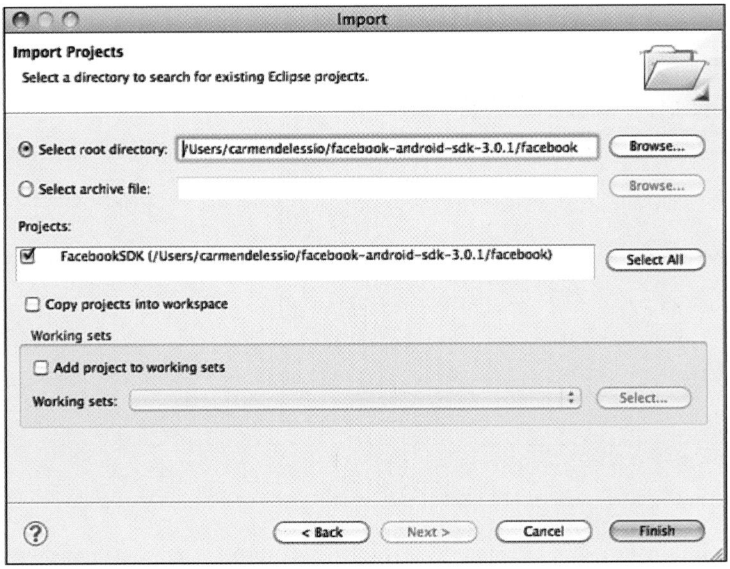

FIGURE 22.4
Selecting the folder and project to import

After you click Finish, your project imports into the Eclipse ADT. It should compile now like any other Android project, but it might not! A challenge in using third-party tools and libraries is getting them set up properly. In Eclipse, you can `Build` and `Clean` the project. Also look at the Android properties by choosing Properties, Android. A Project Build Target should be selected. If it is not, you must select one.

The Android properties window in Eclipse will also show that the Facebook SDK is a library project. See Figure 22.5 where the "is Library" checkbox is selected.

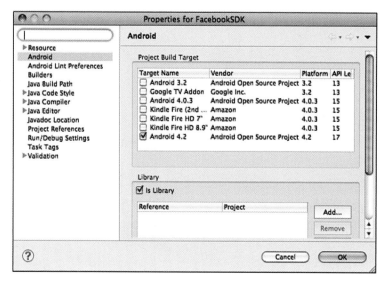

FIGURE 22.5
Library project

Library project are compiled and included in other projects, but they cannot be run on their own.

Both IntelliJ and Android Studio have methods for including library projects. For more on library projects in general, see the Android tools documentation at http://developer.android.com/tools/projects/index.html#LibraryProjects.

The preceding discussion reflects a typical scenario for the use of third-party libraries. Using open source or other Android libraries can offer significant benefits.

Using the Facebook SDK in a Project

At this point, you have set up a Facebook app on the Facebook developer website and imported the Facebook Android SDK. You can now create a new Android project and associate it with the Facebook library. If you have imported the Facebook library, you can follow the steps in the Try It Yourself section. Figure 22.6 shows the result.

▼ TRY IT YOURSELF

Create a Project and Include the Facebook Library

If you have imported the Facebook library project, it is available for use in other projects. Now create a new project and associate the Facebook library project with it:

1. Create a new Android project. The example uses Hour 22.

2. After it is created, go to the project's properties section. (Right-click on the project, and choose Properties.)

3. Click the Add button.

4. Add the FacebookSDK project and click OK.

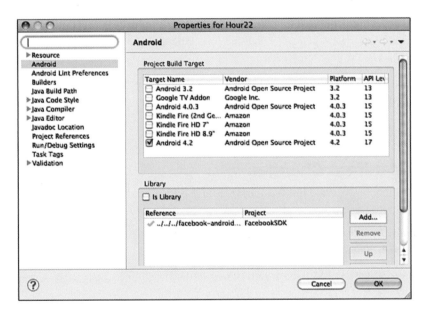

FIGURE 22.6
Facebook library added to project

You have now created a Facebook app, imported the Facebook Android SDK, and associated the Facebook SDK with your new project. You can now make calls to the Facebook SDK in your app, but to log in successfully to Facebook from the app, you have to tie the application id that Facebook generated to your Android app.

CAUTION

Resolving Build Dependencies

The Facebook SDK uses the Android support package for backward compatibility. It is possible for a conflict to exist between the `android-support-v4.jar` used in the new project and the one in the Facebook SDK. One way to resolve this issue is by deleting the jar file from the libs folder of the new project.

Setting the App ID

When you created a Facebook application on the Facebook developer site, an application ID was generated. You can get the application ID by accessing your app at https://developers.facebook. com/apps/.

This application ID is how Facebook identifies the app on its system. It is the key to a user authorizing the app, setting permissions, and getting access.

You must tie this Facebook application ID to your Android project, which takes two steps:

1. Add the Facebook application ID to the String.xml file in the res/values folder. It will look like `<string name="app_id">17-----91</string>` where the value is the application id from Facebook.

2. Update the AndroidManifest.xml file to make the `app_id` string resource known to the Facebook SDK: `<meta-data android:name = "com.facebook.sdk. ApplicationId" android:value = "@string/app_id"/>`.

Making Final Manifest Changes

Two more things are required in Android manifest settings for the Facebook SDK to work properly. You must set the Internet permission and include the Facebook `LoginActivity` from the library.

The Internet permission is as follows:

```
<uses-permission android:name="android.permission.INTERNET"/>
```

The Facebook `ApplicationId` and `LoginActivity` should both be within the application tag:

```
<meta-data android:name="com.facebook.sdk.ApplicationId" android:value="@string/
app_id"/>
<activity android:name="com.facebook.LoginActivity"/>
```

Getting Ready to Code

Setting up the Facebook SDK and getting your project ready for development took a number of steps. You had to create a Facebook app, download and install the Facebook SDK itself, make sure the SDK would build in your environment, and tie it to your project.

At a high level, some of these are common steps when using a third-party SDK that requires developer registration. If you include ads in your app or analytics, you might go through some of the same steps. For ads, you want to make sure that your app gets credit for ads shown, so there will be a mechanism to tie your app to the ad provider.

The Facebook SDK does a lot for us as developers, so you might have to do more setup work with Facebook than with other third-party SDKs. If you have no need to tie the app to a backend, then including a third-party SDK can be a much easier process.

Developing a Facebook Photo Upload App

In this section, you learn to create a simple Facebook photo upload app using the technique from Hour 20 to take a photo using an `Intent`.

The Facebook SDK includes a custom login button that you will use with your app.

Setting Facebook Permissions

Facebook has a permission system in place. When a user authorizes an app, that user is presented with a set of permissions that the app requires. The user has the option to accept or reject the permissions. Facebook makes a distinction between permission to read basic content and permission to write to the site. You need the extended permission `PUBLISH_ACTION` so that you can publish the photo.

Figure 22.7 shows the set of available Facebook permissions.

Much of the app's work will be to handle the Facebook session and permissions properly. The Login button takes care of logging in and logging out.

User Permissions	Friend Permissions	Read Permissions	Publish Permissions
user_about_me	friends_about_me	read_friendlists	ads_management
user_activities	friends_activities	read_insights	create_event
user_birthday	friends_birthday	read_mailbox	manage_friendlists
user_checkins	friends_checkins	read_requests	manage_notifications
user_education_history	friends_education_history	read_stream	publish_actions
user_events	friends_events	xmpp_login	rsvp_event
user_groups	friends_groups	user_online_presence	
user_hometown	friends_hometown	friends_online_presence	
user_interests	friends_interests		
user_likes	friends_likes		
user_location	friends_location		
user_notes	friends_notes		
user_photos	friends_photos		
user_questions	friends_questions		
user_relationships	friends_relationships		
user_relationship_detai	friends_relationship_details		
user_religion_politics	friends_religion_politics		
user_status	friends_status		
user_subscriptions	friends_subscriptions		
user_videos	friends_videos		
user_website	friends_website		
user_work_history	friends_work_history		

FIGURE 22.7
Facebook permissions

Login and Session Management

When a Facebook user logs into Facebook, a session is established with the Facebook server. A token is created that identifies the user's session.

The Facebook SDK provides an infrastructure for login and session management.

Facebook provides a login button widget that you can include in your XML layouts. The LoginButton says either Login or Logout depending on the state of the session.

It is included in the XML layout as the following:

```
<com.facebook.widget.LoginButton
        android:id="@+id/authButton"
        android:layout_width="wrap_content"
        android:layout_height="wrap_content"
        android:layout_gravity="center_horizontal"
        android:layout_marginTop="30dp"
        />
```

To further assist with session management, the Facebook SDK includes a class called UiLifecycleHelper. It is instantiated in the onCreate() method of a fragment as follows:

```
uiHelper = new UiLifecycleHelper(getActivity(), callback);
uiHelper.onCreate(savedInstanceState);
```

The UiLifecycleHelper should be included in each lifecycle method in a fragment or activity. See MainFragment.java to see how it is used in onResume(), onPause(), onDestroy(), and so on.

You want to know whether the user is logged in and whether there is a valid session. To do that, you use a Session.StatusCallback() method. The method is called when the session status changes. When the status changes, the Session.StatusCallback() method fires your internal method onSessionStateChange(). This method is simple. If a session is valid, the photo upload button becomes visible. The following section covers the specific structure of your app implementation.

App Implementation

The Hour 22 project has a MainActivity class and a MainFragment class. The MainActivity class loads the MainFragment class. MainFragment.java shows a Facebook login button. After the user logs in and accepts the Facebook permissions, a photo upload button appears.

The logic of the app is a combination of the photo code from Hour 20 and some sample code from the Facebook how-to section found at https://github.com/fbsamples/android-3.0-howtos.

Facebook gets basic permissions when the app starts. You request extended permissions when the user selects the photo upload button. If the session is valid, then you can check whether the `publish_actions` permission has been authorized by calling the following:

```
session.getPermissions().contains("publish_actions");
```

If this permission is not in place, you request the permission with a call to request new publish permissions:

```
session.requestNewPublishPermissions(new Session.NewPermissionsRequest(MainFragme
nt.this, PERMISSIONS));
```

When you request this permission in your app, the Facebook user will be asked to accept the permission in a dialog. The Facebook SDK handles this user interaction. When you test your app, you can use the Facebook website to unset permissions.

Figure 22.8 shows how Facebook permissions are requested within an app.

If the permissions are in place, you use an intent to take a picture precisely as you did in Hour 20.

After you have the photo saved to a file, you can upload it to Facebook.

Making a Facebook Request

Interacting with Facebook is largely done by making requests and handling responses. In this example, you have a photo file that you want to upload to Facebook. You can use a specific request method for this purpose: the `Request.newUploadPhotoRequest()` method. The complete set of `Request` methods is documented at https://developers.facebook.com/docs/reference/android/3.0/Request.

You use the same method you used in Hour 20 to capture a photo using an `Intent`. The `Intent` is defined by:

```
Intent intent = new Intent(MediaStore.ACTION_IMAGE_CAPTURE);
```

After you set up the intent, you call the `StartActivityForResult()` method. The result is handled in the `onActivityResult()` method. This method is the same you used in Hour 20, but in addition to saving the file, you pass the file as a parameter to a new method called `postPhoto()`.

The `postPhoto()` method creates the Facebook request, sends the request, and handles the result. The specific request is `Request.newUploadPhotoRequest()`. Listing 22.1 shows the `postPhoto()` method. The request is defined on line 4 and executed on line 17. The callback method for the request is defined on lines 6–16.

LISTING 22.1   Facebook Request to Upload Photo File

```
 1:  private void postPhoto(File photoFile) {
 2:   Request request;
 3:   try {
 4:   request = Request.newUploadPhotoRequest(Session.getActiveSession(), photoFile,
 5:                new Request.Callback(){
 6:      @Override
 7:      public void onCompleted(Response response) {
 8:        String resultMessage = null;
 9:         if (response.getError()!=null) {
10:          resultMessage = response.getError().getErrorMessage();
11:         } else {
12:          resultMessage = "Successfully posted photo";
13:         }
14:         new AlertDialog.Builder(getActivity()).setMessage(resultMessage).show();
15:         }
16:      });
17:     request.executeAsync();
18:   } catch (FileNotFoundException e) {
19:       e.printStackTrace();
20:     }
21:   }
```

The app displays the Login button when it starts. The user logs in via the Facebook
LoginActivity. At that point, basic Facebook permissions are requested and the upload button
is enabled. The first time the user chooses to upload a photo, he or she must accept additional
permissions.

The user can then take a photo and it will upload to Facebook.

Figure 22.8 shows the interface for accepting permissions.

Figure 22.9 shows the photo being taken in the app and the uploaded image as it is shown in
the Facebook timeline. Notice how the Facebook image refers to the Hour 22 app. That is one
way that Facebook can be helpful in promoting an app.

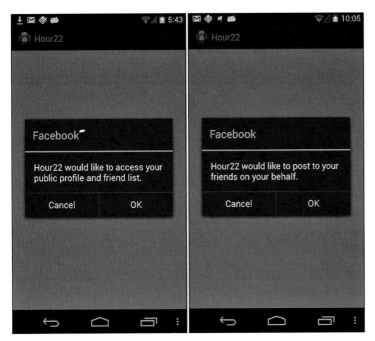

FIGURE 22.8
Accepting Facebook permissions

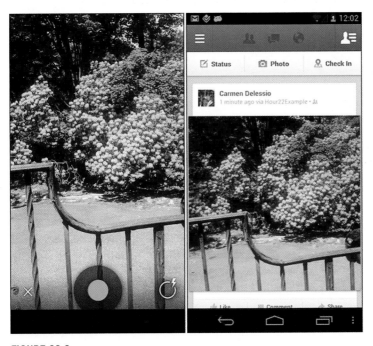

FIGURE 22.9
Taking a photo and seeing the uploaded photo in the Facebook app

Facebook SDK Features

You use the `LoginButton` of the Facebook SDK to log in and the `Request` class to upload a photo. The Facebook SDK also includes UI elements for things such as making friend requests and sharing on Facebook. The ability to invite friends and have the user share achievements or other aspects of your app on Facebook can help promote the app. This is easy to see in a game where the user might ask friends to play or post a high score, but it can be useful in other apps as well. If users post restaurant reviews, check into locations, or log runs in your app, for example, they can promote the app by sharing that information on Facebook.

Facebook SDK Overview

Figure 22.10 shows an overview of the Facebook system. Trying out the sample apps and how-to's can help you get a sense of the Facebook SDK capabilities.

Native UI	LoginButton	FriendPickerFragment		ProfilePictureView	
Graph	GraphUser	GraphObject.Factory		OpenGraphAction	
Core	Session	Request	UILifeCycleHelper	Settings	

FIGURE 22.10
Facebook SDK

Deep Linking

Facebook supports the feature to deep link to an app. If your app is complete and available in the Google Play Store, you can indicate in the Facebook developer console that deep linking should be set to `true`. Then, if a link to your app appears in the Facebook newsfeed on an Android, Facebook will open the app on the device or link to Google Play so that the user can get the app.

Figure 22.11 shows how Facebook deep linking works.

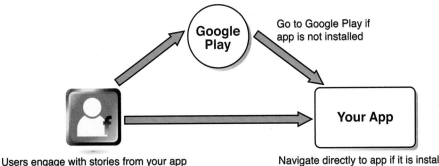

Users engage with stories from your app
in their News Feed on Facebook

Navigate directly to app if it is installed

FIGURE 22.11
Facebook deep linking

Creating Libraries for Your Own Projects

Whether you distribute an SDK or not, creating your own library project can be helpful in managing your own development efforts. In Eclipse, you can directly create a library project when you create a new project or you can identify an existing project as a library project.

Having a library project works well when you design a core set of functions that will be available in every version of your app. Having a core set of functions that work across different apps can be extremely valuable.

Both third-party libraries and internally developed libraries can also be useful to your development process.

Summary

This hour's focus was on setting up and implementing a Facebook Android app using the Facebook SDK. In doing so, you encountered a number of steps that are common to using third-party Android libraries. To create a Facebook app, you had to create a Facebook developer account and get an id for your app. You downloaded, installed, and integrated the SDK into your development environment. You had to resolve issues before development could begin. In incorporating the SDK into the app, you had to include the library and to update the AndroidManifest.xml file. From there, you could use the features of the SDK. You learned you could use third-party libraries to add new features or integrations to your app. Creating your own libraries to use across projects can be a beneficial development approach.

Q&A

Q. What are common issues in Facebook Android development?

A. Facebook development requires coordination between the application defined on Facebook (your Facebook app) and the Android app that you are developing. These are tied together by the `app_id`. Facebook security requires a key-hash from your Android build. These items should all be checked when issues arise. Session management is important, so using the `UIHelper` class and checking and handling Facebook exceptions can make your app more robust.

Q. Do I need to create a web app for Facebook?

A. You can have an Android-only app. If you also create a web app and an iPhone app, use the same Facebook app id. When you do that, your Android app users are promoting the app to your iPhone and web users. Facebook deep linking will do the appropriate thing based on platform.

Workshop

Quiz

1. How are Facebook permissions different from Android permissions?

2. How must the AndroidManifest.xml file be updated to support the Facebook SDK?

Answers

1. With Facebook permissions, the user is authorizing features on Facebook. Those permissions are requested via code. With Android permissions, the Android app is requesting permission to use specific features. Those permissions are requested in the Android manifest.

2. To support the Facebook SDK, the Android Internet permission is required. There must be a reference to the Facebook app id and the Facebook `LoginActivity` must be defined.

Exercise

Much of the required work in this hour is setting up the Facebook SDK to be used successfully. Set up the Facebook SDK and run the sample apps. Download the how-to examples and run them. The samples and how-to examples show a variety of Facebook features and capabilities.

PART V

Wrapping Up

Pro Tips, Finishing Touches, and Next Steps

What You'll Learn in This Hour:

▶ Using `IntentServices` and `BroadcastReceivers`

▶ Adding animation

▶ Incorporating opensource projects

▶ Digging deeper into Android

Professional apps are responsive, pay attention to detail, and include elegant finishing touches. A sophisticated app might use specific Android sensors such as the accelerometer or features such as Near Field Communication (NFC) or Beam. This hour begins with a discussion on how to use an `IntentService`. Services are a fundamental part of Android, and an `IntentService` is a simplified implementation of a service. You can use `IntentServices` to create responsive apps. For finishing touches, you learn how to use Android animations and consider open source libraries that can help you make a slick-looking and responsive app. Finally, this hour covers Android sensors and other features that can be incredibly useful in specific apps.

Responsive Apps: Using IntentService

Sometimes, working in the background makes sense. You have done that with an `AsyncTask`, but an `AsyncTask` is tied to an activity, which can be limiting. An Android service is a background process that lives outside of an activity. Because a service lives outside of an activity, it lives outside of the activity life cycle. A service can keep running in the background even when an activity is destroyed. Whether you use an `AsyncTask` or a service, your goal is to move processing off of the user interface (UI) thread.

A service is created by extending the `Service (android.app.Service)`. Like an activity, the service must also be defined within the AndroidManifest.xml file. A service has a life cycle that includes an `onCreate()` method. Other methods such as `onStartCommand()`, `onBind()`, and `onDestroy()` are part of the `Service` class.

An `IntentService (android.app.IntentService)` provides a simplified way to implement a service. An `IntentService` requires the use of a method called `onHandleIntent()`.

By using an `IntentService`, you can initiate a background process that handles some work and that can occur while the user is still interacting with the application.

In this hour, you create an example that explicitly illustrates this concept and see what is meant by having a responsive app.

The Hour 23 project has a simple MainActivity.java class consisting of a layout with two buttons. One button has the label `No IntentService` and the other has the label `With IntentService`. In the example, the same code is run for each button, with one case using an `IntentService` and the other without using the `IntentService`.

To illustrate app responsiveness, the work done when the user clicks the button is for the app to sleep for 5 seconds. The 5-second delay that we implement simulates work being done in the app that makes the app unresponsive to user input.

When you do that without using an `IntentService`, the button turns blue and remains blue for 5 seconds. The user must wait for control. When you usethe `IntentService`, the button turns blue momentarily when the user clicks it, and then the `IntentService` launches, but the user has immediate control.

Figure 23.1 shows the `No IntentService` button as the user waits.

FIGURE 23.1
Button selected, user must wait for control

Defining an IntentService

As mentioned, to develop an `IntentService`, you must implement an `onHandleIntent()` method. An `IntentService` also requires an empty constructor.

Coding an IntentService

List 23.1 shows the entire FiveSecondService.java code from the Hour23 project.

The empty constructor is included in lines 6–8. The `onHandleIntent()` method appears in lines 9–16. The "work" done in this service is to call `SystemClock.sleep()` on line 11 to have the service sleep for five seconds.

Lines 12–16 of Listing 23.1 define a `BroadcastReceiver`. The `BroadcastReceiver` is used to broadcast that the work is complete. This hour includes more details later on using a `BroadcastReceiver`.

LISTING 23.1   FiveSecondService.java: A Complete IntentService

```
 1:    package com.bffmedia.hour23;
 2:    import android.app.IntentService;
 3:    import android.content.Intent;
 4:    import android.os.SystemClock;
 5:    public class FiveSecondService extends IntentService {
 6:         public FiveSecondService() {
 7:                 super("FiveSecondService");
 8:         }
 9:         @Override
10:         protected void onHandleIntent(Intent intent) {
11:                 SystemClock.sleep(5000);
12:                 Intent broadcastIntent = new Intent();
13:                 broadcastIntent.putExtra("message", "UPDATE:   USING INTENT
SERVICE");
14:                 broadcastIntent.setAction("com.bffmedia.hour23.DELAY");
15:                 sendBroadcast(broadcastIntent);
16:         }
17:    }
```

Updating the Manifest for an IntentService

An `IntentService` must be defined in the `AndroidManifest.xml` file. The definition for a service is like that of an activity. In this case, the service is the `FiveSecondService` class and the `AndroidManifest.xml` includes the following:

```
<service
android:name="com.bffmedia.hour23.FiveSecondService">
</service>
```

Starting the IntentService from an Activity

In MainActivity.java, you define an `IntentService` button and use the `onClick()` method to initiate the service. On line 4 of Listing 23.2, an intent is defined. On line 5, the `startService()` starts the service.

Listing 23.2 shows the complete button definition, the `OnClickListener()`, and the implementation for calling the `FiveSecondService`.

LISTING 23.2   Starting an IntentService

```
1:  runIntentServiceButton = (Button) findViewById(R.id.intentServiceButton);
2:  runIntentServiceButton.setOnClickListener(new OnClickListener() {
3:  public void onClick(View v) {
4:  Intent delayIntent = new Intent(MainActivity.this, FiveSecondService.class);
5:  startService(delayIntent);
6:  }
7:  });
```

That's it. You've created the `FiveSecondService` and launched it from your activity. If you just wanted to launch a background service, you would be done. Ideally, you would want the background service to have a way to indicate that it has completed its task. You can do that using a `BroadcastReceiver`.

Adding a BroadcastReceiver

When the `FiveSecondService onHandleIntent()` method finishes, you want to relay that information to the `MainActivity`. To do that, the service will broadcast an intent using the `sendBroadcast()` method, and `MainActivity` will handle the intent with a `BroadcastReceiver`.

Figure 23.2 shows how this works generically.

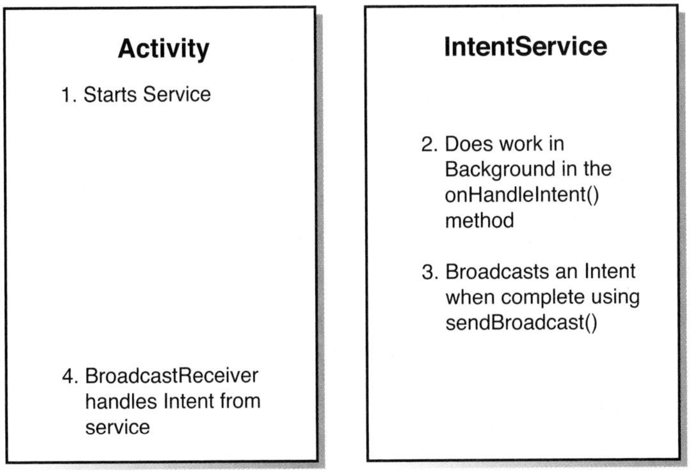

```
┌─────────────────────┐  ┌─────────────────────┐
│      Activity        │  │    IntentService     │
│                      │  │                      │
│  1. Starts Service   │  │                      │
│                      │  │  2. Does work in     │
│                      │  │     Background in the│
│                      │  │     onHandleIntent() │
│                      │  │     method           │
│                      │  │                      │
│                      │  │  3. Broadcasts an    │
│                      │  │     Intent           │
│                      │  │     when complete    │
│                      │  │     using            │
│                      │  │     sendBroadcast()  │
│  4. BroadcastReceiver│  │                      │
│     handles Intent   │  │                      │
│     from service     │  │                      │
└─────────────────────┘  └─────────────────────┘
```

FIGURE 23.2
Interaction between an activity and an `IntentService`

The code in Listing 23.2 starts an `IntentService` in MainActivity.java. Listing 23.1 contains the complete `FiveSecondService` code and includes creating an intent and the call to the `sendBroadcast()` method. The `setAction()` method is called on the intent with the parameter `"com.bffmedia.hour23.DELAY"`. That action identifies the intent. You add extra data to the intent with the `putExtra()` method:

```
Intent broadcastIntent = new Intent();
broadcastIntent.putExtra("message", "UPDATE:  USING INTENT SERVICE");
broadcastIntent.setAction("com.bffmedia.hour23.DELAY");
sendBroadcast(broadcastIntent);
```

The remaining step is to implement a `BroadcastReceiver` in MainActivity.java.

You create a `BroadcastReceiver` class called `DelayReceiver` within MainActivity.java. The `DelayReceiver` will be passed the intent that was created in the service. That intent includes a message as extra data. You display that data in a `TextView`.

After you create a `DelayReceiver`, it must be registered in the activity `onResume()` method and unregistered in the activity `onPause()` method.

Listing 23.3 shows the `DelayReceiver` class.

LISTING 23.3   BroadcastReceiver Implementation (MainActivity.java)

```
1:   public class DelayReceiver extends BroadcastReceiver {
2:        @Override
3:        public void onReceive(Context context, Intent intent) {
4:                String message = intent.getExtras().getString("message");
5:                mDisplay.setText("Finished " + message);
6:        }
7:   }
```

The `DelayReceiver` extends `BroadcastReceiver` and implements the `onReceive()` method, which is passed an `Intent`. Line 4 of Listing 23.3 gets a `message` string by reading the intent extra data. See line 13 of Listing 23.1 to see how this extra data was added to the intent.

The field `mDisplay` in line 5 is a `TextView`. The message extra data from the intent displays on the `TextView`.

To read the action associated with the event, you call `intent.getAction()`. That provides the action that was set in Listing 23.1.

You must also call the `registerReceiver()` and `unregisterReceiver()` methods.

You call the `registerReceiver()` method in the activity `onResume()` method. The field `mDelayReceiver` is of type `DelayReceiver`. The `IntentFilter` parameter passed to the `registerReceiver()` method filters based on the action associated with the intent. In this case, that action is "com.bffmedia.hour23.DELAY":

```
registerReceiver(mDelayReceiver, new IntentFilter("com.bffmedia.hour23.DELAY"));
```

The `BroadcastReceiver` is unregistered in the activity `onPause()` method:

```
unregisterReceiver(mDelayReceiver);
```

Using an `IntentService` and a `BroadcastReceiver` in tandem is a powerful method to invoke a background task and have a notification sent when that task is complete.

Adding Animation

Using animation can convey meaning in an app and make an app feel more responsive. Animation can make an app more fun, but it has the potential to do more. For example, an animation can indicate to users that they need to swipe to unlock their screen.

Animations can get in the way, but if handled wisely, they can add depth to an app.

Several flavors of animation are available in Android. The `ObjectAnimator` (`android.animation.ObjectAnimator`) class is very powerful. It was introduced in Honeycomb (API Level 11).

`ObjectAnimator` provides the ability to animate an object like a button using common graphical transformations. You can translate, rotate, scale, and change the alpha value for an object.

The `ViewPropertyAnimator` (`android.view.ViewPropertyAnimator`) class was added in a later Honeycomb release (API Level 12). This class makes animating a single view easy.

This section shows an example of both `ObjectAnimator` and `ViewPropertyAnimator`. When the Hour 23 app starts, you will animate both the "`No IntentService`" and the "`With IntentService`" buttons.

You define the `doNotRunIntentServiceButton` in the `MainActivity` `onCreate()` method and add `ViewPropertyAnimator`. This button will rotate for two seconds:

```
Button doNotRunIntentServiceButton = (Button) findViewById(R.
id.noIntentServiceButton);
animate(doNotRunIntentServiceButton).setDuration(2000).rotationYBy(720);
```

Listing 23.4 shows the code to animate the `runIntentServiceButton` using `ObjectAnimator` and an `AnimatorSet`. This code is in the `onResume()` method of MainActivity.java. The `AnimatorSet` holds a set of animations and is defined on line 1. The three animation commands are on lines 3 through 6. The scale instructions indicate that the view should grow to 1.5 times the initial size and then return to the original size. Similarly, the alpha command fades the view and then has it return to the original state. Taken together, these commands grow and fade the button before returning it to its original size.

LISTING 23.4 Using ObjectAnimator

```
1:  AnimatorSet set = new AnimatorSet();
2:  set.playTogether(
3:      ObjectAnimator.ofFloat(runIntentServiceButton, "scaleX", 1, 1.5f,1),
4:      ObjectAnimator.ofFloat(runIntentServiceButton, "scaleY", 1, 1.5f,1),
5:      ObjectAnimator.ofFloat(runIntentServiceButton, "alpha", 1, 0.25f, 1)
6:  );
7:  set.setDuration(5 * 1000).start();
```

Figure 23.3 shows one button mid-rotation and the other button as it scales to a larger size.

FIGURE 23.3
Animations in action

As mentioned, these animations are not available on Android before Honeycomb, but there is good news. An open source library called NineOldAndroids provides the ability to do these animations in earlier versions of Android. The support is not absolute, but where there is a similar animation available on the older version of Android, it is implemented in the library.

The library is available as source code and a jar file. If you download the jar file and are using Eclipse, you can import the file from the file systems into the libs folder. You then right-click on the file and add it to the build path. In IntelliJ or Android studio, the jar must be added to the build system.

You can find information on the NineOldAndroids project at http://nineoldandroids.com/.

The source is available on github at https://github.com/JakeWharton/NineOldAndroids/.

You can download the jar from https://github.com/JakeWharton/NineOldAndroids/downloads.

Using open source libraries can be an effective way to add new features or improve an app. The following sections consider several more open source libraries that you might find useful in Android development.

Using Open Source

The NineOldAndroids project, written by Jake Wharton, is one example of a helpful open source Android library. He has written several other helpful Android tools. He works on Android projects at Square, which has released several useful open source projects.

Using open source libraries is common for individual developers and many companies. Most open source code includes a specific license regarding usage. The projects reviewed in this hour are all released under the Apache 2.0 license. You can find more information about that license at http://www.apache.org/licenses/. The FAQ section includes an explanation of the license for non-lawyers.

In addition to the NineOldAndroids project, Jake Wharton has released ActionBarSherlock- and ViewPager-related projects, and Square has released an image library called Picasso. The following sections describe each of these briefly. These projects and other open source projects can help you make better apps.

ActionBarSherlock

ActionBarSherlock extends the compatibility package for Android to provide action bar support for earlier versions. ActionBarSherlock will use a native action bar if available or a custom implementation for versions of Android that do not include a native action bar.

When working with fragments, you will use a `SherlockFragmentActivity`.

For more information on ActionBarSherlock, see http://actionbarsherlock.com/.

ViewPageIndicator

This hour's project works with the `ViewPager` to give an indicator regarding the current page. The ViewPageIndicator can make it clearer to the user that more pages are available to view.

The ViewPageIndicator provides a title for each page being displayed.

For more information on ViewPageIndicator, see http://viewpagerindicator.com/.

Picasso

Handling images in Android might not always be straightforward. You have worked with images and `ImageViews` in the Flickr app and in Hour 21. You know about downloading and caching images and the work required to scale an image to save memory.

The goal of Picasso is to handle working with images and `ImageViews` in an elegant way. It handles disk caching and memory caching of images and keeps overall memory usage to a minimum. Much of the "plumbing" of handling images is kept behind the scenes.

Loading an image from a URL using Picasso is done with one line:

```
Picasso.with(context).load("http://i.imgur.com/DvpvklR.png").into(imageView);
```

For more information on Picasso, see http://square.github.io/picasso/.

Using Open Source in an App

The Hour23OpenSource project uses ActionBarSherlock, ViewPageIndicator, NineOldAndroids, and Picasso.

The app shows Flickr images as the project did in Hour 16. In this app, you retrieve the 12 most recent images. The image data is retrieved in an `IntentService` called `FlickrService`. When the `FlickrService` completes, it broadcasts an intent that includes the photo data as extra data.

A `TextView` is animated for five seconds as the data is retrieved. When the `BroadcastReceiver` fires, the `TextView` is hidden.

A `ViewPager` is used to display each image. The `ViewPageIndicator` shows the title of each image based on the Flickr data. The `ViewPager` displays an `ImageFragment`. The `ImageFragment` includes an `ImageView` to display the FlickrPhoto. Picasso is used to display the image from Flickr in the `ImageView`.

TIP

Adding Jars and Resolving Conflicts

ActionBarSherlock and ViewPageIndicator are libraries that you can include in your app similar to how you included the Facebook library in Hour 22. The possibility exists that a conflict might occur between versions of the Android support library used in your project and in one of the open source libraries. To avoid conflicts, use the latest version of the support library. In Eclipse ADT, you do that by choosing Android Tools, Add Support Library on the project. You can import NineOldAndroids and Picasso as jar files. In Eclipse ADT, import the file into the lib directory and right-click. Choose Add to Build Path.

Digging Deeper into Android

Hopefully this is not a surprise, but 24 hours is not enough time to cover all the interesting and useful features of the Android platform and Android SDK. You've worked on many applications and features over the course of this book.

With the knowledge you have acquired thus far, you might find yourself thinking about your own application ideas. The rest of this hour covers some additional Android features that might help with your applications and point you in the right direction for using the features in your own application.

The Android developer documentation is a good starting point for further exploration of these topics: http://developer.android.com/.

Using Sensors

Using sensors can add interesting and unique features to your app. Android devices come with hardware and software sensors and not all devices will have all sensors. That means that one thing to know about sensors in general is that your app has to check to see whether they exist on a user's device.

This snippet of code checks for the accelerometer sensor:

```
private SensorManagermSensorManager;
mSensorManager = (SensorManager) getSystemService(Context.SENSOR_SERVICE);
if (mSensorManager.getDefaultSensor(TYPE_ACCELEROMETER) != null){
  // Sensor is available
} else {
  // Sensor is not available
}
```

Working with sensors takes a common approach. Like many things in Android, when working with a sensor, you set up a listener and listen for changes produced by the sensor. There is a `SensorEventListener` (`android.hardware.SensorEventListener`) class for this purpose. A `SensorEventListener` implements the `onSensorChanged()` method to listen for `SensorEvents` (`android.hardware.SensorEvent`). From the `SensorEvent`, you can determine the sensor that generated the event and data associated with the event.

The following are some of the device sensors that the Android SDK supports:

- ▶ **Accelerometer**—Measures acceleration in three dimensions.

- ▶ **Light sensor**—Measures ambient brightness.

- ▶ **Magnetic field sensor**—Measures earth's magnetic field in three dimensions.

- ▶ **Orientation sensor**—Measures a device's orientation.

- ▶ **Temperature sensor**—Measures ambient temperature.

- ▶ **Proximity sensor**—Measures whether there is something near the screen of the device.

Handling User Gestures

You already know how to listen for click events. You can also handle gestures, such as flings, scrolls, and taps, by using the `GestureDetector` class (`android.view.GestureDetector`). You can use the `GestureDetector` class by implementing the `onTouchEvent()` method within an activity.

The following are some of the gestures an application can watch for and handle:

- ▶ `onDown`— Occurs when the user first presses the touch screen.

- ▶ `onShowPress`—Occurs after the user first presses the touch screen but before the user lifts up or moves around on the screen.

- ▶ `onSingleTapUp`—Occurs when the user lifts up from the touch screen as part of a single-tap event.

- ▶ `onSingleTapConfirmed`—Called when a single-tap event occurs.

- ▶ `onDoubleTap`—Called when a double-tap event occurs.

- ▶ `onDoubleTapEvent`—Called when an event within a double-tap gesture occurs, including any down, move, or up action.

- ▶ `onLongPress`—Similar to `onSingleTapUp` but called if the user has held his or her finger down just long enough to not be a standard click but also didn't move the finger.

- ▶ `onScroll`—Called after the user has pressed and then moved his or her finger in a steady motion and lifted up.

- ▶ `onFling`—Called after the user has pressed and then moved his or her finger in an accelerating motion just before lifting it.

In addition, the `android.gesture` package enables an application to recognize arbitrary gestures, as well as store, load, and draw them. This means almost any symbol a user can draw could be turned into a gesture with a specific meaning.

Using Styles and Themes

The Android SDK provides two powerful mechanisms for designing consistent user interfaces that are easy to maintain: styles and themes.

A style is a grouping of common view attribute settings that you can apply to any number of view controls. For example, you might want all view controls in your application, such as `TextView` and `EditText` controls, to use the same text color, font, and size. You could create a style that defines these three attributes and apply it to each `TextView` and `EditText` control within your application layouts.

A theme is a collection of one or more styles. Whereas you apply a style to a specific control, such as a `TextView` control, you apply a theme to all `View` objects within a specified activity. Applying a theme to a set of view objects all at once simplifies making the user interface look consistent; it can be a great way to define color schemes and other common view attribute settings across an application. You can specify a theme programmatically by calling the activity class's `setTheme()` method. You can also apply themes to a specific activity in the Android manifest file.

Designing Custom View and ViewGroup Controls

You are already familiar with many of the user interface controls, such as `Layout` and `View` controls, that are available in the Android SDK. You can also create custom controls. To do so, you start with the appropriate `View` (or `ViewGroup`) control from the `android.view` package and implement the specific functionality needed for your control or layout.

You can use custom `View` controls in XML layout files, or you can inflate them programmatically at runtime. You can create new types of controls, or you can extend the functionality of existing controls, such as `TextView` or `Button` controls.

The Facebook `LoginButton` is an example of a custom view, but often custom views are simple extensions of basic views.

Converting Text to Speech

The Android platform includes a TTS engine (`android.speech.tts`) that enables devices to perform speech synthesis. You can use the TTS engine to have your applications "read" text to the user. You might have seen this feature used frequently with Location-Based Services (LBS) applications that allow for hands-free directions.

Converting Speech to Text

You can enhance an application with speech recognition support by using the speech recognition framework (`android.speech.RecognizerIntent`). You use this intent to record speech and send it to a recognition server for processing, so this feature is not really practical for devices that don't have a reasonable network connection.

Using the OpenGL ES Graphics API

For more advanced graphics, Android uses the popular OpenGL ES graphics API. OpenGL ES 1.0 has been supported since Android 1.0. Beginning with Android 2.2, the OpenGL ES 2.0 API is supported. In Android 4.3, OpenGL ES 3.0 support was added. Applications can use Android's OpenGL ES support to draw, animate, light, shade, and texture graphical objects in three dimensions.

Bluetooth

Bluetooth support was included on Android 2.0. With Android 4.3, Android has added support for Bluetooth low energy (LE). Bluetooth low energy makes it possible to build Android apps that communicate with Bluetooth low energy peripheral devices. For example, a phone that includes Bluetooth low energy support that is running Android 4.3 could support an app that interacts with a pedometer.

Android 4.3 introduced the `BluetoothManager` (`android.bluetooth.BluetoothManager`) class to help an app handle Bluetooth management.

More on Bluetooth on Android can be found here:
http://developer.android.com/reference/android/bluetooth/package-summary.html

NFC and Beam

Most Android phones have Near Field Communication (NFC) capability. That means that they have the ability to communicate in short messages from an NFC tag when the phone is very close to the tag. NFC is a set of short-range wireless technologies.

A set of NFC intents is defined in Android. When a tag is read, these intents will be fired. The idea is to create an app that filters for these intents and launches when an NFC tag is read. The details of NFC tags and the relationship between the tags and the application that is launched can get complicated. NFC concepts are covered in the Android developer documentation.

Android Beam is a technology for peer-to-peer NFC communication, which means that two Android devices can communicate through NFC using this technology.

Presentation Class for External Display

The `Presentation` (`android.app.Presentation`) class was introduced in API Level 17 (Jelly Bean 4.2.2). The `Presentation` class is used to present content on an external display. You use it in conjunction with the `DisplayManager` (`android.hardware.display.DisplayManager`) class or the `MediaRouter` (`android.media.MediaRouter`) class.

The `Presentation` class extends `Dialog` (`android.app.dialog`). `Presentation` class is a dialog that displays on an external device.

The `Presentation` class provides the capability for an app to present content on one device and to control it with another. A video could play on a TV and associated content could display on a tablet. It opens up new opportunities for multi-screen apps.

Android 4.2.2 also supports Miracast, a wireless display standard. A Miracast display is treated as another external screen, so you can use the `Presentation` class with Miracast.

Summary

In this hour, you learned about more advanced features of the Android platform including `IntentServices` and `BroadcastReceivers`. You considered how to enhance your apps using open source libraries and animations. In addition, this hour reviewed Android features such assensors, gestures, 3D graphics, NFC, and using external displays.

Q&A

Q. With the contents of this hour, have we covered everything available in Android?

A. No, this book has covered much of the Android system and includes topics such as the use of SQLite, `ContentProviders`, and more that are commonly used in Android, but it is not an encyclopedic view of Android. The goal of this hour was to cover features that are often used in production-level Android apps and to be a guide to new topics.

Q. What happens when new features are added in Android?

A. New features provide new opportunities for developers. Often we need to develop an app for as many people as possible, but developing an app with new capabilities that relies on the latest Android features might provide a good opportunity to create an app that gets noticed and used. In practical terms, developers have learned several patterns that are helpful. Your app should be able to detect new features programmatically. Often new features can be initiated by intents or used with listeners. You might have to learn the new feature, but your approach to implementing the feature in your app will often follow the Android way.

Workshop

Quiz

1. What does the ViewPageIndicator do?

2. How can an `IntentService` communicate with an activity?

3. What class in Jelly Bean would be used with a device that supports Miracast?

Answers

1. The ViewPageIndicator works with the `ViewPager` from the support library. It puts titles or other indicators on the pages that are being viewed.

2. An `IntentService` can send an intent using `sendBroadcast()`. The activity will have implemented a `BroadcastReceiver` to detect the intent.

3. Miracast is a wireless display standard. It can be used with the `Presentation` class to show an external display.

Exercise

The Hour23Opensource project used an `IntentService` and `BroadcastReceiver` to receive photo information from Flickr. Review the source code for that application and for the Flickr application developed in Hour 16. Make a new app based on the Hour 16 app that uses the Picasso library. In that app, replace the `AsyncTask` that is used to retrieve data with an `IntentService` and `BroadcastReceiver`.

HOUR 24
Publishing Your Apps

What You'll Learn in This Hour:

▶ Preparing for release
▶ Publishing to Google Play and other markets
▶ Making money with your app

After you have created an app, you need a way to get that app to your users. In almost all cases, that means making the app available in an app marketplace. Google Play is the Google app marketplace, but it is not the only place to make apps available. Amazon and others can be appropriate options. Selling in an app marketplace requires having your AndroidManifest.xml file set up properly and your app signed. This hour covers that topic as well as some ways to make money with your app.

Preparing for Release

Hour 23 covered adding finishing touches to an app. For an app to be successful, it must be functionally complete, well tested, and as polished as possible. Whether an app is functionally complete is your decision. In general, focusing on key features and doing them well is a good idea. Spend time on the part of the app that users will use all the time.

Releasing an app that you have tested only in an emulator is possible. Except for the simplest of apps, though, this practice is not advised. Your app should be tested on a real device and if possible multiple devices. Test on different-sized devices and on different versions of the Android operating system. If you have internationalized your app, make sure to test in the target locales.

After your app is functionally complete and tested, look for opportunities to add finishing touches. Do you have a great icon? Does the text in the app convey what it should? A silly game might have a different tone from a financial app. Are you able to remove text and use images or animation to convey meaning? Check the Android design principles for inspiration at http://developer.android.com/design/get-started/principles.html.

Preparing the Android Manifest File for Release

Before release, you need to make a number of changes to the application configuration settings of the Android manifest file. Though some of these items seem obvious, the idea is to have them in a checklist to verify the release. Other items are important for showing how the app is made available in an app marketplace like Google Play. Use this list to double-check your Android manifest file.

Android Manifest Checklist

Review the Android manifest file as follows:

▶ Verify that the application icon is set appropriately. Check the various drawable resource directories to ensure that it is set for all densities.

▶ Verify that the application label is set appropriately. This represents the application name as users see it.

▶ Verify the application package name. The app marketplace uses the package name to identify the app. If you do not like your package name, this is the time to change it.

▶ Verify that the application version name is set appropriately. The version name is a friendly version label that developers (and marketplaces) use.

▶ Verify that the application version code is set appropriately. The version code is a number that the Android platform uses to manage application upgrades.

▶ Confirm that the application `uses-sdk` setting is set correctly. You can set the minimum, target, and maximum Android SDK versions supported with this build.

▶ Confirm that the `uses-screens` setting is set properly. This property is not required.

▶ If you had set it, disable the `debuggable` option.

▶ Confirm that all application permissions are appropriate. Request only the permissions the application needs with `uses-permission`.

You can look at the Hour23OpenSource project and consider the Android manifest checklist. First, note that this app really is for demo purposes. It shows toolbar menu choices that are not used for example. It serves just as an example for working through the checklist:

```
package="com.bffmedia.hour23opensource"
android:versionCode="1"
android:versionName="1.0" >
<uses-sdk
android:minSdkVersion="8"
android:targetSdkVersion="16" />
<uses-permission android:name="android.permission.INTERNET" />
```

The package name is `com.bffmedia.hour23opensource`. This is not a particularly good name. You can see the `versionCode` and `versionName`. `VersionName` is what displays to the user. You can use a scheme that includes text and numbers as part of your naming scheme. The `versionCode` is just a number. It is for your internal use and to indicate the latest version to Google Play or other markets. The `versionCode` and `versionName` can be different. You can have `versionName` "1.07a" and a version code of 9. The target and minimum SDK version make sense and so does using only the Internet permission. There is no `uses-screens` option and that is acceptable.

The icon set is `ic_launcher`. It is the default graphic, and it should be changed to represent the app.

TIP

Use the Android Asset Studio

The Android Asset Studio includes an easy way to make icons for your app. The icons are generated into all the desired densities for images. The online tool is easy to use. Other useful features are available in the Android Asset Studio. Check it out at http://android-ui-utils.googlecode.com/hg/asset-studio/dist/index.html.

The app name is included in the application element as follows:

```
android:label="@string/app_name"
```

You can look up the `app_name` in the `strings.xml` resource file and see that the app name is Hour23OpenSource. It is not likely to generate a lot of app sales or excitement.

Using <uses-feature> Wisely

The `uses-feature` tag indicates whether a particular hardware feature is used in the app. For the camera app in Hour 20, this is added to the Android manifest:

```
<uses-feature android:name="android.hardware.camera" />
```

Google Play will filter apps based on this setting.

You can indicate that an app uses the camera, but does not require it, as follows:

```
<uses-feature android:name="android.hardware.camera"
android:required="false" />
```

Signing Your Apps

Android application packages must be digitally signed for the Android package manager to install them. Throughout the development process, Eclipse has used a debug key to manage this process. However, for release, you need to use a real digital signature—one that is unique to you and your company. To do this, you must generate a private key.

You use the private key to digitally sign the release package files of your Android application, as well as any upgrades. This ensures that the application is coming from you, the developer, and not someone pretending to be you.

Self-signing of signatures is standard for Android applications. Code signing allows the Android system to ensure app updates come from the same source as the original app. Because the signature is self-signed, it cannot confirm the identity of the developer, only that the original app and the update come from the same source. You should ensure your private key is kept safe.

Application updates must be signed with the same private key. For security reasons, the Android package manager does not install the update over the existing application if the key is different. This means you need to keep the key corresponding with the application in a secure, easy-to-find location for future use.

WARNING

Keep Your Key Safe!

Your key is critically important—keep it safe! Ideally, only the person in charge of building the release version should have access to the key. Your key should be backed up—preferably with at least one copy kept offsite.

Exporting and Signing the Package File Using Eclipse

Eclipse makes exporting and signing the Android package file easy. This section goes through the steps to create the signed package using Eclipse and then considers the command-line options for using signing packages.

To create the signed package:

1. In Eclipse, right-click on the appropriate project and choose the `Android Tools` option.

2. Choose `Export Signed Application Package`.

3. The Project will be checked for export; click `Next`.

4. On the KeyStore selection screen, choose `Create New Keystore`. Enter a location and name for the keystore and enter and confirm a password.

5. Enter data for key creation. This includes a password, validity in years, and other information. The validity must be more than 25 years. See Figure 24.1.

6. Choose a destination for your APK file and click Finish.

That's it. The APK is the Android package file. It is the Android executable that can be tested and then added to Google Play or other markets.

FIGURE 24.1
Signing an app using Eclipse

Signing Apps Using Command-Line Tools

Knowing something about the command-line tools that are available for creating keystores and signing packages can also be useful.

The command-line tools *keytool* and *jarsigner* are part of the Java Development Kit (JDK). You can use keytool to create a keystore and jarsigner to sign the Android package file.

To get help, you can enter the tool name at a command line. If the tools are not available at the command line, you need to check the path to your JDK. You can find information on keytool and jarsigner at http://docs.oracle.com/javase/6/docs/technotes/tools/#security.

Creating a key with keytool is easiest understood by example:

```
keytool -genkey -v -keystore hour23.keystore  -alias hour23 -keyalg RSA -validity
10000
```

This command creates a keystore in the file hour23.keystore. It is valid for 10,000 days and has an alias of hour23. Figure 24.2 shows the session that occurs after entering this command.

```
Enter keystore password:
Re-enter new password:
What is your first and last name?
  [Unknown]:  Carmen Delessio
What is the name of your organizational unit?
  [Unknown]:  Android in 24
What is the name of your organization?
  [Unknown]:
What is the name of your City or Locality?
  [Unknown]:
What is the name of your State or Province?
  [Unknown]:  NY
What is the two-letter country code for this unit?
  [Unknown]:  US
Is CN=Carmen Delessio, OU=Android in 24, O=Unknown, L=Unknown, ST=NY, C=US correct?
  [no]:  y

Generating 1,024 bit RSA key pair and self-signed certificate (SHA1withRSA) with a validity of 10,000 days
        for: CN=Carmen Delessio, OU=Android in 24, O=Unknown, L=Unknown, ST=NY, C=US
Enter key password for <hour23>
        (RETURN if same as keystore password):
Re-enter new password:
[Storing hour23.keystore]
```

FIGURE 24.2
Creating a keystore with keytool

After you create the keystore, you can use it to sign an APK file using jarsigner. The following assumes you have an unsigned APK called hour23opensource.apk:

```
jarsigner -verbose -sigalg SHA1withRSA -digestalg SHA1 -keystore hour23.keystore
hour23opensource.apk hour23
```

The –sigalg and –digestalg parameters use the Android recommended values. The keystore parameter is specified by the file that you created: hour23.keystore. The hour23opensource.apk file is listed, and the last parameter is the alias name.

This results in a signed Android package. You should run jarsigner - verify hour23opensource.apk to verify the results.

You can do an optimization process for the final APK file by using the Android command-line tool *zipalign*. The command is as follows:

```
zipalign -v 4 hour23opensource.apk hour23opensource-aligned.apk
```

Exporting the Certificate File

Recall from Hour 22 that Facebook required a key hash to identify your app. After you have a private key and have signed the APK file, you can generate the proper key hash for Facebook via the keytool command, as follows:

```
keytool -exportcert -alias hour23 -keystore hour23.keystore  | openssl sha1 -binary
| openssl base64
```

The keystore alias and keystore file are specified. The result is a hash key that is displayed on the command line. That result is what should be populated into the Facebook developer tool.

Testing the Package

Several ways exist to test the signed Android package. The easiest is to email it to an account on an Android device. When you open the attached APK, you should get an option to load the package. Be sure that in the Android Settings app (under Security), you have specified that it's OK to load Android apps from outside the Android market. You specify that unknown sources are allowed.

You can copy the APK file to the device and launch it with a File Manager tool. An app such as Astro File Manager works well for this.

You can also use command-line tool for installing and uninstalling. To install, refer to the apk file:

```
adb install hour23opensource.apk
```

To uninstall, refer to the package:

```
adb uninstall com.bffmedia.hour23opensource
```

Use the command adb devices to list all devices. To specify a device for installation, use the -s flag:

```
adb -s 016B756E0E01C005 install hour23opensource.apk
```

Publishing Your App

With a signed app, you are technically ready to publish your application. This section covers the basics of publishing your app on Google Play and considers some alternative markets. Putting thought and consideration into your presentation and marketing efforts in various app markets is important. The app name, icon, description, and supporting graphics are all important for making a good impression.

Publishing on Google Play

Google Play is Google's app marketplace for Android. It provides an easy way for a developer to publish apps and is probably the most common way that users acquire apps.

To publish applications through the Android Market, you must register as a developer. Registering as a developer verifies who you are to Google and provides a way for Google to pay you when someone buys your app. There is a $25 one-time fee to sign up as a Google Developer. Signing up is a simple online process; go to https://play.google.com/apps/publish/.

After you have your developer account, you can add a new application. You are given the choice to upload the APK or set up the store listing. See Figure 24.3.

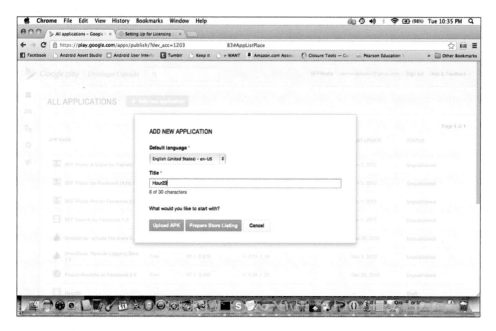

FIGURE 24.3
Adding a new app on Google Play

For an app to have a chance to be successful, take advantage of all the available fields on Google Play when you add an app. Add screenshots, descriptive text, promo text, and so on. You can include screenshots for both phone devices and tablets. The screenshots to include should show key elements of your app and ideally how a user interacts with your app.

Store Listing

You will see additional options for your app including Game Center and other services. Google Play is a helpful area to explore and understand the opportunities for making apps available to users in the best way.

Figure 24.4 gives an idea of some of the screenshot options that are available.

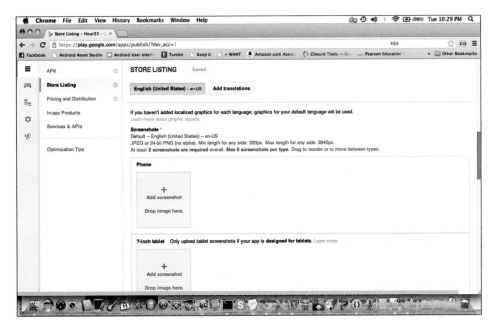

FIGURE 24.4
Store listing in Google Play

Uploading the APK

When you upload an APK to Google Play, Google Play will read the APK file and provide information about the APK such as the number of supported devices. You can upload for alpha and beta testing. To do so, you specify a Google Group or Google+ community.

Figure 24.5 shows the result of uploading the Hour 23 app as an alpha.

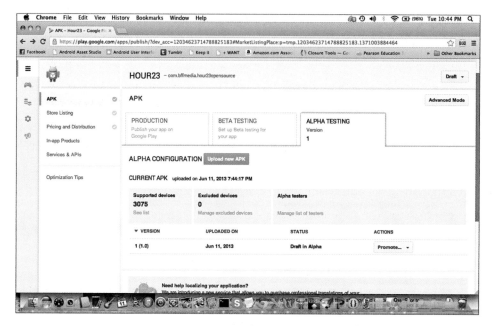

FIGURE 24.5
Uploaded APK in Google Play

You have an opportunity in Google Play to pay for localizing the app. The idea is that your app will include a strings.xml resource file in English that can be pulled from the uploaded APK and translated into other languages. This might be a great option for certain apps. A fee is charged for the translations. See Figure 24.6.

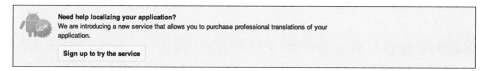

FIGURE 24.6
Translation service in Google Play

Publishing on Amazon

Publishing on Amazon is similar to publishing on Google Play. Choose the Mobile App Distribution option from https://developer.amazon.com/.

You can develop specifically for Kindle Android-based devices or generic Android devices. A Kindle-specific version for the Amazon market might make sense. Kindle Fire is based on Android. If you are developing for the Kindle Fire, getting a device to test on is recommended.

What About OUYA or Other Markets?

OUYA is an Android-based game console that connects to a TV. You can find out more at http://www.ouya.tv/develop/.

If you download the OUYA Developer Kit (ODK), you'll find that it is an Android development environment. Libraries specific to the OUYA cover how to respond to the controller and other specific features.

The development of the OUYA shows that new markets do become available for Android apps.

In Korea, the T-Store is a large app distributor. If you have an app that would do well in Korea, translating it and selling it at the T-Store would make sense.

The T-Store developer center is at http://dev.tstore.co.kr/.

Monetizing Your App

Making apps that people use can be fun and rewarding. Making money with your apps is also fun and rewarding. Many variations exist, but most app monetizaion schemes fall into one of four models: free, advertising, paid, and in-app billing.

Free Apps

With free apps, you can build a user base and work out the bugs in your app and maybe in your idea or product. Some apps become popular first and then you try to figure out how to make money later. Or some apps build a large user base and are acquired by a larger company. Don't dismiss free as a good option for many apps.

Ad Supported

Including mobile ads in your apps is easy to do. You can try AdMob, Amazon, or one of many other ad providers. To include ads in your app, you download an ad SDK and incorporate the ad into your app. You might add an ad slot into your layouts, or determine a good spot within your app to show an ad-based activity. The model is similar to the process you followed for the Facebook SDK in Hour 22.

Paid

The paid model is easy to understand. You set a price level in Google Play and other markets, and users pay for your app. Many apps sell for $0.99 in the U.S., but you might have a specialty app that can sell for significantly more or a great app that can sell for $4.99. Determine the proper price for your app to maximize revenue.

In-App Payments

Google Play and Amazon have different in-app payment options. The classic model for an in-app payment is a game in which there is a virtual currency. Players can earn the currency by playing the game or they can buy the currency with actual money. In-app purchases can give a user the ability to try an app without any upfront expense.

You can mix and match these options. You might decide your app should have an ad-supported version and a paid version without ads. Creating a business around an app always starts with creating a great app. After that part is done, you can experiment with how to make money.

Summary

This hour covered the process of producing a signed Android application and distributing it on various app marketplaces. The signing process is critical for security and for maintaining apps. Multiple app markets exist, including Amazon, and you can take advantage of new opportunities to distribute Android apps on new devices such as the OUYA and in many markets around the world.

Q&A

Q. Is this everything there is to know about selling apps?

A. No, this hour is a good start. You can look into app licenses and privacy policies. This hour mentions in-app billing and using ad SDKs, but does not cover the details.

Q. How can I limit my application to only specific types of devices?

A. Google Play attempts to filter applications available to those compatible with the specific user's device. Each application package includes important information in the Android manifest file. Certain manifest file settings can be used to specify what types of devices your application does or does not support. For example, whether or not an app uses the camera can be determined. After that's done, the app will be available only for appropriate devices.

Workshop

Quiz

1. Is it possible to make an app that optionally uses the camera?

2. What are some common ways of making money with an app?

3. True or false: Google Play provides free translations for your app.

Answers

1. Yes, you can indicate in the Android manifest file that the app uses the camera, but does not require it.

2. Free apps might ultimately make money. Other apps are ad supported, paid, or have in-app billing.

3. False. It offers a paid translation service.

Exercise

Choose any exercise app from this book, export it, and sign it. You can use the Hour23Opensouce app or create a brand-new app. Sign up for a developer account on Google Play and Amazon. Check out OUYA and begin to make great apps that appeal to you. When you begin to create an app, creating one that you care about is ideal.

Index

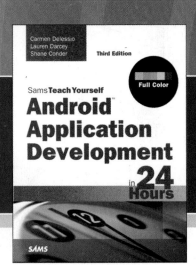

FREE
Online Edition

Your purchase of *Sams Teach Yourself Android™ Application Development in 24 Hours* includes access to a free online edition for 45 days through the **Safari Books Online** subscription service. Nearly every Sams book is available online through **Safari Books Online**, along with thousands of books and videos from publishers such as Addison-Wesley Professional, Cisco Press, Exam Cram, IBM Press, O'Reilly Media, Prentice Hall, Que, and VMware Press.

Safari Books Online is a digital library providing searchable, on-demand access to thousands of technology, digital media, and professional development books and videos from leading publishers. With one monthly or yearly subscription price, you get unlimited access to learning tools and information on topics including mobile app and software development, tips and tricks on using your favorite gadgets, networking, project management, graphic design, and much more.

Activate your FREE Online Edition at
informit.com/safarifree

STEP 1: Enter the coupon code: VJEBYYG.

STEP 2: New Safari users, complete the brief registration form.
Safari subscribers, just log in.

If you have difficulty registering on Safari or accessing the online edition,
please e-mail customer-service@safaribooksonline.com